world of fashion

World of Fashion

People, Places, resources

by

Eleanor Lambert

R. R. BOWKER COMPANY
A Xerox Education Company
New York & London, 1976

Published by R. R. Bowker Co. (*A Xerox Education Company*)
1180 Avenue of the Americas, New York, N.Y. 10036
Copyright ©1976 by Xerox Corporation
All rights reserved.
Printed and bound in the United States of America

Library of Congress Cataloging in Publication Data
Lambert, Eleanor.
World of fashion.

Bibliography: p.
Includes index.
1. Fashion. I. Title.
TT515.L16   746.9'2   75-43904
ISBN 0-8352-0627-0

contents

THE AMERICAS—Cont.

preface

Mass prosperity and mass production have made fashion a key economic factor in virtually every country of the globe. The production of raw and cultivated fibers and textiles; the manufacture of clothing; the efforts of designers, technicians, and workers; and the business of distributing, exporting, presenting, selling, reporting, and promoting wearing apparel account for an estimated one-third of the world's economy. A shortage of wool in Australia, wild-life conservation, even the visit of a discerning "hippie" to the wilds of Afghanistan can (and did) profoundly affect the way people dress during an entire decade.

Explicit facts and pertinent information on the subject of clothing have, however, been hard to come by. Locating basic information, from national export figures to a famous designer's birth date, can often take hours of research. Libraries have sparse material on fashion, microfilm has replaced the old newspaper morgue, and foreign information services are seldom up-to-date.

The aim of this book has been to compile into one reference volume the facts about the creative people, the manufacturing centers, the geographic resources and principal exports, the schools, the costume collections, and all of the other factors which contribute to the gigantic task of clothing the world.

The book is organized geographically—first by continent, then by region, then by country. Each country is briefly summarized in terms of its current contribution to modern dress, whether through inspiration or through its products.

The country's better-known designers, together with young designers of note and promise, are listed alphabetically in the Fashion Designers and Firms section, with a brief biography on each and a note on the typical aspect of his work. Stage and film costume designers who have had traceable influence on general fashion, or have themselves de-

ix

signed clothing for the public, are also included in this section. Influential personalities, other than designers, who in one way or another have played a role in their country's fashion development are listed for many countries in the Fashion Influentials section.

Wherever possible, I have included the country's trade and fashion organizations, honors and awards, schools offering courses in fashion design and clothing production techniques, museums with interesting costume collections, and fashion periodicals. Because of frequent changes in curriculum, tuition, and facilities, some information in the sections on fashion education may already be outdated. Prospective students are advised to write to the director of admissions for up-to-the-minute information.

The amount of information for each country varies, depending on the degree of the country's fashion activity. Instead of disregarding the countries considered inactive in fashion, I have included them whenever information, no matter how scant, was available to me.

Any fashion record intended to assist the student, historian, journalist, or professional designer should record the fashion "greats" who, by their design genius, observations, or visionary leadership, have affected the dress and sometimes the life-style of their epoch. I have listed those who in my judgment are permanently memorable in a separate section called the Hall of Fame. Outstanding personalities whose place in fashion history is, however, not yet clearly established are listed under their native country, either under Fashion Designers and Firms or Fashion Influentials.

The bibliography on fashion history and fashion personalities contains titles which should be available in the average reference library. This is not by any means a vast resource, for the art and impact of fashion have had comparatively few chroniclers or diarists. The few general reference books on the subject have been limited to the main fashion centers of France, Great Britain, Italy, and the United States.

The majority of the material in this book comes from my own research and my files accumulated through 30 years of association with world fashion as publicist, activist, journalist, and fascinated observer. The information on world trade figures, museums, schools, and designers for countries that I have not visited was obtained through questionnaires, telephone interviews, and secondary sources.

I wish to thank the many consulates that provided me with information on their trade associations, schools, and museums. I am indebted to Madeleine Ginsburg of the Victoria and Albert Museum in London; Beatrix Miller, editor-in-chief of British Vogue; and journalists Ernestine Carter and Prudence Glyn of London, Patricia Salmon of Tokyo,

Blance Gallard of Hong Kong, Didder Ronlund of Copenhagen, Hilda O'Farrill de Kelly and Ana Fusoni of Mexico City, and Tuula Saarikoski of Helsinki, all of whom provided me with helpful facts.

Dr. Lazare Teper of the International Ladies Garment Workers Union (ILGWU) was a source of valuable data on foreign clothing imports into the United States. Gordon Stone, librarian of the Costume Institute of the Metropolitan Museum of Art, New York, was extremely helpful and permitted extraordinary use of the Costume Institute's library. The authors, living and dead, of the books I have utilized in my research have not only been helpful, but have provided me with delightful reading.

Janet Goff Harper of my organization gave valuable assistance, as did my staff members Catherine Salsano and Luta Rozental Miller.

Mrs. Olga Weber of the Bowker Company and her associates Julia Raymunt and Filomena Simora have been endlessly helpful in all phases of preparing the book.

The author realizes that in such a fluid universe as fashion no compendium can ever be complete. I shall appreciate all updated information necessary to make forthcoming editions comprehensive and current.

Eleanor Lambert

New York 1976

africa

NORTH AFRICA

Being neither Northern nor African in mentality, North Africa has a look, a life, and an attitude all its own, most vividly illustrated in its clothing.

Although occupied, infiltrated, and linked by trade and culture to the French and Spanish, dress in the North African countries absorbed the best of the West, the nomad, and the Arab into its rich, decorative, and comfortable regional costumes.

Native handicrafts have been scrupulously preserved and taught to the next generation, and in recent years women from wealthy families in almost every country of North Africa have been responsible for utilizing the work of village weavers, potters, and embroiderers in designs which appeal to foreign visitors with discriminating taste.

While no government programs have been set up to create a clothing industry in any North African countries, private enterprise such as Medina Arts in Morocco has worked to improve the styling, sizing, and quality of handmade goods for a wider foreign market.

North Africa's main contribution to world fashion in recent years has been lumped under the one term, caftan. In reality this represents a great variety of silhouettes: the djellaba, a long narrow shirt shape; the gondoura, the loose robe with an opening for the head (generally wrongly called the caftan); and the caftan itself, a two-piece costume of a loose coat tightly belted over a narrow sleeveless underdress.

Most of the North African countries produce wool or cotton for textiles, and Egypt, Morocco, Tunisia, and Algeria have large textile plants. All produce carpets and fine metal work.

Perhaps because of the fashion reputation of several renowned and elegant Moroccan beauties such as Princess Lalla Nezha, Mme Ahmed Benhima, and Mrs. Jahil Tazi, Morocco is best known for its fashion products. The list of Moroccan fashion designers included in this edition can doubtless be equalled in Algeria, Tunisia, or Egypt, but their talents are not promoted nor their clothes available to the visitor.

3

ALGERIA

Costume and Fashion Archives

Musée d'Ethnographie du Bardo (Bardo Ethnographic Museum). 3 avenue Franklin D. Roosevelt, Algiers
This is one of the leading North African centers for collections and information on regional costumes.

Musée National des Antiquités (National Museum of Antiquities). Parc de la Liberté, Algiers
Tel: 60-56-37. Founded: 1897. Curator: Mohammed Temman.
There is a collection of Algerian native costumes, textiles, and jewelry, as well as a selection of Moroccan costumes.

MOROCCO

Fashion Designers and Firms

Rabea Bennani. See Samia

Fadila. Custom caftan makers, 7 rue Aristide Briand, Casablanca
Fadila, owned by the wife of a government official, produces the authentic two-piece caftan costumes (the caftan is a long narrow coat worn over a slim sleeveless dress) in French brocades, chiffons, and silk prints worn by Moroccan women to court functions and formal parties. They are decorated with gold and delicate fine braiding in the coloring of the fabric, and cinched with the wide belt of solid gold or silver gilt encrusted with precious stones which every wealthy Moroccan woman has as her most important family heirloom.
Such caftans are unique and made to order, requiring four or five months to complete. A Fadila caftan costs from five hundred to one thousand dollars.
Fadila's staff of exceptionally gifted beadworkers is drawn from an institute for training young girls established by the owner's family in 1954. Graduates of the Institut Tahara Sebti are also on the staffs of other exclusive boutiques in Morocco.

Zina Guessous. Kenz Boutique, Hotel Mamounia in Marrakesch and other deluxe Moroccan hotels, Avenue des Forces Armées Royale, Casablanca
Morocco's most energetic fashion representative and a prominent international social figure, Mme Guessous is known for updating the classic shapes of her native clothing. In 1968 she caused a sensation by introducing the minicaftan. She uses European fabrics such as silk organza, silk jersey, voile, and lace, as well as the handwoven fabrics of the

4

SUDAN

Costume and Fashion Archives

Sudan Ethnographic Museum. Dept. of Antiquities and Ethnology, University Avenue, Box 178, Khartoum

Tel: 80-935. Founded: 1905. Dir: Sayed Thabit Hassan. Curator: Sayed Aksha Muhammed Ali.

This museum houses collections especially related to the history of costume and textiles. Among the anthropological collections, there are contemporary northern and southern Sudan costumes and textiles.

TOGO

Fashion Designers and Firms

Beverly Majors. Designer of Afro-European fashions, Akuya Boutique, Lomé

At 22, Beverly Majors was a designer and manager of a boutique which set a pattern for many others in developing countries.

Born in 1951 in Chicago, Illinois, Beverly went to Ghana in 1964, at 14, with her family who had grown tired of racial problems in America. A year later she returned to the U.S. to attend Quincy College in Quincy, Illinois. There she took up dressmaking with a local seamstress who taught her the rudiments of construction and finishing.

When her family opened a trucking business in Lomé, she returned and opened her boutique at the leading hotel in Lomé. Her clientele is drawn from the city's active diplomatic life, and Beverly's designs are based on American and Paris styles but made in African tie-dyed or printed cottons and camel's hair blankets brought from the desert tribes.

SOUTH AFRICA

SOUTH AFRICA, REPUBLIC OF

Self-sufficient and self-contained as a European transplant in a remote land, the Republic of South Africa has, of course, no interest in native fashion inspiration. Whatever clothing is not imported follows European models and is produced in highly efficient local factories. The country is highly industrialized, with more than one million factory workers.

A large textile industry produces quantities of polyester fibers and woven fabrics, which together with wool, hides, and mohair, are exported for use in the fashion industries of the world.

In addition to gold and diamonds, the crux of the country's economy, many semiprecious stones are exported to be made into fine or costume jewelry.

The Republic of South Africa has no internationally prominent designers, but there are two or three couture and boutique designers with a devoted following in Johannesburg. Listed below are the designers regarded as most important locally.

Fashion Designers and Firms

Morris Gerald. 16 Uranis St., Observatory, Johannesburg

Chris Levin. 31 Harvard Bldg., 49 Joubert St., Johannesburg

Eric Pugin. 21 Jessie St., Norwood, Johannesburg

Trade Associations and Organizations

National Clothing Federation of South Africa. North State Bldg., Corners Market and Kruis Sts., Johannesburg

Membership organization of clothing manufacturers in South Africa, mainly for internal industry and labor matters.

Costume and Fashion Archives

Africana Museum. Public Library, Market Sq., Johannesburg, Transvaal

Tel: 836-3787. Founded: 1934. Dir: Anne H. Smith.

There are South African costumes from 1652 to the present, including those of the Bushmen and Bantu tribes.

2.

asia

FAR EAST

CHINA, PEOPLE'S REPUBLIC OF

The Chinese were very early international traders on a large scale, having opened the gates of Canton to "the barbarians" in 225 AD. The custom of trading in this manner for one month twice a year, and never otherwise, has continued (with intervals of complete isolation) ever since.

One of the many questions prompted by the new relationship between the People's Republic of China and Western nations is its future role in clothing the world. Mainland China's immense labor potential, and their improved methods of cultivating wool, cotton, and silk point toward a new supply of these fibers in a world where they are growing scarce.

China has made formidable technical advances in producing artificial fibers and when their crafts are freed from the present worn and tacky groove, untold pent-up design talents could be released.

In 1973 it was estimated that mainland China's textile volume amounted to $1,830,000,000, one-fifth of which was exported. More than half a billion dollars worth of cotton fibers were exported to the United States.

While China is officially concerned with the most massive transactions of goods for goods in foreign exchange, it seemed significant to this writer that she was invited to the Canton Fair in 1972 "to survey the future high fashion potential of Chinese resources, crafts and products." In 1975 delegations of Chinese clothing and textile technicians, grouped under the name Chinatex, made an unpublicized but thorough tour of the American fashion market.

CECFA, the Chinese Export Commodities Fair Association, is the modern version of the single all-powerful Imperial Trade Envoy who formerly ruled over the Canton Fair. It is drawn from three Communist government "corporations": China National Textile Import & Export Corporation of Peking, the China National Textiles Import & Export Corporation, Shanghai Branch, and the China National Garments Import & Export Corporation in Canton. During the Canton Fairs held in October

11

and April, that city's Trade Fair complex of modern six-story buildings displays the sum total of China's entire economy, from pickled fish to imperial satin brocades.

As the largest producer of silk and cotton in the world, China has for years supplied those commodities to other countries to be resold as their own. It is not farfetched to speculate that Taiwan receives silk from Communist China in a roundabout way and turns it into one of her lucrative exports.

Among the many differences between Russian and Chinese communism is that China is much more of a consumer society. The wages the people earn can be spent as they like for the limited but unrestricted goods available. The self-discipline and self-criticism preached incessantly by Chairman Mao seem to keep personal belongings down to a minimum, but what they can buy is unexpectedly bright and cheerful. Children and teenagers are gaily and well dressed in pretty coveralls and well-cut shirts and pants, with bright hair ribbons and wristwatches. The idea that Chinese dress is a drab cotton uniform is false. Open fabric stalls along the streets are jammed with shoppers buying vividly colored materials.

The only ready-made clothes for adults are the standard Mao jacket and pants, sold small, medium, and large for less than ten dollars. But colorful yarn-embroidered sweaters are plentiful, as are delicate hand-embroidered organdy blouses.

HONG KONG, SINGAPORE, TAIWAN

Since about 1960, when leading clothing manufacturers in Hong Kong, Taiwan, and Singapore reorganized their operations to develop workers and methods by which they could sell on a broader and more consistent scale to the world market, the ghastly shanty towns that stumbled and slid down the hillsides of Hong Kong Island have all but disappeared. Nearly 200,000 people now work in the Hong Kong garment factories and live in high-rise buildings on the site of their once miserable huts.

Fashion was not the only factor in the vast improvement in Hong Kong's living standard, but the clothing export total of about one billion dollars in 1971 is significant.

Taiwan exports about one-third as much clothing as Hong Kong. Singapore, a late starter in training labor, trails considerably behind.

Taiwan, with an aggressive and protective government, and Singapore, free of Hong Kong's refugee problem, were better off to begin with and have enjoyed a steady rise in employment.

In all these countries, clothing production often depends directly on the styling and technology of foreigners who either own or co-own the factories or hold contracts to supervise production of their products.

The Far East has not yet sought to develop a distinct fashion product for Western use which incorporates the Oriental art heritage. Orientals are important as skilled artisans, and a few Oriental designers have achieved success in Europe and America, but almost no name designers of Western-style clothing have appeared on the local scene.

INDONESIA, KHMER REPUBLIC (CAMBODIA), MALAYSIA

The delicate, graceful bodies of Indonesian and Polynesian women, wrapped in seductive folds of beautiful materials and exquisitely adorned with ornaments and flowers, have inspired fashion for many centuries. Today, when the cult of the body directs much of fashion thinking, the exotic Orient is an omnipresent influence.

These countries, however, have had too many internal troubles to make any more than a half-hearted scramble for a share of the world clothing market. As tourism and other outside contacts increase, the inevitable reflex is to adapt native dress for sale to visitors and eventually to other countries. A foreign resident with an artist's eye and clever hands is usually behind such businesses.

The next step is the establishment of a government agency for the development of a clothing industry for export, advised by textile and fashion experts invited from the West. Such moves toward international recognition are doubtless in progress in the above countries, but only two designers and no trade or educational efforts were found by this writer in 1975.

Fashion Designers and Firms

Iwan Tirtaamijaja. Textile and fashion designer, P. T. Ramacraft, Djl. Panarukan 25, Djakarta, Indonesia

Iwan Tirtaamijaja drifted into fashion after serving as legal adviser to his country's mission to the United Nations. His interest in the native art of batik brought him a commission from the Indonesian government to do a book on the subject. Two years of research during his spare time took him to every little village and kampong of the country. His book *Batik: Pattern and Motif* is an authoritative record of batik patterns and an eloquent plea for the preservation of the ancient craft and its exploitation on the commercial basis.

To practice his belief, he went into the production of batik lengths, drawing original designs based on traditional patterns and motifs and turning them over to hereditary craftsmen.

Dissatisfied with what Djakarta dressmakers and couturiers were doing with his fabrics, he turned to fashion design, using the fabric as a basis for the cut and styling of the garment. He is a couturier catering to Djakarta's elite, and sells ready-to-wear clothes in his own boutiques in Djakarta, Bali, and Hong Kong, and to shops in the United States and Australia.

Iwan has a network of 300 batik makers throughout Java executing his designs, not only on traditional cotton cambric, but on silks and chiffons, and on heavy-weight cottons for furnishing fabrics.

Judith Tumbalaka. Jewelry designer, Hotel Indonesia, Djakarta, Indonesia

An example of the craft-development work being done in outlying countries by transplanted artists, Mrs. Tumbalaka is an American, married to an Indonesian, who became fascinated with the traditional Indonesian jewelry craft and gave it a contemporary feeling. Her work reflects the simplicity of Scandinavian jewelry, yet is delicate and Oriental.

Costume and Fashion Archives

Muzium Negara (National Museum of Malaysia). Damansara Road, Kuala Lumpur, Malaysia
Tel: 80158. Founded: 1963. Curator: Shahrum Yub.
There are costumes of various Malaysian races from ancient to modern times.

National Museum. Vithei Pau-Kambo, Phnom-Penh, Khmer Republic
Tel: 2.20-90. Founded: 1920. Dir: Ly Vouong.
The museum has important Cambodian textile and costume collections.

Sarawak Museum. Kuching, Sarawak, Malaysia
Founded: 1886. Curator: Benedict Sandin.
There is a vast collection of batiks and other decorative textiles, also historical costumes of the region.

Fashion Publications

Wanita. Peti Surat 671, Kuala Lumpur, Malaysia
12 issues/yr. Text in Malaysian.

JAPAN

This most industrious and determined of the Far Eastern countries is also one of the most artistic and patiently perfectionist. The intricate and exquisite wrappings for five eggs (Japanese equivalent of our half-dozen) or an arrangement of fresh shrimp are unique enough to merit a book on that painstaking and ephemeral art. A whole library could be filled with books on Japanese costume and fabrics.

In Japan, it has been the tradition to declare an artist of superlative skill a National Treasure. Modern Japan has one in the fashion field, Kiichiro Yokoyama, designer and painter of kimonos in Kyoto.

Since World War II, when defeat made the Japanese turn eagerly to everything Western, Japan has built a huge industry in ready-made women's and men's clothes in the Western style. They are usually designed by Europeans or Americans under licensing arrangements.

Although there are more fashion and dressmaking schools in Japan than in any other country on earth, the graduates rarely make a reputation in their own industry. Kenzo Takada and Issey Miyake, now important Paris designers, were little known at home. Hanae Mori is an exception, and Sumaka Ito, a designer favored by the Japanese royal family, has shown collections in Paris, London, and New York.

Although Japan was until recently the number one seller of fabrics to the world fashion market, she operates to a large extent as middle man as well as producer. In 1973 Japan purchased the largest portion of silk and textiles of all types produced by the Chinese People's Republic and resold it to the rest of the world. Japan has at times bought so much of the American textile and fiber output that there was a drastic scarcity of domestic materials in America. Even so, she maintains gigantic synthetic combines such as the Tejin Company.

The problem of inflation and high labor costs in Japan, plus the imposition of a strict quota system on Japanese goods by the United States, have prevented the increase in exports which the Japanese had grown to expect each year. Nevertheless, they exported about $467,000,000 in clothing and textiles in 1971 and roughly the same in 1972.

Fashion Designers and Firms

Mohei Ito (1898–1967). Designer and educator

Born in Ohkubo, near Tokyo, September 5, 1898, Mohei Ito shared his generation's growing interest in Western life. He is considered the "father" of Western design in Japan. While attending Keio University, he began to teach himself the technique of cutting and making Western clothes. In 1915 he embarked on the teaching career which resulted in his owning and directing a chain of dressmaking schools all over Japan, most of which continue today, and are still considered the best all-around preparation for a career in fashion design. For names and addresses of some Ito schools, see Fashion Education section.

15

Sumako Ito. Fashion designer and court dressmaker, 39-5-6 Hatanodoi, Shinagawaku, Tokyo

One of the most active of the conservative school of Japanese designers of Western-style clothes, Mrs. Ito was born in Tokyo and at 17 began studying fashion design at the Mohei Ito Design School. She twice (1952 and 1959) won a national fashion design competition sponsored by the Mainichi Press of Japan, with an award given by the American designer Tina Leser. She also developed her own method of speed garment-cutting, now used widely in Japan and known as the Ito cutting method.

After designing for Renown, one of Japan's largest mass manufacturers, she organized her own company and also made an agreement with the department store, Takashimaya, to head their fashion department in Tokyo and their many branches.

Mrs. Ito designs the wardrobes of Princess Michiko and other members of the imperial family.

Like many well-known designers in Japan, Mrs. Ito has her own fashion design school, with about 150 students.

Hanae Mori. Fashion and textile designer, 4-672 Sekimachi, Merima-ku, Tokyo; and 550 Seventh Ave., New York, N.Y. 10018

Born near Kyoto and trained as an artist and textile designer, Hanae Mori married as soon as she left school. Her husband, a prominent textile manufacturer, encouraged her to design prints as a hobby, then produced them commercially.

In the 1950s she began designing Western-style clothes in her prints, with such success that she was asked by a large Tokyo department store to take over its fashion department.

Mme Mori came to America in 1964 to show her collection under the sponsorship of the International Silk Association and after that developed a worldwide reputation.

Hanae Mori was the first Japanese dress designer of couture quality to open branches in other than her native capital. In New York she took over (1973) a large art gallery as a permanent shop.

She received the American Neiman-Marcus Award in 1973.

Kansai Yamamoto. Young-fashion designer, Tokyo Central Apt. 4-3-15, Jingumae Shibuya-ku, Tokyo

Of the school of "young rebel" designers in Japan, Kansai lives and works in the center of Tokyo's artist-and-writers district, and occasionally shows in Europe.

Kansai spent two years in England, where he made a sensation in the British press and far-out boutiques with a collection based on Kabuki costume.

16

His clothes, made in Japan, are a strange blend of Oriental and the English "Mod" style. They have a great vogue in the young boutiques in Japan and are sold in some boutiques in Europe.

Kiichiro Yokoyama. Designer of hand-dyed and tie-dyed fabrics, Motoyama 208, Kami-Kamo, Kita-ku, Kyoto

Considered the finest living creator of the classic type of Japanese kimono silks, Kiichiro Yokoyama is ranked as a National Treasure in Japan.

He was born January 28, 1902, in Kyoto City. He studied silk weaving and printing under the master Yamaga Seika. After passing through the various stages necessary for a craftsman to be regarded as a master, he was invited to exhibit at Nitten, an official showing of masterpieces in textile design. He received Kyoto's textile art prize three times.

Yokoyama's three children have followed in their father's footsteps, and his daughter Toshiko is today Japan's best-known young textile designer.

Toshiko Yokoyama. Textile designer, c/o Kiichiro Yokoyama, Motoyama 208, Kami-Kamo, Kita-ku, Kyoto

This artist, daughter of Japan's master-dyer Kiichiro Yokoyama and the most gifted of his three children, was born in Kyoto, February 3, 1934, and studied design in schools there and in Europe. Her work in textiles is more avant-garde and Westernized than her father's, and she is also well-known in the art of calligraphy. She has had frequent exhibitions of her work in tie-dyed silks and calligraphy at Tokyo art galleries.

Fashion Education

One of the first signs of success on the part of a Japanese fashion designer is to open a dress design school. There are therefore dozens if not hundreds of such schools, each having from 100 to several thousand students. Some of these offer truly professional career training, others are more like home-sewing schools, and few if any combine design and fashion technique with a regular scholastic curriculum.

Since the late Mohei Ito (see Fashion Designers and Firms) appears to be the recognized authority on the teaching of Western fashion design in Japan, having dedicated his entire adult life to this and not to a professional design career of his own, the only Japanese schools listed in this book are those he founded. Among the Ito schools are:

Ito Dressmaking School. 52 Junkei-cho 1-chome, Minami-ku, Osaka

Ito Wardrobe Institute. 15-8 Seijo 5-chome, Setagaya-ku, Tokyo

Ladies Art Dressmaking School. 3-5 Nakano 3-chome, Nakan-ku, Tokyo

Nagoya Ito Wardrobe Institute. 33 Ameo-cho, Naka-ku, Nagoya

Costume and Fashion Archives

Okura Shukokan Museum. 3, Akasaka Aoi-cho, Minato-ku, Tokyo
Tel: (481)0781. Founded: 1928. Dir: Shinkichi Osaki.
This is an important private collection of all types of Japanese art including 18th century No theater costumes. It is now open to the public.

Tokyo National Museum. Ueno-koen, Taito-ku, Tokyo
Tel: 821-3711. Founded: 1871. Curator: Seiroku Nowa.
Collections are related to historical Japanese costume and textiles; they include 7th and 8th century Japanese textiles; court costumes; theater costumes of No, Bugaku, and Kabuki plays; rare kimonos; sacred robes; ornaments; textiles, and costumed dolls.

Fashion Publications

Ai. Shufu-no-Tomo-sha, 1-6 Kanda Surugadai 1-chome, Chiyoda-ku, Tokyo
Founded: 1970. Ed-in-chief: Yasuo Mizuhara. Fashion Ed: Itsu Matsumura. 12 issues/yr. Yen 480/issue. Circ: 200,000. General interest and fashions for the young.

An An. Heibon Shuppan Co., Ltd., 13-7 Ginza 3-chome, Chuo-ku, Tokyo
Founded: 1969. Ed-in-chief: Akira Amagasu. Fashion Ed: Yoichi Akagi. 26 issues/yr. Yen 340/issue. Circ: 450,000. Tie-up with Elle in France.

Bisho. Shogaku-kan Co., Ltd., 3-1 Hitotsubashi 2-chome, Chiyoda-ku, Tokyo
Founded: 1971. Ed-in-chief: Hidenori Sakurai. Fashion Ed: Yuri Nogami. 26 issues/yr. Yen 200/issue. Circ: 750,000. Avant-garde women's fashions.

Dress Making. Kamakura Shobo, 21 Ichigaya-sanai-cho, Shinjuku-ku, Tokyo
Founded: 1949. Ed-in-chief: Nobuko Yasuda. Fashion Ed: Kazuko Mayuzumi. 12 issues/yr (also 5 special issues/yr on styling, fashion, and patterns). Yen 500/issue. Circ: 250,000.

Fujin Gaho. Fujin Gaho-sha, 9-1 Kanda Suda-cho 2-chome, Chiyoda-ku, Tokyo

Founded: 1903. Ed-in-chief: Atsu Takeuchi. 12 issues/yr. Yen 550/issue. Circ: 300,000. One of the oldest fashion magazines for traditional Japanese fashions.

Josei Jishin. Kobun-sha Co., Ltd., 12-13 Otowa 2-chome, Bunkyo-ku, Tokyo

Founded: 1958. Ed-in-chief: Takehiro Hirano. Fashion Ed: Osamu Tsujikawa. 52 issues/yr. Yen 160/issue. Circ: 500,000. Fashions for the business girl and general interest.

Katei Gaho. Sekai Bunka-sha, 2-29 Kudan Kita 4-chome, Chiyoda-ku, Tokyo

Founded: 1958. Ed-in-chief: Mamoru Tsuchiya. Fashion Ed: Shoko Ohshima. 12 issues/yr. Yen 630/issue. Circ: 500,000. General interest with greatest part dedicated to fashion.

Madame. Kamakura Shobo, 21 Ichigaya-sanai-cho, Shinjuku-ku, Tokyo

Founded: 1964. Ed-in-chief: Kooichi Sakaguchi. Fashion Ed: Hiroko Yoshida. 12 issues/yr (4 special issues/yr on fashion styling and patterns). Yen 480/issue. Circ: 400,000. Fashion magazine.

Mode et Mode. Mode et Mode-sha, 75 Ichigaya-yakuoji-cho, Shinjuku-ku, Tokyo

Founded: 1946. Ed-in-chief: Motoi Uchiyama. 7 issues/yr (5 regular fashion issues and 2 complete coverage issues on Paris collections). Yen 750/issue. Circ: 100,000.

No-No. Shuei-sha Co., Ltd., 5-10 Hitotsubashi 2-chome, Chiyoda-ku, Tokyo

Founded: 1971. Ed-in-chief: Rikizo Chino. Fashion Ed: Teruko Aikoo. 26 issues/yr. Yen 300/issue. Circ: 755,000. Fashion magazine, like the French *Elle* but stronger on fashion.

Soen. Bunka Fukuso Gakuin Shuppan-kyoku, Shibuya-ku, Tokyo

Founded: 1936. Ed-in-chief: Mitoko Shinoda. 12 issues/yr. Yen 500/issue. Circ: 300,000. General interest and strong on fashion; also printed in Chinese, Thai, and English.

Yoso. Yoso-sha, 9-12 Kanda Suda-cho, Chiyoda-ku, Tokyo

Founded: 1932. Ed-in-chief: Toshiji Yokoyama. 12 issues/yr. Yen 400/issue. Circ: 80,000. Western fashion magazine.

KOREA, REPUBLIC OF

Although it includes such odd bits of wearing apparel as karate suits, ladies' wigs, and terrycloth scuffs, Korea, the Land of Morning Calm, exports an amazing amount of garments and textiles. In 1973 Korea's fabric exports amounted to $450,833,000 and the world export of Korean finished garments the same year totalled more than $700 million.

In 1971 Korea's total imports of clothing to the United States was $304 million, more than $100 million more than the clothes the United States exported to the entire world, and only $12 million less than the world exports of clothing from the United Kingdom. Korea is also one of the major sources of wigs and false eyelashes.

Many foreign companies of brand-name clothing have licensing arrangements in Korea or maintain branch factories there. Korea has been slow to develop its own designers and has even employed foreign experts to up-date its ancient and historic textile industry, but a few schools teaching fashion and textile design and the construction of Western clothes are gradually preparing native designers to take over. At present there is only one public school, the Korean Design and Packaging Center, which gives fashion courses.

KOTRA, the Korean government's organization for promoting trade with the rest of the world, is a branch of the Ministry of Commerce and Industry and has offices in 69 countries.

The strong restrictions on imports of clothing from the Far Eastern countries imposed by the United States, the United Kingdom, and West Germany were a blow to Korean trade hopes in the early 1970s, but the export figures did not drastically diminish, partially due to Korea's ability to fill gaps in the world demand for textiles.

The Korean Silk Association, formed in the late fifties, has been an efficient and flexible arm of the government's efforts to obtain world markets for its resources. Until the 1960s Japan bought 90 percent of its silk from Korea and re-exported it to the world. Recently, however, Korea has sought to break this hold by directing its efforts to promotion of both fibers and fabrics. In 1973 Korean export of silk amounted to $120 million.

Fashion Designers and Firms

Andre Kim. Ready-to-wear designer, 80 Sakan-dong, Chong-ro, Seoul

Andre Kim has been called the Pierre Cardin of Korea. Using the nation's light and lovely materials and the strong contrast of satin ribbons and braid inspired by Korean costume, Kim makes young Western-style clothes in rather abstract shapes which he exports to other countries.

Princess Julia Lee. Couturiere, Changdok Palace, Seoul

Wife of Crown Prince Kyu Lee and resident of a palace that is no longer royal, the American-born princess has a successful dressmaking business in the palace. Her clothes are adaptations of the elegant and graceful high-bosomed national dress with a kimono neckline and wide wrapped satin sash.

Nora Noh. Dress designer and textile stylist, I.P.O. Box 1370, Seoul

Madame Nora Noh is South Korea's leading designer of ready-to-wear women's clothes.

Born and educated in Seoul, her taste in designing her own wardrobe caught the eye of the wife of a bank president for whom she worked as a secretary. The lady helped Nora Noh find a job in America as assistant designer for Taback of California. In her spare time she studied pattern making and design at the Frank Waggon Technical College in Los Angeles.

Four years later she opened the House of Nora Noh and in another four years, she organized and held the first Western-styled fashion show in Korea at a leading Seoul hotel. Soon her accelerating fame as a designer began to spread overseas through her wide circle of customers, many of whom were wives of foreign diplomats and other officials.

In 1960, she opened her first overseas shop in Honolulu to help stimulate the sales of Korean-made women's apparel and fabrics. Under the aegis of the Korean Silk Association, she now makes annual world tours with her own collection made in Korean fabrics.

Trade Associations and Organizations

Korea Trade Promotion Corporation (KOTRA). C.P.O. Box 1621, Seoul

Founded: 1962. Pres: Kwang-Ho Ahn.

This government-sponsored organization is a branch of the Ministry of Commerce and Industry with centers in 69 countries. The main activity of KOTRA is the promotion of trade with the rest of the world.

Korea Traders Association. 10-1 Hoehyun-dong, 2-ka, Choong-ku, Seoul

Founded: 1946. Dir: Park Choong-Hoon.

A semi-government organization to promote the export of Korean products, it maintains offices in foreign countries.

Korean Silk Association. 15-1 Kwanchul-dong, Chongro-ku, Seoul

Founded: Late 1950s. Chmn: Won-Young Lee.

This organization's main purpose is to promote Korean silk products to foreign markets, cooperating with local manufacturers.

PHILIPPINE ISLANDS

As yet this Pacific country has no self-sustained fashion industry, but it has long been known as a center for embroideries and drawnwork. Many foreign manufacturers occupy the large Philippine work force of handworkers to produce handmade blouses and children's clothes. The sheer, crisp handwoven pineapple cloth used in the famous Philippine national costumes with their decorative butterfly sleeves has occasionally been promoted as a high fashion fabric in the West, but its limited production and fragility prevents any extensive use of the fabric.

Manila's couturiers are both Paris-inspired and ethnic in their concepts. Many nontraditional designs by native dress designers are based on the wrapped Oriental dress and traditional native dress. In the main, however, fashions worn by well-to-do women are copies of European originals, and the young of the Philippines wear jeans.

Fashion Designers and Firms

Christian Espiritu. 1457 Leon Guinto, Ermita, Manila

This Filipino designer has declared that his mission is to liberate the fashions of his country from the restricting confines of traditional couture and copies of European models.

Born January 4, 1934, in Manila, Christian is a qualified architect with a degree from the University of the Philippines. He changed to fashion design in 1960, learning the basic techniques of cutting and sewing from Ramon Valera, considered the doyen of Philippine couture.

Christian counts among his regular clients, the Philippine First Lady, Mrs. Imelda Marcos.

He recently branched out to design menswear.

Romolo Estrada. 1923 San Marcelino, Malape, Manila

Romolo is one of the group of promising young designers serving the young customer in the Philippines.

Jose Moreno. 700 General Malvar St., Manila

This couturier (born 1936), who advocated the development of Philippine cottage industries, is known for his elaborate embroidered gowns made for local women and visitors to Manila.

Guamboy Sotto. 1 Guijo St., San Antonio Village, Makati, Rizal

Born May 29, 1948, Guamboy typifies the current crop of young Filipino designers. He studied fashion design at the San Francisco School of Fashion Design and apprenticed with Filipino designer Christian Espiritu.

He makes custom-order clothes and designs ready-to-wear for export to the U.S.A.

THAILAND

If, like Japan, Thailand were to designate its fashion creators as national treasures, one of them would have to be Sirikit, the doll-like Queen of Thailand.

One of the first women in her country's history to exercise any sort of authority, the Queen is more than personally fashion-minded. Not only has she been regularly cited in the international best-dressed polls, but she is the benevolent dictator of national dress for Thai women. The lowliest vegetable seller in the floating marketplace along the teeming Chaupaya klong as well as princesses and patricians of the court wear clothes of Queen Sirikit's decree.

At Her Majesty's command, the Thai government published a handsome album of colored pictures of Thai women's costumes from 618 AD to today. It is sold to foreigners for charity, and its contents are circulated through schools, organizations, and the press, with the notification: "By the gracious command of Her Majesty The Queen, the national costumes of Thai women are revived and adapted for practical purposes from the old styles."

There are five decreed styles to be worn at various times of day, but not for various stations of life. Only the costliness and formality of the fabric shows any differentiation between the rich and poor. They are the ruan-ton, an overblouse and ankle length, side-wrapped skirt; the chitladda, a similar costume for more formal daytime wear; the amarindra, still similar, but with a rim collar and long tight sleeves; the barompiman, with a tuck-in blouse, a sarong-like skirt, and tight belt in an evening fabric; and the chakri, the full-dress costume for very formal functions, with a folded brocade sarong and a long scarf draped around the bosom and over one shoulder. This is worn with the rich gold and silver filigree belt for which Thai goldsmiths are famous.

Techniques for weaving and printing silks on a scale to export in quantities were originated after World War II by an American resident in Thailand, the late Jim Thompson. With the collaboration of the Crown Princess of Thailand, Thompson set up an atelier to train new weavers and printers and prevent the skill of elder craftsmen from being lost. In addition to printing exquisite traditional patterns on plain, iridescent, and metal-shot silks and cottons, Thompson also created new designs using Thai motifs. He set up quality controls and developed marketing facilities throughout the world. His mysterious disappearance in the early 1960s and the revelation that he had been an American undercover anticommunist agent brought a dramatic end to the story of his artistic, humanitarian, and constructive career. The Thai silks ateliers continue under new management combining Thai and Western experts on design and distribution.

The Queen herself often wears Western clothes, but never on court occasions. Her Western wardrobe is made by Pierre Balmain of Paris, and her Thai costumes by the court dressmaker, Mme Arai Korn-Kaew, a long-established Bangkok couturiere whose privileged relationship to Her Majesty is somewhat like that of Queen Marie-Antoinette's dressmaker, Rose Bertin.

Fashion Designers and Firms

Design Thai. Fashion house, 518/2 Plenchit Rd., Bangkok

This is one of the Far East's major fashion success stories. Founded in 1964 by IBEC (International Basic Economic Corporation), the business established by Nelson and Rodman Rockefeller to put industry in underdeveloped countries on a paying basis, Design Thai produces dresses of native costume inspiration and Western styling formerly designed by a young black American girl, Jackie Ayer. Design Thai clothes are sold in shops throughout Thailand and also exported to the U.S.A., Germany, Great Britain, Japan, and the Caribbean.

Miss Ayer left in 1970, and Design Thai was purchased the same year by Vera and Lou Cyckman, an American couple who own the Star of Siam, another successful operation in Bangkok.

The clothes, more Westernized now, are designed by John Noel Haxo, a French designer formerly on the staff of Lanvin and Nina Ricci in Paris.

MIDDLE EAST

AFGHANISTAN

Afghanistan is a cold, mountainous, and altogether inaccessible country which is nonetheless responsible for the most sweeping fashion of the "hippie" era of the late 1960s, the fur-inside embroidered sheepskin coat.

A young American dropout, Ira Seret, bought all the highly decorative Afghan coats he could carry in the market in Kabul and brought them to America. Designers Anne Klein and Monika Tilley used them with their sportswear, and Ira Seret sold the remainder to Greenwich

Village shops. Within a year he was established in Kabul with 100 leather craftsmen at work, and the sheepskin coats of the Near and Middle East were being worn by a whole generation in Europe and America.

Woolen mills and the export of sheepskins (2,000,000/yr) make up a large part of Afghanistan's economy, but the direct tie-in with the world's fashion market dwindled with changing styles and the internal difficulties of production, transportation, and quality controls. Seret is now an importer of rugs.

IRAN

With a fabulous heritage of fashion inspiration in its miniatures, its mosaics, and embroideries, Iran follows the pattern of the Middle East in forgetting the role clothing could play in its international economy.

The Empress Farah Diba, a woman of great sensitivity and love for her land, has only recently begun to wear clothes made in Iran of Iranian materials. She was formerly known as a faithful client of Christian Dior in Paris. Under Her Majesty's patronage, national handicrafts programs have been set up in the villages and a school established in the historical museum in Teheran. Westernized versions of the national costume are produced to be sold in the handicrafts centers.

The government has not yet made an effort to market its clothing independently of the handicrafts programs, but the House of Iran shops established in Paris, New York, and other capitals are drawing attention to the fine work being done in textiles, embroideries, wood inlay, pottery, and silver by young artists as well as the traditional artisans.

ISRAEL

The dynamism of Israel and its determination to make itself a pilot of progress in the Middle East is demonstrated in the meteoric rise of its clothing industry. Apparel and textiles now rank second and third, respectively, in Israel's gross product of nearly $20 billion. The increasing affluence in Israel itself, plus the energetic efforts of Israel's trade development organizations, have driven the output of textiles and apparel upward by more than 20 percent a year in the 1970s, and even with wartime conditions prevailing, the effort to maintain a steady income from clothing production has never slackened.

The diversity of backgrounds, technical skills, and traditional arts brought to Israel in its 28 years of existence have made its fashion industry as much a melting pot as its population. Designers who have foreseen the advantages of these resources have been the first to draw world attention.

The application of modern, particularly American, procedures in industry has meant that Israel, with union labor and government control of all phases of business, could not enter the world market with low-cost merchandise. It was, therefore, some years before it could compete for volume orders in the more exacting markets. Today, however, production is highly standardized, and the emergence of more creative talents is making Israel an important fashion center.

Fashion Designers and Firms

Miriam Adan. See Kitan Dimona

Beged Or. Fashion house, Factory: Migdal Haemek; Showroom: 45 Ahad Haam St., Tel Aviv

The only Israeli firm with a name in all the countries of the world, Beged Or was founded in 1959 by the Hungarian refugee Leslie Fulop.

Born in Budapest in 1924, Fulop was a law student of 20 when the Germans invaded Hungary. He escaped after the ship he had taken to Istanbul was torpedoed in the Black Sea. He arrived "half naked and without possessions," and managed to work his way to Palestine where he fought in the war of independence and was wounded twice.

A friend from Hungary living in Israel asked him to invest in a leather goods firm. The "friend" vanished, and the "plant" turned out to be a village of unemployed people eager for work but with no premises in which to work. With the help of the government, however, he set up temporary quarters and started the business.

Today Beged Or's leather clothes and fur-lined coats are equal in style and quality to any in the world. The firm has branch offices in New York, Milan, London, Paris, and Dusseldorf and several boutiques in Tel Aviv. They have added other divisions for young versions of their clothes at lower prices.

Rojy (Hananel) Ben-Joseph. Ethnic clothes designer, Rikma, 4 Hatufa St., Tel Aviv

One of the strongest and most identifiable of Israeli fashion talents, Rojy Ben-Joseph was born in Bulgaria and came as a refugee to Israel, living on a kibbutz, where Jews from many countries merged their cultural and physical resources. Her first designs for clothing were adaptations of the traditional costumes of the Jews of North Africa and Yemen, the Druse, and other nomadic tribes of the Middle East.

In 1968 she established Rikma with her brother, Isaac Hananel. The firm utilizes native crafts in garments produced by factory methods. Rikma specialized in beachwear and at-home costumes and found prompt response from local and foreign buyers.

After the Six Day War, Mrs. Ben-Joseph began using accessories and decorations from the Arab regions such as Hebron glass, olive-wood belts, and embroideries and braids from Bethlehem and Gaza.

Dorina. Ready-to-wear manufacturers, 25 Aba Hillel Rd., Ramat Gan
   One of Israel's first ready-to-wear manufacturers, Dorina was established in 1948 to make khaki sweaters for the Israeli army during the War of Independence. Today its knitted fashions, designed by Leah Lessinger, are sold in specialty shops throughout the world, and it manufactures novelty sweaters for designers in many other countries.

Leslie Fulop. See Beged Or

Gottex. 62 Mordechai Anielewicz St., Tel Aviv
   This firm, Israel's largest and leading fashion manufacturer of swimwear and beach clothes, has Leah Gottlieb as its designer.

Leah Gottlieb. See Gottex

Jadoli. Leather designers, 56 Golomb St., Tel Aviv
   Jadoli's high-fashion leather sportswear is designed by Lily Toporek, who owns the firm with her husband, J.T. Toporek. She uses strong basic colors and often combines tweed with leather.

Kitan Dimona. Textile designers, Box 2147, Tel Aviv
   Miriam Adan, the firm's designer, likes to work in pure cotton with bright bold prints. Her look is casual, easy, and young.

Fini Leitersdorf. Designer and teacher, 125 Rothschild Blvd., Tel Aviv
   Called "the godmother of the Israeli fashion image," Fini Leitersdorf is one of the country's most successful designers, and its most dedicated worker for future design stature.
   Born in 1906 in Komarno, Hungary, she came as a refugee from Budapest in 1939 and settled in Jerusalem. She reestablished herself as a dressmaker, but in place of the rich brocades and fine wools she had used before, she experimented with the primitive handwoven wools, leather, and embroideries done by people in the refugee villages and camps. In 1955, with Ruth Dayan, wife of the Israeli general and founder of the Maskit organization to turn the refugee handicrafts into a livelihood for them, Mrs. Leitersdorf set up a shop to sell her dresses and other objects she designed.
   In 1968 she founded Ulpana, a studio–school for young talents, patterned after the Bauhaus workshops in Vienna, where masters and students worked together to create what is now known as Art Deco.
   Married to the well-known Israeli painter Johanan Simon, Fini has a house at Herzlya, the seaside resort, which is a gathering place for Israel's artists.

Leah Lessinger. *See* Dorina

Matzkin. Rainwear manufacturers, 44 Nahlat Benjamin St., Tel Aviv

This firm, one of the largest in Israel was established in 1921, long before Israel became a nation. It is a family business, specializing in raincoats and -suits in a variety of fabrics given a special water-repellant treatment. The designing is done mostly by French couturiers on a contract basis.

Jerry Melitz. Textile and clothing designer, 5 Alharizi St., Tel Aviv

The male member of a husband-and-wife team of designers (now divorced) whose progress has been parallel, yet completely independent since 1964, Jerry Melitz was born and educated in Cordoba, Argentina. He came to Israel in 1949 and studied art at the Bezalel School in Jerusalem.

While serving in the Israeli army he married Miriam Melitz, a fellow student at the Bezalel School, who was also on army duty.

On leaving the service, the Melitzes set up a studio to design interiors, window displays, and textiles. In 1964 Jerry Melitz designed a collection of fashion fabrics. Under the sponsorship of Batsheva de Rothschild, a member of the Rothschild family living in Israel, he presented his first collection of clothes made in his own prints.

He now maintains his own ready-to-wear business, while continuing to design on a free-lance basis for other manufacturers.

In 1966 he won the Israel Export Institute prize for swimwear design.

Miriam Melitz. 63 Nahlat Benjamin St., Tel Aviv

A former textile designer who turned to ready-to-wear, Miriam Melitz designed a small collection for Maskit, the handicrafts organization, before venturing out on her own.

She is known for her designs in white denim with bright appliques. Her ex-husband Jerry Melitz is also a well-known designer.

Nirkam. Industrial Zone, Nir Zvi

This young Israeli firm produces knits in a moshav, a cooperative village. The designer, Judson Oulman, lives in Paris.

Gideon Oberson. Couture and ready-to-wear designer, 11 Lurie St., Tel Aviv

Israel's leading young "name" designer, Oberson was born in 1942 in Italy, but came as a young child to Israel, where he was educated. He received a scholarship to the École de la Chambre Syndicale in Paris and studied there for two years.

On his return he designed for various Israeli manufacturers on contract, then established his own couture house for private clients while continuing to work with wholesale manufacturers.

He is active in many phases of design, creating for the theater and ballet, and was the architect of a cultural hall for the Israeli Air Force. He designed the uniforms for the personnel of El Al Airlines and has coordinated the Bonds of Israel traveling fashion shows sponsored by the Bonds for Israel campaign.

Judson Oulman. *See* Nirkam

Papco. Producers of fashion in stretch materials, 26 Choma Umigdal St., Tel Aviv

A new and highly successful firm known for women's and men's sports and leisure clothes in an unusual type of stretch velour made by their own exclusive process.

Papco clothes are exported throughout the world.

Lily Toporek. *See* Jadoli

Trade Associations and Organizations

The Fashion Center. The Israel Export Institute, 9 Ahad Haam St., Shalom Mayer Tower, Tel Aviv

Dir: Yael Matalon.

This international organization of Israel's fashion and textile manufacturers presents seasonal showings for buyers in Tel Aviv, as well as in New York, Paris, and London.

Government of Israel Trade Centers. Ministry of Commerce and Industry, Foreign Affairs Division, Palace Building, Agroan St., Jerusalem

Deputy Dir: Uzi Nedivi.

This government-sponsored organization maintains offices in many world capitals. Its purpose is to promote Israeli exports to other countries. It produces trade shows for buyers and conducts a constant press campaign through all branches.

The Israel Company for Fairs and Exhibitions (ICOFEX). 48 Kalisher St., Tel Aviv

Founded: 1950s. Dir: Mr. Amnon Shai.

This organization sponsored by the Israeli government arranges "Israel Weeks" in department stores throughout the world.

Maskit. El Al Bldg., 32 Ben-Yehuda Rd., Tel Aviv

Founded: 1955. Pres/Gen Dir: Ruth Dayan.

This handicrafts organization of Israel was started by the Ministry of Labor with the help of a group of prominent women under the leadership of Mrs. Ruth Dayan, then the wife of General Moyshe Dayan. Fini Leitersdorf, one of Israel's earliest designers, organized the Maskit design studio.

Maskit's basic purpose was to find employment for the half-million or more Arab and Palestinian refugees languishing in camps and temporary villages at that time. Their native skills, often of the most primitive nature, were utilized in marketable designs which they could follow.

By 1959, Maskit's efforts began to pay off. Some of the most creative artisans in the country were trained and made independent, and Maskit's distribution was the main source of livelihood for dozens of villages. Muskit clothing, embroideries, hand-woven fabrics, jewelry, and accessories were sold in their own shops in Israel and in foreign countries.

In 1970 Maskit was taken over by a large investors group and is now independent of government support.

Fashion Education

Shenkar College. 24 Anne Frank St., Tel Aviv

Founded: 1970. Pres: Dr. Nathan Brown.

This college offers a two or three year course in design and techniques of all branches of fashion. The school is modelled on the format of the American Fashion Institute of Technology.

Shenkar courses are open to students from all countries. Guest professors from other countries are frequently invited to teach there.

Ulpana. Experimental school for talented young people, c/o Fini Leitersdorf, 125 Rothschild Blvd., Tel Aviv

Fini Leitersdorf, the Hungarian-born Israeli designer, founded Ulpana in 1967 as a studio–school patterned after the famous Bauhaus in Vienna. The experiment, financed by the Working Mothers Association and the government department for the textile industry, groups gifted youngsters with mature artisans, developing their individual skills in the practical act of creating clothing and other articles for use and decoration.

Costume and Fashion Archives

Ethnologic Museum and Folklore Archives. 19 Arlosoroff St., Box 5333, Haifa

Tel: 04/6-85-55. Dir: Dr. Dov Noy.

The collection includes costumes from the Middle East and embroideries and textiles from all parts of the world.

Museum of Ethnography and Folklore. 1 Haifa Rd., Rokach Ave., Ramat-Aviv, Tel-Aviv

Tel: 03/41-52-47. Curator: David Davidowitch.

The museum has a collection of ethnic costumes and textiles from the Middle East.

Fashion Publications

AT. The Israeli Woman's Magazine, Maariv Publishing House, 2 Carlebach St., Tel Aviv

Founded: 1967. Ed-in-chief: Sara Riffin. Fashion Ed: Deborah Levin. 12 issues/yr. IL. 6/issue ($26/yr in U.S.A.)

Israel Fashion Magazine. The Fashion Center, The Israel Export Institute, 9 Ahad Haam St., Tel Aviv

Annual published for the Tel Aviv Fashion Week

La Isha (For the Woman). Nitzan Publishing, 7 Fin St., Tel Aviv

Ed: David Karasick. 52 issues/yr. IL. 4½/issue.

LEBANON

Until civil war devastated Lebanon and set her economy back at least three years, that country was the Arab bloc's most likely pilot into Western ways of raising the living standards of the people.

Due to its long life under French mandate, Lebanon was vastly more Europeanized than its neighbors, with an upper and middle class of prosperous and cultivated people living and dressing in the Western style. Many couturiers and fashion boutiques served the local public and the visitors who filled the rich seaside resorts near Beirut. Tourism, trade with the other Arab countries, and banking, the three main sources of national revenue, brought an international clientele to the fashion creators. It would naturally have followed that Lebanese design, textiles, and clothing manufacture would develop.

As of 1975, however, only 40,000 people of Lebanon's two million population worked in factories of any sort, 6,000 in textile plants, and a minor percentage in clothing shops.

The native fashion item sold in Lebanon (although some originated in Damascus, Syria) was the abaya, the loose, open robe for men and women, made of brocade or sheer, gold-shot silk with hand-worked seams. The typical Middle Eastern tablecloth or handwoven natural silk solidly embroidered with a chain-stitch pattern was also being converted into beachwear in Lebanon.

TURKEY

Being both a crossroad and a fiercely individualistic nation, Turkey has not, at least to this observer, managed to express that interesting blend in its contemporary arts and crafts. Efforts to protect and preserve its heritage and skills in rich embroideries, airy handwoven cottons, gorgeous brocades, silver filigree, and brass brought about a state-controlled handicraft program which maintains a school in Ankara and tourist shops throughout the country. So far, however, only the traditional designs are rigidly followed.

Handwoven silks are still made in Turkey, as are modern copies of the traditional Turkish harem coat. Like most of the less active countries in the international clothing markets, Turkey produces large quantities of Western shirts and slacks at moderate prices for domestic use and for export. Around the city of Bursa is a thriving industry in Turkish towels of amusing design, and well-made towelling bathrobes sold throughout the world.

There are no name designers of international repute in Turkey.

The typical Turkish merchandise with international distribution includes intricate silver or gilt filigree harem belts and jewelry. The yashmak, the Turkish woman's face veil (outlawed by Kemal Ataturk in 1925), is now collected and sold as a scarf. Turkish peasant coats with hand-crocheted or braided borders and buttons and Turkish saddle bags made of carpet squares were widely fashionable as shoulder bags during the mid-1960s in Europe and America.

European boutique designers, especially Thea Porter of London, travel frequently to Turkey to buy the exquisite lengths of French silks and chiffons dating from the 1920s apparently still stockpiled in the huge covered bazaar at Istanbul, a reminder that that city was once an elegant, sophisticated world capital with a lavish court life—a luxurious stopping place for Russian and Eastern potentates.

The jewelry, perfume, and rug markets of Istanbul and other Turkish cities have dwindled in size and quality, but Turkey is still a fascinating center for the traveler with an eye for fashion and the decorative.

Costume and Fashion Archives

Etnografya Muzesi (Ethnographic Museum). Talat Pacha Blvd., Ankara
Founded: 1925. Dir: Enise Yener.

The collection includes Turkish regional costumes and ornaments from the 18th and 19th centuries.

Topkapi Sarayi Muzesi (Topkapi Palace Museum). Sultanahmed, Istanbul

Tel: 27-81-10/27, 81-11/26-53. Founded: 1454. Curator: Firuze Prey-
ger.
There are 1000 examples of royal costumes, plus the incomparable
Topkapi collection of jewels and jewelled objects.

SOUTH CENTRAL ASIA

INDIA

For 4000 years India has recognized and cultivated dress as an art.
Rich and poor alike have draped and decorated their clothing with exquisite artistry and ritualistic meaning since the country's history began.

Fabric dyes were first developed in the Indus Valley, where civ-
ilization is said to have been born. Indian muslins were known in the
1st century AD in Dacca, and are still made in more or less the same way
today. Many of the patterns handblocked on cotton in India today originated in the 12th century. The Indians wove silk for the Roman Empire
with fiber they imported from China.

While silk cultivated in India has never had the delicacy and even-
ness of the Chinese fiber, it is of great beauty and variety. The north of
India is the silk area, and Benares the silk city.

Kashmir, the cool "happy valley" in the north of India, is the source
of the most luxurious of all woolens, cashmere. The underfleece
(pashm) of the Asian goat, woven into the cashmere shawls which were
a major fashion in the 19th century popularized that luxurious material, but the machine woven cashmere woolens we know today come
chiefly from mainland China.

In spite of her heritage, India's present day part in the gigantic job of
clothing the world is no more than that of a humble, discouraged artisan. Internal chaos and the curses of drought and famine have thwarted
the many attempts at foreign industrial aid programs, artisan projects,
and private investments.

Only one firm with a fashion name, Saz, has ventured out of India
into full scale competition with Western fashion businesses. One American designer, Tina Leser, attempted to operate her own factories in India, without enough success to continue. An English woman founded
Malabar, a shop selling attractive Indian fashions for at-home and evening wear. It still exists in the Taj Mahal Hotel in Bombay, but the
founder is no longer active.

33

One successful venture to create a fashion export identity has been the government-operated Handicrafts and Handlooms Exports Corporation of India Ltd., known as SONA. Through this organization, clothing and accessories totally Indian in design, fabric, and pattern are produced under controlled standards of quality and sizing so as to be saleable in Western markets.

Indian jewelry has been a magnificent branch of the art for thousands of years, and the "idol's eye" legend still has the greatest mystique in the world of gems. Though Indians are not precision cutters of jewels nor polishers of metal, the Indian way with cabochon and multicolored stones, colored enamels, and fringes of seed pearls shows a love and skill which challenges the sterile combination of metal and stones known as precious jewelry in other countries.

The tendency of India to stay rooted in its traditions without exerting the patience and imagination of true creativity has brought its modern jewelry into a decline and static insignificance.

Fashion Designers and Firms

Surjit and Ardash Gill. See Saz

Sari "Palaces." Textile shops in various cities of India

In the major cities of India, there are centers called Sari Art Palaces where saris are assembled from the different regions of the country and sold under government supervision at prices which vary according to the need of the region for employment and industrial development. The better-known types such as those in fine silk from Benares are priced high, while saris from the more depressed regions, often extremely attractive in their more primitive hand-woven textures or hand-blocked decoration, are sold at lower prices, sometimes below cost. The government makes up the difference as an inducement to the purchaser.

Saz (Surjit and Ardash Gill). 21C Commonwealth Bldg., Niriman Point, Bombay; 530 Seventh Ave., New York, N.Y. 10018

Two sisters born in Pakistan and displaced by the troubles of the war, Surjit and Ardash Gill were taken by their family, owners of large textile mills, to live in Calcutta. They were brought up in wealth, and educated in India and Europe.

On a trip to New York, they decided to combine their knowledge and talent for fabric designing with their interest in Western clothes. They presented a small collection the following season and quickly attracted elegant women and American buyers.

Alternating every three months, one sister remains in India to design the fabrics and garments and supervise the ateliers for handprinting, dyeing, and beading the dresses, while the other handles the wholesale business end in New York.

Saz dresses for afternoon and evening are cut and shaped in the Western tradition, but made in typical Indian cottons, silks, and chiffon, with characteristic borders, gold embroidery, beading, or paillettes as decoration.

Trade Associations and Organizations

Handicrafts and Handloomed Corporation of India, Ltd. (SONA). 11A Rouse Ave. Lane, New Delhi 1

Founded: 1954. Merged to present corporation: 1964. Chmn: Pupul Jaykar. Exec. Dir: B. Ramadorai.

This is the official government sponsoring organization for the design, production, and distribution of clothing and handicrafts from the various regions of India.

Founded by Mrs. Pupul Jaykar, a well-born Indian lady with a great love of her country's arts, SONA now has a total export of $23 million per year, and eleven sales centers throughout the world.

Costume and Fashion Archives

Bharat Kala Bhavan (Museum of Indian Arts and Archaeology). Benares Hindu University, Benares 5, U.P.

Founded: 1920. Dir: Rai Krishnadasa.

There is a collection of Indian costumes and textiles from the 17th century.

Maharaja of Jaipur Museum. City Palace, Jaipur, Raj.

Tel: 41-46. Founded: 1876. Dir: Kumar Sangram Singh.

There is a large collection of rich antique Indian costumes and textiles.

National Museum of India. Janpath, New Delhi 11

Tel: 38-54-41/42/43/44. Founded: 1949. Dir: Dr. Grace L. McCann Morley.

There is a large collection of Indian textiles and saris, historical and regional costumes.

State Museum. Banarsibagh Lucknow, U.P.

Tel: 2-31-07. Founded: 1863. Dir: Satya Shrava. Keeper of Specialized Collections: M.C. Pande.

There is an excellent collection of Indian costumes, textiles, prints, and embroideries.

NEPAL

This landlocked kingdom with views of two of the highest Himalayan peaks, Mounts Everest and Annapurna, is fascinating to visit, but presents few inspiring moments for the fashion designer. Its proximity to Tibet and the trek of Tibetan refugees who have built villages on the outskirts of Katmandu have introduced colorful costumes and jewelry, whereas the Nepalese costume is comparatively drab.

Nepal produces traditional rugs of thick wool with dragon and lotus motifs very like Tibetan carpets, and offers hand-embroidered blouses and skirts of the hippie variety, which often turn out to have been made in Kashmir and other parts of India.

SIKKIM

Under the patronage of the now-divorced Queen Hope (the former Hope Cook, an American), Sikkim had organized an international trade effort in native handicrafts, jewelry, and perfume. The Queen appeared in person in New York and London when a collection of Sikkimese products was shown for the first time by a leading store, and the project was well underway when a political uprising in Sikkim made it difficult for the royal family.

Prior to the ex-Queen's development project, Sikkim's best-known contribution to modern fashion was the hand-size beaten silver box in the shape of an animal which became fashionable as an evening bag in the late 1960s.

SRI LANKA (CEYLON)

Although the average per capita income of Ceylon is only $108 per year, the island provides the world with some of its finest and most expensive gemstones. The small town of Kandy, in the highlands of Ceylon, is the center of the gemstone mining area. Ceylon sapphires are of a real cerulean blue. Ceylonese craftsmen also do fine carving in precious stones.

In general, Ceylon is a pastoral country of lumber, tea, and coconuts, where the people still wear their native dress. As yet they have not attempted to adapt and market it to the Western countries.

Costume and Fashion Archives

Department of National Museums. Box 854, Colombo 7
   Tel: 95-467/468.
   There are collections of antique costumes, gemstones, and crystals native to the country.

3.

australasia

AUSTRALIA

Although Australia is the world's chief supplier of raw wool, hides, sheepskins, and opals, its remoteness, sparse population, and the exceptionally high tariffs recently imposed on imported fabrics and clothing have held the continent back from the mainstream of world fashion. As a result, Australia's own design forces have developed somewhat in a vacuum.

The few designers who have become known outside their own country have their largest following in Japan.

Australia makes excellent shoes, probably due to a large proportion of first and second generation Italians in the country. Australia also has a large number of amusing and original boutiques, a natural result of its insularity and a testament to its breezy and rugged individualism. Magg, one of the early off-beat clothes shops in Double Bay, Sydney, belonged to Mrs. Harold Holt (now Mrs. Zara Bate) when she was the wife of the late prime minister of Australia. Today boutiques in Melbourne and Sydney sell not only to tourists but to buyers from London, Paris, Germany, and the United States.

Australia's fashion stores such as David Jones, Myers, and George's have been influential in developing a more general fashion consciousness in the Australian public. Fashion and the Australian passion for horse racing join once a year in the Concours d'Elegance, a mass best-dressed competition held on Melbourne Cup Day at the Melbourne race course. Women from all parts of Australia parade in their most elegant outfit, competing for valuable prizes before a jury of international fashion experts.

Fashion Designers and Firms

Gary Bradley. Jewelry designer, 12 Toorak Rd., South Yarra, Melbourne, Vic.

Trained at the London Central School of Art, Bradley prefaced his entry into jewelry-making by touring the world to see the great jewel collections, including the Czarist treasures in Russia and the Persian royal collection in Teheran.

Bradley started a vogue for rings using big organic pearls with modernistic settings.

Kenneth Masbergh. Jewelry designer, 155 King St., Sydney, N.S.W.

Winner of several international jewelry-design awards, Masbergh heads a team of eight associate jewelry designers, all creating abstract designs in precious metal.

Kenneth Pirrie. Ready-to-wear designer, 157 Bouverie St., Carlton, Vic. 3053

One of the pioneers in the sector of the Australian fashion industry catering to the younger market, Pirrie started his own business in 1960. He now has outlets in Hong Kong and the South Pacific, as well as a Japanese manufacturer for whom he designs.

Prue Acton Designs Pty., Ltd. Ready-to-wear designer, 877 Little Collins St., Melbourne, Vic.

A leader in advocating recognition for native fashion talent, Prue Acton has infused her work with the rustic feeling of Australia's past.

Prue Acton's husband, Mike Trelore, is also a popular designer.

Mike Trelore. See Prue Acton Designs Pty., Ltd.

Norma Tullo (MBE) (Mrs. Brian King). Ready-to-wear designer, Tullo Ltd., Tullo Pl., Richmond, Vic. 3131, Melbourne

This young woman was for a time the only Australian fashion designer known by name outside the country. Her dresses and sportswear blend British classicism with a young spirit. They are widely sold in Australia and in the Pacific area, particularly in Japan, where Tullo is a licensed trademark.

She was born in Melbourne on January 31, 1935. Her parents fostered her career and helped her build her business. At 20 she was managing director of her own firm and made frequent world tours. She has won many awards, including the Australian Wool Corporation Award in 1960, the David Jones (department store) Award, Woman's Weekly and Woman's Day Awards.

In 1972 Queen Elizabeth II created Miss Tullo MBE (Member British Empire).

Victoria and Albert. 24 Bay St., Double Bay, Sydney, N.S.W.

This well-known Australian off-beat boutique sells its own creations.

Nelli Vida. 328 New Southhead Rd., Double Bay, Sydney, N.S.W.

Another boutique known for the off-beat styles which they both design and sell.

Fashion Influentials

Bernard Leser. Publisher, *Vogue Australia*, 49 Clarence St., Sydney, N.S.W. 2000

Starting as Australian branch manager for the Condé Nast Publications, Bernard Leser gave impetus to the emerging identity of the Australian fashion industry. Now publisher of the magazine with independent control, he is still working tirelessly to build a core of creativity within the swiftly growing commercial structure of the garment business.

Costume and Fashion Archives

Museum of Applied Arts and Sciences. 659 Harris St., Broadway, Sydney, N.S.W. 2007

Tel: 211-3911. Founded: 1880. Dir: J.L. Willis.

Originally the Sydney Technological Museum, then the Technology and Applied Sciences Museum, this museum was given its present name in 1950. It has 500 items of international costume.

National Gallery of Victoria. Victorian Arts Centre, 180 St. Kilda Rd., Melbourne, Vic. 3004

Tel: 62-7411. Founded: 1943. Dir: Eric E. Westbrook.

There is a small collection of English, Balkan, and Oriental costumes of the 18th and 19th centuries.

Fashion Publications

Australian Bride Magazine. K.G. Murray Publishing Co. Pty., 142 Clarence St., Sydney, N.S.W. 2000

Founded: 1954. 4 issues/yr. Aust.$1/issue. Circ: 15,000.

Australian Fashion News. Peter Isaacson Publishing, 46 Porter St., Prahvan, Vic. 3181

Founded: 1957. 12 issues/yr. Aust.$8/yr.

Australian Women's Weekly. Australian Consolidated Press, 168 Castlereagh St., Sydney, N.S.W. 2000

Founded: 1933. Ed-in-chief: Ita Buttrose. 52 issues/yr. Aust.30¢/issue. Circ: 833,000.

Cleo. Australian Consolidated Press, 168 Castlereagh St., Sydney, N.S.W. 2000

Founded: 1972. Ed-in-chief: Viki Wright. 12 issues/yr. Aust.75¢/issue. Circ: 175,000.

Flair Magazine. K.G. Murray Publishing Co. Pty., 142 Clarence St., Sydney, N.S.W. 2000
Founded: 1956. 12 issues/yr. Aust. 50¢/issue.

Pol. Sungravure Pty., Ltd., 57–59 Regent St., Sydney, N.S.W. 2008
12 issues/yr. Aust.$1/issue. Circ: 33,000.

Vogue Australia. Condé Nast Publications Pty., Ltd., 49 Clarence St., Sydney, N.S.W. 2000
Founded: 1959. Ed: Eve Harman. 10 issues/yr. Aust. $1/issue. Circ: 47,000.

SOUTH SEA ISLANDS

Each of the central islands of the various groups—Tahiti, Fiji, Samoa, etc.—has its indigenous variations of drape and pattern which have inspired local or foreign-resident designers to create Western adaptations. With the growing demand for caftans, muu-muus, and other long loose shapes for beach and evening, many Pacific designers have developed export markets for their wares. Local batiks, sarongs, saris, and exotic printed cottons are also being exported throughout the world.

In every tourist center there is apt to be a designer who adapts native dress to Western fashion. A typical example is Cherie Whiteside of Tiki Togs, Victora Parade, Suva, Fiji.

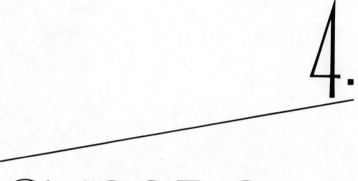

4.

europe

WESTERN EUROPE

AUSTRIA

Austria has for centuries been a resource of particular elegance in classic woolens, embroideries, petit point, braids and trimmings, fine leather goods, simulated stones, and other materials for costume jewelry. It has consistently produced excellent designs in skiwear and hunting clothes.

Since World War II, however, Austrian fashion creativity has remained firmly linked to the past.

In the 1960s, when Austrian imports far exceeded exports, a concerted effort was begun by the government to develop more contemporary, more original fashions. The Foreign Federal Economic Chamber of the Austrian Foreign Trade Office hopes to reverse the trend. Stress has been put on design as well as sales, and monthly bulletins on Austrian fashion merchandise have been issued through what must be one of the most ambitious sales networks in the world: foreign trade delegations in 79 countries. As a result of this program, exports of Austrian goods tripled within 10 years.

Austria is traditionally a country of the independent skilled artisan. In 1974 gem-cutters, goldsmiths, weavers, dyers, knitters, porcelain makers, and tailors still operated more than 150,000 small private businesses in Austria, of which 85,000 are master-craftsmen working alone.

Strass, or the rhinestone, invented in Austria by a Viennese alchemist in the 18th century who had hoped to make diamonds, remains an Austrian specialty, and the firms producing these and faceted colored stones are the largest in that field. Petit point and net embroidery are other Austrian arts still being fed into the fashion stream, although as yet without much imagination.

The remaining clothing classic that is peculiarly Austrian and continuously in fashion is the Tyrolean mountain costume, coats, cloaks, suits, and trousers in the beautiful lichen green loden cloth, and dirndl dresses with embroidered blouses and aprons. Austrian designers have interpreted these for more general use.

Fashion Designers and Firms

Austria has yet no individualized ready-to-wear fashion industry. Fashionable clothing produced there today are either custom-made copies of Paris or Italian couture originals or mass-produced variations on Austrian peasant or classic active-sports styles. Three examples of firms producing such clothing are given here.

Anba of Austria. Fugbachgasse 4, A-1021 Vienna

One of Austria's largest and best sportswear manufacturers, this firm produces trendy beach wear in cotton and knit, and handsomely functional skiwear.

Peter Geiger and Co. A-6130 Schwax

Fine knitwear with the feeling of a Tyrolean costume are the specialty of this company.

Florian Weiser. Hafferlstrasse 3, A-4020 Linz

This is a producer of provincial Austrian clothes for modern use.

Producers of Handbags and Luggage

J. Jolles Studios (Petit point), Andreasgasse 6, Vienna 7
Johann Fröhlich, Hütteldorferstrasse 44-46, A-1120 Vienna
Johann Knechtl, Weggasse 19, A-1060 Vienna
Vogue Grundl & Co., Tuchlauben 12, A-1010 Vienna

Producers of Skiwear

All Sport, A-6850 Rankweil
Paul Bohle, Brüelstrasse 34, A-6922 Wolfurt
Dolomit (Otto Ender), Zollergasse 13, A-1070 Vienna
Exi, Wassergasse 3, A-1050 Vienna
Haslmayer-Grassegg, Wagnerstrasse 5, A-6370 Kitzbühel
Dr. Walter Malin, Bahnhofstrasse 15, A-6850 Rankweil
Heinz Zinke, Rienoblgasse 12, A-1040 Vienna

Trade Associations and Organizations

Bundeskammer der gewerblichen Wirtschaft (The Austrian Federal Economic Chamber). Stubenring 12, A-1010 Vienna

Founded: 1946. Pres: Rudolf Sallinger.

This is Austria's all-encompassing and highly efficient organization for promoting Austrian exports in all areas. It organizes participation in international fashion fairs, publishes well-edited bulletins and periodicals on Austrian fashion, and handles public relations throughout the world. The Austrian Federal Economic Chamber maintains 79 trade delegation offices in foreign countries.

Contact GmbH. Markus-Sittkus Strasse 15, A-5024 Salzburg
Founded: 1971. Dir: Arnold Henhappl.

This organization efficiently promotes and manages international fairs in Salzburg. Contact's fashion fairs are: "Mode-Sport Salzburg—OESFA International," a semiannual trade fair for sportswear, folklore-style fashion, leisure-wear, and accessories; "Jim," a semi-annual fair for ready-to-wear fashion and accessories for the young; "Er," a semi-annual fair for men's wear; and "Es," a semiannual fair for children's wear.

Fachverband der Bekleidungsindustrie (Clothing Industry Association). Schwarzenbergplatz 4, A-1030 Vienna
Founded: 1946. Dir: Dr. Alfred Catharin.

Fachverband der Bekleidungsindustrie, one of the largest organizations in Austria for the apparel industry, promotes the International Vienna Ladies Fashion Week, a semiannual trade fair. Its overall aim is to increase export sales of Austrian women's ready-to-wear and high fashion.

Verein zur Förderung der Schuhindustrie (Association of the Footwear Industry). Krottenbachstrasse 3/2/1, A-1190 Vienna
Founded: 1950.

This membership organization deals with internal matters and also sponsors the semiannual international footwear fashion show "OESMU".

Wiener Messe A.G. Messeplatz 1, A-1071 Vienna
Founded: 1948. Dir: Dr. Friedrich Riha.

This organization sponsors the well-known international Vienna Spring Fair held in March and the Vienna Autumn Fair held in September, a major multiproduct exhibition.

The annual Leather Goods Show is also sponsored by this organization and its main purpose is the development of trade and increase of export of Austrian leather goods.

Fashion Education

Modeschule der Stadt Wien. Hetzendorferstrasse 79, A-1120 Vienna

This fashion school offers a two-year course in dress design and sewing techniques.

Costume and Fashion Archives

Modesammlungen Schloss Hetzendorf (Hetzendorf Palace Collection). Hetzendorfstrasse 79, A-1120 Vienna

Tel: -83-11-46. Founded: 1946. Dir: Dr. Franz Gluck.
Included in this collection are Viennese fashions from 1720 to 1968.

Museum für Kulturgeschichte und Kunstgewerbe am Landesmuseum Joanneum (Joanneum Provincial Museum of Cultural History and Applied Art). Neutorgasse 45, A-8010 Graz
Tel: 76311; 75541. Founded: 1894. Dir: Dr. Walter Modrijan.
There are peasant and period costumes of the 18th and 19th centuries, as well as Coptic, peasant, and Far Eastern embroideries.

Oberösterreichisches Landesmuseum (Upper Austria Provincial Museum). Museumstrasse 14 und Tummelplatz 10, A-4020 Linz
Tel: (07222) 234-55/56. Founded: 1833. Dir: Dr. Wilhelm Freh.
The museum has an extensive Austrian folk-costume collection.

Tiroler Volkskunstmuseum (Museum of Tyrolean Popular Art). Universitätsstrasse 2, A-6020 Innsbruck
Tel: (05222) 2-43-02. Founded: 1888. Moved to present location: 1929. Dir: Dr. Franz Colleselli.
There are 4000 Tyrolean costumes of the 18th and 19th centuries.

Fashion Publications

Astra Mode. Astra Modeverlag GmbH, Bankgasse 1, A-1010 Vienna
Dir: Friedrich Dittrich. 2 issues/yr. S.33/issue. Text in German, French, English, and additional translation sheet in Spanish.

Elegance aus Osterreich (Austria Elegance). Osterreichisches Modesekretariat, Bundeskammer der gewerblichen Wirtschaft, Hoher Markt 3, A-1010 Vienna
Ed-in-chief: Ursula Kehlmann. 2 issues/yr. Complimentary publication of the Bundeskammer der Gewerblichen Wirtschaft. Text in German, English, and French.

Eva. Elke-Zeitschriftenverlag GmbH, Zollergasse 43, A-1070 Vienna
Ed-in-chief: Gertrude Schrofl. 4 issues/yr. S.36/issue.

Ligne Elegante. Maria Minks' Modeverlag Neue Linie, Doblinger Hauptstrasse 87, A-1010 Vienna
2 issues/yr. S.140/issue.

Manteaux et Tailleurs. Astra Modeverlag GmbH, Bankgasse 1, A-1010 Vienna
Ed-in-chief: Friedrich Dittrich. 2 issues/yr. S.40/issue. Text in German, French, and English.

Perfekt Mode. Perfect Verlag, Gentzgasse 121, A-1180 Vienna
Ed-in-chief: Adolf Schnurl. 2 issues/yr. S.35/issue.

La Robe Elegante. Astra Modeverlag GmbH, Bankgasse 1, A-1010 Vienna
Ed-in-chief: Friedrich Dittrich. 2 issues/yr. S.100/issue. Text in German, French, and English.

BELGIUM

Following the establishment of Brussels as the center of the Common Market, Belgium received a wave of new fashion influences. The Avenue Louise, above the old city, blossomed as one of the smartest shopping streets in the world, lined with branches of elegant establishments from Paris, Milan, Stockholm, and London.

So far, however, the stolid Flemish attitude toward style has shown no remarkable reaction. No designers of world note have appeared to challenge the French fashion dominion over both court and popular dress in Belgium, where even the Queen orders her clothes in Paris.

The high standard of living in Belgium rules out a competitive price market for Belgian made goods. Knitted outerwear and leather clothes, however, are exceptionally well made in Belgium, and a fashion center recently built will doubtless spur local manufacturers to more ambitious programs for participation in international fashion commerce.

Trade Associations and Organizations

Belgian Linen Association. 24 rue Motoyer, B-1040 Brussels
Founded: 1955. Dir: Pierre Bodson.

This association of manufacturers of linen textiles and finished articles in linen maintains offices in all major markets of the world, where advertising, publicity, and promotion programs are conducted.

Febeltex. Fédération de l'Industrie Textile Belge, 24 rue Motoyer, B-1040 Brussels
Founded: 1955. Dir: Pierre Bodson.

This is a membership organization of textile manufacturers in various fibers, maintaining its office for industry matters and world promotions of Belgian fabrics in conjunction with the Belgian Linen Association.

Fédération Nationale du Vêtement et de la Confection. 20 avenue des Arts, B-1040 Brussels
Gen. Mgr: J. Docat. Dir: F. Gallez.

This is the largest membership organization in Belgium of manufacturers in all areas of women's apparel.

Fashion Education

There are no specific fashion schools in Belgium. Fashion courses (two and three years) are given at all branches of the Fine Arts Academy, leading to a fashion diploma. The Academy branches are located at:

Mutsaerstraat 31, B-2000 Antwerp

144 rue du Midi, B-1000 Brussels

Academiestraat 2, B-9000 Gent

177 boulevard de la Sauveniere, B-4000 Liege.

Fashion Publications

Femmes d' Aujourd'Hui. 65 rue Hennin, B-1050 Brussels

Founded: 1933. Dir: George Defosse. 52 issues/yr. fr.12/issue. Circ: 1,460,000.

Libelle/Rosita. Tijdschriften Uitgevers Maatschappij N.V., Jan Blockstraat 7, B-2000 Antwerp

Founded: 1945. Ed: J. Jagers. 52 issues/yr. fr.20/issue. Circ: 400,000. Text in French and Dutch.

Officiel du Prêt-à-Porter. Société Européene d' Edition et de Publicité, 265 avenue Louise, B-1050 Brussels

4 issues/yr. fr.600/yr. Text in Dutch and French.

FRANCE

The milestones of French fashion history can be placed at four midcentury points.

When Louis XIV, the future Sun King, ascended the throne in 1643 at the age of five, the mystique of the superiority of French taste dawned. Prior to that, Europe's fashion capitals had been Florence, Venice, Spain, and the rich and rotund trappings of middle-class Holland.

By 1660, when Louis was building Versailles and with it his country's reputation for splendor, enterprising Parisian tailors and dressmakers were doing the same for French fashion. An "export service" in the form of life-size dolls dressed in the "dernier cri" shuttled back and forth to London every month with French art fashion plates, which were also circulated throughout Europe to an avid public.

In 1774, when Louis XVI inherited the throne and the mantle of French artistic and intellectual supremacy from his grandfather Louis XV, Marie Antoinette had already become Europe's Queen of Fashion, and her dressmaker Rose Bertin was popularly known as "minister of fashion." But even then the absolutism of French taste was to be threatened by a breeze from over the water. The English love of nature and outdoor life began to assert itself in softer, more casual English dress. "The costume *a la française* was a permanent party dress," says the Danish historian Henny Hansen. "French costume (was) influenced by English life . . . and English gardens were gradually replacing formal French gardens." By great coincidence, no woman in the world wore "rustic" clothes with more grace and chic than the French Queen, and the English influence was absorbed—to become, in turn, a French export.

In the middle of the next century an Englishman became the expatriate autocrat of French fashion. Charles Frederick Worth, a Britisher from Lincolnshire, founded the haute couture as we know it today, and strengthened its position by his authority, his brilliance as an artist, and his sense of tidy organization.

English influence, in turn, threatened to topple the supremacy Worth had built for French fashion 100 years later. The Youth Revolution, born in the London of Carnaby Street and the Liverpool of the Beatles, rejected the pomp and luxury on which French fashion was based. Then began France's current struggle to prevent its precious legend from becoming a worthless myth.

Between 1965 and 1973 the fortunes of the French haute couture teetered precariously on the verge of extinction while French ready-to-wear sought and gradually found a way to present a cohesive image.

By 1971, France's overall exports of clothing throughout the world amounted to around $550 million, and new French talents in the ready-to-wear field sprang up and flourished.

In 1975 the gap between the grand tradition of French dressmaking and the factory-made fashion product was further closed when the Chambre Syndicale de la Couture Française, formerly restricted to the haute couture, accepted under its wing a coalition organization, the Chambre Syndicale du Prêt-à-Porter des Couturiers et des Créateurs de Mode, conceived and headed by Pierre Bergé, the administrator of Yves Saint Laurent. This group, patterned after the Council of Fashion Designers of America, accepts as members all French designers of note in all areas of fashion.

Fashion Designers and Firms

Alexandre. Influential French hairdresser, 120 Faubourg St. Honoré, F-75008 Paris

The small and dapper Alexandre, possibly the only hairdresser who could confidently invite some of Europe's greatest titles to the wedding of his son, was born in the south of France and was a coiffeur on the Riviera when he first attracted an elegant clientele.

Alexandre was one of the first modern hairdressers to revive the use of false hair, yet he is equally famous for the extreme "artichoke" short cut. He became world famous as coiffeur to Elizabeth Taylor Burton, the Duchess of Windsor, and Mme Hervé Alphand. When Mme Alphand's husband was French Ambassador in Washington, D.C., she made Alexandre the guest star of a "coiffing party" attended by many prominent women.

In 1972, Alexandre's book of memoirs, *Under the Drier at Alexandre*, was published in French and English.

Augustabernard. See Hall of Fame

Loris Azzaro. Haute boutique designer, 65 Faubourg St. Honoré, F-75008 Paris

The Azzaro fashion house specializes in evening clothes made in sizes with a final fitting and finishing done for each individual client.

Born in Tunisia of a Sicilian father and a Tunisian mother, Loris Azzaro studied French literature and taught as a professor in Tunisia and the university in Toulouse, France, from 1957 to 1962.

In 1962 he came to Paris but had to wait four years for his permit to work in fashion. In 1966 he opened a shop near the Opéra selling accessories and beaded evening tops. Among his first noted clients were Princess Soroya of Iran and actress Marisa Berenson.

He now owns four ateliers in Paris and boutiques in Italy, Monte Carlo, and San Tropez.

Cristobal Balenciaga. See Hall of Fame

Pierre Balmain. Couturier and ready-to-wear designer, 44 rue François Premier, F-75008 Paris

Balmain's forte is not the sharp fashion innovation; his quietly luxurious clothes are made for a faithful clientele of established position. He is a consistent favorite of the international aristocracy, including the British "stately home" contingent and such perennial best-dressers as Mrs. Graham Mattison and Queen Sirikit of Thailand.

Balmain was born May 18, 1914, in St. Jean de Maurienne, Savoie, France. He was graduated Bachelor of Science at Grenoble University, and studied architecture at the Academie des Beaux Arts in Paris. Financial problems in his family interrupted his education and he found a job in the Paris couture. In the 1930s and 1940s he worked for Edward Molyneux and Lucien LeLong, where he and another fledgling designer, Christian Dior, shared plans for a couture house of their own. In

1946, however, Balmain opened his own couture house at his present address. One of his friends and early clients was the writer Gertrude Stein.

Tall, handsome, and affable, Balmain is at home in smart international society, a popular lecturer and writer on fashion, and a passionate traveller with a hobby of collecting homes around the world.

He is a Chevalier of the Légion d'Honneur, Officer du Mérite de la République Italienne, and vice-president of the Comité Colbert of Paris.

Beaulard. See Hall of Fame

Rose Bertin. See Hall of Fame

Dorothée Bis. Ready-to-wear firm, 35 rue de Sèvres, F-75006 Paris
This well-known pioneer firm in the fashion boutique business and the production of French ready-to-wear is owned by manufacturer Elie Jacobson. His wife, Jacqueline Jacobson, is the designer. Dorothée Bis is often referred to as the innovator of the early 1970s shorts fashion which *Women's Wear Daily* dubbed "hot pants."

Marc Bohan. Director of design, Christian Dior, 30 avenue Montaigne, F-75008 Paris
Marc Bohan of Christian Dior, one of the most powerful leaders in modern fashion thinking, was born in Paris August 22, 1926. His interest in fashion was encouraged by his mother, a well-known French milliner.

He studied art in French schools, and also took a degree in philosophy. In 1945, he joined the staff of Robert Piguet, where Christian Dior was earlier employed. From 1949 to 1954 Bohan was assistant to Capt. Edward Molyneux, then joined the house of Jean Patou as designer. In 1958 he was engaged as designer for the London branch of Christian Dior. In 1960, after the death of Christian Dior and the interim tenure of Yves Saint Laurent, Bohan took over as designer for the Paris house. He is now design director for both the couture and ready-to-wear operations of Dior throughout the world.

Bohan married in 1952 and was later divorced. He has a daughter, Marie-Anne, born in 1954, to whom he is devoted.

In Paris, Bohan is a prominent social figure and is greatly interested in the theatre, music, and ballet. His apartment directly behind the Dior ateliers holds his extensive modern art collection, including several "Nanas" by sculptress Nicki de Saint Phalle.

Bohan was one of the principal organizers and a participant in the historic French–American Versailles fashion show at the Palace of Versailles in 1973.

Jean Cacharel. Separates producer, 18 rue du Faubourg du Temple, Paris

One of the first successful practitioners of French high-quality mass production. Jean Cacharel was born in 1932 in Nimes, France, and was trained there as a men's tailor. His first designs for women were made in collaboration with Emmanuelle Khanh. His present designer is his sister-in-law Corinne Grandval, a young (born 1945) graduate of the Ecole des Beaux Arts who joined the firm as stylist in 1967.

Cacharel produces many of the fabrics from which his beautifully formed and tailored skirts and tops are made.

Callot Soeurs. See Hall of Fame

Pierre Cardin. Couture and ready-to-wear designer, 118 Faubourg St. Honoré, F-75008 Paris

One of the first Paris couturiers to break with the tradition of elaborate luxury dressmaking and experiment with new, abstract forms and man-made fabrics, Cardin could be termed the "Fauve" leader of French post-World War II fashion. Born July 7, 1922, in Venice of French parents vacationing there, he had his early education in his home town, St. Etienne, France. He studied architecture in Paris, but soon turned to designing dresses. He worked on the staff of a tailor in Vichy during the German occupation, then came to Paris and worked for Paquin, Castillo, and Christian Dior, where he helped create the historic Dior New Look.

In 1957 Cardin opened his own house at his present address and was the first French couturier to sell both ready-to-wear and custom-made clothes on the same premises. He was also the first to present fashions for women and men together, thus sparking the "unisex" idea in high fashion. His stark, short tunics and smock shapes worn over tights and boots, his use of abstract cutouts, and his shiny vinyl clothes worn with hard helmets and goggles launched the Space Age theme in fashion.

Today the Cardin label covers a global fashion empire. His designs in clothing for women, men, and children are produced in Russia, Japan, India, Australia, and the United States as well as throughout Europe, and his name is licensed in fields as far removed from fashion as candy, furniture, and wine.

In 1970, Cardin extended his interests to the art and entertainment fields. He purchased Les Ambassadeurs, a famous 1930s Paris nightclub, and transformed it into l'Espace Cardin, a modernistic complex of experimental theatres, a concert hall, cinema, art gallery, and restaurants. He recently appeared as an actor in a film starring Jeanne Moreau, the actress with whom he has had a long and close relationship.

Cardin's long-time associate, André Oliver, now designs the Cardin ready-to-wear in France and America and collaborates on the Paris couture collections.

Slight in stature, with a fey, remote personality, Cardin is nevertheless a skillful executive. His staff includes Mme Hervé Alphand, wife of a retired French government official and former ambassador to the United States.

Carita Sisters (Rosy and Maria). Influential Paris hairdressers, 11 Faubourg St. Honoré, F-75008 Paris

The Carita sisters, Rosy and Maria, who often collaborate with French couturiers on the coiffures for their collections, were born in Toulouse of a Spanish family.

The sisters had their own salon in Toulouse while in their teens. Established in Paris after World War II, they are credited with bringing earthy feminine reality and hair care to the hitherto flamboyant French coiffure craft. Among the celebrities who helped them foster natural, shiny long hair as the fashion of the 1960s and 1970s were Brigitte Bardot and Catherine Deneuve.

Frederic Castel. Fur designer, Christian Dior, 30 avenue Montaigne, F-75008 Paris

Noted for the elegance and originality of his furs, Castel has submerged his personality within the direction and scope of the Dior name. He is widely credited, nonetheless, with pioneering the use of rich furs such as mink and sable in sports coats and also in the high-fashion use of multicolored dyed mink.

Castillo (Antonio Canovas del Castillo). Couturier (retired)

Member of a patrician Spanish family, Count Antonio del Castillo was born on his family estate near Madrid in 1908 and educated at the University of Madrid and El Sacro Monte in Granada. Instead of following the family profession of law, he left for Paris in 1936, during the Spanish Civil War, to be design assistant to Robert Piguet and Paquin. Leaving Paris in 1942, Castillo came to New York as custom designer for Elizabeth Arden.

In 1950 he was invited by Jeanne Lanvin's daughter, Princesse Marie-Blanche de Polignac, to become designer for the House of Lanvin, where she had succeeded her mother as head of the house. Lanvin then changed its name to Lanvin–Castillo. In 1964 he opened his own couture house on the Faubourg St. Honoré. He retired in 1969, selling the use of his name, but not his talents, to a boutique owner. He has since emerged from private life only once—to design costumes for Sam Spiegel's Russian film epic *Nicholas and Alexandra*.

He now lives in Marbella and Madrid.

Gabrielle Chanel. See Hall of Fame

Cheruit. See Hall of Fame

Chloe. See Karl Lagerfeld

Henri Chombert. Fur designer, 197 rue St. Honoré, F-75008 Paris

This leading French furrier is the second generation in his organization. He was born in Paris, October 23, 1917, and trained as an engineer, but eventually joined his family's fur business. He won the Croix de Guerre and the Medaille de la Résistance in World War II and in 1946 became head of the fur house which bears his name. His daughter is now his assistant.

André Courreges. Fashion designer for men, women, and children, 40 rue François Premier, F-75008 Paris

Courreges, the French designer whose short, childish dresses and coats led the 1960s Youth Rebellion, was born March 9, 1923, at Pau, France, in the Basque district. His father was major domo of a large private estate in the area.

After studying civil engineering and textile and fashion design in Pau and Paris, he applied (1950) to Balenciaga for a place on that master's design staff. He waited six months until he achieved his ambition. In 1961, after 11 years as Balenciaga's chief fitter, Courreges left and opened his own house. Coqueline Barriere, another Balenciaga employee, joined him in the venture. They are now married.

The first Courreges atelier was a small apartment on the Avenue Kleber, with stark white walls and curtains and low chairs suggesting a Flamenco cave, this impression enhanced by constant recordings of Flamenco guitar music. The present-day Courreges building on the rue François Premier still retains the theme of pure white decor, but is otherwise imposingly modernistic.

In 1965 Courreges, concurrently with Mary Quant of London, introduced the mini-skirt, and his stiff flaring "paper doll" coats and dresses, sophisticated versions of children's clothes, made Courreges a household word for the next five years.

Always resentful of imitators, Courreges closed his couture business suddenly in 1966 at the height of his popularity, stating that he would not work until he could benefit from the mass-production of his own ideas. A year later, he reopened with fashions in three divisions, Prototypes (custom-made), Couture Futur (high priced ready-to-wear), and Hyperbole (inexpensive). He also produces and distributes Courreges beach wear and accessories. In 1973 he set up a menswear operation and the following year opened his own retail shop in New York. There are now Courreges boutiques in many other cities.

Jules François Crahay. Designer for Lanvin, 22 Faubourg St. Honoré, F-75008 Paris

Born May 21, 1917, in Liege, Belgium, Jules François Crahay was encouraged by his mother, a Liege couturiere, to study fashion. He attended the Institut Mondial de Coupe in Paris, and then assisted Mme Jouvin, the fashion designer at Paquin. After a brief period of designing on his own in Liege, he returned to Paris as designer for Nina Ricci (1952–1963) and joined Lanvin in 1963.

Crahay is known for his use of bold stripes and vivid colors, and always adds his own dramatic overtones to the current fashion themes.

He received the Neiman–Marcus Award (1962) and the Maison Blanche Award in New Orleans (1963).

House of Creed. See Hall of Fame

Jean Desses (1904–1970). French couturier

Born Jean Dimitre Verginie of Greek parents in Alexandria, Egypt, in 1904, Desses studied law before taking up fashion in 1925 as designer for Mme Jane, couturiere on the rue de la Paix. In 1938 he opened his own house at 37 avenue George V. His evening gowns inspired by classic Greek costume soon became world-famous.

In 1946 he bought the Rond Point Champs Elysées mansion of A.G. Eiffel, designer of the Eiffel tower, and established his ateliers there, with royal and social clients from all over the world. He designed the wedding and bridesmaids dresses for the marriage of Princess Sophia of Greece to Prince Juan Carlos, the Bourbon prince of Spain who succeeded Franco.

In 1960 he closed his couture house to concentrate on ready-to-wear, but soon decided to return to Greece where he continued to design until, overtaken by illness, he sketched his last collection from his hospital bed. He died in August 1970.

Christian Dior. See Hall of Fame

House of Doeuillet. See Hall of Fame

Jacques Doucet. See Hall of Fame

Drecoll. See Hall of Fame

Erté. See Hall of Fame

Jacques Fath. See Hall of Fame

Louis Feraud. Designer for the young, 88 Faubourg St. Honoré, F-75008 Paris

This designer, identified with the "nouvelle vague" mood in young fashion, was born in Arles, France. He fought in World War II and was taken prisoner, passing the time by drawing clothes on the naked women his fellow prisoners scrawled on the walls of the camp.

After the liberation, he opened a dress shop in Cannes, where his talent attracted film stars attending the Cannes Film Festivals. As a favorite designer of Brigitte Bardot, Gina Lollobrigida, Michele Morgan, and others, Feraud designed costumes for 81 films. He opened his Paris house in 1948 and soon after married the designer Mia Fonssagrives. He now has a thriving wholesale and retail business.

Givenchy (Marquis Hubert de Givenchy). Couturier and ready-to-wear designer, 3 avenue George V, F-75008 Paris

This aristocratic designer of super-aristocratic clothes was born February 21, 1927, in Beauvais, France, where his grandfather was director of the Gobelins and Beauvais tapestry organization.

He studied law, but was drawn to a career in fashion and came to Paris at 17. The first sketches he presented won him a position on the staff of Jacques Fath and later he worked with Robert Piguet. He then designed for Elsa Schiaparelli for four years. Cristobal Balenciaga became interested in Givenchy's talents and encouraged him to open his own house in 1951 on the avenue Alfred de Vigny. In 1956 he moved to the building opposite Balenciaga's own, where he remains as the arbiter of classic, yet innovative, European elegance. Givenchy now has a network of high-quality boutiques throughout the world and his own line of menswear, perfumes, and cosmetics.

An elegant, very tall gentleman, Givenchy is a member of international society.

He was one of the five French designers who shared with five American designers in the now-historic Versailles fashion show in 1973.

Louis Antoine Godey. See Hall of Fame

Michel Goma. French couture designer (free-lance)

Michel Goma was well known in French fashion during the 1950s and 1960s, particularly as designer for Jean Patou from 1960 to 1973.

He was born in Montpelier, France, of Spanish descent and studied painting at the Beaux Arts in Montpelier. Arriving in Paris for further fine arts studies, he decided on fashion, and made his living selling sketches. In 1955 he established a connection with a small couture house, La Faurie, and in 1958 bought out the owners. Five years later he joined Patou, where he became a leading name. He severed his connection in 1973 and now does free-lance designing.

Corinne Grandval. See Jean Cacharel

Mme Gres (Alix Gres Barton). Couturier, 1 rue de la Paix, F-75002 Paris

World-renowned as the most skillful designer of intricately cut and exquisitely draped clothes for women, as well as for the subtlety of her neutral colors, Mme Gres wanted to be a sculptor but found it too expensive to work in marble or bronze. She decided to "express the human form through fabric" and, after apprenticing at the house of Premet, made garments in muslin which she sold to Paris couturiers, bringing a new mood of Grecian drapery and free-form sculpture to the fashions of the late 1920s. In 1931 she established the firm of Alix Barton and emerged as a name designer. In 1934, however, she sold the name Alix and in 1942 opened her couture house as Mme Gres. Her first collection, attended by the wives of bigwigs of the German occupying forces, was defiantly designed in red, white, and blue. The Germans closed the house. Since the war, Mme Gres, retiring and secretive as well as stubbornly true to her own exacting standards of workmanship, has become a symbol of the enduring artistry and taste of French fashion. Christian Dior said of her, "Every dress she creates is a masterpiece."

She has served as president of the Chambre Syndicale de la Couture Parisienne since 1972.

Nicole Groult. *See* Hall of Fame

Philippe Guibourge. Creations Chanel, 31 rue Cambon, F-75001 Paris

Philippe Guibourge, now associated with the house of Chanel, was for more than 12 years a designer at Dior. He was born in Paris, July 22, 1931, and studied at the Ecole des Beaux Arts Decoratifs there.

He served in the French army and on his release worked for Jacques Fath for five years. From 1957 to 1960 he assisted Antonio Castillo at Lanvin, then became assistant to Marc Bohan at Christian Dior.

In 1967, when the Miss Dior collections were inaugurated, Philippe Guibourge became the designer. He left Dior in 1975.

Tan Guidicelli. Micmac, 13 rue de Tournan, F-75006 Paris

Tan Guidicelli, designer of the successful Micmac ready-to-wear in France, was born in Paris of Italian and Vietnamese parentage. He learned designing on the staffs of Marc Bohan at Dior, Nina Ricci, and Jacques Heim, but became convinced that the future lay in sprightly young ready-mades and joined Micmac in 1968. His first collection for Micmac (1968) brought his name to prominence. He is credited with launching the maxi-coat, and his polo shirt with epaulets also became a great fad.

He opened his own boutique in 1970, and in 1972 designed the Trell collection in Milan.

John Noel Haxo. *See* Thailand: Design Thai

Jacques Heim (1899–1967)

Jacques Heim, the French couturier credited with being the first to see the possibilities of ready-to-wear as an extension of French couture, took over his parents' fur business (founded in 1898) and shifted to dressmaking in 1920.

A vigorous and dynamic businessman, Heim was a leader in the French couture although his house was seldom a trendsetter. One of the first to sense the coming of a youth-oriented fashion era, he opened Heim Jeunes Filles in 1936 and maintained it as a boutique division until his death. The house of Heim closed in 1969 and was recently reopened by a new organization which purchased the name.

Hermes. House of leather and fashion, 24 Faubourg St. Honoré, F-75008 Paris

Established in the early 1830s by Thierry Hermes, saddle and harness maker, the house of Hermes was opened in its present location in 1837 by the founder's son, Emile.

Hermes supplied riding equipment to crowned heads throughout Europe, including the Emperor Napoleon III and Empress Eugenie. The Czar of Russia commanded Hermes harnesses for the royal carriages and fitted out his Imperial guard with Hermes saddles.

The age of the automobile caused Hermes to diversify into luggage, handbags, and sporting equipment.

Adolphe and Emile-Maurice Hermes, grandsons of the founder, became energetic promoters of Hermes wares. They introduced pictorial silk scarves with the horsey theme that eventually became the Hermes hallmark, and the fittings of their leather accessories forecast the vogue for harness motifs and hardware in sportswear.

In 1922 Emile-Maurice Hermes assumed complete control of the company and modernized the designing, being the first to introduce the zipper to handbags and luggage. He launched jewelry and watches, established wearing apparel as a Hermes division, and created a museum of historic sporting and travel equipment in the Hermes building. The collection includes a spear used at the Battle of Hastings, a trunk made by Hermes for Napolean III, and commemorative scarves made for State Visits to France beginning with that of Queen Victoria.

Hermes is now managed by the fifth generation and employs 600 handworkers in workrooms on the premises. Many of them are the last to follow that craft.

Hermes now has branches in Deauville, Cannes, Monte Carlo, London, Rome, New York, Tokyo, and Beverly Hills.

Mme Jenny. *See* Hall of Fame

Emmanuelle Khanh. Pioneer in French ready-to-wear, 6 Pierre-Lescot, F-75001 Paris

This French designer was born September 7, 1937, and is married to Vietnamese-born interior designer Quasar Khanh, who is now her business associate. They founded the fashion firm in 1960.

The Khanhs are the center of a closely knit group of clothing producers who are not only friends but interlace their talents in various projects.

Emmanuelle, a former model at Balenciaga and Givenchy, had no formal training in fashion, but says she absorbed knowledge while watching Balenciaga work. She began designing for Jean Cacharel and remains intimate with the Cacharel family. Quasar Khanh, her husband, designs Quasar menswear, and his sister Bé Khanh is a well-known textile fashion coordinator. Another friend, Aimer Bruno, organized a firm with Emmanuelle as designer to utilize Rumanian hand embroideries and is now her associate in an additional fashion firm, Emmanuelle Khanh/CINEC.

Part of the "new wave" youth fashion in 1963, Emmanuelle Khanh was to France what Mary Quant was to England and Rudi Gernreich to American fashion.

Sonia Knapp. *See* Emanuel Ungaro

Laferriere. *See* Hall of Fame

Karl Lagerfeld. Ready-to-wear designer, 6 place Saint Sulpice, F-75006 Paris

One of the most versatile and inventive of Paris ready-to-wear designers, Karl Lagerfeld was born in Hamburg, Germany, September 10, 1930, and came to France at 14 when his parents sold their prosperous German dairy business.

In 1954, at 16, he won second prize in the design contest sponsored by the International Wool Secretariat—the same contest which brought Yves Saint Laurent to light as first prize winner. The two designers have been friends ever since.

From 1954 until 1958 he worked as assistant on the design staff at Pierre Balmain, then, bored with the rarefied atmosphere of haute couture, he left fashion to study art. In 1964 he began free-lancing, selling his designs to Krizia Knits in Italy, to shoe manufacturers, designing for films, and working as consultant to textile firms. A temporary assignment with a new firm, Chloe, turned out to be a triumph and he made the house a leader in French prêt-à-porter. He also continues to design furs, shoes, and knitwear.

In 1975, American production of his designs was instigated by Bendel's Studio in New York and Elizabeth Arden launched his perfume, Chloe.

Bernard Lanvin. Administrator, Lanvin, 22 rue du Faubourg St. Honoré, F-75008 Paris

Bernard Lanvin, head of the house of fashion, inherited a great French fashion tradition, and succeeded in moving it into the modern tempo.

Born December 27, 1935, at Neuilly-sur-Seine, he is the grandnephew of Mme Jeanne Lanvin, founder of the house of Lanvin.

He studied in Paris, then at Williams College, Williamstown, Massachusetts, where in 1958 he received his BA after three years study. After a brief period studying at the University of Madrid he served two years in the French Air Force Intelligence.

In November 1963, he married the American model Maryll Orsini, who is now his associate in directing the affairs of Lanvin fashions and perfumes.

Lanvin is Director-General of Lanvin Perfumes and Administrator of la Société Jeanne Lanvin, comprising the Lanvin fashion enterprises. Since 1971 when Lanvin, Charles of the Ritz, and Squibb merged, Bernard Lanvin has been a Director of Squibb.

Lanvin's designer is Jules François Crahay.

Jeanne Lanvin. *See* Hall of Fame

Ted Lapidus. Ready-to-wear designer, 37 avenue Pierre Premier de Serbie, F-75008 Paris

This multifaceted fashion house is built around a designer who was among the first modern menswear designers in France.

Born in Paris on June 23, 1929, of Russian emigré parents, he planned to study medicine, but for income designed and sold clothes in a tiny salon at the Club de Paris. He then went to Japan, studying at a Tokyo technical school to learn clothes construction.

At 20 he left school and opened a salon catering to theatrical personalities, both men and women. His mannequins Capucine and Annabel (later Mme Bernard Buffet) became noted through his clothes. Brigitte Bardot, President Harry Truman, and Geraldine Chaplin were among his clients, helping to spread his philosophy of French ready-mades.

From 1955 onward, Ted Lapidus built a world network of boutiques for men and women, expressing his concepts of a lighter, more uniform, and more sprightly type of dress for both sexes. He owns three large shops in Paris, two in New York, and has extensive distribution in Europe and Asia.

The successful Torrente chain of shops is owned by Lapidus' sister.

Guy Laroche. Couturier and ready-to-wear designer, 29 avenue Montaigne, F-75008 Paris

Known as a designer of individualist clothes and as an inventive showman in his fashion presentations, Laroche has a faithful clientele of European women and his boutique and menswear collections are distributed in many countries.

He was born in La Rochelle, France, in 1923, to a cattle-ranching family. He had no formal training in fashion. He worked on the design staff of Jean Desses for seven years before presenting his first collection (1957) in his own Paris apartment. It was hailed as inaugurating a new "junior look." In 1961 he opened his present house with couture salons and a boutique. It is next door to the Hotel Plaza–Athenee, a center for international fashion buyers. In 1966 he launched a menswear line.

Laroche is rumored to have important Swiss interests as his financial backers.

Yvi Larsen. Paris jeweler, 7 rue Chateaudun, F-75509 Paris

Born in Vienna, Yvi Larsen came to France at the age of four. After studying literature and the history of art in Paris schools, she wrote art and literary reviews. She began designing jewelry as a hobby, selling her whimsical jewels in free-form sculptured gold and jewelled animal shapes to her friends. Mme Pierre Schlumberger, Princess Sadruddin Aga Khan, Baroness Ely de Rothschild, and other best-dressed Europeans have made her name known. She now has three workshops for her thriving international business, affiliated with the French firm of Serge Weisager.

Lucien Lelong. See Hall of Fame

Jacques Leonard (House of Leonard). 19 avenue de l'Opera, F-75001 Paris

This highly successful organization producing printed fabrics and luxury ready-to-wear in the Pucci tradition was founded by Jacques Leonard in 1943. His firm, J. Leonard et Cie., then provided silks and tricots to the couture.

In 1958, with Daniel Tribouillard, his designer, Leonard formed Leonard Fashion to make and distribute ready-to-wear in Leonard's printed fabrics.

Leonard clothes are simply cut and well-finished along classic lines, in bold scarf-like patterns on satiny knits or in combinations of knit and woven fabrics. Leonard Fashion now markets on a worldwide basis sportswear, daywear, evening clothes, bathing suits, and accessories totalling $10 million a year (1975). Besides a general wholesale distribution, Leonard has its own boutiques in Paris, New York, Geneva, Beirut, Tokyo, and Monte Carlo.

Leroy. *See* Hall of Fame

Louiseboulanger. *See* Hall of Fame

Lucile. *See* Hall of Fame

Mainbocher. *See* Hall of Fame

Micmac. French fashion manufacturers and retailers, 13 rue de Tournon, F-75006 Paris

Organized by wealthy German sportsman Gunther Sachs, Micmac was opened in the late 1960s, selling ready-made clothing in avant garde styling. Tan Guidicelli joined the firm as designer in 1968.

Molyneux. *See* Hall of Fame

André Oliver. Designer for Pierre Cardin, 118 Faubourg St. Honoré, F-75008 Paris

André Oliver, associate designer at Pierre Cardin, joined that house in 1955 as its menswear designer soon after he graduated from the Ecole des Beaux Arts in Paris. He is now Cardin's associate designer in all phases of the widespread Cardin design complex which includes women's couture and ready-to-wear, menswear, accessories, and a long list of articles designed under worldwide licensing arrangements.

He was born in Toulouse, France, in 1932. His association with Cardin has been the only one in his career.

Paquin. *See* Hall of Fame

Patou. Couture house, 7 rue St. Florentin, F-75008 Paris

This house, founded by the late Jean Patou in 1914, was almost immediately forced to close when Patou was called up in World War I. Patou served with a Zouave regiment until the Armistice.

In 1919, with his first collection, he caused a sensation—and a fashion revolution—by dropping skirt lengths several inches. In 1924 he travelled to the United States and returned with six beautiful American models who became front-page personalities overnight. In 1929 he repeated his sudden drop in skirt lengths, an act that caused consternation and some cases of financial ruin in the American garment industry, and has also been cited by sociologists and fashion historians as typical evidence of the uncanny relationship between sudden fashion reversals and world unrest.

After Jean Patou's death in 1936, the house continued under the direction of his brother-in-law, Raymond Barbas, a brilliant administrator who was for many years president of the Chambre Syndicale de la Couture Parisienne. Marc Bohan, now Dior's designer, was employed at Patou for several years. The present designer (1973) is Angelo Tarlazzi, an Italian with training in the Italian couture and in the American wholesale industries.

The Patou perfume company, established in 1924, makes the scent "Joy," known for many years as the most expensive perfume in the world.

Mme Paulette. See Hall of Fame

Jeanne Peral. Jewelry designer, 21 rue d'Hauteville, F-75010 Paris

Jeanne Peral is best known in the fashion world for the jewelry she designs for the Paris haute couture collections. Mme Peral, an authority on antiques and a leading expert in updating the jewelry craft in backward countries such as India, was the first to combine antique elements such as metal amulets, ivory and rock crystal carvings, and semiprecious stones with modern costume jewelry findings. The fashionable and rich look this brought to ethnic jewelry had widespread influence.

André Perugia. See Hall of Fame

Robert Piguet. See Hall of Fame

Gerard Pipart. Designer, Nina Ricci, 20 rue des Capucines, F-75001 Paris

Designer for the house of Nina Ricci since 1963, Gerard Pipart is responsible for the highly contemporary Ricci looks.

Born in Paris in 1933, he began as a free-lance designer for the French couture. After serving in the French army, he designed ready-to-wear for L'Empereur, a French wholesale house, and then worked in the United States before joining Ricci in 1963.

Paul Poiret. See Hall of Fame

Paco Rabanne. Avant-garde fashion designer, 7 rue Cherche Midi, F-75006 Paris; Perfume: 58 avenue Marceau, F-75008 Paris

One of the first designers to employ offbeat materials such as steel and plastic disks, aluminum, chains, metal mesh, fluorescent materials, and barnyard feathers in his stark, futuristic clothes, Paco Rabanne is now the center of a worldwide fashion and perfume business, owned by the Groupe Liaison Commerciale International.

Born in San Sebastian, Spain, the son of the seamstress who directed Balenciaga's couture workrooms, Rabanne left Spain with his family during the civil war. He studied to be an architect at the Ecole Superieure des Beaux Arts. After designing handbags, shoes, and embroideries, his first fanciful creations in plastic and feathers were displayed in a Paris art gallery as "pop" sculpture. His idea of welding or moulding clothes rather than sewing them was considered a major breakthrough in modern dress. In the late 1960s his mini-dresses made of chains, hammered aluminum, paper, leather, and knitted fur strips were continuous sensations. One of his plastic dresses, designed for Audrey Hepburn in the film *Two for the Road* was acquired by the Museum of Modern Art in New York in 1967. He is represented in the costume collections of the Musée de Costume in Paris, and the Philadelphia and Dallas museums.

In the 1970s he has concentrated on elements of total environment rather than fashion design and produced one of the most successful perfumes of the period, "Calandre."

Caroline Reboux. See Hall of Fame

House of Redfern. See Hall of Fame

Revillon. 42 rue de la Boetie, F-75008 Paris

The most noted French name in furs, Revillon was founded in 1923 by members of the Revillon family, who braved the blizzards of the Klondike to trap their own furs.

The house of Revillon flourished before and after World War II under the direction of Victor and Mme Jacques Revillon.

Fernando Sanchez is chief designer of the European collections. Revillon also made contracts with various American designers, among them Bill Blass and Adolfo, to create small groups of Revillon furs each year. In 1973, at Revillon's invitation, Bill Blass became the first American to show furs in Paris.

Nina Ricci. Couture and perfume house, 20 rue des Capucines, F-75001 Paris

This house has been known for understated and luxurious fashions since its founding in 1932 by Italian-born Mme Nina Ricci (see Hall of Fame). Her son Robert Ricci took over the administration in the 1950s and has piloted it into an international ready-to-wear and perfume business, while continuing with the couture ateliers. Mme Ricci, a regal white-haired figure, was seen at every Ricci collection opening until her death in 1970.

Ricci clothes are now designed by Gerard Pipart.

Maggy Rouff. See Hall of Fame

Sonia Rykiel. Ready-to-wear designer, 6 rue de Grenelle, F-75006 Paris

Creator of easy, elegant dresses in soft fabrics, Sonia Rykiel was born

Sonia Flis May 25, 1930, in Paris. She is a designer in the high French tradition, although she was never a couturiere. She studied liberal arts and when she married a boutique owner and had two children she expected to remain a housewife.

Her personal dissatisfaction with the type of clothes she could find for herself, however, led her to change the ready-mades available according to her own ideas. At 31, she began to design for her husband's "Laura" shops and in 1968 she established her own business.

She now has her own boutiques in Paris, Hong Kong, and Milan and exports her flowing yet tailored and sportively detailed clothes throughout the world.

In 1975, Mme Rykiel added a boutique of gourmet foods and household articles near her fashion boutique.

Yves Saint Laurent. 5 avenue Marceau, F-75016 Paris

Yves Saint Laurent, France's most renowned designer since Christian Dior, was born in Oran, Algeria, on August 1, 1936. His parents were French colonials.

Although he planned to be a political scientist, his teachers in the local lycée recognized his design ability and urged him to enter a contest judged by Christian Dior. He won the prize and also an offer to assist Dior in Paris.

In 1953, at 17, he came to Paris and from 1954 worked with Dior as his assistant until the great designer died three years later. He designed the next collection on his own, but his introduction of such "hippie" clothes as black leather jackets and pants brought about disputes with the Dior management. Then, Saint Laurent was unexpectedly drafted into the army. He suffered a nervous breakdown in army camp and was released from further service, but was not asked to return to Dior. He brought suit against the House of Dior for damages and was in turn countersued for enticing workers to the new business he was then in the process of organizing together with Pierre Berge, a well-known art entrepreneur who had earlier fostered the career of the painter Bernard Buffet.

The House of Saint Laurent opened January 29, 1962, at 30 bis rue Spontini. Among his backers were an American business man from Georgia, Jo Mack Robinson, and the American cosmetic firm, Charles of the Ritz.

In 1966, Saint Laurent opened Saint Laurent Rive Gauche, a boutique on the rue de Tournon on the Left Bank in Paris. A wave of smart boutiques followed in the boulevard Saint Germain area, and, as many predicted, eventually rang the death knell for the rarefied atmosphere of haute couture.

Saint Laurent's small prints in murky colors, his revival of crêpe de Chine and high platform shoes, his loose tent shape, and his pleated skirt with the stitched down hemline all became basic 1930s-inspired trends in the 1960s and 1970s.

A slender, perennially boyish young man, with blond hair and intellectual eyes behind huge glasses, Saint Laurent is shy and diffident, but very articulate. He designs frequently for the French revue theatre and the ballet, and created an amusing little character named "Naughty Little Lulu" in a book which he wrote and illustrated.

He has won every honor in fashion, and is one of the rare fashion designers to have a celebrity rating equal to a movie idol. He was one of the five French couturiers who shared with five Americans in the historic Versailles fashion show in 1973.

Jean-Louis Scherrer. Couture and ready-to-wear designer, 51 avenue Montaigne, F-75008 Paris

One of the few French couture houses to emerge successfully in the 1970s, Scherrer had important political figures as his first business backers and the house was then bought by an industrial conglomerate.

Born in Paris, the son of a surgeon, Scherrer trained for a career in ballet at the Paris Conservatory, but a back injury put a stop to his studies. He made fashion sketches to amuse himself while convalescing and on his recovery got a job on Christian Dior's staff. When Dior died and Yves Saint Laurent was chosen to succeed him, Scherrer left, and found backers for his own house.

Scherrer clothes have a following of smart international women. They are traditional in feeling, but young and well-priced, both at the couture and ready-to-wear level.

Elsa Schiaparelli. *See* Hall of Fame

Jean Schlumberger. Jewelry designer, 4 rue de Ponthieu, F-75001 Paris

Jean Schlumberger, internationally known jewelry designer, was born in Mulhouse, Haut Rhine, now Alsace-Lorraine, on June 24, 1907. His parents removed the family to Switzerland after World War I, and he was educated there. He feels his career began in the Paris flea market in 1937, when he purchased a tray of dusty Dresden china flowers and later turned them into amusing jewel-studded clips. This led to doing costume jewelry for Schiaparelli. Clients of that house—Mrs. Harrison Williams, Daisy Fellowes, Millicent Rogers, and Audrey Pleydell-Bouverie among them—asked him to design precious jewelry for them.

His independent career was interrupted by World War II. He was in the Battle of Dunkirk and was able to reach England, then America, as a worker with the Free French.

In 1947 he became associated with Tiffany in America and in 1956 he was made vice-president of the firm.

Schlumberger is credited with originating the combination of colored semiprecious stones with rare gems, and is noted for creating lifelike flowers and animals in jewels.

Kenzo Takada (Jap). Ready-to-wear designer, 46 rue Sainte Anne, F-75002 Paris

This Japanese-born (February 28, 1940) designer, called "the idea man of French ready-to-wear," is the son of a couple who kept a traditional Japanese inn in Himegi, a small town 50 miles from Osaka.

He studied in Osaka, intending to be a teacher of languages, but at 17 he left for Tokyo and the Bunka School of fashion where he spent three years. He gained his first prominence as a fashion artist for Japanese publications and continued to earn his living at drawing after he came to Paris in 1965.

Under the sponsorship of the Pisanti textile group, he presented showings of mad but provocative ready-to-wear fashions which caused great excitement in the late 1960s, and in 1970 he and a partner, Gilles Raysse, opened Jap, a boutique at 28 passage Choiseul, an Art Deco glass-roofed shopping area in Paris.

He now has three Jap shops in Paris, and one each in London, Munich, and Rome. He manufactures his own collections of clothing, accessories, shoes, and scarves and has licenses to design menswear, winter sportswear, beachwear, and household linens under his name for European firms.

Vicky Tiel. Ready-to-wear designer, 21 rue Bonaparte, F-75006 Paris

One of the first Americans to make a name in French ready-to-wear, Vicky Tiel was born October 21, 1943, in Washington, D.C. She studied art and costume design at Pratt Institute and the Parsons School of Design in New York, also attending the Parsons branch in Paris.

With Mia Fonssagrives, another Parsons girl in Paris, Vicky designed costumes for the film *What's New, Pussycat?*, gaining so much attention that they opened a Paris boutique.

Vicky Tiel now has her own business, partially financed by film star Elizabeth Taylor, for whom she has designed many film costumes.

Jacques Tiffeau. Ready-to-wear designer, 25 rue Faubourg St. Honoré, F-75008 Paris

Born October 11, 1927, in Chenevelles, France, Jacques Tiffeau served in the ground troops of the French Air Force.

After his demobilization he went to Paris and was "discovered" by Christian Dior. He worked as Dior's assistant until coming to America

(1952) as designer for Monte-Sano & Pruzan. With Beverly Busch, Pruzan's daughter, he formed Tiffeau-Busch, Inc., designing sportswear and tailored clothes.

In 1970 he went into business under his own name, but returned to France in 1971 and joined Saint Laurent as supervisor of the Rive Gauche collections of ready-to-wear the following year.

As of 1976, Tiffeau became designer for Originala, a New York coat and sportswear house (512 Seventh Ave., New York, N.Y. 10018).

Tiffeau received two Coty Awards, in 1960 and 1966, and the London Sunday Times Award, 1966. He has an apartment in Paris and a farm in Mougins, France.

Tiktiner (Dina Tiktiner Viterbo). Ready-to-wear designer, 55 promenade d'Anglaise, Nice

This well-known French ready-to-wear house, whose designer, Dina Viterbo, her husband and two daughters run the various branches of designing, manufacturing, and retailing sportswear with a Riviera look, originated as Mme Viterbo's hobby.

In 1949, Mme Viterbo began to make and sell beachwear in Nice under her maiden name, Tiktiner. Its success brought other shops and wholesale orders from stores in America.

Henri Viterbo is now president of two wholesale manufacturers' trade associations in the south of France. Their daughter is married to the prominent American dress manufacturer Mort Schrader.

Emanuel Ungaro. Couturier and boutique designer, 2 avenue Montaigne, F-75008 Paris

Emanuel Ungaro, leader of the avant-garde Paris couturiers, was born in Aix-en-Provence, France in 1933, of Italian parentage. His father was a tailor and trained Emanuel in that craft. "My father," he says, "taught me to recognize line and quality, and to respect every stitch."

At 23, Ungaro went to Paris and through family friends obtained a post on Balenciaga's design staff. He remained six years, then in 1962 joined another Balenciaga "graduate," André Courreges, in setting up a new fashion house. After one collection, however, Ungaro branched out on his own in a one-room studio on the Avenue McMahon. His organization is now established in an 18th-century mansion transformed into an ultramodern setting for the Ungaro clothes.

The famous Ungaro print patterns, mingling abstract and flower motifs, are designed by the designer's close friend Sonia Knapp.

Rose Valois. See Hall of Fame

Philippe Venet. Couturier and ready-to-wear designer, 62 rue François Premier, F-75008 Paris

This designer, trained in the Givenchy ateliers, is particularly known for his beautifully cut coats and suits. He was born in Lyons, France, about 1930. He learned the tailoring craft from the age of 14 and from 1951 to 1953 worked on Schiaparelli's staff in Paris. A fellow worker, Hubert de Givenchy, employed Venet as his master tailor when he founded his own house, and Venet remained with Givenchy until 1962 when he in turn established his own couture business.

Today, Venet's couture and ready-to-wear have a wide following and boutiques in Paris, Monte Carlo, and in other cities. He opened a boutique in the Philippines in 1973.

Victorine. See Hall of Fame

Madeleine Vionnet. See Hall of Fame

Roger Vivier. Shoe designer, 73 quai d'Orsay, F-75007 Paris
Among the best-known contemporary shoe creators, Vivier was born in Paris on November 13, 1913, and at 13 began working for a shoe manufacturer to earn funds to study sculpture at the Beaux Arts.

Delman, the American shoe manufacturer, brought Vivier to fashion prominence, introducing a Vivier collection in America in 1943.

In 1953, Vivier joined the house of Christian Dior to design the Dior shoe collections. Ten years later he opened his own business in association with Michel Brodsky, a relative of Marc Chagall, and now designs for shoe companies in the United States, Japan, Spain, and France.

Vivier's apartment on the quai d'Orsay is one of the showplaces of Paris, filled with his collection of ancient and modern sculpture and abstract paintings.

He has won the Neiman–Marcus Award and the Mare Moda Tiberio d'Oro Award.

One of his most famous assignments was to create the coronation slippers for Queen Elizabeth II.

House of Worth. See Hall of Fame: Charles Frederick Worth

Fashion Influentials

In France, the haute couture designer's ivory tower is rarely shared with anyone, least of all with members of the press. The fruitful interchange of opinions and helpful "log-rolling" and press promotion so familiar in America and England were until recently unknown in Europe.

There have been, however, notable exceptions: the influence wielded on French fashion designers of the 20th century by their artist friends Leon Bakst, Christian Berard, Jean Cocteau, Salvador Dali, and Raoul

71

Dufy and by editors such as Marie-Louise Bousquet and Helene Gordon-Lazareff.

Today a more relaxed atmosphere prevails in France and the press has been more instrumental in adding impetus to the careers of numerous designers, particularly in ready-to-wear. The availability to a wider public of ready-made clothing has made the fashion writer an instrument of propaganda and guidance, appreciated equally by the designer and the wearer of the new fashion. Thus the newspaper columnist may be as vital to a designer's career as the famous artist whose work inspired him in the old days.

Christian (Bebé) Berard (1902–1949)

This fashion artist of great talent and power from about 1924 through the 1940s had profound influence on several Paris designers of the period and brought about major fashion changes.

The son of a wealthy family who owned a string of funeral parlors in France, Berard was born August 20, 1902, in Paris and trained as an architect before turning to painting. Although he had a tremendous and serious talent, it was dissipated by both frivolous and serious weaknesses. His mania for the fashionable nightlife and petty gossip hampered his work, and an addiction to opium wrecked his health and caused his early death.

In spite of Berard's ungainly bulk, his stained red beard and dirty clothes, he was lionized by fashionable Paris. He loved to sketch on restaurant tablecloths, suggesting ideas to designers; he is said to have sketched the prototype of the New Look for Christian Dior in a bistro and to have suggested to Schiaparelli some of her most original color combinations and print motifs. The necessity of meeting deadlines for the fashion magazines which supported him, however, often reduced him to tears.

Berard's fashion sketches and his designs for the theatre are now classics of those arts. In his fashion sketches he introduced primitive colorings and inaccurate but interesting outlines which did not reflect the real clothes, but sparked the designers' imagination to new proportions. He often left the faces off his figure sketches, prompting one of his employers, William Randolph Hearst, to dub him "Faceless Freddie." Mrs. Edna Woolman Chase, editor of Vogue, was so annoyed at the inaccuracy of his drawings that she cabled, "Who would ever want to own that hat as you have pictured it?"

After he died on February 11, 1949, Berard was given a celebrity's funeral, with his adored "tout Paris" in attendance.

Claude Berthod. Fashion editor, Elle, 100 rue Reaumur, F-75002 Paris

Following the tradition established by Helene Lazareff, Mme Berthod was for about five years the editor most directly responsible for interpreting fashion through the pages of France's leading magazine for young people. She made innovations of her own and had a keen understanding of the potentials of French ready-to-wear.

She was replaced in 1973 by Daisy de Galard.

Marie-Louise Bousquet (1887–1975). Editor and fashion arbiter

One of the great catalysts of the Paris fashion and intellectual world for nearly half a century, Mme Bousquet was perhaps its last great lady of the literary salons.

Born in the late 19th century, she was married to Jacques Bousquet, a popular dramatist through whom she met the leading literary figures of the time. During World War I, to pool rations, the group met in Mme Bousquet's flat for dinner once a week. The habit never lapsed and her salon became a Parisian social tradition and entree to success.

In 1921, after meeting Carmel Snow, editor of the American fashion magazine *Harper's Bazaar*, Mme Bousquet became the magazine's Paris editor and an effectual and perceptive liaison between French arts and letters and the American public, introducing such writers and artists as Colette, Jean Cocteau, Louise de Vilmorin, Erté, Drian, Christian Berard, and Henri Cartier-Bresson through the pages of *Harper's Bazaar*. Together, Mme Bousquet and Mrs. Snow also furthered the international renown of many designers including Chanel, Vionnet, Gres, Molyneux, Rochas, Balenciaga, and Dior.

A tiny, birdlike woman crippled by arthritis, but sparkling with wit and energy, Marie-Louise Bousquet continued to flourish until the late 60s when her health failed. She retired in 1971. She lived bedridden in the apartment on the Place du Palais Bourbon, from which she helped to launch many of the immortals of French creativity, and died there on October 13, 1975.

Claude Brouet. Editor, *Marie Claire*, 51 rue Pierre Charron, F-75008 Paris

This editor covers high fashion for a broad readership and interprets trends thoroughly for every type of consumer.

Francine Crescent and **Françoise Mohrt.** Editors, French *Vogue*, 4 place du Palais Bourbon, F-75007 Paris

The two women responsible for French *Vogue*'s fashion coverage, both are in intimate contact with and have advance information on French fashion at all price levels.

Contrary to the earlier tradition of having titled personages on the French *Vogue* staff, both Mme Crescent and Mme Mohrt rose from the ranks in the magazine.

Helene de Turkheim. Fashion editor, *Figaro*, 14 Rond-Point des Champs-Elysées, F-75008 Paris

As fashion arbiter of the most prestigious French newspaper, Mme de Turkheim is an important critic of French fashion. Her associate, Viviane Greymour, is also a well-known figure on the French fashion scene.

Hebe Dorsey. Features writer, Paris *Herald Tribune*, 21 rue de Berri, F-75380 Paris

This Tunisian-born journalist is a key interpreter of French fashion to the English-speaking residents of Europe. She is a trenchant reporter and a trained observer. She also writes special articles for French periodicals.

Gerald Y. Dryansky. Former European editor, *Women's Wear Daily* (Fairchild Publications), 39 rue Cambon, F-75001 Paris

A journalist as well as novelist, Gerald Dryansky brings a quiet, dry humor plus skilled assessment to reports on European fashion and society for the Fairchild Publications. His commentary on fashions, personalities, and the Parisian lifestyle in *Women's Wear Daily* will form a valuable future record of the 1960s and 1970s.

Born in New York City, he went to Princeton (AB), Harvard (AM), and the Columbia School of Journalism. He came to Paris in 1964 after writing for the Philadelphia *Inquirer*.

In 1975 Dryansky left Fairchild to join a French textile company.

Helene Gordon-Lazareff. Chairman and editor, *Elle*, 100 rue Reaumur, F-75002 Paris

Probably the most powerful individual in the French press during the rise of young French fashion and the prêt-à-porter in the 1960s, Mme Lazareff was editor of *Elle* when it emerged after World War II as the voice of the liberated generation of French girls.

The wife of the late Pierre Lazareff, a brilliant newspaperman who later organized and was publisher of the Paris newspaper, *France Soir*, she shared her husband's life as an envoy of the Free French Movement in the United States during the war, returning to France on the arrival of General de Gaulle. During the war years she worked on *Harper's Bazaar* in New York.

Suzanne Guilley. Editor, *Officiel*, 226 Faubourg St. Honoré, F-75008 Paris

As selector of the fashions to be pictured in the magazine which is used for copying by dressmakers, large and small, throughout the world, Mme Guilley has been a strong force in the maintenance of French fashion prestige.

Rebecca Stickney Hamilton. Paris editor, *Harper's Bazaar* and *Queen*, 12 rue d'Astorg, F-75008 Paris

As a fabric and fashion expert reporting those fields from Europe to the U.S.A. and Great Britain, Rebecca (Becky) Hamilton is a skilled observer of changes which eventually affect dress in America and the British Isles.

Born in Arlington, Massachusetts, and a graduate of Wellesley College, Mrs. Hamilton went to Europe for the American Red Cross in 1945 and remained after the war as associate editor of British *Harper's Bazaar*.

Since 1948 she has lived in Paris as interpreter of European fashion for the home markets.

Françoise Mohrt. *See* Francine Crescent and Françoise Mohrt

Susan Train. French editor, American *Vogue*, Condé Nast Publications, 4 place du Palais-Bourbon, F-75007 Paris

Since 1951, Susan Train, born in New York City, has been responsible for reporting French fashion to readers of American *Vogue*. She is an expert on every aspect of the French fashion scene and a friend of many of its leading personalities.

Trade Associations and Organizations

Chambre Syndicale de la Couture Parisienne. 102 Faubourg St. Honoré, F-75008 Paris

Pres: Mme Gres. Perm. Off: Jacques Mouclier.

This organization, founded in 1868 at the instigation of Charles Frederick Worth as an outgrowth of the French guilds, has as its aim the coordination of all activities of haute couture. It provides legal protection against style piracy and sets dates for the semiannual couture showings. It issues credentials to the world press for couture openings, sponsors promotional activities, etc.

In 1973 the Chambre revised its policies to allow some prêt-à-porter firms to become members.

In 1930 the organization founded a training school for student designers and technicians, called l'Ecole de la Chambre Syndicale de la Couture (*see* Fashion Education).

In 1975 a new organization of couture and ready-to-wear designers was formed as another arm of promotion within the Chambre Syndicale. It is called Chambre Syndicale du Prêt-à-Porter, des Couturiers et Créateurs de Mode.

Chambre Syndicale du Prét-à-Porter des Couturiers et Créateurs de Mode. Designers organization, 100–102 Faubourg St. Honoré, F-75008 Paris

Founded: 1973. Pres: Pierre Bergé.

The recently organized designer group, affiliated with but still separate from the Chambre Syndicale de la Haute Couture, aims to guide and promote activities of the high fashion designers with ready-to-wear divisions. It will act independently of the French mass-production manufacturers in setting dates for showings and in propaganda functions.

L'Union Française des Arts du Costume (French Union of Costume Arts). 105 bd. Malesherbes, F-75008 Paris

Tel: 387-19-26. Founded: 1945. Pres: Bruno du Roselle. Dir: Yvonne Deslandres.

This trade and promotion organization represents the French couture and the French textile and clothing industries. Founded in 1945, and originally affiliated with the Musée Carnavalet in Paris, the organization in 1961 joined with the Chambre de Commerce et d'Industrie de Paris in opening the Centre de Documentation du Costume, an archive of books and documents pertaining to French fashion, including collections of sketches donated by famous couturiers.

At present admission is by appointment only.

Fashion Education

Note: The pamphlet "Study of Art in France" prepared by the cultural services of French embassies states that an inquiry to a French school must be accompanied by three international reply coupons.

Ecole A. Gogel des Cadres Couture. 15 rue de Chateaudun, F-75009 Paris

The school gives a two-year course leading to Certificat de Maitrise Formation Cadres. Training is offered for couture designers or directors of fashion houses, with courses in the history of costume.

L'Ecole de la Chambre Syndicale de la Couture. 45 rue de Saint Roch, F-75001 Paris

This is Europe's leading fashion school for French and international students.

Founded in 1930 under the leadership of Jacques Worth, then president of the Chambre Syndicale de la Couture Parisienne, the school was originally intended to provide talents and skilled labor for the French fashion houses; courses were given to train apprentices and aspiring French designers.

The school was soon urged to offer its superior courses to foreign students, many on scholarships from art or fashion schools of their native countries.

French students complete a three-year course. Foreign students follow a two-year course in fashion design, sketching, pattern-cutting, and draping. Well-known Paris designers conduct conferences and admit students to see their collections.

Ecole de L'Union Centrale des Arts Decoratifs. 6 rue Beethoven, F-75016 Paris

A four-year course is given in art studies including costume design.

Ecole des Beaux-Arts et des Arts Appliqués. 5 quai de la Daurade, Toulouse 31

This art school offers evening courses in fashion design. Students must have the authorization of the assistant mayor of Toulouse.

Esmod Guerre-Lavigne. Ecole International de Modelistes, 130 rue Reaumur, F-75002 Paris

There are one- or two-year courses according to the level of the student with an accelerated three- to six-month course in fashion design leading to a diploma.

Costume and Fashion Archives

Centre de Documentation du Costume. See Trade Associations and Organizations: L'Union Française des Arts du Costume

Musée de l'Homme, Laboratoire d'Ethnologie du Musée National d'Histoire Naturelle (Museum of Man, Ethnology Laboratory of the Museum of Natural History). Palais de Chaillot, Place du Trocadéro, F-75016 Paris

Tel: Pas. 74.46. Founded: 1878. Dir: Robert Gessain.

There are collections and archives of European and Asian dress.

Musée Departemental Breton (Museum of Brittany). 1 rue de Roi Gradlon, F-29000 Quimper

Curator: M. Quiniou.

This is an important collection of Breton costumes, antique and typical of the region.

Musée des Arts Decoratifs (Museum of the Decorative Arts). Palais du Pavillon Louvre de Marsan, 107 rue de Rivoli, F-75001 Paris

Tel: 7-42-22-84. Founded: 1880. Curator: François Mathey.

There are costumes, lingerie, and accessories from the 16th to 20th centuries.

Musée du Costume de la Ville de Paris (City of Paris Costume Museum). 14 avenue New York, F-75016 Paris. Correspondence: 9 rue Gaston Saint Paul, 75016 Paris
Tel: 727-92-98. Founded: 1956. Dir: Jacques Lanaigne.
There is an extensive collection from the 18th century to the present, including costumes from the Carnavalet Museum. Temporary exhibitions are presented to document the evolution of a style or to display new acquisitions. The museum publishes catalogs of its exhibitions.

Musée du Tissu d'Art et du Costume (Museum of Fabrics and Costumes). Chambre de Commerce et d'Industrie de Tourcoing, Place Charles-Roussel, F-59200 Tourcoing (Nord)
Tel: 74-89-16. Gen. Secy: J.E. Van Den Driesche.
Extensive collections of costumes and documents for the study of ancient and modern fabrics can be seen at this museum.

Musée du Vieux Toulouse (Museum of Old Toulouse). 7 rue Dumay, F-31000 Toulouse
Dir: Pierre Salies.
There are local costumes, examples of antique printed calico designs, and costume dolls. There is also an excellent collection of old photographs of local costumes.

Musée Felibréen de l'Art Provençal (Felibres Museum of Provençal Art). Château Gombert, 5 place des Héros, F-13001 Marseilles
There are French provincial costumes from the 17th to 20th centuries.

Musée Fragonard (Fragonard Museum). 2 rue Mirabeau, F-06130 Grasse
Tel: 161. Curator: Georges Vindry.
There is a collection of 18th century costumes and accessories and costume dolls.

Musée Municipal de Dinan (Municipal Museum of Dinan). Château de la Duchesse Anne, F-22100 Dinan, Brittany
Tel: 2.43 (Mairie). Dir: M. Rochereau.
There is an extensive collection of Breton regional costumes.

Musée Pyrénéen (Pyrenees Museum). Château-Fort, F-65100 Lourdes, Hautes Pyrénées
Tel: 204. Curator: Jean Robert.
There are regional peasant costumes and old photographs and costume plates of local costumes.

L'Union Française des Arts du Costume. See Trade Associations and Organizations

Fashion Publications

L'Art et la Mode. 17 Faubourg Montmartre, F-75009 Paris
Dir: Charles Mandel. 4 issues/yr. $25.00/yr. in US. Circ: 35,000.

Collections/Femme Chic. Publications Lauchel, 8 rue Halevy, F-75009 Paris
Founded: 1953. Ed: Pierre Lauchel. 6 issues/yr. $24.00/yr. in US. Circ: 109,744.

Couture Internationale. Publications Lauchel, 8 rue Halevy, F-75009 Paris
4 issues/yr. $19.00/yr. in US.

Dépêche Mode. Ed. "Edition et Communication," 3 rue de Teheran, F-75008 Paris
Founded: 1925. Dir: Hervé Coquerelle. 12 issues/yr. $82.00/yr. in US. Circ: 12,346.

Echo de la Mode. Ste. Unide, 9 rue d'Alexandrie, F-75002 Paris
Dir: A. De Smaele. 52 issues/yr. $55.00/yr in US. Circ: 501,591.

Elegance Masculine—Mylord. Edition Asteria, 5 rue Greffuhle, F-75008 Paris
Founded: 1932: 6 issues/yr. $12.00/yr. in US.

Elle. Soc. France Editions et Publications S.A.R.L., 100 rue Reaumur, F-75002 Paris
Founded: 1945. Dir/Founder: Helene Gordon-Lazareff. Ed-in-chief: Daisy de Galard. 52 issues/yr. $45.00/yr. in US. Circ: 600,000.

Femme. Publications Lauchel, 8 rue Halevy, F-75009 Paris
4 issues/yr. Circ: 5,811.

Femme d'Aujourd'Hui. 25 avenue Matignon, F-75008 Paris
Ed-in-chief: Marthe de Prelle. Fashion Eds: Janine Vivot and Nathalie Mantovani. 52 issues/yr. $35.00/yr. in US. Circ: 1,046,470.

Femme Pratique. 25 avenue Matignon, F-75008 Paris
Ed-in-chief: Michele Butten. Fashion Ed: Gilette Saint-André. 12 issues/yr. $30/yr. in US. Circ: 355,021.

L'Homme (Le Maître Tailleur). 8 rue d'Aboukir, F-75002 Paris
Dir: M.J. Ph. Vauclair. 6 issues/yr. $75/yr. in US.

Jardin des Modes. 100 rue Reaumur, F-75002 Paris
Founded: 1920. Dir: Guy Letellier. 12 issues/yr. Circ: 139,310.

Jours de France. 7 Rond-Point des Champs-Elysées, F-75008 Paris
Founded: 1954. Dir. Gen: Gal de Benouville. 52 issues/yr. $52.00/yr.
in US. Circ: 644,523.

Jours de France—Special Prêt-à-Porter. Additional copies of the *Prêt-à-Porter* included to subscribers.

Lui. 63–65 avenue des Champs-Elysées, F-75008 Paris
12 issues/yr. $20.00/yr. in US. Circ: 454,533.

Mariages. Publications Lauchel, 8 rue Halevy, F-75009 Paris
Founded: 1960. Eds: Pierre Lauchel and André Thiebaut. 6 issues/yr.
$16/yr. in US. Circ: 57,958.

Marie-Claire. 51 rue Pierre Charron, F-75008 Paris
Founded: 1954. 12 issues/yr. $12.00/yr. in US. Circ: 677,772.

Marie-France. 114 avenue des Champs-Elysées, F-75008 Paris
Founded: 1944. Dir. Gen: J. Sangnier. 12 issues/yr. $15.00/yr. in US.
Circ: 534,225.

Mode Chic de Paris. 14 rue Duphot, F-75001 Paris
Founded: 1928. 4 issues/yr. Circ: 61,844.

Modes de Paris, Pour Vous Madame. 2 rue des Italien, F-75009 Paris
Founded: 1948. Ed-in-chief: Mme Jolivet. 52 issues/yr. Circ: 1,272,033.

Modes et Travaux. Editions Edouard Boucherit, 10 rue de la Pepiniere,
F-75380 Paris
Founded: 1919. Dir: Edouard Boucherit. 12 issues/yr. $16.50/yr. in
US. Circ: 1,735,228.

Officiel de la Couture et de la Mode de Paris. Officiel de la Couture
S.A., 226 Faubourg Saint Honoré, F-75008 Paris
Founded: 1921. Eds: Marcel G. Peres and George Jalou. 8 issues/yr.
$49/yr. in US.

Officiel du Prêt-à-Porter. 17 Faubourg Montmartre, F-75009 Paris
Dir: Charles Mandel. 4 issues/yr. $25.00/yr. in US.

Vogue (French edition). Les Editions Condé Nast S.A., 4 place du
Palais-Bourbon, F-75007 Paris
Founded: 1921. Ed-in-chief: Mme Mohrt and Mlle Crescent. 10 is-
sues/yr. $42.00/yr. in US. Circ: 44,179.

Vogue-Homme. Les Editions Condé Nast S.A., 4 place du Palais-Bourbon, F-75007 Paris

Founded: 1974. Pres/Gen. Dir: Daniel Salem. 4 issues/yr. $20/yr. in US.

GERMANY, FEDERAL REPUBLIC OF

Of all the clothing sold within the European Common Market, West Germany produces 69 percent, and thus is the largest garment center in Europe.

Its clothing industry has been a major factor in the postwar economy of Germany. This statistic is historically related to Berlin, where ready-made clothes were produced as early as 1837. In West Berlin, clothing is the third largest consumer industry today, employing 40,000 workers and bringing in an annual revenue of more than $500 million.

As so frequently happens, however, the feast of German fashion production is accompanied by a near-famine in German fashion creativity. Clothes made in Germany continue to be (a) derivative of Paris or Rome, (b) produced more by precision methods than the soft dressmaking techniques now used for every type of garment, with the result that they are rather square and hard in line, and (c) except in rare instances lacking in the wit and personality intrinsic to original designs.

Through the medium of frequent and beautifully organized trade fairs in Munich, Dusseldorf, Berlin, and Frankfurt, Germany has shown signs of awakening to the spirit of creative fashion. To its power as a mass-production center will probably be added an individual fashion message.

Fashion Designers and Firms

Willi Bogner. Skiwear designer, Box 800280, D-8000 Munich 80

This ski and sportswear house has two famous skiers, Mr. and Mrs. Willi Bogner, as designer–owners. They are known for the innovative use of lighter insulated fabrics and the introduction of tasteful colorings in ski wear.

They now have a branch manufacturing firm in New York.

Uli Richter. Couturier and ready-to-wear designer, Uli Richter Modelle, 15 Kurfürstendam, D-1 Berlin West

Couturier and wholesale manufacturer Uli Richter was born December 28, 1926, in Potsdam, Germany and brought up in that city.

He was expected to follow the family profession of pharmacy, but after a brief study of chemistry he turned to designing textiles. In 1945, at 19, having escaped from Potsdam when it became part of East Germany, he apprenticed at the House of Horn, West Berlin's leading women's specialty store. His first independent design was a hit, and he was soon Horn's chief designer.

In 1959 he established his own fashion house, Uli Richter Modelle, in Berlin, then added salons in Dusseldorf and Munich. His custom clientele includes well-known German women, among them Mrs. Willy Brandt and members of the Hohenzollern family. His ready-to-wear is sold throughout Europe.

Talented, handsome, and a fine linguist, Uli Richter is West Germany's frequent "fashion envoy" to other countries.

He won the German Textile Board's Golden Scissors Award in 1966, and served on the jury of the Swiss Production Board in St. Gallen, Switzerland.

Walter Rupp. Couture and ready-to-wear designer, Rupp and Taureck, D-8897 Pottmes

This designer shares a successful partnership which owns an international chain of boutiques for ready-to-wear.

Edith Schmid (Werner). Designer of far-out clothes, Herrenstrasse 30, Munich

A member of Munich's colorful social and artistic circle, Edith Schmid designs for the theater and television as well as for her own boutique, where her following is drawn from the young and wealthy set of Munich. She also owns a popular nightclub called "Why Not?"

Fashion Influentials

Jan H. Friedländer. Paris representative, *Madame und Elegante Welt*, 69 boulevard Beausejour, F-75016 Paris, France

Representing Germany's leading women's magazines, Friedländer is in touch with all fashion activities in Europe, and the *Madame* annual gala of international fashion is built around the Paris collection he considers the most significant of the year.

Margarete Schüssel. Fashion editor, *Madame und Elegante Welt*, Verlag H. Heilmaier, Altheimer Eck 13, D-8 Munich 2

As fashion editor of *Madame und Elegante Welt*, Germany's leading high-fashion publication, Mme Schüssel is an expert at explicitly interpreting international trends for her readers in terms of cut. She is a former teacher of sewing techniques.

Trade Associations and Organizations

Fashion Fairs (Cavin and Tubiana, OHG). Organizers of international trade fairs, Heyes Strasse 20-22, D-12 Dusseldorf 12

See United States: Trade Associations and Organizations.

Frankfurter Rauchwaren-Messe GmbH (Frankfurt International Fur Fair). See Verband der Deutschen Rauchwaren-und Pelzwirtschaft e.v.

Igedo Internationale Mode-Messe GmbH. Freilegrath Strasse 28, D-4000 Dusseldorf 30.
Founded: 1950. Dirs: J.A. Baum and Manfred Kronen.
This group organizes international high-fashion ready-to-wear showings in Dusseldorf four times a year. It attracts both German and foreign buyers.

Interstoff Messe und Austellungs GmbH. Friedrich Elbert Anlage 57, Postfach 970 126, D-6 Frankfurt/Main 97
Founded: 1952. Dir: D. Peter Graf von Wedel.
This group organizes the important trade showings of fashion fabrics twice a year (May and November) in Frankfurt, attracting thousands of international buyers.

Mode-Woche-München GmbH. Theresienhöhe 15, D-8000 Munich 12
Founded: 1947. Dir: Alfred Wurm.
This international trade fair in Munich attracts hundreds of German and foreign exhibitors and thousands of buyers twice each year. The fair, in March and October, is aimed at showing better-quality merchandise of interest to expensive boutiques.

Verband der Damenoberbekleidungsindustrie e.v. (German Association of Ladies Wear). Kaiserstrasse 46, D-4000 Dusseldorf North
Dir: Helmut Gilbert.
This organization founded soon after World War II, deals with all internal and external trade interests of the large and efficient German clothing industry.

Verband der Deutschen Rauchwaren-und Pelzwirtschaft e.v. (Association of German Fur Manufacturers). Bettinaplatz 1, D-6000 Frankfurt/Main
Founded: 1950. Pres: Walter Wurker. Dir: Gunter Fix. Dep. Dir: Walter Langenberger.
This organization, with a membership composed of all branches of the German fur trade, deals with internal matters and also sponsors Frankfurt's annual International Fur Fair which is rapidly becoming a forecast point of the world fur trends and technology of furs.

Fashion Education

West Germany has a number of schools teaching textile and clothing design, although there is no school where the creative element is particularly stressed. A sampling of the schools with courses in both fashion and textiles follows.

Deutsche Meisterschule für Mode. Rossmarkt 15, D-8 Munich 2
This school has a different French couturier each year as guest lecturer and critic.

Institut für Modeschaffen der Stadt Frankfurt. Morfelder Landstrasse 277, D-6 Frankfurt/Main

Kunstschule Westend. Liebigstrasse 3, D-6 Frankfurt/Main

Lette-Verein-Berlin. Victor-Louise Platz 6, D-1 Berlin 3

Meisterschule für Mode. Werkkunstschule für Textil, Grafik, Werbung, Armgartstrasse 24, D-2 Hamburg 22

Modeschule Düsseldorf. Uhlandstrasse 38, D-4 Dusseldorf

Studienstatte für Textilkunst Krefeld. Frankenring 20, D-415 Krefeld

Costume and Fashion Archives

Bayerisches Nationalmuseum (Bayern National Museum). Prinzregentenstrasse 3, D-8000 Munich 22
Tel: 22-25-91. Founded: 1855. Gen. Dir: Dr. Hans Robert Weihrauch.
There are collections of fashions and peasant costumes, textiles, and needlework from the 16th to the 19th centuries.

Deutsches Ledermuseum (German Leather Museum). Frankfurterstrasse 86, D-6050 Offenbach/Main
Tel: 81-39-82. Founded: 1917. Dir: Dr. Phil Günter-Gall.
There are antique leather costumes and shoes from all over the world.

Historisches Museum (History Museum). Untermainkanal 14, D-6000 Frankfurt/Main
Tel: 2-12-33-70. Founded: 1878. Dir: Dr. Hans Stubenvoll.
There are costumes and uniforms of the 18th and 19th centuries.

Kostümforschungs Institut (Costume Research Institute). Kemnatenstrasse 50, D-8 Munich 19
Dir: Hermine V. Parish.
There is a fine collection of costume plates, lithographs, rare editions and other documents illustrating all aspects of costume.

Fashion Publications

Note: Two East German publications, Modische Linie and Sibylle, are included in this section.

Brigitte. Gruner and Jahr Verlag, Presshaus, D-2000 Hamburg 1
Founded: 1957. Ed: Volker. 12 issues/yr. DM.3.50/issue.

Burda Mode. Verlag Aenne Burda, Am Kestendamm 2, D-76 Offenburg
Founded: 1950. Ed-in-chief: Irene Baer. 12 issues/yr. DM.3.50/issue
($19/yr. in US). Circ: 2,000,000.

Chic. Ross-Verlag, Spichernstrasse 12, D-5000 Cologne 1
Founded: 1948. Ed: Dr. Hellmuth Kobusch. 4 issues/yr. DM.6/issue
($21/yr. in US). Circ: 100,000.

Die Frau. Verlag Welt am Sonnabend, Adlerstrasse 22, D-4000 Dusseldorf 1
Founded: 1965. Ed: P. Preiss. 4 issues/yr. DM.10/issue.

Die Linie. Verlag Heber, Stadtwaltgurter 46, D-5000 Cologne 41
Founded: 1950. 4 issues/yr. DM.12/issue ($29/yr. in US).

Frau im Spiegel. Verlag Ehrlich & Sohn KG, Postfach 2139, D-24 Lubeck
Founded 1946. Ed: Jochen Seelhoff. 12 issues/yr. DM.3.50/issue.

Frauenwelt und Modeblatt. Verlag Klampt, Postfach 58, D-6720 Speyer
12 issues/yr. DM.2.80/issue.

Madame und Elegante Welt. Verlag Dr.H. Heilmaier, Altheimer Eck 13,
D-8000 Munich 2
Founded: 1948. Ed-in-chief: Jochen Willke. Fashion Ed: Margarete
Schüssel. 12 issues/yr. DM.4.50/issue ($28/yr.in US).

Modische Linie. VER Fachbuchverlag, Karl-Heine Strasse 17, DDR-
7031 Leipzig
Founded: 1969. 4 issues/yr. M.13.60.

Neue Mode. H. Bauer Verlag, Burchardstrasse 11, D-2000 Hamburg 1
Founded: 1948. 4 issues/yr. DM.8.40/issue ($23/yr. in US).

Sibylle. Verlag für die Frau, Friedrich-Ebert Strasse 76-78, DDR-7001
Leipzig
Founded: 1958. 4 issues/yr. M.4.50/issue.

GREAT BRITAIN

It is not general practice to credit Great Britain with anything like the
global fashion domination attributed to France; even so, British influence and British talents have played an impressive role in the history of
world fashion.
The designer who actually established the French haute couture tra-

dition was the Englishman Charles Frederick Worth. Lucile, Lady Duff-Gordon, one of the first fashion designers to conduct business on an international scale, was born in Canada and started her career in London. One of her British assistants, Captain Edward Molyneux, carried the dash and freedom of the Prince of Wales' Mayfair set across the channel to Paris, where he starred twice during his lifetime.

English-bred Elizabethan, Victorian, Regency and pre-Rafaelite (Art Nouveau) fashions dominated world fashion for long periods, followed in the 1960s by the Mod, the Carnaby Street and the King's Road "looks," all originally British. The godmother of all three was the young British designer Mary Quant (who also launched the mini-skirt). Another dynamic Briton was Janey Ironside, brilliant teacher at the Royal College of Art in the 1950s and 1960s, who fostered a new fashion generation.

The Industrial Revolution, without which there could be no mass production of garments, American ready-to-wear, or French prêt-à-porter, began in 19th-century England. Britain's most pervasive fashion influence, however, lay in the incomparable hand-tailoring techniques developed there in the 18th and 19th centuries. This skill, combined with the inbred understanding of functionality seen in English sports clothing, influenced all of 20th-century fashion; comfort and freedom, more than visual effect, are the prime elements of modern dress.

England gave fashion its most learned fashion historian, James Laver, and its keenest and most vivid contemporary chronicler of the fashionable life, Sir Cecil Beaton.

In terms of clothing as a resource of world trade, however, the British Empire's contribution has been weak. The British Clothing Export Council has sponsored numerous trade tours and clothing exhibits throughout the world, and cites an increase in the export of clothing of £20 million each year. Yet the creative talents who express the unhopeful, fatalistic spirit of Britain in the home market find a restricted public elsewhere. The slow uptake of British-made exports was recently attributed by Sheila Black in the Financial Times of London to "poor-quality merchandise, made too fast and too cheaply." In 1972, however, it was officially reported that the United Kingdom's efforts to spur exports had resulted in a nearly 40 percent increase in earnings.

The British couture houses which dressed the wealthy of pre-war days have almost disappeared, without being replaced on any large scale by important wholesale firms. British fabrics are produced in sizable quantity, but significant names like Sekers, Ascher, Harris, Donegal, Liberty, and Moygashel have lost much of their aura.

In men's clothing, the dominant world market that was British until World War II has disappeared, although highly gifted men's fashion designers continue to create in England.

ENGLAND

Fashion Designers and Firms

Hardy Amies. 14 Savile Row, London W1

This leading English fashion designer is now better known for his menswear, although he still designs for Queen Elizabeth II "by command" and maintains a successful London fashion business.

Born Edwin Hardy Amies on July 17, 1909 in London, he was educated at Brentwood School and studied in France and Germany.

He received his early fashion training at W & T Avery, a Birmingham dressmaking house. In 1934 he came to London to design for Lachasse, a well-known couture house where his mother was employed. He was quickly promoted to designer, then manager as well.

Amies served during World War II in British Army Intelligence, reaching the rank of lieutenant-colonel. He was appointed head of the Special Forces mission to Belgium, where he was made Officier de l'Ordre de la Couronne (1946).

In 1946 he opened his own couture house at the present address, which now has the insignia, "By Appointment to Her Majesty Queen Elizabeth II," beside its doorway. His boutique, opened in 1950, was one of the first to offer high-fashion ready-to-wear in a London couture house.

In 1967 Amies was asked to restyle men's fashions for a large Scottish tailoring firm and his reputation in that field has since grown steadily. He is now under contract with Genesco of America to design men's clothing and accessories there.

Tall, thin, and an excellent example of his clothes creed of classic British cut with contemporary coloring and detail, Amies also exemplifies the modern commuting spirit of international fashion. He travels monthly between London and New York, maintaining an apartment in New York and a handsome early Victorian house in London.

He was chairman of the Incorporated Society of London Dress Designers from 1959 to 1960.

His awards include Harper's Bazaar Award (1962), the American Caswell-Massey International Award for men's fashions (1962, 1964, and 1968), and the London Sunday Times Special Award (1965).

Annacat. Boutique (wholesale & retail) and designers for boutiques, 270 Brompton Rd., London SW3

Opened as a boutique by British socialites Janet Lyle and Maggie Cheswick in 1965, Annacat expanded to wholesale production in 1970. The neoromantic clothes designed for the shop attracted international attention when worn by the young aristocratic set in London and New York. Janet Lyle now operates Annacat in partnership with Leslie Poole.

Aquascutum. Tailored clothing producers, 100 Regent St., London W1

This firm, widely known for rainwear, was founded in 1851 by a Regent Street custom tailor who introduced the first showerproof finish on wool and coined his label from the two Latin words "aqua" (water) and "scutum" (shield). Today Aquascutum makes tailored clothes in British fabrics for both men and women which are sold internationally and in their own London shop.

Laura Ashley (Mrs. Bernard Ashley). Ready-to-wear designer–manufacturer, Rhayader, Wales. London office: 157 Fulham Rd., London SW3

Laura Ashley, whose clothes are derived from the romantic, earthy costumes of her native Wales, is one of Great Britain's most widely distributed designers. She and her husband Bernard Ashley began by making hand-blocked scarves (1955) and opened their first shop in London in 1965. They now own a network of nearly 20 shops in Europe and licence their label in Japan, Australia, and Canada.

The Laura Ashley business is based in Rhayader, Wales, where their factory finishes and prints the fabrics, before local people make up the clothes for distribution.

Baccarat. Ready-to-wear producers, 40 Great Marlborough St., London W1

The first large-scale wholesale firm to make and distribute the young, nonconformist fashions by new name designers in England during the 1960s, this firm was founded by Claire Black and her husband Monty Black. Claire Black edits the typical Baccarat look of neoromantic softness, with a staff of several young designers under her supervision. Bill Gibb, now on his own, got his start with Baccarat.

There are Baccarat boutiques in leading stores throughout the British Isles and Ireland, and the firm exports to many foreign countries.

Maureen Baker. See Susan Small

John Bates. Designer for Jean Varon, 19-21 Noel St., London W1

Known for producing trendy English clothes at a moderate price, John Bates attributes his down-to-earth attitude towards design to his early life in the rugged mining area of Newcastle, Northumberland. He trained to become a journalist for two years, but instead took his first job on the staff of a London couture house where he picked up pins, ran errands, and "emptied waste baskets filled with my design sketches." After four years, he decided to try the ready-to-wear opportunities and sold his sketches to wholesale firms in London.

His fortunes changed when he re-met two young men from his couture days; they had been searching for him to join them as the designer in a new company, Jean Varon Ltd.

In 1965 Bates won the British press Dress of the Year Award for his see-through mini-dresses. They are now on display in the Museum of Costume in Bath. The following year he won the Yardley London Look Award which carried with it a trip to New York.

Bates was the first designer to do fashions for television, notably the popular "Avengers" series. A subsidiary company, Capricorn (John Bates' sign) produces his coats and suits. John Bates' designs are now exported to 44 countries.

Belinda Bellville. Bellville Couture, 185 Sloane St., London SW1

This wholesale house, founded in 1956 by Belinda Bellville, specializes in romantic evening clothes in the stately tradition. David Sassoon is now co-designer.

Manolo Bianchek. *See* Chelsea Cobbler

Biba (Barbara Hulanicki). Avant-garde wholesale and retail designer, (no business address in 1975).

Barbara Hulanicki and her husband Stephen Fitz-Simon founded one of the most colorful fashion businesses in England and continue to contribute to British fashion prestige.

A leader of the 1960s antiestablishment fashion movement, Barbara studied fashion illustration at the Brighton Art School. She was the daughter of a Polish diplomat who spirited his family to England in advance of the German invasion. When an original dress design she submitted in a newspaper contest brought 12,500 orders, she started a mail-order dress business which quickly established her reputation for fashion in soft young lines, good fit, whimsical touches, and low prices.

In 1964 when the exaggerated British "teddy boy" and "bird" fashions swept in, Biba opened a shop in a small mid-Victorian house off the King's Road. It became the most popular and crowded spot in the area. Couples with their infants in market baskets thronged the shop to buy her matching unisex costumes.

Since then Biba has moved to larger quarters five times, most recently to the renovated Art Deco building formerly occupied by London's Derry and Tom's department store, with a roof-garden restaurant and 150,000 square feet of selling space. This closed in 1975. Since 1970 the Biba company, now comprising men's clothes, cosmetics, and home furnishings as well as women's fashions, has been part of the Dorothy Perkins chain of retail shops.

Claire Black. *See* Baccarat

Blades. Men's tailors, 8 Burlington Gardens, London W1
This is one of England's trend-setting "bespoke" tailors, headed by Rupert Lycett-Green, making menswear on a limited basis, but with widespread inspirational power.

Hylan Booker. Cannibal Clothes Ltd., 11 South Molton St., London W1
Hylan Booker, one of the very few Americans to have entered and made good in British fashion, is a black ex-soldier born in Detroit, Michigan. He served in the U.S. Air Force from 1958 to 1962, and then took his GI studies at the Swindon College of Art and the Royal College of Art. At the latter institution, where his fashion sketches won him a three-year scholarship, he studied under the inspiring Professor Janey Ironside.

Hailed as a brave young talent of English "Mod" fashion, Booker briefly operated his own London dress firm, but soon closed it and joined the venerable house of Worth as a couture designer.

Since 1972 he has designed sports clothes in the young but more classic spirit for Cannibal.

Moya Bowler. Shoe designer, Moya Bowler, Ltd., 5 Norland Sq., London W1
This shoe designer who emerged in the Carnaby Street days is now designing and styling for English, continental, and American shoe firms.

Born in Reading, Berkshire, on June 9, 1940, Moya grew up at Battle, Sussex, the site of the Norman-Saxon Battle of Hastings.

In 1957 she entered the Brighton College of Art, graduating in art and dress design, then studied at the Royal College of Art under Professor Janey Ironside, who encouraged her to free-lance as a shoe designer while still a student.

In 1964 she started Moya Bowler, Ltd. She now designs on a free-lance basis in partnership with an American, Richard Joseph. Shoe manufacturers in Greece, Japan, and the United States are their clients.

Burberrys. Rainwear and sportswear for men and women, 18–20 Haymarket, London SW1
Burberrys was founded in 1856 by London tailor Thomas Burberry

(1835–1889) to make waterproof gabardine clothes for gentlemen's field sports. The firm later produced Army and Navy uniforms as well. The Burberry raincoat eventually became internationally known, and a generic term after King Edward VII developed the habit of saying "Give me my Burberry."

Burberrys now produces classic sportswear and accessories of all types for men and women.

Busvine. See Hall of Fame

John Cavanagh. Dress designer, 26–27 Curzon St., London W1

Irish-born on September 28, 1914, John Cavanagh studied at St. Paul's School in England and trained on the staff of Edward Molyneux (1932–1940). In Paris when World War II broke out, he joined British Intelligence and also served in the Camouflage Corps. In 1945 he joined Pierre Balmain as assistant to that Paris couturier and remained until 1951. He opened his own business in London in 1952, designing for members of the Royal family and for chic English women. Clive is now associated with John Cavanagh as designer of his ready-to-wear collections.

He was vice-chairman of the Society of London Dress Designers (1956–1959).

Chelsea Cobbler. Shoe designers and manufacturers, 37 High St., London NW1

Influential in world fashion for fanciful boots in the mid-1960s, the Chelsea Cobbler produces full-scale shoe collections and retains its trend-setting reputation. Richard Smith is director of the firm, and Manolo Bianchek its designer.

Ossie (Raymond) Clark. Ready-to-wear designer, 6 Burnsall St., London SW3

Known as one of England's most daring and innovative designers, Ossie Clark was born in Liverpool on June 2, 1942. His mother worked as a charwoman so that he could study fashion design at the Manchester School of Art (1957–1961). He won a scholarship to the Royal College of Art in London and studied there until 1964.

With his wife Celia Birtwell, who designs all of his prints, he launched his first dress collection in the spring of 1966 for Quorum, a firm started earlier by Alice Pollock who now designs a separate collection under her own name. Since then, he has done the Quorum collections and was among the first foreigners to design for the French ready-to-wear firm, Mendes. Ossie Clark clothes are sold all over the world, with the largest sales in Germany and America. Although first known for his "young rebel" fashions, mini-skirts and see-through clothes, Ossie changed in the early 1970s to "sophisticated-women" clothes inspired by the 1940s.

A sprightly fashion epigram-maker, Ossie Clark's "mots" include: "Designing for the future is impossible because the future never comes," "Fashion is to stop people being bored," and "I shall always design for people my own age."

Clive (John Quentin Evans). Free-lance designer, 4 Palliser Court, Barons Court, London W14

Now design consultant for several British and European companies and designer of John Cavanagh's ready-to-wear, Clive was one of the few young British style stars of the 1960s who preferred designing couture to off-the-peg fashion. He opened his own couture house in 1962, when the Carnaby Street fashion movement was just beginning. He managed to be successful, but in 1971 the difficulties of producing luxury clothes forced him to turn free-lance.

Born on December 16, 1933, he went to Bradfield College to follow his father's career by studying medicine. After spending two years in the Royal Navy he decided to be a designer and worked for London couturiers John Cavanagh and Michael before setting up his own firm. In 1970, Clive designed the uniforms of the BOAC stewardesses and ground staff.

House of Creed. See Hall of Fame

Maxwell Croft. Wholesale fur designer, 105 New Bond St., London W1

Maxwell Croft, England's best-known furrier, is vice-president of the British Fur Trade Association. In 1973 Maxwell Croft was the first fur designer to have a shop within a British department store.

Barbara Daly. Makeup specialist, 10 Westbourne Gardens, London W2

Barbara Daly has been responsible for many trends in makeup and feature emphasis during the 1970s, particularly in replacing sharply drawn eye outlines with a misty rainbow of tinted eye shadows. She designs unusual makeup for avant-garde and period films, including The Clockwork Orange and Barry Lyndon, both produced by Stanley Kubrick.

Mr. Fish (Michael Fish). Menswear designer, 100 Mount St., London W1

This "trendy" men's fashion firm led the high-fashion side of the male fashion insurgence in the 1960s.

Michael Fish, the designer for what the London Times called a "boutique for rich gentlemen," was born in London and at 15 was a delivery boy for a London haberdasher. He went on to work as a salesman at Sulka and later was designer at Turnbull & Asser, exclusive Jermyn Street shirtmakers.

Barry Sainsbury, a member of the Sainsbury biscuit family of England, helped Michael Fish start Mr. Fish and shared in the strong promotion of its extravagantly patterned shirts, its variation on the Nehru jacket, and its collections of period coats, waistcoats, ruffled shirts, and Beau Brummell slacks. He has now withdrawn from the firm.

Mr. Fish designs are now more conservative but always distinctive and have international distribution.

Foale & Tuffin, Ltd. *See* Sally Tuffin, Ltd.

Gina Fratini. Dress designer, 21–22 Great Castle St., London W1

This ready-to-wear designer is known for her distinctive blend of romantic lines with contemporary coloring and fabrics.

Born in Japan, Miss Fratini was brought to England as a baby and stayed until she was seven. Then the family moved to Canada, Burma, and India within five years. She later attended school in England and spent three years at the Royal College of Art.

She joined the Katherine Dunham Dance troupe for two years as a costume designer, travelling around the world. After returning to England, she designed for the stage and films and in 1964 started her own business.

Mr. Freedom (Tommy Roberts). Boutique fashion designer, City Lights Studio, 54 Shorts Garden, London WC2

Best known for having introduced Pop Art and cartoon characters as decorations on shirts and sweaters, Mr. Freedom, founded by Tommy Roberts as a shop on Kensington Church Street, was a center for the "freak-out" men's and women's fashions of the late 1960s, also selling furniture and children's clothes.

In 1972, Tommy Roberts opened his City Lights Studio, where he and a group of associate designers create wild, fanciful clothing for both sexes.

Bill Gibb. Bill Gibb Ltd., 67 Knightsbridge, London SW9

Leader of the 1970s crop of avant-garde English designers, Bill Gibb was born in 1943 on a farm in northeastern Scotland.

Encouraged by his grandmother and his teacher in Fraserburgh Academy, he came to London in 1962 to study at St. Martin's School of Art. He left four years later with honors as the top student. He won a scholarship to the Royal College of Art (RCA) in 1966 to study under Professor Janey Ironside. During this period Bill and three friends owned and designed for their own boutique. As a participant in the Yardley Award he came to New York, where he attracted international attention before he was out of school.

After leaving the RCA, he did free-lance designing for the English wholesale firm Baccarat, then joined their design staff. With textile designer Kaiffe Fassett, Bill made a collection which combined Scottish tartans with hand knits and helped establish the fashion for mixed textures and patterns. One of these garments is now in the permanent collection of the Museum of Costume in Bath.

Vogue selected Bill Gibb "Designer of the Year" in 1970. That year he was invited by the Federation of the Embroidery Industry of Austria to design their fashion collection in Japan. A Bill Gibb dress was chosen for the exhibition "British Design" at the Louvre in Paris in 1971.

In 1972, Bill Gibb Ltd. was established and Gibb's modern clothes in the elaborated mood of the early 1900s, influenced by Poiret and Erté, continued to attract attention to the designer.

Norman Hartnell. Court dressmaker, 26 Bruton St., London W1

Born on June 12, 1901, in London, Hartnell attended Magdalen College, Cambridge University, where he designed costumes for his class plays. He began designing professionally in 1923 for an exclusive London dressmaker. In 1927 and again in 1930, he showed collections in Paris with success both with private clients and professional buyers.

His elaborate fur-trimmed and beaded evening gowns and his majestic afternoon clothes made him a natural choice for the ladies of the Royal family, whom he has dressed by Royal Warrant for three generations.

During World War II he designed prototype utility clothes to demonstrate how to save fabric. He designed the uniforms of the women of the Royal Air Corps and the Red Cross.

Hartnell, a witty and gregarious gentleman, was one of the founders of the Incorporated Society of London Fashion Designers. He received the M.V.O. (Member Royal Victoria Order) in 1953.

He received the Neiman–Marcus Award in 1947 for his contribution to world fashion. Hartnell's autobiography, *Silver and Gold* (Evans Brothers, 1955), and his book on the history of royal dress, *Royal Courts of Fashion* (Cassell, 1970), (see Bibliography) are delightfully chatty and full of unusual historical information.

Jaeger. Sportswear producers, 57 Broadwick St., London W1

Jaeger was founded in London in 1884 by Dr. Gustav Jaeger, a native of Stuttgart, Germany, in line with his theory that wearing natural wool next to the skin was "a year-round source of bodily well-being." His ideas became a cult, with such followers as George Bernard Shaw,

Rudyard Kipling, and Edward VII, and eventually expanded his scope to produce smart ready-made woolen outerwear for men and women.

Jaeger now has wool farms in Australia, 14 factories in Britain, a separate American wholesale organization, and 62 retail shops throughout the world.

Leonard (Leonard Lewis). Hairstylist, 6 Upper Grosvenor St., London W1

Best known for introducing the fad for vividly colored streaks in women's coiffures, Leonard is London's most talked-of hair stylist. He also designs the coiffures for films and produces hair-treatment products of natural substances and vitamins. He created the 18th-century wigs for the Stanley Kubrick film *Barry Lyndon*.

Leonard has now added a London shop for male hairdressing.

John Lobb. Bootmakers, 9 St. James St., London SW1

Lobb has been the status name in British men's shoes for five centuries and has a branch in Paris. Lobb also created one of the male luxury fashions of recent years, velvet house slippers with the man's monogram embroidered in gold on the front.

Lucile. See Hall of Fame

Luke (Gordon Luke Clarke). Boutique designer, 184 King's Rd., London SW3

A New Zealander with a Scottish father and Maori mother, Luke was born Gordon Luke Clarke in Auckland on August 9, 1945. At 12 he won a design award sponsored by Air New Zealand, and by 18 he was a member of Hardy Amies design staff in London. He designed Amies ready-to-wear for five years, then toured India for 18 months.

On his return to London he opened a shop in the new center of far-out fashion, the King's Road, where his clothes soon found a following. Luke's colorful and highly individualistic clothes are also sold in American stores.

Molyneux. See Hall of Fame

William Morris. See Hall of Fame

(Henry) Digby Morton. Fashion designer (retired)

Digby Morton, known in England for his quiet tailored sports clothes and in America as the initial designer of Lady Hathaway shirts, was born November 27, 1906, in Dublin, Ireland. He studied at the Dublin Metropolitan School of Art and the Polytechnic Art School in London.

His designing career began in 1930. In 1936 he married journalist

Phyllis Mary Panting, daughter of the editorial writer Pendennis of the *London Observer* and goddaughter of H.G. Wells.

Digby Morton's wartime uniform for the Women's Voluntary Services was worn by 1,000,000 women and is still the official uniform of that British organization.

Morton was the first London couturier to show in Paris after World War II (1948), and in 1952 he was the first London couturier to show in New York. In 1953 he designed the first Lady Hathaway shirt collection for the Hathaway Shirt Company and was appointed vice-president of the company in 1955. In 1958 he became designer–director of the London firm, Reldan-Digby Morton, producing ready-to-wear casual sports clothes. He retired in 1973 and the Mortons now spend most of the year in the Bahamas.

Digby Morton was a founder–member of the Incorporated Society of London Fashion Designers. He received the Aberfoyle (Ireland) International Fashion Award in 1956.

Jean Muir (Mrs. Harry Leuckert). Designer of ready-to-wear, Jean Muir Ltd., 22 Bruton St., London W1

Jean Muir, the diminutive British fashion dynamo whose soft, seductive clothes in misty colors have a recognizable stamp, was born in London. She had no formal schooling in design, but her fashion sketches eventually brought her a job with the Jaeger company. Her first assignment as designer was with Jane and Jane, a London wholesale house.

She opened her own business in 1960 and throughout the "Mod" and "Hard Chic" periods retained the diffused charm of her clothes. In 1964 a Jean Muir dress was chosen by the British fashion press as the Dress of the Year and placed in the collection of the Museum of Costume in Bath. In 1965 Miss Muir received the Ambassador Magazine Achievement Award "for applying the highest professional standards to British ready-to-wear which has made her an authority among young fashion designers."

Jean Muir fashions are now produced in France as well as in England and America and are sold throughout the United States.

Tommy Nutter (Thomas Anthony Nutter). Men's fashion designer, Nutters of Savile Row Ltd., 35A Savile Row, London W1

Tommy Nutter, leading British tailor of the 1970s, is credited with restoring technical perfection to masculine British fashion after the haphazard workmanship of the "swinging London" period.

Born April 17, 1943, in Barmouth, North Wales, Nutter studied architecture at Willesden Technical College, but disliked it. A boy-wanted sign in the window of Ward & Co., fine old London tailors, set Nutter on his professional career at 19. Seven years later, in 1969, Nutter designed and built his own tailoring establishment on the site of Ward & Co.

On the International Best-Dressed List himself, Nutter makes the clothes of many other fashion pacesetters, among them Lord and Lady Harlech, Hardy Amies, Twiggy, and Mick and Bianca Jagger.

He is a member of the Federation of Merchant Tailors and serves on the Committee of the Clothing Institute of Great Britain. He is a guest critic and lecturer of the Royal College of Art in London.

Alice Pollock. See Quorum

Thea Porter (Dorothea Naomi Seale Porter). Dress designer, 8 Greek St., London W1

Half French and half English, this designer was born in Damascus, where her parents were missionaries. She spent her early life in the Middle East, attended London University on a scholarship, but was "sent down" after two years. She married Robert Porter, a British economist attached to the Foreign Service, and returned to live in Lebanon for the next 14 years where she gained attention as a painter.

In 1964 she went back to London and opened a shop selling Oriental antiques and fabrics and doing interior decorating. Her use of exotic fabrics and embroideries extended to designing at-home and evening clothes. Her delicately sensuous gowns of Oriental and Art-Deco materials expressed the mystery of the seraglio in the idiom of current fashion. Her first professional clients were London's far-out pop singers.

She received the British Clothing Institute's Designer of the Year Award in 1972, and was one of the seven designers chosen for the special British design exhibit at the Louvre in Paris.

Thea Porter clothes are exported throughout the world. She designs in other fields, including fabrics and children's wear.

Mary Quant. Mary Quant, Ltd., 3 Ives St., London SW3

The English designer called the "Mother of Mod," and credited with launching the mini-skirt and sparking the Youth Revolution in British fashion was born February 11, 1934, in London. Her parents were Welsh-born schoolteachers. She studied illustration at the Goldsmith's College of Art, where she met and married a fellow student, Alexander Plunket-Greene. They have one son, born in November, 1970.

After designing hats for a time, she and her husband set up Bazaar, the first Quant clothes shop in the King's Road, the Bohemian section of London. It was the first shop to cater directly to independent young girls. Other Bazaars followed and in 1961 she contracted to design special collections for the American firm, J.C. Penney. She now has licenses in many countries for her clothes, lingerie, furs, hosiery, shoes, and hats.

In 1963 the firm expanded, adding its Ginger Group of low-cost clothing. That year Mary Quant received the London Sunday Times Fashion Award. In 1966 Mary Quant cosmetics were launched, the first beauty line strictly for the young, and are now an international success.

In 1967, Miss Quant was created an Officer of the Order of the British Empire (O.B.E.), and the same year was elected a Fellow of the Society of Industrial Artists, receiving their design medal. In 1969 she was named a Royal Designer for Industry by the Royal Society of Arts.

Quorum. Ready-to-wear designers, 52 Randor Walk, London SW3

This swinging fashion design house was formerly a partnership between Bill Gibb and Alice Pollock, but Alice Pollock is now its sole designer.

Edward Rayne. Shoe designer and manufacturer, H & M Rayne, Ltd., Tileyard Road, King's Cross, London N7

Edward Rayne was born in London on August 19, 1922, and at 18 joined the firm founded by his grandparents in 1889 as an apprentice. By the time he was 29 he was chairman and managing director of Rayne's.

The firm expanded to retailing in 1920, adding the exclusive Bond Street shop now patronized by the Royal family (and the first British shop to feature American fashions).

The present-day Rayne organization holds a half interest in Delman in America and in 1967 became associated with the American Genesco Corporation, which in 1973 sold its interest in Rayne to Debenham and Freebody, the English retail chain.

In October, 1970, a Rayne shop was opened in Paris.

A champion bridge player, Edward Rayne played on the English bridge team which won 10 European titles (1948).

Edward Rayne has been a prime mover in group efforts to promote British fashion talents and further an international exchange of fashions. He served 10 years on the Export Council for Europe, and is chairman of the Incorporated Society of London Fashion Designers and a member of the European Trade Committee of that body.

House of Redfern. See Hall of Fame

Reldan, Ltd. 214 Oxford St., London W1

This is a wholesale firm producing classic British separates for which Digby Morton was for many years the designer.

House of Reville. See Hall of Fame

Zandra Rhodes. Dress and textile designer, 64 Portchester Rd., London W2

England's most romantic and influential avant-garde designer, Zandra Lindsey Rhodes was born September 11, 1940, in Chatham, Kent. Her mother, Beatrice Rhodes, was a former fitter at Worth in Paris and later became senior lecturer on fashion at Medway College of Art in Kent.

Zandra studied textile printing and lithography at Medway and at the Royal College of Art, where she developed her skill at hand-screening textiles.

She graduated in 1964 with first-class honors entitling her to add Des.RCA (Designer of the Royal College of Art) after her name.

She taught part-time in English art schools in order to set up her own print works. In collaboration with Alexander McIntyre, she made fabrics for the new wave of British "Mod" designers, particularly Foale & Tuffin. She also opened her own boutique, the Fulham Road Clothes Shop, to sell dresses made of her prints. It was a success and in 1968 she established her own dress firm.

A curious blend of almost poster-like exaggeration and old-world romanticism, Zandra Rhodes fabrics seem to embody the ambivalent modern life, particularly of Britain.

Known as the "girl with green hair" for her personal proclivity for rainbow-tinted hair and bizarre eye makeup, Zandra nonetheless launched (1973) the ultraromantic revival of the crinoline in ruffled tulle.

In 1972 the British Clothing Institute named Zandra Rhodes Designer of the Year. She also received the National Diploma of Design, given by a committee of experts appointed by the British government.

Sally Tuffin, Ltd. (formerly Foale & Tuffin, Ltd.). Ready-to-wear, 4 Ganton St., London W1

Sally Tuffin and Marion Foale, leaders in the Carnaby Street period in British fashion, were fellow students at the Walthamstow School of Art and the Royal College of Art. They finished training in 1961 and became partners in a private dressmaking business. Sensing the swing toward youth-oriented fashion, they then concentrated on young "kicky" ready-to-wear. With limited capital they took premises in Carnaby Street and their company, Foale & Tuffin, Ltd., helped to make that area famous as the fashion heart of the Youth Rebellion of 1965.

In 1973 the partnership was dissolved, and the firm continues as Sally Tuffin, Ltd.

Sekers Fabrics Ltd. (West Cumberland Silk Mills). 190 Sloane St., London SW1

This prominent English fabric manufacturer was founded by the late Sir Nicholas Sekers.

From World War II until his retirement in 1968, "Miki" Sekers was one of the most dynamic figures in the fabric industry. Sekers silks, sheer weightless woolens, and mohair textures starred in couture collections throughout the world.

A Hungarian-born gentleman of wide interest in the arts, Nicholas Sekers was knighted by Queen Elizabeth II for his contribution to fashion and to music. Family dissension, particularly policy differences with his son-in-law Jean Baudrand, led to Sir Nicholas' final retirement, and he lived abroad until his death in 1972.

Sekers is now directed by Mr. Baudrand and his wife, the former Christine Sekers.

Mme Handley Seymour. *See* Hall of Fame

Susan Small. Ready-to-wear designer, 76 Wells St., London W1

This British ready-to-wear firm was one of the first strictly ready-to-wear operations in England.

The firm, founded in the early 1960s for wholesale distribution only, is an acquisition of the Courtaulds fabric empire, and now has a retail shop on Sloane Street in London.

Maureen Baker, designer with the firm since its inception, is a favorite of Princess Anne. One of her fashion triumphs was the precedent-shattering announcement by Buckingham Palace that Susan Small, rather than one of the official Royal dressmakers, was Princess Anne's choice to design her wedding gown and going-away costume when she married Captain Mark Phillips.

Teddy Tinling. Designer of tennis clothes, 26 Avon Trading Estate, London W14; and 147 N. 12 St., Philadelphia, Pa. 19107

Born in 1910, Tinling gravitated early to his passion, tennis. He was a ballboy at Wimbledon for 26 years before beginning to design and manufacture clothes for the sport. When Suzanne Lenglen returned to tennis in the 1930s to play against the new champion Alice Marble, Teddy Tinling designed Lenglen's "answer" to Alice Marble's revolutionary shorts—a brief pleated skirt with attached panties underneath.

Now over 60 and still the champion's favorite (he designed Billie Jean King's shiny multicolored costume for her historic "battle of the sexes" match against Bobbie Riggs in 1973), Tinling is an ebullient, witty personality much loved and chosen by the British Clothing Institute as its Designer of the Year in 1971.

In 1975 Tinling sold his business in England and now spends the majority of his time in the U.S.A. working out of Philadelphia.

Turnbull and Asser. Shirtmakers and haberdashers, 71 Jermyn St., London SW1

One of the first of the elegant old-time London haberdashers to link with the international ready-to-wear demand, Turnbull and Asser now exports throughout the world as well as continuing to serve clients in their Regency premises on Jermyn Street.

Worth House of Fashion. 50 Grosvenor St., London W1

This successor to the London branch of the historic fashion house founded in Paris by Charles Frederick Worth (see Hall of Fame) was purchased by Sydney Masson and is operated as a ready-to-wear shop.

Fashion Influentials

Alison Adburgham. Fashion writer, Tredore Cottage, Little Petherick, Wadebridge, Cornwall PL27 7QT

Alison Adburgham, fashion editor of the *Guardian* for many years, is the author of several books relating to British fashion and England's famous shops and fashion thoroughfares. Her no-nonsense fashion journalism, while totally factual, never downgrades the importance of dress in modern life.

Her books and articles on the history of English fashion and London's fashionable shops and streets have made her an authority on costume in the 20th century.

She is now retired from active journalism and living in Cornwall.

David Bailey. Fashion photographer, 177 Gloucester Ave., London

This young camera artist effectively captured the look and mood of "rebel" British fashion in the 1960s. Among the beauties and fashion innovators of the period starred in his fashion studies were Jean Shrimpton, Penelope Tree, and Catherine Deneuve (to whom he was married for a time).

Bailey was reputed to have inspired the character of the fashion photographer in the film *Blowup*.

Now much less insurgent, Bailey continues to be a leading British fashion photographer, working chiefly for British *Vogue*.

Sir Cecil (Walter Hardy) Beaton (C.B.E.). Reddish House, Broadchalke, Warwickshire

As author, photographer, costume designer, and fashion historian, Cecil Beaton's observations and influence significantly touched world fashion for 30 years.

Born Cecil Walter Hardy Beaton on January 14, 1904, in London, of wealthy and social parents, he was educated at Harrow and Cambridge.

In school he experimented with photography. Later his diffused, strangely posed portraits of well-known personalities of the 1920s ran in *Vogue* and *Vanity Fair*.

As official photographer to the British Royal family from the time of King George V, he made historic photographs of King Edward VIII before and after the abdication and was the only photographer to record the marriage of that ex-monarch to Wallis Simpson. He made the official coronation portraits of George VI and Queen Elizabeth II. In 1968 the National Portrait Gallery in London held an exhibition of his photographs.

Beaton's books, particularly *The Glass of Fashion* (Doubleday 1954), are virtual textbooks on the fashions and manners of his favorite period, 1900–1930.

Beaton's costumes for the stage and screen have had definite influence on contemporary fashion. His designs for *My Fair Lady*, both stage and screen versions, influenced the shapes, colors, and mood of clothes during the early 1960s.

In 1971 Beaton was asked by the Victoria and Albert Museum in London to assemble a major exhibition, "Cecil Beaton's Anthology of Fashion." It was one of the most popular attractions in the museum's history and later (1973) Beaton was knighted by Queen Elizabeth II.

Sheila (Psyche) Black. The *Times*, Printing House Square, London EC4

Sheila Black was women's editor of the *Financial Times* of London and now writes on women's interests for the London *Times* and British magazines.

A former actress who worked in a machine factory during the war, Ms. Black's sound analysis of fashion economics in terms of the average consumer broadened understanding of the subject in Britain.

Ernestine Carter (O.B.E.) (Mrs. John Carter). 113 Dovehouse St., London SW3

The former associate editor of the London *Sunday Times* is now writing books and special articles.

This American-born writer was a leader of the effort to establish British fashion designers as creative identities, and to widen the British public's appreciation of world fashion talents.

Her fashion pages in the influential London *Sunday Times* brought a lively, knowledgeable new tone to British fashion reporting. She is said to have discovered a number of England's now well-known designers, including Foale and Tuffin, Jean Muir, Bill Gibb, John Bates, Gina Fratini, and jeweler Andrew Grima.

In 1970 she received the Fashion Writer of the Year Award from the Clothing Institute.

Her book *With Tongue in Chic* (Michael Joseph, London, 1974) is an amusing and informative record of international fashion happenings and personalities between 1950 and the present day.

Madge Garland (Lady Ashton). 57 Melbury Rd., London WI4 8AD

This former fashion editor of British *Vogue* was a dynamic spirit in the postwar British fashion resurgence and author of some of the most interesting books of fact and comment in fashion. She helped to organize the London Fashion Group, later renamed the Incorporated Society of London Fashion Designers. Her books on fashion and beauty are widely read.

Miss Garland joined the *Vogue* staff as a receptionist in 1922 and remained with the magazine more or less steadily until the fall of Paris, "when we were all out of jobs."

In 1947, after working for some years with a London shop and launching ready-to-wear by young designers of the day, including Hardy Amies, she was asked by the Royal College of Art to develop a format for its fashion school. Using the American Parsons School of Design as a blueprint, she insisted, over the opposition of British educators, on combining practical guidance from industry with theory and academic instruction.

Her marriage to Sir Leigh Ashton ended in divorce after a short period. She is now retired and living in London.

Prudence Glyn (Lady Windlesham). Fashion editor, the *Times*, Printing House Square, London EC4

Prudence Glyn is England's leading fashion editor and one of the most powerful and energetic people behind the scenes of British fashion.

The daughter of a British army officer, Prudence Glyn at 18 worked as a sales representative at the ready-to-wear house of Belinda Bellville, then entered journalism on the staff of the *Woman's Mirror*. She became its fashion editor in 1964 and in 1966 joined the *Times* as fashion editor. She brought a cultivated and literary but distinctly non-fluffy style to fashion writing.

In 1973 she single-handedly presented a large and ambitious international fashion show under official auspices at Lancaster House to celebrate the entry of Great Britain into the Common Market.

Miss Glyn is married to Lord Windlesham (David James George Hennessy) a member of the cabinet of the British government. She is a member of the Council of the Royal College of Art, a member of the consultative committee on fashion of Leicester Polytechnic, a member of the marking committee of the Quality Assurance Council of the British Standards Institution, member of the committee of the National Council for Diplomas for Art and Design, and a judge of the Duke of Edinburgh's Design Prize (1970, 1971, and 1972).

In 1971 she won the Clothing Institute's award as fashion writer of the year.

Felicity Green. International Printing Corporation, 14 New Fetter Lane, London EC4

A former newspaper fashion editor, she is now a powerful and effective disseminator of fashion news and the first woman appointed to the Board of the International Printing Corporation, owners of numerous newspapers and women's publications.

Rebecca Stickney Hamilton. See France: Fashion Influentials

Prof. Janey Ironside (Jane Acheson). Fashion educator, 17 Queensdale Pl., London W11

Born Jane Acheson in Simla, India, where her father was a diplomat (Sir James Acheson was later British Resident in Kashmir), she came to England in 1938 and attended dressmaking school in London. After marrying the interior designer Christopher Ironside at the beginning of World War II, she worked in the camouflage department of a hydraulic brake factory. After the war she set up a small couture business designing special collections of children's clothes for stores.

In 1949 she joined the staff of the newly organized Fashion School of the Royal College of Art as assistant to Madge Garland, founder of the school and its first professor. In 1956 Miss Garland resigned and Janey Ironside succeeded her.

She immediately instituted a strong departure from usual teaching methods by encouraging her students to express their fantasies in their design, and at the same time seeking practical outlets for their work in industry. Professor Ironside is often credited with being the guiding hand behind the Carnaby Street and "Mod" fashion movements.

In 1967 she fought against having the Fashion School segregated from the university degree status accorded to the rest of the Royal College of Art, and lost. Her resignation was accepted and she retired. Her book, *Janey* (see Bibliography) is an autobiographical reflection of England's struggle to establish a true identity in fashion.

Winifriede Jackson. Fashion editor, *London Sunday Telegraph*, 135 Fleet St., London EC4

This fashion editor has established a large following for her quiet but forceful expression of the more conservative attitude toward dress in Britain.

Anthony King-Deacon. c/o *Harpers & Queen*, Chester Gate House, Vauxhall Bridge, London SW1

King-Deacon is a leading writer on British fashions for men. His articles appear in the *London Evening News*, the *Observer* and *Harpers & Queen*.

Willy Landels. Editor, *Harpers & Queen*, Chester Gate House, Vauxhall Bridge, London SW1

Mr. Landels edits *Harpers & Queen*, the new combined magazine of fashion and smart activities in Europe.

Doris Langley-Moore (O.B.E.). 5 Prince Albert Rd., London NW1

Mrs. Langley-Moore is one of the world's most knowledgable collectors of costumes and an outstanding authority on fashion documentation.

After writing many books and lecturing on fashion history, Mrs. Langley-Moore helped to found (1955) the Museum of Costume in the Assembly Rooms at Bath and presented her entire collection to it. She later established the Fashion Research Center at Bath.

She is the author of numerous books and articles on period fashion (*see* Bibliography).

James Laver (C.B.E.) (1899–1975).

Fashion historian, lecturer, and writer of a number of books of great value in fashion history, James Laver had an important part in engendering interest in fashion as an art form.

Formerly in charge of all activities having to do with fashion and costume at the Victoria and Albert Museum in London, Laver was born in Liverpool on March 14, 1899. He was a well-known poet in his early years, then became Keeper of Prints and Drawings at the Victoria and Albert, a title he retained long after his lectures and books had made him a renowned fashion authority.

The ease of dating prints and paintings by the costumes worn in them inspired him to study the cycles of fashion. He became a lecturer and a most fertile writer on the subject, with a dozen books on clothes and fashion to his credit (*see* Bibliography).

Mr. Laver was a Commander of the Order of the British Empire, an Honorary Fellow of the Royal Society of Arts, a Fellow of the Royal Society of Literature, and vice-president of the Internal Faculty of Arts.

He died in London on June 3, 1975.

Beatrix Miller. Editor, British *Vogue*, Hanover Sq., London W1

Britain's leading fashion magazine editor today, Beatrix Miller came to *Vogue* from *Queen* magazine. She is a strong champion of the pre-

Rafaelite, neoromantic clothes, hairdos, and makeup with which England's designers made their contribution to world fashion in the 1970s.

William Poole. Textile designer (retired), Ampleforth Abbey, York

William Poole, English fabric designer, led the revival of Art Nouveau prints about 1959 with his collections for Liberty of London. Poole later worked briefly in America for the Onondaga textile firm, but returned to England in 1968 to enter the Monastery of the Benedictine Order at Buckfast Abbey, Devon, where, as Brother Simon, he taught art.

In 1974 Poole left the monastery but entered Ampleforth Abbey the following year.

Vidal Sassoon. Hairdresser, Main offices: 171 New Bond St., London W1. American headquarters: 803 Madison Ave., New York, N.Y. 10022

Credited with launching both the very short and very long hairstyles during the 1960s, Vidal Sassoon also introduced the hairdressing salon with a show window in which customers could be seen under the driers. By lifting the shroud of mystery and self-consciousness from hair care, he helped to establish the era of the natural look.

Vidal Sassoon was born January 17, 1928, in London. His family are well-known London carpet dealers with roots in the Middle East. He was apprenticed to a hairdresser at 14 and at 26 he opened his own shop on Bond Street, where he introduced his method of blunt-cutting hair and blowing it in contours without the use of rollers.

There are 19 Sassoon shops in the British Isles and the United States.

He is married to former film actress Beverly Adams. With their two children, they live in New York.

Alison Settle (O.B.E.) (Mrs. M. Towers Settle). 6 Church St., Steyning, Sussex

Mrs. Settle, now retired, is remembered as the grande dame of the British fashion press. She was editor of *The Lady*, British *Vogue* and fashion editor of the *Observer*, and later adviser to the British textile industry. She received the Silver Medal of the Royal Society of Arts in 1952.

Serena Sinclair. Fashion editor, *London Daily Telegraph*, 135 Fleet St., London EC4

She is a highly competent but impish writer whose observations on the international fashion scene have a large following.

The Earl of Snowdon (Antony Charles Robert Armstrong-Jones, Viscount Linley). Fashion photographer, artistic advisor on design, Kensington Palace, London W8

As Antony Armstrong-Jones, Lord Snowdon was a successful fashion photographer before his marriage in 1960 to Princess Margaret, sister of Queen Elizabeth II. He continues to photograph for British *Vogue* and other publications as well as to compile photographic documentaries in books and films. He has official appointments to supervise government-sponsored design projects.

Born on March 7, 1930, he was educated at Eton and Jesus College Cambridge. He was in charge of the decorations for the investiture of Prince Charles as Prince of Wales in Caernarvon Castle, and designed the Snowdon Aviary at the London Zoo.

He has been a consultant to the British Council of Industrial Design since 1962 and serves as a Fellow or is on the boards of numerous art and theatre societies. He is the author of several books of photographic studies and made a notable TV documentary on the condition of the elderly in Britain.

Cherry Twiss. *London Telegraph*, 135 Fleet St., London EC4

This author of special fashion features for the *London Weekend Telegraph* supplement both writes and supervises photographs reflecting new fashion trends.

Trade Associations and Organizations

The British Fur Trade Association. 68 Upper Thames St., London EC4 3AN

Founded: 1919. Reorganized: 1963. Chmn: Simon Reiss.

This is the national British organization of designers, fur technicians, manufacturers, and retailers of fur garments and the allied trades, which merged with the British Fur Trade Alliance.

Maxwell Croft, leading London furrier, was one of its most zealous and effective leaders for many years.

The Association has an information service for its members.

Clothing Export Council of Great Britain. Academy House, 26–28 Sackville St., London W1X 1DA

Pres: Lord Rhodes. Dir: T.P. Randle.

This is Britain's official organization fostering the export of clothing; it has a membership of manufacturers of ready-to-wear for women, men, and children.

The Council sponsors seasonal trade shows for international buyers, many of which are held at Earls Court and Grosvenor House. To attract buyers, the Council has also organized special showings of British high fashion as window dressing for the mass-production market periods in London. British fashion has toured the world under the Council's aegis.

The Clothing Export Council announced in 1973 that a World Fashion Center for the British clothing industries was being planned in London.

The Clothing Institute. 17 Henrietta St., London WC2E 8QN

The Clothing Institute is a membership organization of clothing manufacturers and producers of articles and machinery pertaining to the industry.

The Institute's activities include providing up-to-date information of use to fashion designers, manufacturers, and clothing engineers, setting and maintaining standards of training and expertise in all areas of clothing production, and sponsoring courses and research projects to improve techniques, design, and quality of British-made clothing. It publishes a bimonthly journal, a newsletter, and a yearbook. It conducts seminars and world conferences and a designers' convention.

Its most far-reaching fashion activity is the Clothing Institute Diploma Awards in various fields of design and technology, given after examinations held for graduate students and for professionals who wish to improve their rating in the industry. A committee of experts judges the papers submitted.

The Institute has 34 branches in Great Britain, Ireland, Africa, and Australia.

The Costume Society. 157 Pope's Lane, London W3

Founded: 1965. Secy: Anne Thomas.

This membership organization was established within the Victoria and Albert Museum Department of Textiles in 1965 to further the study and preservation of historic and contemporary dress, their accurate documentation, and the study of the decorative arts allied to dress.

The Society's activities include lectures and illustrated monographs. Membership carries a subscription to its journal, *Costume*, reduced rates on its publications, and invitations to its special seminars and lectures.

It provides bibliographies on costume books and other aids to study for students and professionals in the field of fashion and theatrical design.

Design Council. 28 Haymarket, London SW1Y 4SU

Founded: 1944.

The purpose of this organization is to promote and improve the standard of design in many fields.

Formed by the British government in 1944, the Council was at first concerned only with industrial and engineering design, but is now expanded to cover fashion, particularly as taught in schools and colleges.

It has an information center and publishes a monthly magazine, *Design*. It also issues books and an annual directory of the design courses available in the United Kingdom. It maintains a placement service for designers.

Incorporated Society of London Fashion Designers (no official address).

Founded: 1942. Chmn: Edward Rayne.

This more-or-less inactive membership organization was once restricted to private couturiers, and later expanded to include accessory designers.

Founded through the leadership of fashion editor Alison Settle and advertising executive Margaret Havinden, the Society had as its first chairman the designer Edward Molyneux and two prominent women, Mrs. Ian Fleming and Lady Hartwell, for many years acted as official spokesmen for the cause of London's fashion creators.

Affectionately known as "Inc Soc," the Society became dormant as the haute couture in Great Britain dwindled, but it still existed in 1974. Edward Rayne, London shoe manufacturer, has served as chairman of the organization since 1960.

International Institute for Cotton. 17–19 Maddox St., London W1

Founded: Mid-19th century.

This international organization, started in Manchester when that city dominated the cotton industry, promotes the use of cotton in fashion throughout the Commonwealth.

It carries on a promotion and information service for designers, textile manufacturers, and the press. It publishes a fashion-trend bulletin with fabric swatches and resources, sponsors fashion shows, and prepares and distributes fashion press material in a regular program.

International Wool Secretariat (IWS). 6 Carlton Gardens, London SW1

Tel: (01) 930-7300. Founded: 1937. Mging Dir: Kenneth Clarke.

This central organization for the promotion of wool, with branches in 24 countries, was founded in 1937. The Secretariat maintains a large staff in London to report and publicize the use of wool in all types of wearing apparel.

London Fashion Fair International. See Clothing Export Council of Great Britain

Honors and Awards

The Clothing Institute Awards (Designer of the Year)

This organization (17 Henrietta St., London WC2E 8QN) gives Designer of the Year Awards for outstanding work by a professional designer, as well as to writers on women's and men's fashion (See Trade Associations and Organizations: Clothing Institute).

Design Medal of the Society of Industrial Artists and Designers

This medal can be won by a fashion designer; Mary Quant received it in 1967. The recipient is chosen by a committee of the Society of Industrial Artists and Designers whose address is: 12 Carlton House Terrace, London SW1.

Designer of the Year Award. See Clothing Institute Awards.

Designer, Royal College of Art (Des.RCA)

This honor is conferred on British designers who attended the Royal College of Art (Kensington Gore, London SW7) when their later achievements are considered exceptional.

The Diploma in Art and Design

Awarded to designers in competition under the aegis of certain schools, approved by the National Council for Diplomas in Art and Design, and designated by a committee of fashion authorities appointed by the Council. Address: 16 Park Crescent, London W1N 4DN.

London Sunday Times Fashion Award

In 1963 the London *Sunday Times* established an international fashion award patterned after the American Coty Awards, but discontinued it in 1967.

The Queen's Award to Industry

This was established in 1965 by the Office of the Queen's Award to Industry, One Victoria St., London SW1H OET, and is given annually to 100 British companies with outstanding records in export, and for technological innovations. It has occasionally been won by fashion firms.

Royal Designer for Industry Awards

These annual awards, established in 1936, are given to artists working in any branch of industry, and are designated by a committee appointed by the Royal Society of Arts, John Adam St., London WC2N 6EZ. Fashion designers have occasionally received one.

Royal Honors List

British fashion personalities have occasionally been included in the Royal Honors List. In 1957 Cecil Beaton was named C.B.E. (Companion of the British Empire) and was knighted by Queen Elizabeth II in 1972. Mary Quant, the designer, has been twice honored by her monarch—

she was named O.B.E. (Order of the British Empire) in 1967 and Royal Designer for Industry of the Royal Society of Arts in 1969. Others prominent in English fashion who have received royal recognition in recent years include James Laver, the fashion historian; designers Norman Hartnell, Hardy Amies, and Jean Muir; and fashion editors Alison Settle and Ernestine Carter.

The Royal Warrant
The Royal Warrant, entitling a business house to place the royal lion and unicorn with arms emblazoned with "By Appointment to . . ." at its door and on its stationery, is the sovereign's sign of esteem for products used regularly by any of three members of the Royal family, the King or Queen, the royal spouse, and the Prince of Wales.

The Royal Warrant was first granted by Queen Elizabeth I and was very frequently given by King Charles II. Queen Victoria put the matter in the hands of the Association of Her Majesty's Tradesmen, now the Royal Warrant Holders Association (7 Buckingham Gate, London SW1). A Royal Warrant is valid usually through two reigns, that of the monarch who bestowed it and that of his successor. Sometimes, however, it is extended by the Association. Thus some old and highly respected firms still display their warrant from Queen Victoria, Edward VII, George V, and Queen Mary. Among fashion houses with the current right to display the Royal Warrant are Norman Hartnell, Hardy Amies, Edward Rayne, and Burberrys.

Fashion Education

Barnfield College. Barnfield Ave., Luton, Bedforshire
There is a three-year program in fashion plus a one-year foundation leading to City and Guilds of London Institute certificate (CGLI).

Berkshire College of Art. Marlow Rd., Maidenhead, Berkshire
A two-year fashion program plus a one-year foundation leading to a regional diploma are offered.

City of Birmingham Polytechnic Art and Design Center. Corporation St., Birmingham B4 7OX
There is a three-year program in fashion design plus a one-year foundation leading to a Polytechnic diploma, Licentiate of the Society of Industrial Artists and Designers. There are additional courses in fashion/textile leading to a Diploma in Art and Design (DipAD), considered the equivalent of a university first degree. The program was founded in 1971.

Bolton College of Art and Design. Hilden St., Bolton, Lancashire

There is a four-year program in fashion leading to a regional diploma, Diploma of Associateship (DA), City and Guilds of London Institute certificate (CGLI), and Licentiate of the Society of Industrial Artists and Designers certificate (LSIA).

Brighton Polytechnic. Faculty of Art and Design, Grand Parade, Brighton, Sussex BN2 4GJ

There is a three-year program (begun in 1970) in fashion design and textiles leading to City and Guilds of London Institute certificate (CGLI) and Licentiate of the Society of Industrial Artists and Designers (LSIA).

Bristol Polytechnic. Faculty of Art and Design, Clanager Rd., Bower Ashton, Bristol, Gloucestershire

This school offers a three-year program (begun in 1969) in fashion or textiles plus a one-year foundation leading to a regional diploma or Licentiate of the Society of Industrial Artists and Designers (LSIA).

Canterbury College of Art. 1/3 St. Peter's Lane, Canterbury, Kent

There is a two-year program in dress design leading to City and Guilds of London Institute certificate (CGLI) and Licentiate of the Society of Industrial Artists and Designers certificate (LSIA).

Chesterfield College of Art and Design. Penmore House, Hasland, Chesterfield, Derbyshire

Offered here are a three-year program and a one-year foundation leading to a college diploma, City and Guilds of London Institute certificate (CGLI), or Licentiate of the Society of Industrial Artists and Designers (LSIA).

Derby & District College of Art. Kendleston Rd., Derby, Derbyshire

There is a three-year fashion program leading to college diploma, City and Guilds of London Institute certificate (CGLI) or (plus 1 year) to Licentiate of the Society of Industrial Artists and Designers (LSIA) certificate.

Epsom School of Art and Design. One Church St., Epsom, Surrey

There is a three-year program in fashion design plus a one-year foundation leading to City and Guilds of London Institute certificate (CGLI).

Gloucestershire College of Art and Design. Pittville, Cheltenham, Gloucestershire

Fashion courses are given leading to a Diploma in Art and Design (DipAD) which is equivalent to a university first degree. The school was founded in 1968.

Harris College School of Art and Design. Corporation Sta., Preston, Lancashire

There is a three-year program in dress design plus a one-year foundation leading to a Licentiate of the Society of Industrial Artists and Designers certificate (LSIA).

Hartlepool College of Art. Church Sq., Hartlepool, Devon

There are two- or three-year programs in dress design leading to City and Guilds of London Institute Certificate (CGLI).

Hastings College of Further Education. Archery Rd., St. Leonards on Sea, Sussex

A three-year program is offered in fashion design, textiles, and marketing leading to a college diploma.

Hornsey College of Art. Crouch End Hill, Hornsey, London N8

There is a three-year program in fashion design and textiles leading to the Diploma in Art and Design (DipAD), considered the equivalent of a university first degree.

Kingston Polytechnic. Faculty of Art and Design, Knights Pk., Kingston upon Thames, Surrey KT1 2EE

There are fashion design courses leading to a Diploma in Art and Design (DipAD), considered the equivalent of a university first degree. The school was founded in 1970.

City of Leicester Polytechnic. Box 143, Leicester, Leicestershire LE1 9BH

There is a three-year program (begun in 1969) in shoe design and lingerie leading to a Polytechnic diploma and additional programs in fashion and textiles leading to the Diploma in Art and Design (DipAD), the equivalent of a university first degree.

Liverpool Polytechnic. Faculty of Art and Design, Hope St., Liverpool, Lancashire L1 9EB

Now considered one of the leading fashion-design schools in Great Britain, it was founded in 1970 and offers a three-year program leading to the Diploma in Art and Design (DipAD), the equivalent of a university first degree.

London College of Fashion and Clothing Technology. 20 John Princes St., London W1

There are three-year programs in fashion design, clothing, and millinery, leading to a regional certificate.

Manchester Polytechnic. Faculty of Art and Design, Cavendish St., All Saints, Manchester M15 6BR

There is a three-year program (begun in 1970) leading to the Diploma in Art and Design (DipAD), the equivalent of a university first degree.

Medway College of Design. Fort Pitt, Rochester, Kent

There is a three-year program in dress design leading to Licentiate of the Society of Industrial Artists and Designers certificate (LSIA).

Newcastle-upon-Tyne Polytechnic. Faculty of Art and Design, Ellison Bldg., Ellison Pl., Newcastle-upon-Tyne, Norfolk NE1 8ST

There is a three-year program (begun in 1969) in fashion design leading to a Polytechnic diploma, Licentiate of the Society of Industrial Artists and Designers certificate (LSIA).

North East London Polytechnic. Forest Rd., London E17

A three-year program is offered in fashion and textiles plus a one-year foundation leading to a Polytechnic diploma, Licentiate of the Society of Industrial Artists and Designers (LSIA).

Odham Further Education Center. Union St., Oldham, Lancashire

There is a two-year program leading to a regional certificate.

Plymouth College of Art and Design. Palace Court, Plymouth, Devon

There is a three-year program in fashion and in textiles.

Portsmouth College of Art and Design. Hyde Park Rd., Portsmouth, Hampshire

There is a two-year program plus a one-year foundation leading to a regional diploma, Licentiate of the Society of Industrial Artists and Designers certificate (LSIA).

Ravensbourne College of Art and Design. Rookery Lane, Bromley, Kent

There is a three-year program leading to the Diploma in Art and Design (DipAD), equivalent to a university first degree in fashion.

Royal College of Art. Kensington Gore, London SW7

One of the two leading schools in Europe teaching fashion design. (The other is l'Ecole de la Chambre Syndicale, Paris.)

The Royal College is generally credited with giving impetus to the extraordinary upsurge of young rebel talents in the early 1960s and became world famous and a worldwide influence as the "Mod" and "Youth Kick" fashion crazes progressed. The majority of the designers who made Carnaby Street, the King's Road, and later the Fulham Road synonymous with far-out clothing studied at the Royal College under a remarkable teacher, Professor Janey Ironside. Prof. Ironside not only inspired and encouraged her students to move away from tradition, but she rallied industry to help them realize their ideas in merchandise. The Mod fashion movement was in this way similar to the Art Nouveau, Art Deco, and Bauhaus movements.

Internal conflicts caused Professor Ironside's resignation in 1968. The fashion department, now under the direction of Joanne Brogden (Des.RCA), follows the new policy of the school to balance fine and applied art.

The Royal College of Art, opened in 1857, was a particular interest of Queen Victoria and Prince Albert. The objects purchased for the students to copy later formed the nucleus of the Victoria and Albert Museum. In 1896, Queen Victoria established the school as the Royal College of Art. In 1947, the courses in fashion were established.

The school gives its special designation of Designer, Royal College of Art, in the form of an honor (see Honors and Awards).

St. Martins School of Art. 109 Charing Cross Rd., London WC2H 0DU
There are fashion design courses leading to a Diploma in Art and Design (DipAD).

Salford College of Technology. Department of Art and Industrial Design, Salford, Lancashire M6 6PU
There are two- and three-year programs in fashion design leading either to a Diploma of Associateship—Salford (DA–Salford) or Licentiate of the Society of Industrial Artists and Designers (LSIA).

Salisbury College of Art. New St., Salisbury, Wiltshire
There is a three-year program in fashion design leading to a regional diploma.

Southend College of Technology. School of Art and Design, Caernarvon Rd., Southend on Sea, Essex
A three-year program in fashion leading to a college diploma is available here.

Thanet School of Art. Hawley Sq., Margate, Kent
There is a three-year program in dress design leading to City and Guilds of London Institute certificate (CGLI).

Trent Polytechnic. School of Art and Design, Burton St., Nottingham, Nottinghamshire NG14 4BU
There is a three-year program in textiles leading to a Polytechnic diploma and additional fashion design courses leading to a Diploma in Art and Design (DipAD), the equivalent of a university first degree.

Costume and Fashion Archives

Bankfield Museum. Ackroyd Pk., Haley Hill, Halifax, Yorkshire
Tel: Halifax 54823. Founded: 1897. Dir: R.A. Innes.
There are interesting collections of costumes and textiles from ancient Egypt through the 18th century.

City of Birmingham Museum and Art Gallery. Congreve St., Birmingham B3 3DH
Tel: 021-235-2834. Founded: 1885. Dir: Dennis Farr.
This is a large and interesting collection of English costumes from the 18th to the 20th centuries.

The Bowes Museum. Barnard Castle, Durham, County Durham
This museum has a large collection of late 18th century and Victorian costumes.

Castle Howard Costume Galleries. Castle Howard, Yorkshire
Tel: Coneysthorpe 333. Founded: 1963. Curator: Cecile M. Hummel.
Said to be the largest private costume collection in Britain, the castle houses more than 2000 period costumes displayed in appropriate settings aimed at giving the viewer a total impression of life in each era, from the 17th to the 20th centuries.

Central Museum and Art Gallery. Guildhall Rd., Northampton
Tel: Northampton 34881 (day); 39131 (Sat. and evenings). Founded: 1865. Dir: W.N. Terry.
This is a small but interesting costume collection.

Leicester Museums and Art Gallery, Newarke Houses Museum. The Newarke, Leicester M14 5LL
Tel: 0523-26832. Founded: 1849. Dir: T.A. Walden.
The collection includes English costumes from the 16th century to the present.

London Museum. Kensington Palace, The Broadwalk, Kensington Gardens, London W8 4PX
Tel: 01-937-9816. Founded: 1912. Dir: John Hayes.
Coronation robes and other royal costumes are displayed here. The costumes, arranged in period settings, illustrate the life and history of London from the earliest settlement to the present.

City of Manchester Gallery of English Costume. Platt Hall, Rusholme, Manchester M14 55W
Tel: 061-224-5217. Founded: 1948. Dir: G.L. Conran. Curator: Anne M. Buck.

The Gallery houses a collection of complete costumes from the 17th century to the present. The museum publishes picture books of different periods of English costume.

Museum of Costume. Assembly Rooms, Alfred St., Bath, Somerset
Tel: Bath 28411. Founded: 1963. Founder and Honorary Advisor: Doris Langley-Moore. Dir: J.W. Munn.

This museum is said to have the largest costume collection in the world. Chronologically it ranges from the 16th to 20th centuries and is arranged to demonstrate fashion evolution. Much of the collection is the gift of the fashion historian, Doris Langley-Moore.

The collection includes clothing worn by famous personages, among them Lord Byron, Lady Byron, Queen Victoria, Queen Alexandra, and Queen Mary.

City of Nottingham Museum and Art Gallery. The Castle, Nottingham NG1 6E1
Tel: 0602-43615. Founded: 1878. Dir: E.J. Laws.

The museum's collections include costumes from 1600 to 1955 with special attention to laces, since Nottingham was historically the center of the British machine-made lace industry.

Royal Albert Memorial Museum. Queen St., Exeter, Devon EX4 3RX
Tel: 5-6724. Dir: Patrick J. Boylan.

There are costumes of the 18th century and Victorian periods.

Snowshill Manor. Broadway, Gloucestershire
Founded: 1951. Dir: Paul Crosfield.

An outstanding collection of English costumes dating from the 17th to 19th centuries, originally the personal collection of Charles Wade, the clothes are shown in room settings of the period.

Victoria and Albert Museum, Costume Court. South Kensington, London SW7
Tel: 01-589-6371. Founded: 1852. Costume Court: 1962. Dir: Roy Strong. Dir. Costume Court: Madeleine Ginsburg.

Although the Victoria and Albert Museum dates back to the mid-19th century, its vast costume collections were only recently concentrated within one area of display. The department is now under the direction of Madeleine Ginsburg, who was trained by the Victoria and Albert's scholarly historian and writer on fashion, James Laver.

In October 1971, the Costume Court presented a major fashion exhibition, "Fashion, an Anthology by Cecil Beaton."

The collection ranges over about 400 years of costume, including many examples of royal garments spanning all reigns from Queen Elizabeth I to Queen Elizabeth II. There is an excellent accessories collection which includes a number of Queen Mary's famous toque hats. Mrs. Ginsburg administrates a library of 250,000 books and periodicals on costume and fashion.

Fashion Publications

Flair. I.P.C. Magazines, Ltd., Tower House, 30–32 Southampton St., London WC2
Founded: 1960. 12 issues/yr.

Harpers & Queen. National Magazine Co., Ltd., Vauxhall Bridge Rd., London SW1
Ed: Willie Landels. 12 issues/yr. £8 (£9 overseas)/yr.

Hers. I.P.C. Magazines, Ltd., Tower House, 30–32 Southampton St., London WC2
Founded: 1966. Ed: K. Walker. 12 issues/yr. $6/yr in US.

Men's Wear. Textile Trade Publications, Ltd., Knights House, 20 Soho Sq., London W1V 6DT
Ed: C.T. Waller. 52 issues/yr. £8.50/yr. Circ: 15,000.

Vogue. Condé Nast Publications, Ltd., Vogue House, Hanover Sq., London W1
Ed-in-Chief: Beatrix Miller. 16 issues/yr. £10.75 (£11.50 overseas)/yr. High fashion.

SCOTLAND

The perennial charm, historical associations, and romantic variations of Scottish tartans have intrigued fashion designers since Queen Victoria and Prince Albert first "discovered" Scotland as a vacation land. In the 1840s tartan plaids, from sashes to carpets, swept the world. A Scottish envoy of Queen Victoria at the court of Siam so intrigued the King with his tartans that Thai silks have been made in shimmering plaids ever since.

Textiles and clothing have been an important factor in the Scottish economy. Popular Ballantyne knits are known worldwide, and Harris tweeds and Shetland woolens have become almost generic fashion terms. The commercial manufacture of fabrics and clothing occupies about 200,000 people of Scotland's 5,000,000 population.

Since World War I, the Dawson spinning and weaving mills around Kinross, Scotland, have gradually become dominant in producing fine cashmere. The unique properties and purity of the water in Scotland are said to contribute as much to the washing of cashmere wool as it does to the distilling of Scotch whiskey. Experts say that Scottish cashmere is softer and more pliable than any in the world for this reason.

Cottage weaving and knitting have been a worthwhile assist to the family income in many regions. Bonnie Cashin of America, Scottish-born Valerie Louthan, and ladies-of-the-manor such as Mrs. Alwyn Farquharson, wife of the laird of Invercauld, have contributed importantly to keeping these industries abreast with fashion demand and opportunities for distribution.

Fashion Designers and Firms

Valerie Louthan (Mrs. David Louthan). Designer of sweaters and knits, Galashiels

This designer, with her own knit mill in Scotland, has what to most women would represent the dream life. She is married to a leading financial consultant and with her husband and four children commutes between homes in Marbella, Spain; Gstaad, Switzerland; and Galashiels, Scotland, with stopovers in London and New York.

She was born in the north of England in 1936 and studied art at the Nottingham School of Fine Arts, Oxford University, and the London Royal College of Art. She always loved "fiddling with knitted textures," and was naturally drawn to that area when she decided to design. She designed knitwear collections for an Austrian firm, for Braemar and John Lang of Scotland before starting her own business in 1972. She has also designed tweeds and served as color consultant in America for Monsanto fibers.

Trade Associations and Organizations

The Scottish Committee of Design Council. The Scottish Design Center, 72 St. Vincent St., Glasgow G2 5TN

This Scottish organization performs a function similar to that of the Design Council of Great Britain with which it is affiliated. See England: Trade Associations and Organizations—Design Council.

Fashion Education

Edinburgh College of Art. Lauriston Place, Edinburgh EH3 9DF

There is a two-year program in fashion leading to Scottish Certificate of Education (SCE), and additional courses in English and four O's (ordinary-level exams) leading to a Diploma of Art.

Costume and Fashion Archives

Dumfries Burgh Museum (formerly the Society Museum). The Observatory, Corberry Hill, Dumfries

Founded: 1835. Joined with the Dumfries Burgh Museum: 1934. Dir: A.E. Truckell.

There is a large collection of local fashions from 1790 to 1890, as well as a photo collection of life in the area.

National Museum of Antiquities of Scotland. One Queen St., Edinburgh EH2 1JD

Tel: 031-556-8921. Founded: 1781. Dir: R.B.K. Stevenson.

There are objects from Scotland's past from prehistoric to recent times, including period costumes.

Paisley Museum and Art Galleries. High St., Paisley, Renfrewshire

Tel: Paisley 2484. Founded: 1870. Curator: David R. Shearer.

There is a definitive collection of Paisley shawls made here in the 19th century. This museum is a valuable resource for textile designers.

Fashion Publications

Annabel. D.C. Thompson Co., Ltd., 80 Kingsway East, Dundee
Founded: 1966. Ed: W. Scott Smith.

WALES

Although this rugged pastoral country still retains its national costume in about the same relation to daily life as it preserves its native language, its direct contribution to world clothing is so minimal that no mention is made of the category in its national production or employment statistics.

One designer at least has helped to make fashion use of the quaint Welsh dresses in small flower-patterned, striped or eyelet cotton with flounced skirts, low-necked bodies, decorative aprons, and ruffled mob caps. Welsh-born Laura Ashley (see England: Fashion Designers and Firms), now a leading designer of romantic fashions catering to the English and European markets, bases her collections chiefly on Welsh costume and has her own production center in Wales.

Fashion Education

Cardiff College of Art. The Friary, Cardiff, Glamorgan

There is a two-year program in fashion plus a one-year foundation leading to a college diploma.

Denbighshire Technical College. Mold Rd., Wrexham

There are two-year fashion courses leading to a City and Guilds of London Institute certificate (CGLI).

Newport College of Art. Clarence Place, Newport, Monmouth

There is a three-year program in fashion leading to City and Guilds of London Institute certificate (CGLI) and a three-year program plus a one-year foundation leading to Licentiate of the Society of Industrial Artists and Designers (LSIA).

Costume and Fashion Archives

Welsh Folk Museum. St. Fagans Castle, Cardiff CF5 6XB

Tel: Cardiff 561352/8. Founded: 1947. Dir: Iorwerth C. Peate.

There are Welsh peasant costumes and embroideries from the 17th to 20th centuries. The museum is affiliated with the National Museum of Wales.

IRELAND, NORTHERN

Although part of the British Isles, Northern Ireland has never shared in the creative side of the British clothing industry. The country's production of linen and other textiles, representing a large portion of the economy of the Six Counties, suffered greatly from the troubles of the 1970s. Spun rayon had begun to take much of the demand away from Irish linen, and although Northern Ireland produces rayon and mixtures of cotton and rayon for household use, the process of adjusting to these new techniques has been interrupted.

Moygashel linens are still supplied to the fashion industries in America and Europe, but in smaller and smaller quantities and at higher prices. Flax-growing has dwindled in Ireland, and the flax for linen weaving is now largely imported from Belgium.

Belfast and Londonderry have large clothing factories employing nearly 50,000 workers, but they produce chiefly men's shirts and pyjamas.

There are no designers of note in Northern Ireland and few, if any, fashion education or training programs are available.

IRELAND, REPUBLIC OF

The Irish Free State, stemming from the intense nationalism of the people of southern Ireland, reflects its national characteristics in a small but clearcut contribution to world fashion. The handknit, natural colored and bulky Aran fisherman's sweater has been absorbed into classic sportswear, as have Donegal and other handwoven tweeds, and the typical Irish hooded cloak. Ireland was a pioneer in introducing the cottage industry idea, consequently helping to revive handwork as a viable element of modern clothing.

Such designers as Sybil Connolly and Cyril Cullen groomed cottage workers to execute knits and tweeds in their designs. Sybil Connolly revived almost-defunct weaving centers, including the centuries-old looms that produced the silk and wool poplin known as "the Pope's linen" originally woven exclusively for the Vatican. Miss Connolly also brought Carrickmacross lace and Irish crochet into high fashion use.

Ireland produces a large amount of sewing threads for export and is more or less self-supporting in the production of machine-made clothing.

The Irish Trade Development Board, established after World War II, has been vigorous in promoting Irish design through group showings and trade fairs throughout the world. Since the Republic of Ireland entered the Common Market in 1973, exports have risen, but six years of conflict between northern and southern Ireland have hampered progress.

Fashion Designers and Firms

Clodagh (Aubry). Designer in Dublin and New York, 53 Pembroke Rd., Dublin, and 156 E. 82 St., New York, N.Y. 10028

One of Ireland's younger name designers, Clodagh was born October 8, 1937, in Galway, Ireland.

She literally "fell" into designing. A riding accident put her in the hospital for a year. An ad in the newspaper for a fashion school said "Be a designer." At 17, after a year at the Grafton Academy, Dublin, she presented her first couture collection. She soon opened a boutique and also wrote a weekly fashion column for the *Irish Times*. She designed knitwear, children's clothes, shoes, and towels under contract to other houses.

Clodagh, now divorced from her first husband, Desmond O'Kennedy and married to American screenwriter Daniel Aubry, recently closed her boutique in Dublin and now makes one-of-a-kind "collectors pieces" for private customers in her custom salons in Dublin and New York.

Sybil Connolly. Couturiere, 71 Merrion Sq., Dublin 2

Known for reviving such unique Irish textiles as pleated handkerchief linen, Carrickmacross lace, and "the Pope's poplin" (a plain or watered silk-and-wool ribbed fabric), Sybil Connolly was born in Swansea, Wales, on January 24, 1921, of an Irish father and Welsh mother who had migrated from County Waterford. She is related to the celebrated Dunsany family of Ireland. When her family settled in Waterford she was educated at the Convent of Mercy there.

At 17, she joined Bradley's, exclusive London dressmaker, as an apprentice on the design staff. When war broke out in 1940 she returned to Dublin and worked as buyer for the fashion house of Richard Allen. At 22 she became a director of the firm, then its designer.

In 1957 she opened her own couture house in Dublin's historic Merrion Square, with special permission from the government to convert one of the square's Georgian mansions to business purposes. Her clientele is now worldwide. Jacqueline Kennedy (Onassis) chose a Sybil Connolly dress for her official White House portrait.

An authority on the Celtic and Georgian arts of Ireland, Miss Connolly served on the Historical Arts Council of Ireland and is a member of the Irish Georgian Society. In 1958 she was acclaimed one of the "Women of the Year" of the British Isles.

Cyril Cullen. Knitwear designer, Carrick-on-Shannon, County Leitrim

Cyril Cullen is a former civil servant in Ireland's Welfare Department who became a designer to help the indigent. He is now a leader in the field of Irish cottage industries. Having noted that many of the unemployed, particularly women, were eager to find work of any sort, he looked up knitting in the encyclopedia and taught himself the basic process. He then worked out new designs for the women volunteers to follow. The informal group's first efforts were sold successfully at the Shannon Airport duty-free shops and in 1967 Cullen resigned from his government job to give all his time to the home knitters.

In 1969 he bought an 18th century building in Carrick-on-Shannon and turned what was an abandoned hospital into workrooms, offices, and shipping center. He distributes his collection to England, Europe, Canada, and the U.S.A.

He employs more than 1100 hand knitters and handloom workers, and is a participant in Irish export promotions throughout the world.

Cullen was born in Cork and is married to a girl from the same area; she is also his business associate.

Donald Davies. Designer-manufacturer, Charleville, Inniskerry

Ireland's most successful wholesale operation, Donald Davies of Dublin was founded in 1954 with Donald Davies as administrator and his wife Mary as designer, using handwoven Irish tweeds, handknits, and linens. Their shop in Inniskerry is in the village near Charleville, the historic Georgian estate they own and occupy with their family of four children.

In 1971 Donald Davies opened a successful shop in New York. His fashions are also featured at Ireland House, 150 New Bond St., London.

IB Jorgensen. Dublin couturier, 24 Fitzwilliam Sq., Dublin 2

Danish-born (January 23, 1935) IB Jorgensen came to Ireland with his family when they moved from Denmark as farmers. He studied at the Grafton Academy of Dress Design in Dublin where he won two awards in 1953. He worked three years for Dublin fashion houses and in 1956 opened his own firm. He now occupies a Georgian mansion on Fitzwilliam Square in Dublin. His wife, Patricia, is his associate.

Trade Associations and Organizations

Irish Export Board. Merrion Hall, Strand Rd., Dublin 4

This well-organized and effective organization to foster and aid businesses both large and small is financed by the government.

The Board sponsors group trade shows in hotels in various capitals during the traditional buying periods. It issues fashion press releases and photographs to the international press and provides a staff to receive and assist buyers at group shows.

Young businesses which show promise are given financial aid for promotional and selling trips, and in some cases they receive aid in organizing their factories.

Fashion Education

Grafton Academy of Dress Designing. Grafton St., Dublin 2

Established soon after World War II, this school has become The Republic of Ireland's chief training center in fashion design. Although it offers only a one-year course, it has excellent standing with the Irish garment producers.

Costume and Fashion Archives

National Museum of Ireland. Kildare St., Dublin 2

Tel: Dublin 65521. Curator: Dr. A.T. Lucas.

There are English and Irish costumes from 1600 to 1850, laces, and textiles. There is also a fabulous collection of Celtic gold ornaments and 1000-year-old stone carvings showing costumed figures.

ITALY

In Italy, fashion creativity burst out like fireworks immediately after World War II, only to succumb to the same apathy and desperation which followed the country's strike-ridden lack of leadership. By the 1970s the most fertile designers were stymied by the problems of labor and obtaining materials. Italy's export figures are uncertain due to the unsettled conditions, but by 1975 official statements spoke of an improved outlook.

The Italian government has always been an ally of Italian fashion in financial and promotional assistance. This alliance was obvious in the summer of 1973 when the President of Italy formally received international buyers and the press at the Palazzo Venezia on the eve of the Rome couture showings. One speaker, Senator Radi, termed high fashion "the research sector of the clothing industry; a vital part of our economy." Accordingly government subsidy (sometimes a major portion of the cost of producing a couture collection) continues to be granted to designers whose export sales would not warrant such encouragement in other private-enterprise countries.

Italy has for centuries been the center of design and production of the finest fashion materials such as printed and slubbed dupioni silks, textured cotton damasks and brocades, and sheer woolens. Lake Como, the traditional capital of the fabric industry, now has competition from other centers in the north, near Milan, where synthetics are produced in vast quantities.

The silk industry has been indigenous to Italy from the 14th century when the silk worm was supposedly brought from China by Marco Polo. There is virtually no silk grown in Italy now, and its silk companies are largely dependent on imported silk fibers and even imported finished goods to which the Italian labels are added. Dupioni silk suitings, for instance, come to Italy in the finished state from Mainland China or Japan. Much of Italy's reputation for fine leather goods now depends primarily on outside production in Yugoslavia and other leather-working countries.

Rome continues to be the artistic core of Italian high fashion, but several important designers now work in Milan and the north of Italy, and its burgeoning ready-to-wear industry is centered in Milan and Turin.

Sardinia and the southern part of Italy, where poverty has been desperate for many years, are now being slowly rehabilitated by the government-sponsored infusion of fashion and cosmetic factories under a system of tax-reduction to manufacturers and training programs for the workers. Foreign as well as native employers are welcomed by the government and given special concessions under the Mezzogiorno and other Italian work-development plans.

Fashion Designers and Firms

Albanese. Shoe creators, Via Lazio 18, Rome

Founded in the early 1940s by Armando Albanese as a custom-order shoe atelier with a small clientele of elegant Romans, Albanese is now international in scope, with Armando's son, Enzo Albanese as its head. Albanese designs are now done by the owner's wife, Teresa (Mezzitesta) Albanese, who trained as a painter and joined the firm in 1952.

Among shoe-fashion milestones credited to Albanese are the introduction of the transparent shoe, shoes combining black patent leather and colored suede, and the flat-soled street shoe.

Walter Albini. Ready-to-wear designer, c/o Trell, Via Masaccio 12, I-20129 Milan

One of Italy's most successful exporters of fashions, Walter Albini was born May 9, 1941, in Busto Arsizio, near Milan. He studied at the Istituto di Belle Arti e Moda in Turin, where he graduated.

He went to Paris where he worked as an illustrator and designed boutique fashions. Upon his return to Italy in 1965, he formed his own firm in Milan and designs women's, men's and children's fashions for various manufacturers.

Albini commutes between Milan and Venice, and has a house in Tunisia.

Renato Balestra. Couturier and ready-to-wear designer, Via Gregoriana 36, I-00187 Rome

Born in Trieste to a well-known family in the construction business, Renato Balestra studied to be a civil engineer. As a student he made a bet with friends that he could create the direct opposite of the solid forms of building construction in beautiful yet functional clothing. The fashions he stands for today, however, have an aloofness and angularity that one journalist described as "traditional futurism."

Basile. Ready-to-wear for women and men, Via Jennes 51, I-20145 Milan

Named for Gianfranco Basile, a small tailoring establishment parlayed into a flourishing moderate-priced fashion manufacturer under the creative business leadership of Aldo Ferrante, Basile became a key factor in Italian wholesale fashion in the mid-1970s. Today it is owned by FTM, a triumvirate of Ferrante and his two partners Tositi and Monti.

Beginning as a corset salesman, Ferrante entered the fashion world in 1949 by designing an innovative range of men's neckwear, then worked in textiles and later as sales agent for Krizia and Missoni. In 1967, FTM was formed as the production organization for knitwear designed by a variety of talents: Missoni, Walter Albini, Cerruti, and others.

Since 1972, Basile has concentrated on women's fashion in the highly elegant tradition, designed by Muriel Grateau.

Battistoni. Haberdashers, Via Condotti 61, Rome

This leading maker of Italian menswear, particularly shirts and ties, was established in the 1930s and was the training ground for several well-known designers including Carlo Palazzi. It has an international clientele and is one of the status tourist shops in Rome.

Biki. Couture house, Via San Andrea 8, Milan

This fashion house, owned by a powerful and dynamic business woman, has a following of smart Milanese and Roman ladies, as well as many Italian stage and screen personalities.

The founder, Signora Elvira (Biki) Leonardi is the granddaughter of the famous composer Giacomo Puccini. Through her mother she inherited one of Milan's largest newspapers, Il Corriere della Sera.

The colorful and dramatic Biki collections are edited by Sra. Biki, but designed by her son-in-law, the American-born Alain Reynaud. Reynaud previously designed for Jacques Fath in Paris and Maurice Rentner in New York.

Brioni (Gaetano Savini Brioni). Via Barberini 79/81, Rome

Brioni has been a symbol of traditional Italian tailoring since the 1930s.

Gaetano Savini Brioni, head of the house, was born September 10, 1909, in Termi, Italy. He has been a leader of the Italian menswear industry from the time his impeccable but nontraditional suits were discovered by such world figures as the Prince of Wales, later the Duke of Windsor, and film star Douglas Fairbanks.

Brioni again led the resurgence of Italian menswear creativity after World War II.

He has won many awards throughout the world.

Bulgari. Jewelers, Via Condotti 11, Rome

This jewelry establishment, well known in Europe and the Far East since the early 1900s, was founded by two brothers, Constantine and Giorgio Bulgari, as a small atelier in Rome. Their regal and decorative jewels, mixing stones and elaborate gold work with Byzantine splendor, soon brought them clients among royalty, Eastern potentates, and the very rich everywhere.

The Bulgari minaudiere, a ribbed gold and jewelled evening box inspired by the Russian court jeweller Fabergé, became a world fashion in the 1960s, and they were among the first to establish the fashion for ornate chains and pendants.

Constantine, who died in 1973, was a collector and historian of rare and precious period jewelry.

His sons Gianni and Nicola Bulgari now head the firm, which has several international branches.

Cadette. Via Eustachi 45, I-20029 Milan

Founded in 1966 by Enzo Clocchiati and Christine Tidmarsh, Cadette today represents a trio of talents: Christine, a former Saint Laurent mannequin; Enzo, a young businessman–sportsman with an uninhibited approach to sportswear; and Walter Albini, a trained fashion creator. When Enzo took over a small clothing factory to update its management, he recruited the taste and expertise of the two others.

Among the first Italian houses to own and operate independent boutiques in Italian cities and in Paris, Cadette helped establish Milan as a fashion center by withdrawing from the long-established Florence showings.

Cadette clothes play up abstract forms and motifs inspired by modern artists such as Van Gogh, Giacometti, and Matisse. They are off-beat and dramatic, yet always contemporary, thus appealing to a celebrity clientele as well as to a broad world of wholesale distribution.

Roberto Capucci. Italian couturier, Via Gregoriana 56, I-00187 Rome

The wonder-boy of Italian fashion just after World War II, Capucci was only 20 when he established his couture house in 1950 and was hailed as a genius. For the next 10 years he contributed to Italy's reputation as a center of audacious, "dolce-vita" fashion.

In 1962 he opened a couture salon in Paris, but his star waned somewhat and he returned to a more faithful clientele in Rome. In 1970 he was asked by the Indian government to go to India to study its textiles and their application to Western fashion. The same year he introduced a new version of the monastic dress which he termed the Giotto line and offered it in place of the unpopular midi-skirt. Although first known for "Hard Chic" clothes, his always-interesting cut is today soft and flowing, with a feeling of classicism and timelessness.

Patrick de Barentzen. Couturier and ready-to-wear designer (retired)

This Danish-born designer was one of the bright talents who made the Roman fashion scene electric after World War II. In the 1960s he was one of Italian fashion's important trend-setters, maintaining his atelier and boutique at Via Gregoriana 5. He closed his house suddenly in 1971 and now lives in retirement.

Marchesa Olga de Gresy. See Mirsa

Roberta di Camerino (Roberta of Venice). Designer and boutique owner, Campo Santa Maria Formosa 6123, Venice. New York address: Olympic Tower, 645 Fifth Ave., New York, N.Y. 10022

Born Giuliana di Camerino but widely known both as Roberta di Camerino and Roberta of Venice, this designer is one of the leading business successes of her native city, Venice, and one of its best-known citizens. Her fashions are infiltrated with Venetian colors and motifs, and her Venetian cut-velvet handbags have been status symbols for 25 years.

Born December 8, 1920, in Venice, Roberta's career began immediately after World War II when she and her banker husband Guido di Camerino returned from Lugano, Switzerland, where they had spent three years to escape the Nazi domination of Italy. To earn pin money during their enforced exile, Giuliana designed handbags and had them made by a local saddlemaker.

Returning to Venice, she set up a small studio and workshops in an old gondola factory. Stanley Marcus of Neiman–Marcus of Dallas, Texas, was first to introduce Roberta of Venice designs outside Italy, and in 1956 she received the Neiman–Marcus Award.

Today, Roberta's organization is the only wholesale fashion manufacturing business in the city of Venice, maintained as a cooperative since the designer gave the factory to her employees. She owns other factories throughout Italy, including a tannery for her leathers, an umbrella factory, a plant where her famous "trompe d'oeil" sheer wool or cotton jerseys are printed, and workshops for frames and hardware for her bags and luggage. Parts of her leather products are now manufactured in Yugoslavia.

Roberta di Camerino fashions are sold throughout the world. Roberta boutiques are established in New York, Chicago, most Italian cities, Paris, the Riviera, and the larger centers in Germany, Austria, Switzerland, Sweden, Denmark, Belgium, Holland, and Lebanon.

Alberto Fabiani. Couturier and ready-to-wear designer, Via Condotti 11, I-00187 Rome

Especially noted for tailored clothes of innovative cut and impeccable workmanship, Alberto Fabiani was born in Rome, the son of an artisan tailor and clothing manufacturer. He learned his craft from his father who established the house of Fabiani in 1909.

In 1952 he married Donna Simonetta Visconti (now the Duchess di Cesaro), a rival fashion designer in Rome. After working separately in Italy they opened (1962) a joint venture, Simonetta et Fabiani, on the rue François Premier in Paris. It was a financial success, but the necessity of choosing between Italy and France as a domicile brought a division between them, both personal and professional. They closed the couture house in 1964 and were divorced in 1972. Simonetta remained in Paris with her own Simonetta Haute Boutique for high fashion ready-to-wear. Fabiani returned to Rome and his couture establishment, continuing to stand for the best in skillful cut and tailoring for women and for brilliant variety in simple day dresses.

The Fabiani ateliers are in a magnificent palazzo, once the home of Marchese Guglielmo Marconi, the inventor of radio.

Fendi. Fur designer and manufacturer, Via Borgognona 39, I-00817 Rome

Italy's best-known fur-fashion producer, Fendi is a family-run business founded by Adele Fendi about 1918. Her five daughters (Carla, Franca, Paula, Anna, and Alda) and their husbands are now associated with her in the business. Karl Lagerfeld of Paris designs many of their collections.

Fendi furs are well-known throughout the world with both private clients and stores in Germany, the United States, Switzerland, and Japan. The furs are notably trendy, in unusual pelts, colors, and treatments. In 1974 Fendi launched the idea of unlined fur coats.

Aldo Ferrante. See Basile

Fortuny. See Hall of Fame

Irene Galitzine. Designer and cosmetician, Via V. Veneto 84, I-00187 Rome

Best known for launching the "palazzo pajama," Princess Irene Galitzine was born in Tiflis, Russia, of the noble Russian Galitzine family which traces its ancestry to Catherine the Great. Her family fled to Italy in the Russian Revolution, and she was educated in Italian and English schools. She learned five languages and studied art in Rome, but her urge was toward fashion. For three years she worked with a Rome couture house, then in 1959 presented her first personal collection. It immediately won awards, including the Filene (Boston) Award for new talent.

Galitzine's historic palazzo pajama was introduced in 1960 at the Pitti Palace in Florence. In 1962 the Italian fashion press voted Galitzine "best designer of the year." In 1964 she was the first Italian designer to show her collection in the Italian Embassy in Washington. The following year she received the London Sunday Times International Fashion Award and the same year received the Italian Government's Isabella d'Este Award given to outstanding women of achievement from different countries. She was the first Italian designer to be sponsored in the Far East when the Japanese group, ISETAN, introduced her clothes.

Gucci. Leather goods creators, Via Tornabuoni 73, I-50123 Florence

Leather goods designers and manufacturers for more than five centuries, this family business was established in the 15th century by an ancestor of the present head, Dr. Aldo Gucci.

After World War II, the high quality and simple good taste of Gucci handbags refocused international attention on Italian styling as competitive to the elegant French handbag. In the 1960s, the low-heeled Gucci moccasin with a brass harness bit across its tongue became a world craze, speeding the trend to sporty, low-heeled footwear. Today the tackroom hardware and the red and green canvas stripes used on Gucci accessories and luggage represent possibly the most imitated and status-making fashion look in the accessory world.

Since about 1970, Dr. Gucci has steadily expanded his retail empire with a string of Gucci shops in cities throughout the world.

In 1972, the members of the Gucci family signed an agreement to keep the business in their private domain for the next 100 years at least. Dr. Gucci's two brothers, three sons, and 19 grandchildren are at present involved in the designing, selling, and distribution of Gucci products.

Krizia. *See* Mariuccia Pinto Mandelli

La Mendola. Ready-to-wear and textile designers, Piazza Trinita dei Monte 15, Rome

This house, owned by two Americans, Michael La Mendola and Jack Savage, is known for its vibrant original prints around which the clothes are designed. It was founded in 1964 after the two partners had met on their jobs in the film industry and decided to collaborate in fashion.

Michael La Mendola, born June 6, 1929, in Champaign, Illinois, came to Rome to study painting, but found a job with a movie unit. Jack Savage, a native of Herminie, Pennsylvania (born April 4, 1931), attended the University of Pittsburgh and the Pittsburgh Playhouse School of the Theater. He served four years in the United States Air Force and came to Rome to act in films and dub Italian films into English.

La Mendola's silk jersey dresses and scarves, in original prints, first attracted professional buyers and tourists staying at the Hotel Hassler, across the Piazza from their boutique. They now export to the United States and all of Europe and live nearby in an historic frescoed villa once the property of the Vatican.

Pino Lancetti. Couturier, Via Condotti 61, I-00187 Rome

A designer who began as a painter, Pino Lancetti was born in Perugia in 1932, studied fine arts at the Perugia Academy, and came to Rome to continue his painting. Princess Giovannelli, who had opened a maison de couture in Rome, persuaded him to apply his talents to making clothes. Gradually learning the techniques of dressmaking, he then designed for Simonetta, Fabiani, Carosa, and de Luca. In 1961 he opened his own house at his present address.

Very shy and retiring, Lancetti continues to relate painting to his work which he terms "classical, subtle, and lyrical." He is an instructor to young designers in a school in Rome and designs decorative fabrics for a large Japanese textile company.

Heavily influenced by nostalgic moods and art periods, Lancetti clothes are always flowing, graceful, subtly colored, and dramatic.

Andre Laug. Couturier and ready-to-wear designer, Piazza di Spagna 81, I-00187 Rome

One of the most thoroughly trained and technically skilled of Roman designers, Andre Laug was born in Gravelines, France, on December 29, 1931. He worked five years for Nina Ricci in Paris and once offered to quit his job to work as an apprentice to Andre Courreges, whose technical perfection he greatly admires. He came to Rome as designer with the house of Antonelli and in 1968 opened his own establishment.

Laug's precise, clean lines, his architectural use of pleats and slim, "split-level" silhouettes, and his unusual handling of stripes blend the simplicity of Chanel and Molyneux outlines with the abstract art themes of today's fashion.

Elvira (Biki) Leonardi. See Biki

Angelo Litrico. Menswear designer, Via Sicilia, Rome

This designer, best known for tailored clothes, was born in Catania, the son of a fisherman. He came to Rome in 1950, with no funds, but his childhood training as a men's tailor brought him employment. He soon opened his own shop and his unusual details and colorations in men's suits brought him a prominent clientele, including members of the Rothschild family and King Hussein of Jordan.

In 1967 he extended his activity to include a collection for women.

Mariuccia Pinto Mandelli. Krizia, Via Agnello 12, I-20121 Milan

One of Europe's first advocates of the extremes of modern fashion, the midi- and maxi-skirts, Mariuccia Pinto Mandelli also launched the opposite length, called "hot pants," in 1970 and made those shorts briefly a world fashion.

Born to a family of educators, she began her professional life as teacher in a primary school near Milan. With a friend, Flora Dolci, she organized a firm (1953) to design dresses for women and children in the light, unconstructed forms which were revolutionary in 1957, their founding date. The name Krizia was taken from one of Plato's dialogues on the vanity of women. In 1964 Krizia showed a memorable collection in Florence, winning the fashion critics award.

Before her marriage to Aldo Pinto, who now manages her knitwear and ready-to-wear businesses, Mariuccia Mandelli collaborated with two other designers who are now well known—Walter Albini and Karl Lagerfeld.

Krizia's characteristic is an amplitude of thick fabric combined with thin or sheer fabric in graceful, picturesque lines.

Like many fertile fashion creators, Mandelli now has a group of manufacturing divisions: for knits, for sportswear, and for children. She also works on license arrangements with firms in America and other countries.

In 1971 she received the Tiberio d'Oro Award in Capri's Maremoda promotion of Italian fashion.

Mirsa. Knitwear designer and manufacturer, La Robinia, I-28066 Galliate, Novara

Mirsa, one of Italy's keystone knitwear houses, was founded by the Marchesa Olga de Gresy in 1937 in Milan. She had previously designed for firms in Turin. During the war years the family Gresy and the Marchesa's flourishing handloomed knitting ateliers moved to the family estate, "La Robinia," in Galliate.

The label Mirsa is derived from the names of Marchesa Olga's two children, Mirella and Sandro.

Mirsa remains a family-run organization, headed by the Marchesa and assisted by various members of her family who design, supervise production, and promote the worldwide sale of their knitwear collections.

In 1953 Mirsa received the Neiman–Marcus Award.

Ottavio and Rosita Missoni. Knitwear designers–manufacturers, Sumirago, Varese

Ottavio and Rosita Missoni, Italy's leading creators of knit fashions, whose lacy textures and rainbow-shaded patterns have affected style in many areas, began their business in 1953 soon after their marriage. Ottavio, born in Ragusa, Yugoslavia, in 1921, was an Olympic hurdle racer and met his wife Rosita Jelmini during the Olympic games in 1948. Rosita had been brought up to know one phase of clothing manufacture through her family's loungewear business.

Sensing the growing interest in knits, the Missonis started a small business with five workers. Their vivid color sense expressed Rosita's suave, simple designs and the unusual stitches Ottavio worked out on the very sophisticated knitting machinery they invested in brought them instant acclaim.

Today their model factory, with more than 200 workers, is part of their own compound of antique and modern buildings, including a house for the Missonis and their three children.

The Missonis received a Neiman–Marcus Award in 1973.

Ognibene–Zendman. Via Toscana 1, I-00187 Rome

This fashion house has an American, Peter Zendman, as its designer and an Italian, Sergio Ognibene, as administrator. Zendman, son of an

American textile family, worked five years for Balenciaga in Paris, and his sense of cut and texture are original.

Carlo Palazzi. Menswear designer, Via Borgonona 7, Rome

Born May 3, 1928, in Urbino, Italy, Carlo Palazzi worked for a men's haberdasher in Bologna, then came to Rome as director of the menswear firm of Battistoni. In 1965 he opened his own custom and ready-to-wear atelier in the Via Borgonona and recently expanded his quarters to occupy the beautiful Piazza Torlonia nearby.

Known as one of the most elegant and original Italian designers for men, Palazzi created a number of menswear collections for the British firm of Jaeger, but now distributes his own ready-to-wear throughout the world.

Palazzi is a member of the Camera Nazionale dell'Alta Moda Italiana and winner of a number of Italian fashion prizes for fashion excellence.

Emilio Pucci (di Barsento). Palazzo Pucci, Via dei Pucci 6, I-50122 Florence

The man who made the Pucci print dress the fashion uniform of a generation was born Marchese Emilio Pucci di Barsento in Naples, November 20, 1914. His family tree has a Russian branch descending from Peter the Great and Catherine the Great. He and his family now occupy the ancestral palace in Florence, where family portraits and art works by Botticelli, Raphael, Leonardo da Vinci, and Donatello are to be seen.

Pucci studied at the University of Milan, then attended the University of Atlanta, Georgia, and Reed College in Portland, Oregon, where he received his Master of Arts degree in social sciences in 1937. In 1941 he was made a Doctor of Political Science by the University of Florence. While serving his military training the war started and he served as a captain in the Italian Air Force for 14 years.

He opened his fashion business in 1950 and almost overnight established the soft, easy silk jersey Pucci print dress as a status uniform throughout the world. It was the first of the all-purpose little jersey dresses to be combined with status symbol identification in its prints and thus pointed ahead to today's more casual interpretation of elegance.

In 1959 Marchese Pucci married Cristina Nannini di Casabianca. They have two children, Allesandro and Laudomia.

In 1965 he was elected to Italy's Parliament as a Liberal member for Florence. He has been a leader in efforts to focus world attention on Italian fashion and an emissary of Italy on many international Italian fashion tours. His foreign designing activities included designing the first sprightly, highly colored air hostess wardrobes for Braniff Airways, a move which started a world trend in that direction. He designs foundation garments, mail-order fashions, sportswear, ski clothes, and housewares for companies in America and elsewhere.

Pucci received the Neiman–Marcus Award (1954), the Burdine's Sunshine Award (1955), and the Sports Illustrated Award (1961).

Alain Reynaud. See Biki

Evan Richards. See Tiziani

Heinz Riva. Couturier and ready-to-wear designer, Piazza di Spagna 86, I-00187 Rome

Born in Zurich on March 16, 1938, Heinz Riva attributes his intense unwavering interest in a fashion career to the encouragement of his mother who was directrice of a Swiss fashion house. He studied at the Beaux Arts of Zurich and went on to l'Ecole de la Chambre Syndicale in Paris. He worked briefly for Paris and London couturiers before coming to Rome in 1963 as assistant designer with Irene Galitzine.

In 1966 he opened his own house at his present address. His clothes are lively and young, yet sophisticated.

Sanlorenzo. Couture and knitwear house, Corso Vittorio Emanuele 68, I-10121 Turin

This couture house, founded in 1950, is now run by Marisa and Paola Sanlorenzo, the two daughters of the original designer. Both are still in their twenties (1975).

Sanlorenzo was noted for its svelte suits and soignee dresses, with a clientele of wealthy north Italian ladies. The daughters of Signora Sanlorenzo, however, brought a younger, more contemporary flavor and instituted the ready-to-wear knitwear branch of the business.

Fausto Sarli. Via Filangieri 34, I-80121 Naples

This designer, best known for his tailored clothes, was born in 1927 in Naples of a wealthy family who lost everything in World War II. He was able to study fashion designing and in 1954, after winning a national design competition, he presented his first collection at the Pitti Palace in Florence.

Although he has a salon in Rome, Sarli's chief atelier is in Naples, where he creates, designs, and prepares his collections. He has five children, and his two elder sons work with him.

Mila Schon (Shon). Couturiere and ready-to-wear designer, Via Monte Napoleone 2, I-20121 Milan

This custom and ready-to-wear designer was the first one to introduce double-faced wools into the couture, and brought that difficult technique to its highest perfection. She is to Italian fashion what Mme Gres is to French, but the Schon look is much more angular and stark, avoiding mannishness by a willowy hairsbreadth. Mila Schon is also noted for her abstract shaping and ombre shading. Her extraordinarily worked beaded dresses are unique.

Born in Trau, Dalmatia, of an aristocratic Yugoslav family, she came to Italy as a child when her parents fled from the Communists. After some years in Trieste, she moved to Milan. She went frequently to Paris and was a faithful client at Balenciaga until financial reverses forced her to earn her living. She started by opening a small Milan atelier to copy Paris models, but her first independent collection shown in Florence in 1965 was a brilliant success. At that time she initiated ready-to-wear to parallel her custom-made clothes, calling it Alta Moda Pronta.

Her ateliers, like her clothes, reflect her highly distilled artistic sense. She utilizes the best architects and best artisans to display and decorate her designs, having been the first designer in recent times to use fine cloisonne buttons and other jewelers' touches in her clothes.

Ken Scott (George Kenneth Scott). Textile and fashion designer, Via Corridoni 37, I-20137 Milan

The first American to make a name in Italian fashion, Ken Scott was born November 6, 1918, in Fort Wayne, Indiana, the son of a local photographer whose family had provided portraits for many generations of American family albums.

Ken's mother, widowed and financially wiped out at the beginning of the Depression, managed to send Ken to New York to study at the Parsons School of Design. He also studied painting with the American artist Moses Soyer.

"I was the first to put sequins on Easter eggs. It was no achievement, but it bought meals," says Ken. He worked for a florist on weekends, and his "crazy" flower arrangements inspired the prints which were later to make him famous as a member of the Falconetto textile organization in Milan.

Ken Scott scarves, characterized by solid patterns of huge flowers, were framed as well as worn in the 1950s. In 1964 Ken launched a collection of ready-to-wear, sold internationally and in his own Milan boutique. His boldly printed stretch bathing suits can be said to have started the vogue for colorfully printed swimwear. He was the first European-based designer to develop entire collections in one synthetic fabric, such as Bancroft's Banlon®.

Simonetta (Duchess Simonetta di Cesaro) (retired). Via Gregoriana 5, Rome

This Italian-born couturiere, now retired, is the daughter of a Russian mother and the Sicilian Duca di Cesaro. She was first married to Count Galaezzo Visconti. Their daughter, Verdi Visconti, is a well-known Roman interior designer.

Having begun to design clothes in the mid-30s, Simonetta was one of Rome's leading dressmakers when (1952) she married Alberto Fabiani, a rival designer. Their son Bardo Fabiani is a photographer in London.

Simonetta and Fabiani successfully maintained separate couture establishments in Rome for several years, then in 1962 opened a Paris couture house together, called Simonetta et Fabiani, at 40 rue François Premier. Fabiani returned to Italy in 1965, but Simonetta remained in Paris to establish the first of the "haute boutiques" of expensive ready-to-wear now familiar throughout the world.

The Fabianis were subsequently divorced, and Simonetta sold her Paris boutique and the use of her name to French interests. She travelled to India on a religious pilgrimage, and in 1973 she established a colony for the care of lepers there. She developed a training program for weaving and the making of rugs and handwoven clothing to partially support the afflicted and provide modern treatment for the disease.

Simonetta now lives in Rome and Paris part of the year, while continuing her studies and charitable projects in the Far East.

Luisa Spagnoli. Knitwear designer, Via Po 16A, Rome

This organization stems from the hobby of the wealthy Luisa Spagnoli, owner of the famous Perugina candy company. She kept a small zoo on the estate and ordered some angora rabbits from Turkey. Their magnificent fur appealed to her so much that she hired some local workers to spin it into yarn for knitted fashions.

When Signora Spagnoli died in 1935, her ideas were still in the experimental stage, but after World War II her descendants developed it into a successful "vertical" fashion business.

Spagnoli sweaters and clothing are now designed and produced from the fiber on by the most sophisticated modern machinery producing angora, lamb's wool, angora mixtures, merino, cashmere, silk, cotton, and orlon yarns.

Spagnoli exports to 5000 outlets in 75 countries. There is a chain of 150 Spagnoli shops in Italian cities, and in Dallas, Texas.

Tiziani. Via Gregoriana 41, I-00187 Rome

This Italian couture house founded in 1963, is owned by an American from Texas, Evan Richards. In rather flamboyant taste, expressing current fashion trends in colorful and highly alluring ways, Tiziani's clothes are in demand by film stars such as Elizabeth Taylor and Gina Lollobrigida.

Born in Jacksboro, Texas, he received his Master's degree in music at North Texas University, then went to Rome to study singing. He found himself dabbling in costume designing and in 1963 decided to open a small fashion house. He now has added a boutique and sells his ready-to-wear in America, Mexico, and West Germany.

Bergin Usberk. Couturier, Via Gregoriana 12, Rome
This designer, now working in Rome, was born in Istanbul, Turkey. His wealthy family wanted him to become a diplomat, but he was more interested in designing.

After studying at the American College in Istanbul, he graduated from the Turkish Academy of Fine Arts, where he was recommended for the l'Ecole de la Chambre Syndicale de la Haute Couture in Paris. After his graduation, he worked for three years on the staff of Pierre Cardin.

In 1965 he returned home and opened his couture house in Istanbul, where he soon became Turkey's best-known designer. In 1971, he opened his Rome house, commuting between the two cities.

Usberk clothes are colorful and graceful, with consistent overtones of Oriental but nonethnic decoration.

Valentino (Garavani). Via Gregoriana 24, Rome
Valentino Garavani, the best known Italian designer of the 1960s and 1970s, was born in 1932 in Voghera, Italy. He studied fine arts in Milan and at 18 went to Paris to study fashion design and cutting. He worked for five years on the staff of Jean Desses and three more for Guy Laroche.

In 1960 he returned to Italy and worked briefly for Irene Galitzine, then opened his own atelier. His stress on day clothes tailored in pure white and brown and white, his unique soft tailoring and suave simplicity brought him immediate acclaim. His early clients included Mrs. Jacqueline Kennedy Onassis, Elizabeth Taylor Burton, and the Empress of Iran.

In 1968, the American Kenton Corporation acquired Valentino's name and all his interests outside Italy. In 1973 Valentino repurchased these.

His couture salons and boutique in Rome occupy a house above the Spanish steps belonging to the Vatican. He has a shop in the Via Condotti where home furnishings and household linens of his design are sold. There are Valentino boutiques in various cities throughout the world.

Valentino's business administrator and partner, Giancarlo Giammetti, is credited with a major contribution toward the international success of the House of Valentino.

Mario Valentino. Shoe designer, Via Frattina 58, Rome

Formerly known under his registered label, Valentino, Mario Valentino designed custom-order and ready-made shoes for his family firm founded in 1890. He also designed collections for shoe manufacturers in other countries.

When Valentino Garavani emerged as a famous couturier, a conflict developed over the use of the Valentino label and resulted in a law suit. Although still unresolved in 1974, the fashion world generally uses the full name, Mario Valentino, when referring to the shoe designer.

Jole Veneziani. Fur and clothes designer, Via Montenapoleone 8, I-20100 Milan

Jole Veneziani, known for her clean cut and elegant clothes and furs, was born in Taranto, Italy. Her father was a lawyer and writer, her brother Carlo a well-known poet and playwright. She studied acting, design, and painting. For a short period she worked as a journalist. Later she was manager of an English fur company in Milan.

In 1943 she opened, at the present address, her own fur atelier and in 1946 added a couture collection. In 1969 she introduced ready-to-wear collections.

Today her activities include couture, a sportswear line, knitwear, and accessories (shoes, stockings, handbags, umbrellas, and perfume).

Her awards include the "Giglio d'Oro" presented to her at the Pitti Palace in Florence by the Italian and foreign press. In 1972 she was named "Cavaliere al merito della Repubblica" by the Italian Republic. In 1973 she received the "Ape d'Oro" and in 1974 the "Maschera d'Argento"—the international Oscar award for her artistic merits in the field of high-fashion fur creations.

Fashion Influentials

Countess Consuelo Crespi. Editor, American *Vogue*, Condé Nast Publications, Palazzo Odescalchi, Piazza Santi Apostoli 81, Rome

An international beauty and social leader, Countess Crespi is an important catalyst and expert critic of Italian fashion.

Born Consuelo O'Connor in New York, she and her twin sister Gloria were popular fashion models before she married Count Rudolfo Crespi, the well-known public relations executive in Rome. Their daughter Pilar Crespi followed in her mother's path as a noted beauty and cover girl. Pilar is now married to Gabriel Echevarria of Bogota, Colombia.

Elisa Massai. Milan representative, Fairchild Publications, Corsa Porto Nuova 48, Milan

Mrs. Massai, the daughter of a famous Italian general, has been an important observer and recorder of Italian fashion and economics since World War II.

Brunetta Mateldi. Fashion artist and reporter, Via Bagutta 1, Milan

Diminutive, dynamic Brunetta is one of the most popular and powerful press personalities in Italy. Her lively cartoonish sketches capture the spirit of the season and her phoned-in reportage has a sprightly bite to it.

Beppe (Giuseppe) Modenese. Fashion consultant, Via Borgospesso 19, I-20100 Milan

For many years Beppe Modenese has been involved with Italian fashion in the field of public relations and as fashion consultant to designers and textile manufacturers.

As advisor to Dupont in Europe, he is responsible for surveys of the collections and for summaries and photographs to the press.

Born in 1928 in Alba, he attended l'Accademia Albertina of Turin, studying economics and business administration.

Giorgio Pavone. Organizer and publicist of fashion events, Via Monte della Gioie 9, Rome

Pavone, formerly partner of Count Rudolfo Crespi, now heads a number of Italian fashion public relations programs, among them the Mare Moda di Capri. An elegant socialite himself, he is active in the introduction of new fashion ideas, particularly in the area of men's clothing.

Maria Pezzi. Fashion writer, *Il Giorno*, Via A. Fava 20, I-20125 Milan

An elegant woman and an excellent writer, Signora Pezzi is noted for her critiques of fashion events which are considered the most important in the Italian press.

Bianca Maria Piccinino. TV fashion commentator, RAI—Radio-televisione Italiana, Viale Mazzini 14, I-00195 Rome

Italy's leading fashion reporter on the air, Mme Piccinino plans and produces a regular fashion report in daily and special news shows.

Lucia Rafaelli. Fashion editor, *Vogue Italia*, Edizioni Condé Nast S.p.A., Piazza Castello 27, I-20121 Milan

Lucia Rafaelli is a woman of taste and judgment who has made *Vogue Italia* an accurate mirror of current fashion.

Count Franco Savorelli. Viale Beatrice d'Este 4, Milan

Count Savorelli, a leading promoter of Italian fashions and of international products sold in Italy, is also an elegant figure in Italian social life. He has been in charge of the press attending the semiannual ready-to-wear Italian collections concentrated at the Palazzo Pitti in Florence.

Pia Soli. Fashion writer, *Il Tempo di Roma*, Via Santa Valeria 5, Rome

One of the few Italian fashion writers who has covered the collections in other style capitals including New York, Pia Soli is a trained interpreter of fashion for a large public.

Trade Associations and Organizations

Associazione Italiana Produttori Maglierie e Calzetterie (National Knitwear and Hosiery Association of Italy). Via Moscova 33, I-20122 Milan

Founded: 1945. Dir: Dr. Bruno Bianchi.

This organization represents nearly 2000 knit-goods and hosiery manufacturers with the aims of internal, export, and promotional cooperation.

It also conducts seminars and research projects for technical development and gives study grants in technology and design.

Camera Nazionale della Moda. Via Panama 26, I-00198 Rome

Founded: 1947. Dir/Pres: Luciano Goracci.

This official organization, now affiliated with l'Ente Italiano Moda, was organized soon after World War II to regulate practices and promote interest in Italian high fashion.

With government aid, the Camera has presented Italian high fashion in group showings throughout the world. Its main international function, however, is to organize a schedule of couture showings in Rome for buyers and press twice a year.

In spite of opposition to the subsidy of rarified couture operations by the government, Luciano Radi, a member of the Italian parliament, persuaded Italy's President Giovanni Leone to formally open the Alta Moda collections in July 1973. In his speech the president referred to the high-fashion designers as "a research sector of the clothing industry; a vital part of our economy."

Membership in the Camera includes about 50 houses of clothing and accessories in Rome, Milan, Florence, Venice, and Turin.

Centro Internazionale delle Arti e del Costume. Palazzo Grassi, San Samuele 3231, I-30124 Venice

Founded: 1951.

This nonprofit organization founded by Dr. Franco Marinotti, president of Snia Viscosa, with a membership of leading Italian fiber producers, maintains a center in Venice for research, conventions, and the documentation and display of period fashions and textiles.

141

The center now owns a collection of antique textiles and a library of 6000 texts on textiles, costumes, and the history of dress.

Comitatto Moda Industriali dell'Abbigliamento. Via Giovanni de Grassi 6, I-20123 Milan
Founded: December 1961. Dir: Antonino Evangelisti.
This association of textile producers is a liaison group between fashion designers and the textile industry.

Ente Italiano della Moda. Corso Galileo Ferraris 2, I-10121 Turin, and Piazzale Flaminio 19, I-00196 Rome
Founded: 1947. Dir. Gen: Amos Ciabattoni.
This trade and promotion organization founded after World War II has as its members manufacturers of all types of couture, ready-to-wear, textiles, and accessories.
Amos Ciabattoni was formerly director of an association representing high fashion, the Camera Nazionale della Moda Italiana, which has now been linked with l'Ente Italiano della Moda.

Ente Mare Moda Capri. Camera di Commercio di Napoli, Via San Aspreno 2, I-80100 Naples
Founded: 1965. Pres: Pasquale Acampora.
This group showing of Italian resort and summer sportswear is held every fall in Capri. Sponsored by the Camera di Commercio of Naples and Neapolitan businessmen, the festival combines the promotion of fashion talents with tourism. An award, the Tiberio d'Oro, is given during Mare Moda to fashion designers and a beauty pageant is also held.

Istituto Nazionale per il Commercio Estero (I.C.E.) (Italian Institute of Foreign Trade). Via Liszt 21, I-00100 Rome
This government department, affiliated with the Ministry for Foreign Trade (Ministero del Commercio con l'Estero) was set up to organize the participation of groups, representing every Italian industry in foreign trade fairs outside Italy. The Italian Institute maintains branch offices in every large country to which Italian exports go.

Milanovendemoda (Group Fashion Week). c/o Assomoda (Associazione Nazionale Italiana Rappresentanti Moda), Piazzetta Guastalla 15, I-20122 Milan
Founded: 1975.
This organization seeks to establish Milan as the buying center for Italian ready-to-wear.

Honors and Awards

Emanuele Nasi Prize
Given by Ente Italiano della Moda, Corso Galileo Ferraris 2, I-10121 Turin, the four annual awards are given for the best graduate theses on fashion. Only Italian students are eligible.

Tiberio d'Oro Award. See Trade Associations and Organizations: Ente Mare Moda Capri

Fashion Education

Accademia Italiana di Costume e Moda. Via S. Maria dell'Anima 16, I-00186 Rome
Pres: Gilberto Bernabei. Dir: Rosana Pistolese.
This school's fashion courses are planned to create professionals in various fields including fashion for women, men, and children, costume design for the stage, films, and television, textile design, accessories, fashion-show production, fashion promotion, and fashion journalism.
The two-year course of nine months each year is supervised by practicing designers in each field and students also may work as apprentices.

Costume and Fashion Archives

Centro Internazionale delle Arti e del Costume (International Center of Art and Costume). Palazzo Grassi, Venice
There is a collection of ancient and modern textiles and a display of typical costumes illustrating the history of dress.

Museo Degli Argenti (Silver Museum). Palazzo Pitti, I-50125 Florence
Tel: 270323. Founded: 1919. Dir: Marco Chiarini.
There is a large collection of Italian costumes, rare laces, and textiles.

Museo Etnografico Giuseppe Pitré (Giuseppe Pitré Ethnographic Museum). Parco della Favorita, I-90146 Palermo, Sicily
Tel: 516141. Founded: 1909. Dir: Gaetano Falzone.
Grecian, Albanian, and Sicilian peasant costumes are presented in realistic displays.

Museo Giuseppe Garibaldi (Giuseppe Garibaldi Museum). Piazza Medaglie d'Oro 1, Como
Tel: 268053. Founded: 1932. Dir: Ferrante Rittatore Vonwiller.
There is a large collection of historic costumes dating from the Italian Renaissance, European peasant costumes, and examples of fine textiles.

Museo Nazionale delle Arti e Tradizioni Popolari (National Museum of Arts and Popular Traditions). Piazza Marconi 8, I-00144, Rome
Tel: 596148. Founded: 1906. Opened: 1956. Dir: Dr. Tullio Tentori. There is a large collection of Italian regional peasant costumes from the 19th century up to the present day.

Raccolte del Settecento Veneziano (The 18th Century Venetian Collection). Ca' Rezzonico, Grand Canal, Venice
Tel: 706480. Founded: 1660 (second floor: 1745). Relocated: 1936. Dir: Giovanni Mariacher.
This is a small but exquisite collection of 18th-century Venetian costumes, ornaments, and fabrics, some of the latter very rare.

Fashion Publications

Amica. Editoriale del Corriere della Sera, Via Solfernino 28, I-20100 Milan
Founded: 1962. Dir: Paolo Pietroni. Fashion Ed: Roberta Marioni. 52 issues/yr. L.300/issue ($36/yr in US). Circ: 445,000.

Annabella. Rizzoli Editore S.p.A., Via Civitavecchia 102, I-20132 Milan
Founded: 1933. Dir: Paulo Ochipinti. Fashion Ed: Luciana Omicini. 52 issues/yr. L.300/issue ($32/yr in US). Circ: 438,000.

Arbiter. Largo Toscanini 1, I-20122 Milan
Founded: 1927. Ed: Michelangelo Testa. 4 issues/yr. L.2500/issue ($21/yr in US). Circ: 40,000.

Cherie Moda. Edizioni Moderne Internazionali, Via Burlamacchi 11, I-20135 Milan
Founded: 1955. Dir: Alfredo Pietracini. 3 issues/yr. L.600/issue ($7.00/yr in US). Circ: 225,000.

Cherie Moda—Speciale. Edizioni Moderne Internazionali, Via Burlamacchi 11, I-20135 Milan
Founded: 1961. Dir: Alfredo Pietracini. 2 issues/yr. L.1000/issue ($7.50/yr in US). Circ: 52,500.

Confezione Italiana. Edizioni Aurelio Canevari s.r.l.
Founded: 1960. Ed: Aurelio Canevari. 4 issues/yr. L.1000/issue. Circ: 41,000. Text in Italian, English, French, German, and Spanish.

Cosmopolitan-Arianna. Arnoldo Mondadori Editore, Via Banca di Savoia 20, I-20122 Milan
Founded: 1973. 12 issues/yr. L.600/issue ($13/yr in US). Circ: 230,000.

Donne Eleganti. Edizioni Ibi, Via Finochiaro Aprile 5, I-20124 Milan
Founded: 1949. Ed: Ida Biondi. 4 issues/yr. L.1100/issue ($11/yr in US).

Eva. Rusconi Editore S.p.A., Via Vitruvio 43, I-20124 Milan
Founded: 1933. Dir: Lillo Tombolini. 52 issues/yr. L.250/issue ($22/yr in US). Circ: 368,947.

Gioia. Rusconi Editore S.p.A., Via Vitruvio 43, I-20124 Milan
Founded: 1938. Dir: Silvana Jacobini. 52 issues/yr. L.300/issue ($28.00/yr in US). Circ: 478,702.

Grazia. Arnoldo Mondadori Editore, Via Bianca di Savoia 20, I-20122 Milan
Founded: 1938. Dir: Renata Sidoti. Fashion Ed: Carla Vanni. 52 issues/yr. L.300/issue ($40.50/yr in US). Circ: 450,000.

Harper's Bazaar (Italian Edition). Editore Syds, Via Nino Bixio 45, I-20123 Milan
Founded: 1969. Dir: Isabella Niechi. 10 issues/yr. L.1000/issue ($36.00/yr in US). Circ: 38,000.

Linia Italiana. Arnoldo Mondadori Editore, Via Bianca di Savoia 20, I-20122 Milan
Founded: 1965. Dir: Fabrizio Pasquero. 7 issues/yr (also 4 large issues/yr). L.1500/reg. issue (L.3000/lg issue). $45/yr in US. Circ: 30,000. Text in Italian with summary in English and German.

Linia Maglia. PAN—Periodici Aracne Nuova Editrice Milano, s.r.l., Via Solfernino 32, I-20121 Milan
Founded: 1950. Dir: Dr. Mario Bonetti. 4 issues/yr. L.1500/issue ($20.00/yr in US). Circ: 8000.

Moda Maschile. Sartetecnica S.p.A., Via Y.B. Vico 18, I-20135 Milan
Founded: 1925. 6 issues/yr. L.5500/yr ($9/yr in US). Circ: 10,000.

Playboy (Italian Edition). Rizzoli Editore S.p.A., Via Civitavecchia 102, I-20132 Milan
Founded: 1972. Dir: Paulo Mosca. 12 issues/yr. L.1500/issue ($22.00/yr in US). Circ: 120,000.

La Sposa. Edizioni Moderne Internazionali, Via Burlamachi 11, I-20135 Milan
Founded: 1962. Ed: A. Maria Pietracini. 2 issues/yr. L.1700/issue. Circ: 34,000.

L'Uomo Vogue. Edizioni Condé Nast S.p.A., Piazza Castello 27, I-20121 Milan

Dir: Dr. Franco Sartori. 6 issues/yr. L1500/issue ($13.00/yr in US). Circ: 55,000.

Vestire. Gruppo Finanziario Tessile, Corso Giulio Cesare 31, Turin Founded: 1959. 2 issues/yr. $14/yr in US.

Vogue Italia. Edizioni Condé Nast S.p.A., Piazza Castello 27, I-20121 Milan

Founded: 1950. Dir: Franco Sartori. Fashion Ed: Lucia Rafaelli. 13 issues/yr. L.2500/collection issue. L.1500/regular issue ($36.00/yr in US). Circ: 50,000.

NETHERLANDS

Without any fanfare, and with only two or three designers of any pretension to international fame, the Dutch clothing industry has made tremendous strides since the midsixties when ready-made clothing manufacture became a factor in the European economy.

By 1973, the Dutch government's trade figures showed clothing exports of more than $100 million a year in women's suits, blouses, foundation garments, and lingerie, plus the men's and boys' clothing which Holland has made for some time. This figure is about one fifth of the total exports achieved by France, where the fashion climate has been conducive to far quicker growth of a ready-to-wear market.

Diamonds, for generations a virtual Dutch monopoly, suffered the effects of the last war, but Amsterdam continues as an important center for the handling of diamonds for jewelry as well as for industry.

Holland is also developing a fashion-rated production in fine leather goods and gloves.

Fashion Designers and Firms

The Netherlands has no internationally recognized designer labels. The two designers listed below are the only Dutch designers who occasionally appear in European fashion reports.

Ernst Jan Beeuwkes. Noordeinde 62b, The Hague

Dick Holthaus. Van Baerlestraat 12, Amsterdam

Trade Associations and Organizations

Amsterdam Fashion Export Center (Amfec). Van Eeghenstraat 101, Amsterdam

Founded: 1968. Dir: Leon Kusters.

This is a purely trade-relations organization of about 20 Dutch women's and children's ready-to-wear manufacturers centered in and around Amsterdam.

Costume and Fashion Archives

Het Nederlands Kostuummuseum, Kabinet van Mode en Smaak (Netherlands Costume Museum, Cabinet of Fashion and Taste). Lange Vijverberg 14, 070 The Hague. Correspondence: Dienst Voor Schone Kumsten, Box 72, 070 The Hague
Tel: 657394. Founded: 1952. Dir: Dr. L.J.F. Wijsenbeek.
There are costumes from the 18th century to the present.

Rijksmuseum, AFD. Nederlandse Geschiedenis (National Museum, Department of Dutch History). Stadhouderskade 42, 020 Amsterdam
Tel: 732121. Founded: 1808. Dir. Gen: Dr. A.F.E. Van Schendel.
This is one of the world's great museums, inspiring to fashion designers through the costumes in early Flemish and Dutch paintings and the actual clothing in the museum's rich collection of costumes and rooms.

Rijksmuseum Zuiderzeemuseum (National Zuiderzee Museum). Wierdijk 13, NL-02280 Enkhuizen
Tel: 3241. Founded: 1948. Dir: Dr. G.R. Kruissink.
There are traditional Dutch costumes in authentic settings.

Fashion Publications

Damesmodevakblad. De Gederlander Vakpars, Postbus 16, Nymegen
Founded: 1969. 4 issues/yr. fl.25/yr. Circ: 5000.

Herenmodevakblad. De Gederlander Vakpers, Postbus 16, Nymegen
Founded: 1969. 4 issues/yr. fl.25/yr. Circ: 4000.

Sir. Oberschuedstraat 170, Amsterdam
Founded: 1936. 4 issues/yr. fl.84/yr. Men's international fashion and textile trade journal. Text in Dutch, French, English, German, Italian, and Spanish.

PORTUGAL

Without name designers in ready-to-wear, and no couturiers known outside the country, Portugal nonetheless has a generic stamp of gaiety and vivid colors plus its ancient and still-preserved tradition of handicrafts.

Through these qualities, and with some government assistance, Portugal exports sweaters, cotton dresses, woolen garments, and soft, young, bright-colored shoes of great charm.

Filmoda, an international fair for clothing and shoes, was organized by the Portuguese Export Promotion Board and the Secretariat of the International Lisbon Fair in 1970. In 1971, according to Filmoda's report, the number of exhibitors doubled over those showing in 1970, and exports in shoes and wearing apparel rose from 40 to 50 percent in 1972.

The unrest in the following years has seriously disrupted international trade.

Note: A discussion of the island of Madeira immediately follows the Portugal Costume and Fashion Archives section.

Fashion Designers and Firms

Calcado Marina—P.C. Castro & Irmao, Lda. Shoe manufacturers, Felgueiras

Makers of well-designed open sandals and boxed sports shoes, characterized by vivid combinations of two leathers or several colors. These are produced under the Marina and their labels.

Empresa Fabril Eicorte, Lda. Ready-to-wear manufacturers, Rua Neves Ferreira 3-B, Lisbon 1

This large producer of ready-to-wear for women makes everything from jeans to evening gowns. Although still concentrated on the domestic market, Empresa Fabril Eicorte was in 1973 gearing up to export. The designs are mostly Paris-inspired and "trendy" rather than classic.

Jonex—J. Fernandes da Silva. Shoe manufacturers, Rua Padre Americo, S. Joao da Madeira

This firm makes and exports interesting sports shoes using Portugal's large natural resource, cork.

Josefina Modas. Couture house, Casa Cela Nova-Viveiro, Estoril

Most Portuguese women of wealth buy their clothes in the main European fashion centers, but such houses as Josefina in Estoril and Nelson and Sonia in Cascais manage to maintain couture businesses, producing Paris copies and original designs.

Murrell. Makers of crocheted fashions, Avenida Frei Miguel Contreiras 54, Lisbon

Murrell clothes are typical of Portugal's small but prosperous handcrochet industry. Murrell began to export in the early 1970s.

Trade Associations and Organizations

Fundo de Fomento de Exportaçao (Portuguese Export Promotion Board). Avenida 5 de Outubro 101, Lisbon

In 1972 this government-sponsored body for the development of foreign trade made clothing a priority item in its program. As part of the European Economic Community, Portugal set out to claim its share of the revenue from fashion. Under the board's jurisdiction, Portuguese clothing producers take part in "fashion weeks" in many countries, and also mount their own in Lisbon each year.

The board is also active in forming associations within industry to standardize and improve quality and styling and to set higher technical goals.

Costume and Fashion Archives

Museu de Arte Popular (Folk Art Museum). Avenida de Brasilia, Belém, Lisbon 3

Tel: 611282 and 611675. Founded: 1948. Curator: Maria Helena Coimbra.

There are regional costumes, textiles, laces, and embroideries.

Museu-Escola de Artes Decorativas (Museum-School of Decorative Art). Fundação Ricardo Espirito Santo Silva, Largo das Portas do Sol 2, Lisbon 2

Tel: 86-21-84. Founded: 1953. Dir: António Maria Pinto Leite.

This historic palace, beautifully arranged and preserved in 15th, 16th, 17th, and 18th century rooms, originally belonged to the Espirito Santo Silva family, and included specimen examples of Portuguese costumes, fabrics, tapestries, tiles, leather work, and furniture.

Adjoining the museum are the Espirito Santo workshops where artisans supported by the banking family's cultural foundation restore art objects and teach the art of tooling leather, reproducing period furniture, tapestry, carpets, and embroidery.

Visits to the museum and workshops are by application only, except on certain days when the museum is open to the public.

THE ISLAND OF MADEIRA

This Portuguese island in the Atlantic has preserved the early art of appliqué and embroidery on sheer fabrics such as handkerchief linen and organdy. Although used chiefly in table linen, Madeira embroidery has occasionally figured in fashion when it has been used by designers for evening dresses. In recent years the idea was taken up by Roxanne of Samuel Winston in New York and Valentino in Rome.

Being a cottage industry, Madeira embroidery remains a small element of the island's economy and is applicable solely to luxury fashion.

SPAIN

It is an ancient and curious truth that the Spaniard's inborn vision of beauty is usually coupled with wanderlust. Some of the greatest Spanish talents have flourished outside Spain's boundaries, and Spanish fashion is no exception. Like the expatriate artists Picasso and Miro, Cristobal Balenciaga left Spain to become the dominant fashion influence of the world in the mid-20th century.

At home, oddly enough, Spanish fashion is an ineffectual, though persistent, contender for world interest. In a country where handwork is a living heritage, where leather and wool have been superbly crafted for centuries, and where the labor force is strongly controlled and therefore uninterrupted by strikes, the production of clothes is neither a cohesive luxury trade nor a profitable mass industry.

The complicated Spanish government system of export control for many years discouraged foreign buyers from seeking to bring Spanish goods into their countries. In 1965, a coalition of four Spanish ministries —Interior, Tourism, Information, and Labor—sought to alter that situation in relation to clothing. The Alta Costura Española (now called Camera de la Moda Española) was set up with government financing and the famous best-dresser Countess Aline Quintanilla y Romanones as its honorary but active patroness. Protocol and inner politics, however, prevented the list of participating designers from being dispassionately edited to include only those with definite export possibilities. Overlong and lacking impact, the schedule of couture showings failed to impress buyers and journalists.

Spain's ready-to-wear industry for men and women, largely centered around Barcelona, has, however, found a market. Firms like Mitzou, Ledaspain, and Loewi are world-renowned in leather fashion. A remarkable artist, Jose Maria Fillol, designs 11 different collections in Barcelona within one successful fashion conglomerate called Moda del Sol. Manuel Pertegaz has done in ready-to-wear what he could not do single-handedly in the couture—attract a large international clientele.

In a country with endless wealth of inspiration in the richness and variety of its regional costume, Spain's contemporary designers remain deliberately aloof from ethnic influence. The tradition has always been that no Spanish lady would consider wearing anything with a "native" flavor other than her heirloom mantillas and shawls at bullfights and her ruffled polka dot cotton dresses at the Feria in Seville. The authentic gypsy and flamenco dresses made in Seville and Granada have found a market in boutiques outside the country, and one flamenco dancer, Lucero Tena, has made the attempt to market flamenco dresses internationally.

Textiles, particularly woolens, are beautiful and expertly made in Spain, but most are "jobbed" to France and England to be resold as if they originated there.

Spanish glass beads and other trimmings have an international market at the wholesale level.

Spanish-made shoes are among the best in the world, but few are labelled with the names of Spanish designers. The sizable industry is largely producing under contract with manufacturers in other countries.

Fashion Designers and Firms

Cristobal Balenciaga. See Hall of Fame

Asunción Bastida. Paseo de Gracia 96, Barcelona; and Hermosilla 18, Madrid

Asunción Bastida, a pillar of the Spanish ultraformal fashion tradition, was born in Catalonia, the daughter of a knitwear manufacturer, and was taught the art of cutting and sewing at home.

Her professional debut was in 1926, and the first Asunción Bastida Salon was inaugurated in Barcelona in 1931, with a Madrid branch opened shortly after.

Sra. Bastida pioneered in efforts to promote Spanish fashion abroad and helped to organize a number of government-sponsored showings in world capitals.

Elio Berhanyer. Designer of young fashions, Calle Ayala 124, Madrid 6

A Spanish designer who works in abstract lines, like Courreges, but whose work also often suggests the cool, nonsensual thinking of Givenchy, Berhanyer is recognized as a positive if not magnetic international talent.

Born in Cordoba and a shepherd in his early years, he later trained as an architect. Berhanyer is far more handsome, gregarious, and mundane than Pertegaz, but shares the elder designer's passion for inventive cut and is equally absorbed in his work. During the early 1960s Berhanyer had a tie-up in the United States with the firm of Jerry Silverman.

José Maria Fillol. Multifaceted designer, Moda del Sol, Calle Lauria 5, Barcelona

Spain's most versatile and one of its most successful designers of boutique fashion, José Maria Fillol was born in Valencia and trained for 15 years in the French couture and prêt-à-porter industry. He returned to Spain in the late fifties and began designing beachwear.

When a group of 11 manufacturers of coats, suits, dresses, beachwear, and leather fashion banded together to show to local and foreign buyers, Fillol gradually added design assignments. His creativity, sense of fashion timing, and wit were so productive that he is now fashion director of the entire group.

Herrera y Ollero. Almirante 9, Madrid 4

This team of designers has a following of well-known Spanish ladies. Theirs is one of the few houses which occasionally use themes of native Spanish costume in their clothes. Their first success in fashion outside Spain was an adaptation of the flamenco dancer's shirt with a buttoned neckband and tucked, embroidered front.

Rafael Herrera, born in Seville, and Ollero, whose birthplace was Caceres, a tiny village in the Estremadura section of Spain, were both trained in tailoring by their fathers. They met while at school in Madrid and started their business in the early 1960s.

Induyco. Tomas Betron 61–62, Madrid 7

They are manufacturers of top-quality classic sportswear for women and men.

Ledaspain. Leather fashion house, Napoles 249, Barcelona 13D

Well-known producers of ready-to-wear in leather and suede, Ledaspain makes the most fashionable of Spain's excellently worked leather clothing. Manuel Pertegaz has designed a number of Ledaspain collections.

Lino (Martinez). Couture and ready-to-wear designer, Plaza de Santa Bárbara 3, Madrid

Lino hails from Madrid and began his fashion career in 1930, designing on a free-lance basis for several high-fashion houses. He now maintains a large establishment in Madrid and is active in efforts to create a Spanish fashion image outside his country. He has served as president of Madrid's Alta Costura Association and has frequently shown his collection in other countries.

Loewe. Leather fashion house, Serrano 26, Madrid; and Paseo de Gracia 35, Barcelona 7

Though not as well-known internationally as Gucci of Italy or Hermes of France, Loewe has equal standards of excellence in workmanship and taste. Like Gucci and Hermes, Loewe is now opening branches in other world capitols.

Marbel Jr. Avenida de Nazaret 1, Madrid 7

Youngest and most energetic of the well-known Spanish designers, with a strong local following for his offbeat clothes, Marbel Jr. opened his couture business at 19, in the small apartment he still occupies in a residential district on a hilltop overlooking Madrid. He does not design everyday clothes, but concentrates on arresting creations for evening. He says he is interested in only about 300 faithful clients, but his melodramatic showings are unfailing news sensations.

Carmen Mir. Couturiere, Provenza 245, Barcelona

Carmen Mir, known in Spain for her crisp but graceful day clothes, was born in Manresa. At 13, she cut her first tailormade suits for friends. Her fashion salon in Barcelona is now managed by Carmen Mir's daughter-in-law, Elisa Lacambra. Her husband and son handle the administrative end of the business.

Mitzou (Izquierdo). Leather fashion designer (retired), Serrano 27, Madrid

Although she vacillates between working and retiring, Mitzou is one of the most innovative and perennially influential creators of leather clothing in Spain. Born in France, Mitzou is married to Jose-Maria Izquierdo, well-known antique dealer who recently set up a highly successful Spanish version of Mme Tussaud's wax museum in Madrid.

Mitzou's design of a fur-bordered suede coat with frog fastenings for Julie Christie in the film *Doctor Zhivago* set a world fashion and the designer made a promotional tour through America with the picture's stars. Her perfectionist traditional suede and leather shooting and riding clothes for Spanish ladies brought her initial acclaim. She treated suede with the same ease of woven fabric, making curvaceous dresses and low cut evening gowns never before attempted in that medium. Her use of sweet colors and pastels in leather was also trend-setting.

She maintained her own factories in Barcelona and Madrid, but has recently closed that end of her business and works for private clients only.

Manuel Pertegaz. Couture and ready-to-wear designer, Avenida Generalissimo Franco 401, Barcelona 7

The undoubted monarch of Spanish fashion, tiny (about five feet), intense Manuel Pertegaz was born in Aragon and grew up in Barcelona. He was so intent on making clothes that his pastime at 8 was making buttonholes, and at 12 he apprenticed himself to a tailor. At 13 he cut and made clothes for his sister, and although the tailor he worked for made only men's suits, Manuel was soon designing and sewing the wardrobe of the tailor's wife. He began to work independently from his studio, with his sister as helper, and in 1942 moved to the large luxury apartment which has been converted into his present Barcelona salon. There he began working in the double-faced wool technique which brought him his first international notice. In 1968 he opened a handsome modern house in Madrid which he maintains in tandem with his Barcelona business.

A lone worker but conscientious about cooperating on efforts to improve Spain's overall international fashion image, Pertegaz stands apart, by his own merits, from all competition in Spain today. Typically family-minded, he employs numerous relatives in his business, and his niece Sionine is his able directrice.

Pedro Rodriguez. Couturier, Paseo de Gracia 8, Barcelona 7; and Alcala 54, Madrid 14

Pedro Rodriguez stands as the exemplar of the ultra-formal fashion tradition in Spain, as does Norman Hartnell in England.

Born in Valencia, he was a tailor's apprentice in Barcelona at 10 and began working independently while still in his teens. Although he had his own couture house in 1923, his fashion show at the Barcelona Fair in 1929 brought him to the attention of elegant Spanish women, and his spectacularly beaded gowns soon became the classic dress for court functions throughout Europe.

He has fashion establishments in Madrid, Barcelona, and San Sebastian, and boutiques in the leading Spanish resorts.

Pedro Rovira. Couture and ready-to-wear designer, Rambla de Prat 7, Barcelona

Born in the Catalonian town of Badalona, near Barcelona, Pedro Rovira studied medicine at the University of Barcelona, but left to apprentice to a local tailor. His first effort on his own was a success, and his meticulously cut daywear and beautiful beaded dresses have become classic in Spanish society.

Santa Eulalia. Couture house, Paseo de Gracia 60, Barcelona

One of the oldest dressmaking houses in Spain (dating from 1900), Santa Eulalia has dressed rich Spanish ladies for generations. Today the house owns boutiques throughout Spain, selling ready-made clothes and accessories.

For the past 28 years, the couture house has been directed by Santiago Lopez Gabarro, and the collections are designed by Pedro Formosa.

Trade Associations and Organizations

Camera de la Moda Espanola. Rosario Pino 6, Madrid

Founded: 1965. Dir: Pedro Leon.

This is a government-subsidized organization founded jointly in

1965 by Spain's Ministries of Interior, Trade, Tourism, and Labor, together with the syndicates of textiles and leathers. The new organization (1973) is still under the government, but now concentrated within the Ministry of Commerce. The purpose is to promote Spanish high fashion and ready-to-wear, textiles, leathers, and accessories through press and buyers showings, and participation in trade fairs. Countess Alina Quintanilla y Romanones, American-born wife of a Spanish grandee and a perennial member of the international best-dressed list, was the first Honorary Directrice.

Moda del Sol. Lauria 5, Barcelona 10
Founded: 1960 (?). Dir: Luis Luque.
This membership organization conducts fashion shows for its participants, and promotes the beachwear and sportswear of eleven houses, all with collections designed by a single talent, José Maria Fillol.

Servicio Comercial de la Industrias e de la Confeccion. Avenida de José Antonio 32, Madrid 13; and Avenida de José Antonio 670, Barcelona 10
This organization is subsidized by the Ministry of Commerce and sponsors fashion shows for all groups of the industry and manufacturers. It also deals with internal and labor matters.

Costume and Fashion Archives

Museo de Historia de Sabadell (Sabadell Museum of History). Calle San Antonio 13, Sabadell, Barcelona
Tel: 295-1462. Founded: 1931. Dir: Juan Farell Domingo.
There is a collection of ancient garments and textiles of Coptic, Gothic, French, Oriental, Moroccan, and Spanish provenance; 18th and 19th century Spanish costumes; and looms and weaving implements.

Museo del Pueblo Español (Museum of Spanish Folklore). Plaza de la Marina Española 9, Madrid 9
Tel: 228-50-39. Founded: 1934. Opened: 1940. Dir: Maria Luisa Herrera Escudero.
This museum has collections of costumes and textiles; historic costumes from the 18th century and a few earlier; and 162 complete regional costumes, toreador costumes, and military uniforms.

Museo del Tejido y de Indumentaria (Museum of Textiles and Costumes). Calle Hospital 56, Barcelona
Tel: 319-76-03. Founded: 1965. Honorary Dir: D. Manuel Rocamora Vidal. Exec. Dir: Doña Pilar Tomas Farell.
The total of 2000 items at this museum includes textiles, European

civil dress, liturgical robes from the 13th century, laces, costumes, and accessories assembled by Don Manuel Rocamora.

Museo Etnologico y Colonial de Barcelona (Ethnologic and Colonial Museum of Barcelona). Escuela del Mar, Parque de Montjuich, Barcelona

Tel: 2-23-73-64. Founded: 1952. Dir: Auguste Panyella Gomez.

There are collections especially related to the history of costume and textiles of many countries.

Museo Federico Mares (Federico Mares Museum). Calle Condes de Barcelona 10, Barcelona

Tel: 310-58-00. Founded: 1946. Dir: D. Federico Mares Deulovol.

The collections here are especially related to the history of costume and textiles; there are also garters, stockings, fans, and parasols of the 18th and 19th centuries and regional Catalan and Valencian costumes.

Museo Municipal de Madrid (Madrid Municipal Museum). Calle Fuencarral 78, Madrid

Tel: 222-5732. Founded: 1927. Dir: Enrique Pastor Mateos.

There is a small costume collection and a larger collection of prints depicting men's and women's costumes of the early 19th century (Modas de Madrid 1804).

Museo Municipal de San Telmo (Municipal Museum of San Telmo). Plaza del Pintor Zuloaga, San Sebastián

Tel: 426600, ext. 231. Founded: 1932. Dir: D. Gonzalo Manso de Zuniga.

There is a room of costumes of popular dancers of the region on life-size manikins; a collection of Basque bonnets of the 15th, 16th, and 17th centuries; exemplars of the 18th and 19th centuries; and Basque embroideries and lace.

Museo Nacional de Artes Decorativas (National Museum of Decorative Art). Calle de Montalbán 12, Madrid 14

Tel: 221-3440, 222-1740, 232-6499. Founded: 1913. Dir: Dolores Enriquez Arranz.

This museum's collection has approximately 100 examples of rare fabrics (brocades, brocatelle, damasks, silks, etc.) from the 15th to the 19th centuries.

Museo Textil Biosca (Biosca Textile Museum). Calle de San Pablo 7, Tarrasa, Barcelona

Tel: 297-3557. Founded: 1946. Dir: Dr. F. Torrella Niubo.

There are collections of costumes and textiles—Coptic, Spanish, Arabic, Moroccan, and North African from the 10th to the 18th centuries; Oriental (Byzantine, Arabic–Syrian, Persian, Chinese–Japanese, Turkish) from the 6th to the 17th centuries; pre- and post-Columbian textiles (Peruvian and Mexican); Italian and Spanish textiles from the Gothic–Renaissance period covering the 13th to the 16th centuries; European textiles from the 15th to the 18th centuries (peasant textiles of various origins and periods); and masculine and feminine apparel from the 18th and 19th centuries.

Fashion Publications

Belleza y Moda. Editorial Quiris S.A., 104 Rocafort Street, Barcelona 15
Founded: 1969. Ed: Felix Estrada Mengod. 12 issues/yr.

Dandy. Pub. E. Oromi, Rda Universidad 31, Barcelona
Ed: E. Oromi. 2 issues/yr. $7/yr.

El Hogar y La Moda. Diputacion 221, Barcelona
6 issues/yr. US $15.60/yr.

SWITZERLAND

Swiss fashion has been described as "like Swiss cooking—a little bit of everybody's." Considering that Switzerland in 1972 exported more clothing and textiles than France, the fact that the country has never taken the trouble to develop an indigenous fashion personality may not seem too important.

Switzerland's preeminence in the field of fine textiles dates back more than a hundred years. Firms like Stehli, Abraham, Forster Willi, and Braunsweig have been and still are shining names in world fashion.

Switzerland is one country which produces and features clothing for women with ample figures in expensive price ranges.

In clothing, however, only one Swiss name—Bally—has achieved world recognition. Characteristically, the Bally Shoe Company's enclave of 30 shoe designers is totally anonymous.

Long known as the center for the finest novelty fabrics in pure silk and pure cotton such as silk organza, organdy and other embroidered cottons, guipure lace, reembroidered lace, and decorative braids and trimmings, Switzerland is now also a leading producer of synthetic fibers and fabrics.

Fashion Designers and Firms

Gilbert Albert. Jewelry designer, 7 rue de Simplon, Geneva
Gilbert Albert, designer of real jewelry with an imaginative rhythm and airiness, has won the International Diamond Award several times.

He is also known as designer of the luxury range of Patek-Philippe watches.

Bally Schuhfabriken A.G. CH-5012 Schoenenwerd

This renowned shoe firm, founded by Dr. Max Bally in the late 19th century, is still controlled by the Bally family.

Bally has a large staff of designers, but uses no designer names in their shoes. They have also, occasionally, asked dress designers from other countries to do small collections for them.

Bally's general reputation is in sport shoes, but the shops they now own in the major capitals show a full range of shoes for all occasions.

Forster Willi and Co. St. Gallen

Makers of embroidered and appliquéd organdies and eyelet cottons, Forster Willi has served high-fashion designers throughout Europe and America for several decades.

H. and A. Heim A.G. Gartenhofstrasse 15, CH-8036 Zurich

One of Switzerland's better quality ready-to-wear firms, Heim now has a separate division which manufactures similar clothes at lower prices.

Handschin and Ronus A.G. (Hanro). CH-4410 Liestal

Hanro knits for women, men, and children are known throughout Europe for high quality and conservative good taste.

Humbert Entress A.G. Strickwarenfabric, CH-8355 Aadorf

Entress is well known as specialists in knitted dresses trimmed with leather or fabric.

Pius Wieler Söhne A.G. Bahnhofstrasse 15, CH-8280 Kreuzlingen

This well-known firm makes chic winter knit costumes, ski clothes, and stretch-fabric bathing suits.

W.A. Meyer (WEA). Seestrasse 247, CH-8038 Zurich

Meyer designs and produces much of Switzerland's fashionable leisure and after-ski wear in fabric, leather, lambskin, and imitation fur.

Walter Stark A.G. Unterstrasse 4, CH-9000 St. Gallen.

One of the better ready-to-wear producers in Switzerland, Stark manufactures women's clothes with a French look in excellent fabrics.

Fashion Influentials

Dr. Charlotte Peter. Editor, *Elle (Suisse)*, Gotthardstrasse 61, CH-8002 Zurich

Dr. Peter, an excellent journalist and expert on feminine interests, has adapted for Swiss readers the *Elle* concept of the young "doer." While Switzerland has many writers on fashion, her writing is the most balanced in relation to Swiss women.

Trade Associations and Organizations

Office Suisse d'Expansion Commerciale. 18 rue de Bellfontaine, CH-1001 Lausanne

Switzerland's government export office is set up to aid manufacturers who export in all fields. It has branches throughout the world and conducts campaigns of propaganda and trade development.

Schweizer Modewochen Zurich. Seegartenstrasse 2, CH-8008 Zurich

This private organization assembles and administers semiannual fashion weeks in Zurich. Most of the exhibitors are Swiss, but manufacturers from other countries are invited to participate.

Swiss Clothing Manufacturers Association. Uto quai 37, CH-8008 Zurich

Dir: F. Loeb.

This membership organization of clothing manufacturers for men, women, and children deals principally with internal industrial matters.

Fashion Education

Note: A good working knowledge of either German or French is important in Swiss schools.

American Fashion College of Switzerland. Bahnhofstrasse 7, CH-6000 Lucerne

Tel: (041) 22-46-31. Swiss Telex: (845) 72303. Founded: December 1970. Pres: Phillip J. Markert. Dir. Academic Affairs: William J. French, II.

The American Fashion College of Switzerland is a nondenominational, coeducational, degree-granting American college offering an Associate of Arts Degree in fashion and a Bachelor of Arts Degree in merchandising.

All classes are taught in English. The majority of the students are American; 90 percent of these are from the United States and 10 percent are Americans living abroad or English-speaking students of other nationalities.

The college is on the quarter system; and a normal academic load is 20 credit-hours per quarter.

Dormitories and meals are available.

Industrie- und Gewerbemuseum mit Textile- und Modeschule. Vadianstrasse 2, CH-9000 St. Gallen

Dir: E. Fick.

This school gives a three- to four-year course in the design of printed and embroidered textiles. It grants a diploma to students of Swiss citizenship only.

Kunstgewerbeschule der Stadt Zurich (Zurich School of Applied Art). Austellungsstrasse 60, CH-8005 Zurich

Dir: Dr. Mark Buchmann.

This professional school offers courses in jewelry and ornament, fashion, and textile design.

In jewelry and ornament there are one- and two-year courses leading to an attestation and three-year courses leading to a diploma.

In fashion design, there are three- or four-year courses, with preparatory training if there is no apprenticeship, leading to a Leaving Certificate.

In textile design, there are four-year courses, including one year practice, leading to a Leaving Certificate.

The school has no dormitories.

Modeschule Bruenn. Beethovenstrasse 45, CH-8002 Zurich

Founded: 1951. Co-Dirs: H. Camastral and B. Frederiks.

Established by Paulo Bruenn as a small school for the training of students in fashion drawing, fashion design, costume history, and pattern-making for the couture, this school gives a two-year course with a diploma.

Costume and Fashion Archives

Fédération Nationale des Costumes Suisses (National Federation of Swiss Costumes). Weinbergastrasse 145, CH-8042 Zurich

Tel: (01) 26-2366. Sec. Gen: Ambros Eberle.

This is a "living museum" of 20,000 people who preserve and wear the traditional costumes of the regions of Switzerland. The association holds costumed gatherings and publishes bulletins on national costume in French and German.

Musée Gruyèrien (Museum of the Gruyere District). Rue Victor Tissot, CH-1630 Bulle

Founded: 1923. Dir: Henri Gremaud.

There is an excellent collection of folk art, including an important collection of Swiss regional costumes and ornaments. There is also a photographic collection of local events showing peasant costumes.

Musée Jurassien (Jura Museum). Grand-Rue, CH-2800 Delémont

Tel: 066-29-12. Founded: 1909. Curator: André Rais.

There is a remarkable collection of regional historic material, including peasant costumes, some Louis XIV costumes, and 18th-century bonnets.

Schweizerisches Landesmuseum (Swiss National Museum). Museumstrasse 2, CH-8000 Zurich
Founded: 1898. Dir: Dr. E. Vogt.
Included in this collection are Stone-Age textile fragments and 17th-century costumes.

Fashion Publications

Annabelle. Verlag Annabelle, CH-8000 Zurich
6 issues/yr. Circ: 100,000.

Elegance Suisse. Office Suisse d'Expension Commerciale, 18 rue de Bellefontaine, CH-1001 Lausanne
Founded: 1968. Ed: Peter Pfister. 6 issues/yr. Trade publication. Text in French, German, English, and Spanish.

Elle (Suisse). Gotthardstrasse 51, CH-8002 Zurich
Ed-in-chief: Dr. Charlotte Peter. 6 issues/yr. *Elle (Suisse)* appears in German and French editions.

Femina. Femina Verlag, CH-8000 Zurich
6 issues/yr. Circ: 80,000.

Femme d'Aujourd'Hui & Patrie Suisse-Actualités. Editions Meyer, Cie., 5 rue Bovy-Lysberg, Geneva
52 issues/yr. Circ: 44,54l.

Meyers Modeblatt. Verlag G. Meyers Erben, Klausstrasse 33, CH-8000 Zurich
Founded: 1924. 52 issues/yr.

Tout Pour Vous. Editions Claspy Zurich, Hinterbergstrasse 27, CH-8044 Zurich
Founded: 1935. Ed: H.R. Weber. 2 issues/yr. Text in French, German, Italian, and English.

SCANDINAVIA

The creative talents producing clothing in the Scandinavian countries are at once so homogenous and so individual that it was recently proposed in print by one of their number: "The Finns should design, the Swedes manufacture and the Danes do the selling. The Norwegians could handle complaints."

It is more than an idle observation. The pure, strong outlines and vivid glowing colors of Finnish design have permeated and are beginning to revitalize the nearly sterile restraint of modern Scandinavian design. To clothes, as to architecture, pottery, glassware, and carpets, the Finns have brought their own verve and earthiness. Sweden, though a country of great sophistication, has in recent years produced only one name designer in the women's field, and she was trained and worked for years in America. Sweden's production methods are first rate, however, and its rainwear and skiwear are outstanding. In menswear, Sweden has a designer of international reputation.

Danish designers, like the Finns, are multitalented and dedicated to the idea of creating an entire environment rather than concentrating on clothing. Design in both countries is inspired by the collective ideal of the Bauhaus, William Morris, and Frank Lloyd Wright.

Norway, with no designers known by name beyond its borders, nevertheless has a large wholesale industry in which most firms produce clothing for men, women, and children under one roof. Their heavy outerwear is of good quality.

All Scandinavian countries have made a strong bid for the world market. Textiles and clothing in Finland, for example, represent the country's third largest export since the war. In 1961 Finland exported clothing in the amount of 4 million marks; 10 years later, in 1971, the export of clothing was 500 million marks. Only wood processing and metals exceed that figure.

DENMARK

Fashion Designers and Firms

Margit Brandt. Designer for Erik Brandt, Østergade 6, DK-1100 Copenhagen K

Margit and Erik Brandt are Denmark's most famous husband-and-wife team. She designs clothes in the New Wave feeling; he is the businessman who has arranged her distribution in 20 countries and established a string of Bistro Brandt boutiques in Denmark. Margit Brandt also designs silverware, kitchenware, and lingerie for other firms.

Born in 1945, Margit Brandt trained at the Margaretheskolen fashion school in Copenhagen and worked in Paris on the staffs of Pierre Balmain and Louis Feraud. At 23, she and her husband, 25, were already embarked on their own business.

Finn Birger Christensen. Fur designer, Birger Christensen, Østergade 38, DK-1100 Copenhagen K

The fourth-generation head of his family's 100-year-old fur business, Finn Birger Christensen was born March 14, 1926. In the family tradition, he was educated for the administrative responsibilities he was expected to assume. He studied at a business college in Copenhagen and finished his scholastic education in Sweden. He then trained with the Hudson Bay Company to learn furs from their source and worked in fur businesses in London, Paris, and New York.

When he became head of the Birger Christensen Company, it took on both a heightened fashion aura and international scope. He heads a large staff of designers whom he imbues with his own feeling for each season's trends. He has 20 Birger Christensen fur departments in stores throughout the world which he visits regularly. He is among his own country's most active and patriotic citizens, heading several civic and charity organizations, including the urban renewal project for Copenhagen.

An affable and handsome gentleman, Christensen is often unofficial ambassador of his country at international events.

Sos Drasbek and Ib Drasbek. Dranella, Frederiksberggade 26, DK-1459 Copenhagen K

This successful and versatile husband-and-wife team of designers produce clothes of the young "kicky" school, mainly sportswear and dresses, but including shirts, shoes, clogs, rubber boots, and children's wear.

Sos Damgaard Drasbek, born in 1938, studied art in Copenhagen and at 20 married Ib Drasbek, an interior designer, and with him formed Dranella. Today they manufacture in Jutland and sell throughout the world in addition to licensing their designs in other countries, including Finland and Japan.

Sos Drasbek serves on the Selections Committee of the Danish Ministry of Education for the training of industrial and fashion designers.

Mugge Kølpin. Designer in various fields, Fredensvej 14, DK-2950 Vedbaek, Copenhagen

With her husband, Jes Kølpin, Mugge Kølpin has an extensive fashion business for which she is both designer and sales director, but not manufacturer. The Mugge Kølpin Collections are produced by five different factories in Denmark, America, Australia, and Italy. The designs are siphoned through the Kølpin sales offices into stores throughout the world.

Born February 15, 1945, in Copenhagen, Mugge attended the Margaretheskolen Fashion School there, graduating in 1964. The next year she married Jes Kølpin, an architect. He continues his profession while administrating the Mugge Kølpin enterprises.

Lennart Raaholt. Free-lance designer, Vesterbrogade 45, DK-1620 Copenhagen V

Born June 10, 1947, in Ringe, Funen Islands, Denmark, Raaholt worked as a boy for Danish dress factories, then attended the Royal College of Art in Copenhagen, where he won prizes in menswear design. He free-lanced for three years in Paris, Rome, and London, returning to Copenhagen to form his own company, Lennart, making teen-age dresses on a modest scale. American department store buyers discovered him and channelled his designs to larger manufacturers for mass production.

Raaholt designed whimsically decorated jeans for Levi-Strauss in America, dresses for Australian and Finnish companies, fabrics, menswear, furs, and leather fashions. Tall, ebullient, and a leader of the young bohemians in Copenhagen, Raaholt is considered one of Denmark's "comers" in fashion.

Fashion Influentials

Didder Ronlund. Fashion writer, *Berlingske Tidende*, Pilestraede 34, DK-1147 Copenhagen K

One of the few European journalists who covers fashion in every fashion capital, Mrs. Ronlund has also been influential in relating Scandinavia's fashion designers to the rest of the world. Her factual and sparkling accounts of fashion trends and personalities have made her a recognized mover in the development of Scandinavian fashions.

Trade Associations and Organizations

Scandinavian Clothing Council. Vester Voldgade 115, DK-1552 Copenhagen V

Founded: 1972. Pres: Olav Hauge.V-P: E. Strom-Hansen.

This trade association of clothing manufacturers handles industry problems. It also sponsors the twice yearly Scandinavian Fashion Weeks for ready-to-wear fashions for women and men. On the Fashion Weeks, the Council collaborates with the Scandinavian Fashion Center.

Scandinavian Fashion Center. Bella Center, Center Blvd., DK-2300 Copenhagen S

Founded: 1970. Dir: John Ljunggreen.

This membership trade association made up of fashion manufacturers interested in the promotion of Scandinavian fashions was the initiator of the Scandinavian Fashion Week, which is now mainly coordinated by the Scandinavian Clothing Council.

Fashion Education

Danish School of Arts and Crafts. Hans Christian Andersen Boulevard 10, DK-1553 Copenhaven V

Although this is not a fashion school, a number of successful designers received their basic art training there.

Margaretheskolen. School of Fashion and Textile Design, Ostergade 55, DK-1100 Copenhagen K

The art and techniques of fashion are taught by this school which has turned out many well-known Danish designers.

Fashion Publications

Alt For Damerne (Everything for the Ladies). Gutenberghus-Bladene, Vognmagergade 11, DK-1148 Copenhagen K

Founded: 1946. Ed: Kay Dorph-Petersen. 52 issues/yr. Kr.169/yr. Circ: 167,811.

Soendags-B.T. Berlingske Tidende, Pilestraede 34, DK-1147 Copenhagen K

Founded: 1921. Ed: Nele Poul Soerensen. 52 issues/yr. Kr.130/yr.

FINLAND

Fashion Designers and Firms

Marjetta Heikkila. Ready-to-wear designer, Kaisu Heikkila, Kalevantie 7, SF-33100 Tampere 10

Born in 1947, Marjetta studied in Helsinki and started designing for her parents' dress business when she was 20. She has added to the typical bright, printed-cotton body tent, which is a Finnish hallmark, some much more fitted and bare shapes of her own. The Heikkila family owns a series of boutiques.

Karen Hellemaa. Leather designer, Friitala Nahka Oy, SF-28400 Ulvila

A Finnish-born artist who spent her childhood in Argentina and studied painting in New York, Madrid, and Helsinki, Karen Hellemaa of Friitila was a well-known painter before she became interested in fashion. She now designs for Finland's best-known leather fashion firm, and also for Delta Couture Corporation in Switzerland. On the side, she continues to paint and, like many Scandinavians, designs interiors for homes and offices.

Lapponia Jewelry, Ltd. Makelankatu 60A, SF-00510 Helsinki 51

This center of artist-designed, sculpturesque real jewelry was established in 1960 by Pekka Anttila. The company now employs 160 craftsmen in gold, silver, and precious stones. The head designers, Bjorn Weckstrom and Poul Havgaard, creators of three-dimensional silver jewelry, have won many prizes. Examples of Lapponia jewelry are owned by the Royal Goldsmith's Society, Princess Anne of England, the Prince of Wales, Mrs. Aleksei N. Kosygin of Russia, and Empress Fara Dibah of Iran.

Marimekko Oy. Fashion–production company, Vanha Talvitie 3, SF-00500 Helsinki 50

Marimekko, a firm producing clothing, dress and interior fabrics, graphics, and products for use in the home, was founded in 1951 by Armi Ratia, artist, textile designer, and leader of the vital Finnish modern design movement. Mrs. Ratia is still director.

Operating internally like a cooperative of artists, and externally as a highly efficient international business, Marimekko has been a model for followers of the art-for-industry plan in many countries. Its annual turnover in 1973 was 21 million Finnish marks. Fifty percent of Marimekko products are exported to 23 countries.

The typical Marimekko dress, a full, printed tent shape, has gone into the language like "cardigan," "bloomer," and "Levi's."

Armi Ratia founded the modern school of Finnish fashion, both spiritually and practically, by training many of the country's now-independent designers.

She was born in Karelia and escaped to Helsinki when her homeland was annexed by Russia. One of the circle of creative people who established Finland as the magnetic center of new Scandinavian design in the first postwar years, she is now a member of Ornamo, the important society of outstanding talents established in 1911 which has brought world recognition to Finnish arts and crafts.

Today the Marimekko workshops produce printed cottons for fashion and home decoration, clothes, accessories, and household linens, wrapping paper, plastic tableware and many other articles.

Vuokko Nurmesniemi. Clothing and textile designer, Merikatu 1, SF-00140 Helsinki 14

Known in several areas of Finnish design, Vuokko is one of the leading fashion names in Finland.

Born February 12, 1930, in Helsinki, she studied ceramics at the Athenaeum Institute of Industrial Design. In 1952 she joined the design staff of Arabia, Finland's famous pottery and glass design studio; then she designed clothes and printed cottons for Marimekko from 1954 to 1960.

Following her marriage to Antii Nurmesniemi, one of Finland's leading industrial designers (he designed the Helsinki subway), she designed wallpapers and settings for industrial fairs with him and also established her own company for making clothes in the strong, cottony Finnish tradition with an individually youthful, crisp, and sturdy stamp. She maintains a design studio with 45 assistants and her own factory and shops in Helsinki. Half of her production is now exported.

Vuokko won the Georg Jensen prize for design in 1953 and the Gold Medal of the XIth Triennial in Milan.

Tua Rahikainen. Fur designer, B. Rahikainen & Co., Kasarmikatu 48, SF-00130 Helsinki 13

Tua Rahikainen designs interesting and elegant collections for her family's fur business, founded in 1948 when she was four years old.

Born on August 29, 1944, to Birgit and Ake Rahikainen, both fur technicians, she graduated from the Helsinki School of Industrial Design in 1969 and continued her training in Paris. She is now chief designer for the firm and one of Finland's recognized fashion talents.

Armi Ratia. See Marimekko Oy

Sirkka Vesa-Kantele. Designer, retailer and journalist, Puzzle, Frederikinkatu 37, Helsinki

An archetype of the multifaceted Scandinavian designer, Mrs. Vesa-Kantele is editor-in-chief of Finland's leading fashion magazine, *Muotisorja*, also owns Puzzle, one of Helsinki's chic young boutiques, and supplies it from her own ready-to-wear business which also exports her designs.

Born in the countryside near Helsinki, Sirkka studied at the Central School of Industrial Arts and received a scholarship to l'Ecole de la Chambre Syndicale in Paris. While there, she won a pan-European young designer's competition, sponsored by Jacques Heim.

Returning to Helsinki, she made her first fashion impact designing original buttons, then took over the fashion magazine which she still edits.

Going against the Finnish tradition of bright bold prints and loose tent shapes, Mrs. Vesa-Kantele established her own style in the young, crisp tradition of Courreges and Mary Quant, and designed clothes for Leninki Tiklas and furs for G-Product.

In addition to her own business, she supervises a design studio which creates on a contract basis for firms in every area of fashion and home products.

Bjorn Weckstrom. Jewelry designer, Lapponia Jewelry, Ltd., Makelankatu 60A, SF-00510 Helsinki 51

This outstanding designer–sculptor in metal and stones was born February 8, 1935, in Finland. He graduated from the Helsinki Jewelry School in 1956. In 1963 he joined Lapponia, where his jewelled abstract forms in precious metals became world famous.

Fashion Influentials

Anna-Liisa Ahtiluoto. Fashion editor, *Helsingin Sanomat*, Ludwiginkatu 2/10, SF-00130 Helsinki 13

Mrs. Ahtiluoto is the representative of a powerful newspaper whose influence on both designers and industry is felt at both the creative and consumer end of fashion.

Kerstin Fried. Fashion editor, *Hufudstadsbladet*, Mannerheimintie 18, SF-00100 Helsinki 10

Interested in all phases of design and in international fashion, Mrs. Fried is an important observer and catalyst in the growing Finnish clothing industry.

Trade Associations and Organizations

Central Federation of Finnish Clothing Industries (VATEVA). Fredrikinkatu 41C, SF-00120 Helsinki 12

Founded: 1959. Mging. Dir: Jussy Peitsara.

Finland's clothing trade association has a membership of 95 percent of the nation's manufacturers. All promotional activities and trade studies come under its program.

Finnish Fashion Designers Association (MTO) (affiliated with Association of Finnish Designers, ORNAMO). Unioninkatu 30, SF-00100 Helsinki 10

Founded: 1965. Mging. Dir: H.O. Gummerus.

The purpose of this organization of about 100 professional designers is to expand their own horizons via lectures, advisory sessions, study tours, and competitions. All members are graduates of the Institute of Industrial Arts.

The group maintains an information service and issues publications.

The Finnish Foreign Trade Association. Etelaesplanadi 18, SF-00130 Helsinki 13

Founded: 1919 (under the name of Finnish Export Association). Reorganized: 1938 (under present name). Dir: Harri Malmberg.

This organization is one of the oldest in Finland. Since 1970 it has been partly sponsored by the Finnish government which together with members of the association promotes Finnish products, including fashions. It maintains 15 branches in foreign countries.

Fashion Education

Fine Arts Academy of Finland. Kaivokatu 2–4, SF-00100 Helsinki 10

This school provides a four-year course of practical and theoretical training in fine arts: painting, graphics, and sculpture.

The teaching staff consists of well-known artists, many of whom speak English.

Applicants must pass a three-week test course (for a fee) on various subjects, beginning in August. Applicants are required to present in person or by proxy samples of their work. Mail applications are not considered. The school does not grant scholarships to foreign students.

Taideteollinen Oppilaitos (The Institute of Industrial Arts). Kaivokatu 2–4, SF-00100 Helsinki 10

The aim of the Institute is to provide training in a four-year course for the various branches of industrial art, and training for art teachers. Students, who must have sufficient general school education, will receive practical and theoretical training in industrial arts. The Institute is also open to professionals for additional training.

The Institute has departments in graphic arts, camera arts, ceramics, metal design, fashion, furniture and interior design, textile weaving and design, and art education.

Professionals having graduated from the Institute or other recognized schools or with long-standing experience may take advance studies on an individual program.

Since foreign students seldom master the Finnish language, they usually enroll as nonmatriculated students; certificates of former school work or practical experience are required. A nonmatric student can earn a special version of the Institute certificate.

Costume and Fashion Archives

Kansallismuseo (Finnish National Museum). Mannerheimintie 34, SF-00100 Helsinki 10

Tel: 441181. Founded: 1893. Dir: Riitta Pylkkanen.

There are collections of Finnish and European regional costumes dating from the 1830s.

Fashion Publications

Eeva. Kustannus Oy Eeva, Annankatu 18, SF-00120 Helsinki 12

Ed-in-chief: Ulla Leskinen. 12 issues/yr. Fmk.34.00/yr.

Kauneus Ja Terveys. Kustannus Oy Eeva, Annankatu 18, SF-00120 Helsinki 12
Ed-in-chief: Marja-Leena Markkula. 12 issues/yr. Fmk.34.00/yr.

Me Naiset. Erottajankatu 11, SF-00130 Helsinki 13
Ed-in-chief: Helena Ahti. 12 issues/yr. Fmk.64/yr.

Muoti Ja Kauneus (formerly *Muotisorja*). Yhtyneet Kuvalehdet Oy, Hietalahdenranta 13, SF-Helsinki 18
Founded: 1944. Ed-in-chief: Sirkka Vesa-Kantele. 6 issues/yr. Fmk.40.00/yr. Circ: 58,159.

Uusi Anna (formerly *Anna*). Hitsaajankatu 10, SF-00810 Helsinki 81
Ed-in-chief: Kirsti Lyytikainen. 52 issues/yr. Fmk.68.00/yr.

NORWAY

While Norway has no designers of international renown and is still so conservative that coats are listed as "mantels" in their clothing directories, there are about 100 Norwegian manufacturers of rainwear, outerwear, sportswear, children's wear, caps, shirts, blouses, and lingerie selling throughout Scandinavia and Europe.

Norway is attempting to build up a design entity through the preservation and revival of its native handicrafts and by laying increased emphasis on the design of textiles, clothing, and ornament in the State School of Arts and Crafts.

Trade Associations and Organizations

Export Council of Norway. Drammensvn 40, Oslo 2
Founded: 1945. Dir: Jarman.

This organization of Norwegian manufacturers and exporters is backed by the government. Its main purpose is to develop trade and increase export of Norwegian products. It is considered the largest and most important export organization in Norway, with 24 branches throughout the world. It is the consultative body for the Ministry of Commerce and the Ministry of Foreign Affairs on trade and export policy.

National Federation of Clothing Manufacturers. Økernvn 145, Oslo 5
Founded: 1955. Dir: K. Christiansen.

This organization of 80 members represents about three quarters of Norway's clothing production. It deals with labor contracts.

Norwegian Textile Manufacturers Association. Prinsens gt. 2, Oslo 1
Founded: 1898. Dir: E. Brwstaard.

This membership organization, comprising all groups of the textile industry, conducts promotional events for consumer education, provides sales assistance, and also deals with labor contracts.

Fashion Education

State School of Arts and Crafts. Ullevalsvn 5, Oslo 1
Founded: 1818. Dir: H. Stenstadvold.

There is a three-year program in fashion design, fashion drawing, and ornamental design, leading to a diploma. Four-year courses lead to a diploma in textile design.

Costume and Fashion Archives

Historisk Museum (Historical Museum). University of Bergen, Joachim Frieles Gate 3, N-5000 Bergen
Tel: 21-00-40. Founded: 1825. Dir: D. Anders Hagen.

There are urban and peasant costumes from western Norway, embroideries and rural tapestries, jewelry, and bridal crowns, as well as an extensive photographic collection.

Norsk Folkemuseum (Norwegian Folk Museum). Museumsveien 10, ̄Bygdy, Oslo 2
Tel: (02)55-6395. Founded: 1894. Dir: Reidar Kjellberg.

This museum was founded to preserve a record of "the old way of life" in rapidly industrializing Norway. Lifelike figures wear the appropriate costume of the time and region in settings of actual houses of the old Norway. The guides also wear costumes of the various districts.

The museum, a showplace for tourists and a place of inspiration for designers, has a large section devoted to Norwegian arts and crafts. In summer there are folk festivals and dances where regional costumes are worn.

Fashion Publications

Alle Kvinner (Magazine for Women). Gyldendal Norsk Forlag, Sehenstedsgt 4, Oslo 1
Founded: 1938. Ed: Brita Ruud. 52 issues/yr. Kr.155/yr.

SWEDEN

Fashion Designers and Firms

Sighsten Herrgård. Designer for men and women, Upplandsgatan 32, S-11328 Stockholm

Like Katja of Sweden in the women's field, Sighsten Herrgård is the only designer of menswear in the Swedish market who is known outside his country. Born in Helsinki on January 8, 1947, he graduated from Stockholm University at 20, and attended Croquis, the Academy of Couture, and the Anders Beckman School of Fashion in Stockholm and the Academy of Couture in Copenhagen.

Herrgård has received many menswear awards from various countries: England, France, Mexico, and the United States. He has also been on the International Best-Dressed list.

Katja of Sweden (Karin Hallberg Geiger). Clothing designer, MMT Tricot Ab, Fack, S-20070 Malmo 5

The daughter of Sweden's leading ceramist, Karin Hallberg, whose label is Katja, was born in Ekeby on January 12, 1920. She attended the Art Industrial School in Stockholm and studied art with Arslers Beckman.

She became a fashion illustrator for the Stockholm newspaper *Dagens Nyheter* and from 1942 to 1945 designed clothes for MEA, the local exclusive Stockholm store.

At that time, she discovered the work of American designer Claire McCardell in a fashion magazine and determined to follow the McCardell concept of fashion based on today's living but stemming from the culture of one's own country.

In 1946 Katja went to America to attend the Parsons School of Design, where Claire McCardell was lecturing.

In 1949 she founded Katja of Sweden in New York with success, and in 1953 transferred her firm to Sweden. Today she is Sweden's most powerful fashion voice and was recently responsible for the establishment of a studio for young designers in every field, patterned after Taliesen West which the late American architect Frank Lloyd Wright organized in Arizona.

Katja of Sweden, producing apparel, prints, shoes, and accessories under Katja's design, is now owned by a large Swedish conglomerate.

Katja is married to Rod Geiger, formerly a film producer and now her associate. He invented a photographic process for printing on fabric which brought added fame to Katja fashions.

Fashion Influentials

Baroness Anne-Marie Ehrenkrona. Fashion editor, *Aftonbladet*, Box 157, S-10518 Stockholm

Sweden's high-style fashion reporter, Baroness Ehrenkrona covers fashion worldwide in a critical and informative way.

Fashion Education

Konstfackskolan (State School of Arts and Design). Valhallavägen 191, Box 27117, S-10252 Stockholm 27
Founded: 1844. Reorganized: 1945. Dean: Ake Huldt.
This school, with no exact place in the Swedish educational system, is considered the leading training school for fashion design in the country.
The departments for the arts and design give courses in textile, jewelry, and fashion design on a four- to five-year basis, with scholarships to Swedish students only except in the case of special arrangements between governments.
There are no dormitory arrangements.

Costume and Fashion Archives

Borås Museum. Ramnaparken, S-50265 Borås
Tel: (3033)110200. Founded: 1914. Dir: Ingegärd Vallin.
There are collections of peasant costume, fashions, and textiles from the end of the 18th century to about 1940.

Malmö Museum. Malmöhusvägen, S-21120 Malmö
Founded: 1901. Dir: Ingemar Tunand.
An excellent collection, this one includes fashions and Swedish peasant costumes.

Nordiska Museet (Nordic Museum). Djurgården, S-11521 Stockholm
Tel: (08)630500. Founded: 1873. Dir: Dr. Hans Hansson. Keeper of Textiles: Anna-Maja Nylen.
This museum has a large collection of peasant costumes and fashions from 1600 to 1960.

Statens Etnografiska Museet (National Museum of Ethnography). Norra Djurgården, S-11527 Stockholm
Tel: (08)603122. Founded: 1902. Dir: Karl Erik Larsson.
There is a large collection of folk costumes and fashions from all parts of the world.

Fashion Publications

Damernas Varld. Ahlen & Akerlunds Foerlags AB, Torsgatan 21, S-10544 Stockholm
Founded: 1971. Ed: Gunny Widell. 52 issues/yr. Kr.2.50/issue.

Femina. Allers Foerlag AB, Landskronavagen 23, S-25185 Helsingborg
Ed: Sidney Grahn. 52 issues/yr. Kr.2.50/issue. Circ: 25,000.

Habit. Foerlags AB Habit, Humlegaarsgatan 19, S-11446 Stockholm
Founded: 1961. Ed: Olav Rebane. 16 issues/yr. Kr.50/yr. Circ: 10,049.

EASTERN EUROPE

ALBANIA

Costume and Fashion Archives

Museum of Archaeology and Ethnography. c/o Institute of Scientific
Research in History and Linguistics, State University, Tirana
Founded: 1948. Dir., Ethnographic Section: Rrok Zojzi.
There is a rich photograph collection showing Albanian peasant
costumes.

CZECHOSLOVAKIA

Costume and Fashion Archives

Moravské Múzeum, Etnografický Ústav (Moravian Museum, Ethno-
graphic Collections). Gagarinova třida č.1, Brno
Founded: 1804. Dir: Ludvik Kunz.
There are nearly 50,000 examples of folk costumes.

GREECE

To fashion manufacturers and stores throughout the world, Greece
has been a recurrent thought which frequently ended in frustration.

Its huge pool of labor with a heritage of clever hands, its inherent
sense of line and earthy sun-filled colors, and the traditional crafts of
weaving, embroidery, leather, and metal work still practiced in scores
of villages as a chief source of livelihood, have constantly tempted,
then baffled and discouraged the joint efforts of foreign buyers and the
Greek government. With a worldwide potential, clothing production in
Greece has remained scattered and erratic. Periodic official programs
for promotion and export revealed the presence of imaginative designers, but lack of quality control and merchandising expertise meant that
much of the clothing ordered was never delivered.

The Greek government offered inducements to foreign and local firms willing to build or develop clothing, knitting, and leather factories and bring in capital and technical experts. Production in shoes, men's clothing, textiles, children's clothing and inexpensive ready-to-wear got a start in 1969, but faded away with the change of government and the Cyprus upheaval.

Two modern Greek talents, at least, have appeared on the world fashion scene: Ilias Lalaounis, the goldsmith who revived fine reproductions of ancient Greek jewelry, and Yannis Tseklenis, a consistent producer of interesting ready-to-wear.

Fashion Designers and Firms

Dozia. Ready-to-wear designer, 26 Herodotou St., Athens

Using Greek peasant hand-blocked silk scarves and native printed cottons, Dozia creates young clothes in the folk manner, blending peasant and Byzantine overtones. Although her production is limited, Dozia is well known to individualist clothes collectors within and visiting Greece.

Amalia Frontzou. 47 Botsari Yannena St., Athens

This prominent society woman has built up an interesting cottage industry using handwoven woolens from the Greek mountain villages to make coats with colorful handworked seams.

Ilias Lalaounis. Jewelry designer, 6 Panepistemiou Ave., Athens

The jeweler credited with starting the vogue for ethnic fashion jewelry well before the time of hippie thongs and beads, Ilias Lalaounis began as designer for the firm of Zolotas. He sought and received authorization from the Athens Museum to make exact reproductions of ancient Cretan and Byzantine gold jewelry from the museum's collections. His later interpretations of the flat Cretan collars with raised geometric designs, his bracelets of twisted gold with lion's and ram's heads, and his woven gold chains are now collectors' pieces almost as precious as those that inspired him.

Lalaounis now has his own independent and international business and signs his pieces with his own name. Zolotas continues as a separate firm.

After making many variations on the classic and preclassic Greek themes, Lalaounis has branched out into abstract designs.

Efi Melas. 18 Voulis St., Athens

Greece's most famous fashion model, Efi Melas now produces inexpensive ready-to-wear for her own boutiques and for export.

She designs her own prints in simple, childish motifs and signs her work with the symbol of her Greek name, an apple.

Nikos and Takis. Boutique designers, 10 Lisiou St., Plaka, Athens

Partners in designing original and simple leisure and sportswear with a Greek Flavor, Nikos and Takis have fashion boutiques in several Greek island resorts and also export to other tourist centers.

Yannis Tseklenis. 18 Voulis St., Athens

The creator of his own Greek-motif prints from which he designs thematic fashion collections with the same signature effect as in fashions by Pucci or Roberta di Camerino, Yannis Tseklenis is also known for almost single-handedly launching ready-to-wear in Greece.

Born November 6, 1923, into an aristocratic Greek family with generations of textile interests behind him, Tseklenis went to school with King Constantine and was an usher at the royal wedding. He studied art and designed fabrics in Paris and London before taking over the family fabric business and adding clothing factories.

Today he owns a string of 11 boutiques in Athens and the Greek islands and sells his clothes for men and women to speciality shops in Europe and America.

He was one of the organizers of the Hellenic Fashion Institute, a joint promotional effort of Greek designers and government departments.

Zolotas (Dr. Zenophone Zolotas). Jewelers, 10 Panepistemiou St., Athens

This jewelry firm originated the idea of making reproductions of historic gold ornaments in the Athens Museum. Ilias Lalaounis was then the Zolotas designer, and his uncle, Dr. Xenophone Zolotas, was its founder. Dr. Zolotas, a prominent Greek banker and archeological authority, continued the business with other designers after Lalaounis opened his own ateliers.

Trade Associations and Organizations

Hellenic Fashion Center. 50 Omirou St., Athens 135

Founded: 1975. Dir: George Koutsoubelis.

This membership organization promotes showings of its participants, comprising high fashion; ready-to-wear for women, men, and children; jewelry; swimwear, as well as accessories. Its main purpose is to develop trade and increase the export of Greek products.

Hellenic Fashion Institute. 34 Amalias Ave., Athens

Founded: Late 1960s. Pres: John Tsobanelis.

This organization was founded by a coalition of Greek designers and government agencies to establish standards and obtain a wider market for fashions made in Greece. Due to changes in the government, the institute has been relatively inactive during the 1970s, but it is still empowered to prepare periodic group showings in Greece and foreign countries.

It also sponsors courses in fashion design and fashion techniques.

Costume and Fashion Archives

Benaki Museum. Koumpari 1, Athens

Founded: 1930. Curator: Lambros Entaxias.

There is a superb collection of Greek regional costumes beautifully displayed.

HUNGARY

Fashion Designers and Firms

Clara Rothschild. Rothschild Szalon, Vaci St., Budapest

Virtually the only high-fashion designer and interpreter of French fashion in Eastern Europe, Clara Rothschild (born in 1903) has bridged the gap between capitalism and communism with apparently serene adjustment. Until 1950, when she turned her business over to the state, remaining its "artistic director and designer," Mme Rothschild was a couturiere continuing her family heritage as court dressmaker. Her father, Abraham Rothschild, made clothes for Empress Elizabeth of Austria–Hungary and her court. In 1937, Clara Rothschild opened her own business in Budapest and until 1944 it flourished. When the Germans invaded Hungary, she and her husband hid in the house of a Swedish diplomat, but her husband was discovered and killed.

Although officially socialized, the Rothschild ateliers are conducted in the same way as any high-fashion establishment in Paris, London, or New York. The clientele includes Empress Farah Diba of Iran, Mrs. Andrei Gromyko of the U.S.S.R., the wives of communist leaders in Mongolia and Yugoslavia as well as of Hungary, and many prominent visitors from the West.

Costume and Fashion Archives

Iparmüveszeti Muzeum (Museum of Applied Arts). Ullöi-utca 33–37, Budapest 9

Tel: 189-676. Founded: 1872. Dir: Eszter Geszti.

The huge collection here contains Hungarian peasant and court dresses, fabrics and embroideries from the 16th to 18th centuries.

Neprajzi Museum (Museum of Ethnography). Könyves Kálmán-körút 40, Budapest 8

Tel: 140-058. Founded: 1872 (prior to 1872, part of the National Museum). Dir: Dr. Tamás Hoffmann.

There is a vast collection of Hungarian and Near Eastern costumes and textiles from the 17th century.

Pálóc Museum (Paloc Museum). Pálóc liget 1, Balassagyarmat (Nógrád)
Founded: 1891. Dir: Jószef Zólyomi.
There is an extensive collection of Hungarian peasant costumes from the 19th and 20th centuries, as well as a photographic section.

POLAND

Trade Associations and Organizations

Textil-Limpex. 25 Traujacuwtta, Lodz
The purpose of this enterprise is to build foreign markets for Polish fabrics.

Costume and Fashion Archives

Muzeum Archeologiczne i Etnograficzne w Łodzi (Lodz Archaeological and Ethnographic Museum). plac Wolności 14, Lodz
Tel: 339-13, 348-90, 322-97, 297-14 (director). Founded: 1929. Dir: Konrad Jażdżewski.
There is a good collection of Polish garments and handicrafts.

Muzeum Etnograficzne we Wrocław (Wroclaw Ethnographic Museum). Kazimierza Wielkiego 33, Wroclaw
Tel: 433-13. Founded: 1953. Dir: Magdalena Rostworowska.
This museum's collection of folk art includes regional costumes.

Muzeum Kultury i Sztuki Ludowej w Poznaniu (Poznan Museum of Folk Culture and Handicrafts). ulica Grobla 25, Poznan
Tel: 530-06. Founded: 1911. Dir: Stanislaw Blasczyk.
There is a collection of regional costumes and fabrics of Poland.

Muzeum Narodowe w Poznaniu (National Museum in Poznan). ulica Marcinkowskiego 9, Poznan
Tel: 580-11. Founded: 1857. Independent Research Worker: Kazimierz Malinowski.
There are sections of folk art, including embroideries and costumes.

Museum Naradowe w Warszawie (Warsaw National Museum). ulica Jerozolimskie 3, Warsaw
Tel: 21-10-31. Founded: 1862. Dir: D. Stanislaw Lorentz.
In this collection there are historic national costumes, embroidery, laces, and handwoven belts.

Państwowe Muzeum Etnograficzne w Warszawie (National Museum of Ethnography in Warsaw). Kredytowa 1, Warsaw
Tel: 27-76-43. Dir: Kazimierz Pietkiewicz.
This collection contains textiles and garments.

RUMANIA

After 1955, when Rumania joined her national policies and even her army with the Russian Soviet, production of consumer goods such as clothing fell so low that it is not even listed on the national production index of 1970. One year before that, however, an organization called the Foreign Trade Company of the Handicrafts Co-operatives had been formed to attempt an economic reform that would move Rumania into the world clothing trade.

ICECOOP, as the new blend of government and artisans is called, comprises about 600 state-owned factories, small and large, all working under the control of a director of design. A curious sideline of ICE-COOP, described in the promotional booklet it issues to prospective buyers, is "a great variety of services with the payment in freely convertible currency for foreigners in Rumania: repairs and maintenance of cars and household devices, translations and typing, and the restoring of funeral monuments."

In 1864 Rumania was one of the first European nations to manufacture ready-made clothing. In 1948 a concerted effort was made to establish a flourishing business in clothing such as sportswear, knits, and menswear, but lack of purchasing power for textiles caused it to dwindle to nearly nothing. Until recently the only production of any size was in embroidered peasant blouses from the different regions, sold sparsely to other countries along with peasant carpets and other handicrafts.

To increase exports to the United States, Rumania now employs a consulting designer, Isabel Mueller. Mrs. Mueller lives in New York, but commutes to Bucharest to supervise a corps of designers at ICE-COOP.

ICECOOP now issues a seasonal catalog of its nationally produced clothing in wool, real and synthetic leather, imitation fur, and synthetic fabrics made by 20,000 workers. In 1973 they recorded an annual output of 10 million men's shirts, 1½ million men's suits, 2 million women's dresses, children's clothes, and accessories sold to 20 countries.

A central design center in Bucharest, headed by Mrs. Blumeta Darie, provides more than 6500 new models as well as fabric and print designs, patterns, undergarments, and stockings.

The address of this paragon of fashion combines is: Foreign Trade Company of the Handicraft Co-operatives, 12 Marin Serghescu St., Sector II, Bucharest.

Costume and Fashion Archives

Muzeul de Arta al Republicii Socialiste Romania (Museum of Art of the Socialist Republic of Rumania). Strada Stirbei Vodă 1, Bucharest
Tel: 133-030. Founded: 1949 (new wing: 1962). Dir: Mircea Popescu.

There are Rumanian court costumes from the 15th to 19th centuries; also national and regional textiles from Rumania and other countries.

Muzeul de Arta Populara al Republicii Socialiste Romania (Museum of Folk Art of the Socialist Republic of Rumania). Calea Victoriei 107, Bucharest
Tel: 16-71-59. Founded: 1906. Dir: Tancred Banateanu.

There is an interesting collection of national costumes, embroideries, textiles, and ornaments.

UNION OF SOVIET SOCIALIST REPUBLICS

In 1973, the U.S.S.R. Dom Modeli, house of fashion, hitherto a nameless, faceless, but omnipotent, power over the production and selling of clothing, began a trickle of designer credits in the captions under the fashion pictures in their propaganda magazines. The names were not Russian, but those of presumably fretting fashion creators in the satellite city of Riga, Latvia.

Any credit at all, however, was a significant breakthrough. The Soviet Union has always listed fashion among the "official" arts (not until 1969 and the establishment of the National Endowments on the Arts did this happen in America), yet in all those years only one designer had been personally identified. He is Vyacheslav Zaitsev, a man in his 30s, responsible for the original models which Dom Modeli translates into ready-to-wear.

Soviet propaganda calls Zaitsev the country's Number One designer; up to 1973 he was to all intents and purposes the only one.

With the problem of standing in line for hours in any shop where a clothing shipment has been received, of being frustrated by the lack of variety in stores, and of feeling poorly dressed among the thousands of present-day visitors to Russia, the attractive and increasingly liberated young Russian woman has made her annoyance felt to the point that the government now siphons clothing in large quantities from Czechoslovakia, Poland, Hungary, and Latvia into Russian consumer stores.

Both Polish and Latvian styling and workmanship are good, although the quality of fabrics I observed a few years ago was very poor. The Czechs and Hungarians made chic haute-couture clothes before World War II, but so far have not carried that quality into their mass-produced items.

A major black-market item in Russia is the simple knit or jersey shirtwaist dress smuggled in from Finland or Denmark.

Although Russia remains far behind in its many five-year plans to increase the manufacture and distribution of consumer goods including clothing, the Russian government frequently sponsors foreign trade exhibitions which include high fashion. The American exhibit in Moscow in 1959 had the largest cross-section fashion show of American designs ever presented. It was one of the fair's most popular attractions. In 1967 the Soviet Union invited 29 nations to participate in an international clothing exhibit in Moscow. It was a gigantic undertaking, brilliantly staged and supervised by the director of the Bolshoi Theatre, and open to the public. The crowds filled an Olympic-size stadium holding 10,000 people for five shows a day.

The gap between the supply and demand for clothing domestically has not kept Russia from seeking foreign markets. This includes precious furs, such as sable, lynx, fox, karakul, and fur plates, plus furs such as broadtail, ermine, and squirrel which Russia distributes for China and other countries without trade ties to the West. All these are sold at three auctions each year in October, January, and July in Leningrad, and are attended by fur experts from all over the world.

Fashion Designers and Firms

Riga, Latvia House of Fashion

In a break with precedent, the U.S.S.R. in 1973 published a series of fashion pictures from the Riga, Latvia House of Fashion with the names of the designers identifying each dress. Although no information about the designers was given, the unique situation makes even their names historic. They are Bruno Korn, Gunta Zile, Rita Peterson, Arija Pupenova, Rasma Baitman, and Mara Nezdulkina.

Trade Associations and Organizations

Dom Modeli (House of Fashion). Verkhnaya Krasnoselskaya ulitsa 15, Moscow B-140. For information: V.O. Raznoexport at same address.

Dir. of Design: Vyachleslav Zaitsev.

This is the internal organization responsible for styling and production of all clothing in Russia. Designer Zaitsev is the only "name" designs, patterns, undergarments, and stockings.

Costume and Fashion Archives

Note: Countries of the Soviet bloc do not provide detailed factual information either on management or content of the collections. Therefore information of that nature included here may not be up-to-date.

Muzeĭ Etnografii Narodov CCCP (State Ethnographic Museum of the Peoples of the USSR). Inzhenernaja ulitsa 4/1, Leningrad D-11
Dir: L.M. Saburova.
The museum has 250,000 documents on life and culture in Russia from the 18th century to the present.

Palata Moskovskogo Kremlia (Kremlin Armory Palace Museum). Moscow
Founded: 1906. Dir., Kremlin Museums: I.I. Tsvetkov.
The State Armory collections are enormous and unique, comprising Byzantine, Oriental, Turkish, European, and Russian costumes and fabrics, including textiles, embroideries, and costumes from the 11th to the 19th centuries. Personal clothing of Empress Catherine the Great and Peter the Great is on display and a rich collection preserved but not displayed can occasionally be seen by special arrangement.

State Hermitage Museum. M. Dvortsovaya naberezhnaya 34, Leningrad
Founded: 1764. Dir: B.B. Piotrovsky.
The collection includes Western embroideries, textiles, and laces, Russian costumes and textiles from the 16th to 19th centuries. A rich collection preserved but not displayed can occasionally be seen by special arrangement.

Zagorskiĭ Gosudarstvennyĭ Muzeĭ i Zapovednik (Zagorsk State Museum). Zagorsk, Moscow
Founded: 1920. Dir: M.A. Popesky.
There are Russian folkloric costumes from the 19th century to 1920.

YUGOSLAVIA

This small country, with its ethnic riches in costume and its unforgotten skills of weaving and decoration, is beginning to threaten Italy as a center for industrialized clothing production. The socialist government of Yugoslavia gives a measure of incentive to the people through a form of profit-sharing and encourages contracts with companies from strike-plagued Italy and other countries with higher labor costs. Since the mid-sixties, foreign manufacturers of leather clothes, handbags, men's clothing, and sportswear have made part or all of their merchandise in Yugoslav factories.

A number of native designers have become well known in Yugoslavia. Some of these are promoted in government-sponsored fashion trade shows and style magazines distributed throughout the world. No clothing with designer labels is exported, as yet, although the first move toward exchanging fashion identities was made by Modfest, an international fashion conference held in Zagreb under the sponsorship of Creations Zagreb. Designers from England, France, and Italy were invited to meet in the town of Trogir to show their collections with Yugoslavian designers and exchange views in a seminar.

Through a program of fashion fairs and other promotions, Yugoslavia has increased its exports as much as 27 percent a year. Its total export of clothing in 1972 was $53 million, and in textiles $22 million.

Fashion Education

Beogradska Universitet (University of Belgrade). Akademija za primenjene umetnosti (Academy of Applied Art), ulica 7 Jula 4, YU-11000 Belgrade
There are four-year courses in fashion design and textile design, leading to a diploma from the Academy.

Viša Tehnićka Škola. Smetanova ulica 17, YU-62000 Maribor
This is a higher technical school, offering two-year courses in fashion design and textile design, leading to a diploma.

The following three technical junior colleges are part of the public school system and offer two-year courses in fashion design and textile design.

Školski Tekstilni Centar. ulica Ribara 126, YU-41000 Zagreb

Tekstilni Školaski Centar. Jasenićka 10, YU-11000 Belgrade

Tekstilni Centar. Stan. Zagarja 33, YU-64000 Kranj

Costume and Fashion Archives

Dubrovaćki Muzej (Dubrovnik Local Museum). Knežev Dvor, Prid Dvorom, YU-50000 Dubrovnik
Tel: 26469. Founded: 1872. Dir: Ante Kalmeta.
There are rich collections of regional costumes, embroidery, and textiles.

Etnografski Muzej (Ethnographic Museum). Studentski trg 13, Belgrade
Tel: 625-922. Founded: 1901. Dir: Slobodan Zečević.
There is a large collection of folk costumes and fabrics of Yugoslavia,

ancient Balkan costumes, and local costumes; there are also peasant carpets and native ornaments.

Etnografski Muzej (Ethnographic Museum). Mažuranićev trg 14, YU-41000 Zagreb
Tel: 449-886. Founded: 1919. (Opened: 1920). Curator: Marijana Gušić.
There are 30,000 examples of costume and textiles of Yugoslavia.

Gradsk Muzej (Sombor Town Museum). trg Republike 4, YU-25000 Sombor
Tel: 025/27-28. Founded: 1883. Dir: Milan Konyovitch.
There is a collection of richly ornamented national costumes formed in the 19th century, also antique handwoven woolens.

Fashion Publications

Model. Novinsko-Izadavocko Poduzece Republika, Gunduliceva 37/1, Zagreb
Official clothing magazine.

5.

the americas

NORTH AMERICA

CANADA

Canada, a divided land ethnically and politically, presents a united front in its hopes of making the production and export of clothing a consequential part of its economy. British, French, Eskimo, and Indian, together with Europeans more recently arrived, make up the Canadian population, and consequently the variety of skills available to a developing garment industry.

In 1974 more than 2000 manufacturing firms were making clothing for women, men, and children in five areas of Canada. Nearly 65 percent of Canadian clothing producers are based in Montreal and Quebec. Montreal has the highest concentration of designers, many foreign-born and most trained in Europe or the United States.

Toronto has long-established firms with fine designers, mostly conservative in their approach, who have already gained a market in other countries. Ontario contains several hundred clothing factories and accounts for roughly one fourth of Canadian-made clothing.

Winnipeg, Manitoba, derives its clothing skills from its severe climate. The heavy outdoor clothes made there represent 10 percent of the total produced in Canada.

Edmonton, Alberta, has a number of manufacturers of volume merchandise such as jeans and active sportswear.

The Canadian apparel industry has experimented with the labor possibilities of the Méti (half-breed Indians) and of cottage industries in Mennonite religious settlements where the people prefer not to go far from the family circle. Satellite plants in other rural areas are seeking to maintain a cottage-industry system in Canada and also to preserve the Indian and early colonial crafts.

As a result of a concerted plan of design development, trade and press promotion, Canadian clothing exports more than tripled in the years between 1967 and 1974, from $27 million (Canadian) to more than $115 million. The total industry produces $1.8 billion in clothing.

In 1972 the Ministry of Industry and Commerce sponsored an annual Press Weekend patterned after the American Designer Showings Press

Weeks in New York, to which fashion editors from many countries were invited. Market weeks are held in all the Canadian fashion centers.

Canada has a large corps of fashion designers who do collections in many different fields under separate contracts. A single designer frequently produces separate collections of ready-to-wear, lingerie, furs, menswear, sportswear, maternity wear, and children's clothes for different manufacturers.

Fashion Designers and Firms

Leo Chevalier. Montroy Coat Co., 140 Cermenzie Blvd., Montreal, P.Q.

This Montreal-born designer is one of the leaders in his city's drive for international fashion attention. He designs complete collections in two widely different fields: elegant coats, suits, and knitted separates for the Montroy Coat Company and sophisticated dresses and loungewear for Nadio/Van Essa. Both are produced at higher price ranges.

He was born October 8, 1934, and attended Montreal's School of Art and Design. He did window displays at a Montreal specialty shop and free-lance designing before opening his own couture business. He entered the wholesale field in 1971.

He received the Designer of the Year Award given by the International Ladies Garment Workers Union of Canada (1967) and the Merit Award of the Province of Quebec in 1973.

Tom d'Auria. Junior fashion designer, Lee Parker, 1435 Bleury, Montreal, P.Q.

This American-born designer, now among the top ten in Canada, was born in Pennsylvania and studied at the Fashion Institute of Technology in New York. He designed far-out clothes for The Factory, a Montreal wholesale firm, and took his collection to Paris for the French prêt-à-porter showings with great success. He joined Lee Parker in 1973.

Vali Dubsky. Vali Designs, 163 Bellechasse, Montreal, P.Q.

One of a number of European-born Canadian designers of note, Vali Dubsky was born in Budweis, Czechoslovakia, on March 31, 1929, and attended Prague College, the Rotter Art School, and the University of Prague.

She is often inspired by film themes and period costume but her clothes are never violently nostalgic.

Elvia Gobbo. Lingerie and loungewear designer, Daisy Fresh, 450 Dorchester St., Quebec City, P.Q.

One of Canada's most advanced designers, who has shown at the Paris prêt-à-porter collections, Elvia Gobbo was born in New York and trained at the Traphagen School there. She opened a boutique in Montreal before becoming designer for various manufacturers, including dresses, sportswear, lingerie, and knits.

Flemming (Sorenson). Avant-garde hat designer, Canadian Hat Manufacturers, 1250 St. Alexander, Montreal, P.Q.

Born in Copenhagen, Denmark, in a family which had made shoes for generations, Flemming has been designing in Canada for about 10 years. He is a colorful personality and is much promoted by his sponsors and stores.

Starting as a custom milliner in Montreal, he now designs for the largest wholesale millinery distributor there, but lives in Toronto.

Flemming hats were worn by the hostesses at Montreal's Expo and his designs are often chosen for international millinery shows.

Marielle Fleury. Rainwear designer, Sport Togs, 7130 St. Urbain, Montreal, P.Q.

Montreal-born and an active booster for her city's acceptance as a fashion center, Miss Fleury is a former boutique owner who also designed handwoven fabrics before entering the wholesale industry.

Hugh Garber. Designer for Margo Dress (Canada), Ltd., 7101 ave. du Park, Montreal, P.Q. H3N 1XQ

Hugh Garber was born in Montreal in 1945 and studied at the Hornsey College of Art in England and at the Fashion Arts Academy in Montreal.

In 1966 he went to Rome where he spent two years, first as assistant designer to Patrick de Barentzen and then as designer with Roberto Capucci. In July, 1968, Hugh Garber returned to Montreal to design for Margo Dress (Canada), Ltd.

Margaret Godfrey and Nicola Pelly. Co-designers, Boutique Bagatelle, 1193 Carre Philippe, Montreal, P.Q.

These two young English women design young tailored fashions for large Canadian firms. Margaret Godfrey was born February 20, 1944, in Cheshire, England, and studied at the Hastings School of Art. Nicola Pelly, born February 18, 1948, in Warwickshire, went to art college at Kingston-upon-Thames.

Bagatelle clothes are not exported from Canada to the United States, but the firm has factories in Pennsylvania. The two also do a menswear line.

Alan Goldin. *See* Toby Kline and Alan Goldin

Claire Haddad. Lingerie and loungewear designer, Claire Haddad, Ltd., 110 Spadina Ave., Toronto, Ont.

The daughter of a well-known Canadian manufacturer of cold-weather bathrobes, Claire Bardwell Haddad gained her own reputation as a designer of filmy lingerie and seductive loungewear.

She studied art in Toronto and New York. Following her marriage in 1964, she and her husband established their firm, which now sells internationally and is shared by their children.

Mrs. Haddad, active in all phases of the Canadian fashion growth efforts, serves on the advisory committee of Seneca College and is a member of the Canadian Fashion Group. She was one of the founding members of the Association of Canadian Fashion Designers.

In 1967 she won the Coty Award of Canada and holds six Eedee Awards from the Ontario Department of Economic Development.

(Hester) Elen Henderson Children's wear designer, Elen Henderson, Ltd., 1262 Don Mills Rd., Toronto, Ont.

One of Canada's internationally known designers and a leader of the Canadian fashion industry, Mrs. Henderson was born March 25, 1906, in Birmingham, England, and educated in Leeds, England. She was apprenticed to a milliner in Leeds and taught herself the techniques of dressmaking. She came to Canada during the war and founded Elen Henderson, Ltd. in 1946 when her two small daughters inspired her designs for children.

Elen Henderson clothes are widely sold in the United States and England as well as Canada.

She received the Eedee Award of Ontario government six consecutive years, from 1965 through 1970, and was chosen to design the uniform of the Canadian Girl Guides and Brownies.

Jacqueline Karene. Knitwear designer, Cortina Knitters, 642 de Courcelles, Montreal 207, P.Q.

She designs colorful, interestingly patterned knits with a folk flavor.

Toby Kline and Alan Goldin. Designers of junior fashions, The Market Montreal (Fashions), Ltd., 372 St. Catherine St. W., Montreal, P.Q.

They are designers of lively junior fashions with wide distribution in the United States and Europe as well as Canada.

Pat McDonagh. Pat McDonagh & Associates, Inc., 111 Peter St., Toronto, Ont.

One of Canada's most dynamic and successful fashion designers, Pat McDonagh was born March 17, 1934, in Manchester, England. She studied languages at Manchester University and the Sorbonne in Paris. Instead of teaching school, however, she went to London and Paris as a fashion model, then returned to set up fashion boutiques in the English provinces. She designed costumes for the Beatles and for British television. After her marriage to television director David Main, she came to Canada, where they settled with their three children. She opened Canadian versions of her English boutiques and designed the clothes she sold. Her firm is now part of the Sterling Knitting combine of Great Britain and her designs are sold throughout the United States and the United Kingdom.

She received the Ontario government's Eedee (Excellence of Design) Award five times.

Nicola Pelly. See Margaret Godfrey and Nicola Pelly

Irving Posluns. Coat manufacturers, 637 Lakeshore Blvd., Toronto, Ont.

This is one of Canada's largest and most widely distributed manufacturing organizations, producing cloth, leather, and raincoats for women in the medium price range. It was founded in the 1950s and now has branch offices in Montreal and New York.

The design staff is not featured by name, but Albert Sung is listed as one of the group.

Donny (Donald) Richer. Fur designer, 415 Mayor St., Montreal, P.Q.

Called "Montreal's Liberace," fur designer Donny Richer is Canada's most flamboyant fashion personality. His furs are show-stoppers and he makes fur the crux of his personal life as well.

The son of a Canadian fur manufacturer, he attended Sir George Williams University to study business administration. He joined his father's fur business in the early 1960s as assistant designer, later assuming full responsibility for the collections.

Michel Robichaud. Designer for Auckie Sanft, Inc., 1193 Carre Philippe, Montreal, P.Q.

Born June 9, 1939, in Montreal, Robichaud was sent to Paris as an apprentice in a couture house. He worked with Nina Ricci and Guy Laroche before returning home to open his own boutique and design wholesale ready-to-wear in the Paris tradition. His work is very high-style and meticulously detailed.

Robichaud was named first president of the Association of Canadian Fashion Designers when it was founded in 1974.

Albert Sung. See Irving Posluns

John Warden. Multifaceted designer, 1407 Bishop St., Montreal, P.Q.

One of Canada's most versatile and active young designers with an international reputation, John Warden was born December 28, 1939, on the Canadian side of Niagara Falls, and studied fashion design in the United States at Parsons School of Design in New York.

He designed for a Canadian coat and suit house before opening his own Montreal boutique. His simplistic, yet individual, fashion approach and his understanding of his medium soon brought him contracts to design for a variety of manufacturers, including dresses, sportswear, knits, furs, loungewear, jewelry, accessories, and shoes. He maintains a studio in Montreal where his numerous enterprises are centered. His work is exported to 14 countries.

Fashion Influentials

Joyce Carter. Fashion editor, *Toronto Globe and Mail*, 444 Front St. W., Toronto, Ont. M5W 2S9

A fine journalist and believer in high quality, Joyce Carter has been a factor in raising the standard of taste in both designing and at the customer level in Canada.

Wini Rider. Fashion editor, *The Gazette*, Box 6036, Montreal 101, P.Q.

An American with long training in retailing and a degree from the Tobe-Coburn School of Fashion Careers in New York, Wini Rider stresses the reader viewpoint in her fashion reporting and believes in reality as the primary focus of fashion coverage. She has been a vigorous and effective crusader for the recognition and appreciation of Canadian fashion talents.

Betty Runcie. *Vancouver Province*, 2250 Granville St., Vancouver, B. C. V6H 3G2

One of the leading members of the well-coordinated and jointly effective fashion press in Canada, Miss Runcie has been particularly vocal on the subject of greater promotion of Canadian fashion by Canadian retailers.

Joan Sutton. Women's and fashion editor, *Toronto Sun*, 322 King St. W., Toronto, Ont.

One of Canada's most dedicated and knowledgable fashion press women, Miss Sutton is an active crusader for the development of an independent fashion image in Canada.

Lissa Taylor. Fashion advisor and coordinator, c/o Department of Industry, Trade and Commerce, 112 Kent St., Ottawa, Ont. K1A 0H5

Since the early 1950s, Mrs. Taylor has been an outstanding mover–doer in the progress of Canadian fashion. She began her career with

T. Eaton Co., Ltd., the department store complex, as a free-lance public relations consultant for the eastern and middle-western provinces. In 1952 she joined Duplan of Canada as director of fashion and promotion and in 1955 was loaned by that textile organization to present the first-ever Canadian fashion show held outside the country at the Brussels World's Fair. In 1957 she became director of Dupont's Canadian fashion bureau and in 1967 organized Dupont's biannual "Canadian Designers of Tomorrow" competition, an effort which spurred much of Canada's present-day fashion talent.

In 1973 Mrs. Taylor was instrumental in the official establishment of Fashion Canada, with members among the apparel and textile designers and the backing of the federal and provincial governments of Quebec, Ontario, Manitoba, and British Columbia.

Vivian Wilcox. Fashion editor, *Style*, 481 University Ave., Toronto, Ont. M5W 1A7.

This leading fashion journalist has been instrumental in the development of Canadian fashion.

She was born in Aurora, Ontario, and interested herself in fashion from her girlhood when she got her first job as campus fashion advisor at Simpson's department store in Toronto. She worked on several magazines as fashion editor before helping to set up *Style*, the Canadian magazine devoted to fashion.

Sybil Young. Fashion editor, *Canadian* Magazine, The Simpson Tower, 40 Bay St., Toronto, Ont. M5W 2Y8

An Englishwoman with family and personal background in retailing, Miss Young came to Canada in the 1950s and worked on *Style*.

She has drawn the Canadian designer closer to the Canadian public by the excellent visual presentations she makes in her color pages. She recently commented that Canadian fashion has gone "light years ahead" in adventurous designing in her 20 years of observation.

Trade Associations and Organizations

Apparel Manufacturers Council of Canada. 214 Merton St., Suite 102, Toronto, Ont. M4S 1A6

Founded: 1937. Exec. Dir: F. Bryan.

This trade group is concerned with internal affairs and export development.

Canadian Textiles Institute. 1080 Beaver Hall Hill, Suite 1002, Commerce House, Montreal, P.Q. H2Z 1T6

Founded: 1935. Pres: J. Armstrong.

This membership organization of textile and fiber manufacturers deals with industrial affairs only.

Fashion Canada. c/o Department of Industry, Trade and Commerce, Tower B, Suite 838, 112 Kent St., Ottawa, Ont. K1A 0H5

Founded: 1973. Exec. Dir: Lissa Taylor. Pres: Bill Wilton.

This organization is the first unified attempt to promote creative fashion representing all of Canada rather than separate sections of the country.

Still in its initial program stage, Fashion Canada organizes seminars between design students and professional designers, presents coordinated fashion shows for the press, students, and buyers, and sponsors working scholarships in Paris, London, Milan, and New York for established designers, internships for graduate students, and training-in-industry opportunities for undergraduate students of fashion.

Fashion Canada supports the Fashion Designers Association of Canada in its activities.

Working in collaboration with Canadian industrial trade associations and regional fashion organizations, Fashion Canada assists in promotional programs in various areas, from Canadian furs to shoes and children's wear.

Fashion Designers Association of Canada, Inc. 1411 Crescent St., Montreal, P.Q. H3G 2B4

Founded: 1974. Exec. Dir: Mary Stephenson.

This national organization is Canada's first effort to project the creative work of the country's fashion designers.

Encouraged and partially financed by Fashion Canada, the Canadian government's department dealing with the apparel industries, the Fashion Designers Association holds group showings for press, buyers, and students, as well as establishing a code of ethics and practices in the profession.

Footwear Bureau of Canada. *See* Shoe Manufacturers Association of Canada

Fur Fashion Council of Canada. 4626 St. Catherine St. W., Montreal, P.Q. H3Z 1S3

Founded: 1964. Pres: A. Cleven. V-P: Bernard Friedman.

This membership organization includes fur manufacturers, retailers, skin dealers, and all primary producers of ranch furs.

The Council's purpose is to act as liaison between the Canadian Fur Trade and the International Fur Trade Federation with its head office in London, England, to promote fur fashions internationally. The Council also arranges fashion shows and issues consumer information.

Leather Bureau of Canada. Box 182, Station H, Montreal, P.Q. H3G 2K7

Founded: 1967. Dir: E. Hammond.

This promotional agency does regular press mailings and conducts internal and external promotional activities.

Montreal Manufacturers Council (Apparel Division). 400 de Maisonneuve Blvd. W., Suite 1055, Montreal, P.Q. H3A 1L4

Founded: 1974. Exec. Dir: Laz Peters.

The Montreal Manufacturers Council is an organization made up of smaller associations, representing about 750 manufacturers. This association has as its purpose the promoting of showings of the Canadian apparel manufacturers in Canada and other countries, and participates in trade fairs. The main function, however, is dealing with internal and labor matters.

Shoe Manufacturers Association of Canada. 1010 St. Catherine St. W., Suite 711, Montreal, P.Q. H3B 3R4

Founded: About 1950. Exec. V-P: Jean-Guy Maheu. Dir: Francis Kelly.

An industrial membership organization, the Shoe Manufacturers Association is concerned with internal matters. It has its own promotional setup known as the Footwear Bureau of Canada, which handles publicity releases and cooperates on fashion shows.

Tanners Association of Canada. Box 294, Kleinburg, Ont.

Founded: During World War I. Dir: Fred A. Glasser.

This organization represents the leather and fur handlers of Canada. They sponsor the Leather Bureau of Canada's yearly promotional campaigns.

Honors and Awards

Eedee (Excellence of Design Award).

This award was presented annually by the Ontario Ministry of Industry and Tourism in conjunction with the fashion industry from 1965 to 1971.

Fashion Education

College du Vieux-Montreal. 200 E. Sherbrooke St., Montreal, P.Q. H2X 3M8

Gen. Dir: André Trudel.

Besides offering a three-year program in marketing and retailing, this community college also teaches sewing skills, often leading to fashion careers. Design, however, is not a part of the curriculum.

Douglas College. 322 Columbia St., Box 2503, New Westminster, B.C. V3L 5B2

Tel: (604) 588-4411. Founded: 1970. Chmn, Fine Arts: David Peterkin.

This community college offers two-year courses in fashion design and couture, leading to a college diploma.

George Brown College of Applied Arts and Technology. Kensington Campus, 21 Nassau St., Toronto, Ont. M5T 1M3

Tel: (416) 967–1212. Founded: 1967. Dean: S. Schipper.

This college offers two- and three-year programs in fashion design and apparel management, leading to an official college degree.

LaSalle College. 2015 Drummond St., Montreal 107, P.Q.

Tel: (514) 842–3823. Founded: 1959. Pres Dir. Gen: Jean-Paul Morin.

Established in 1959, LaSalle College has been offering a fashion program since 1967. It offers three-year programs leading to an official college degree in fashion designing, fashion production, and fashion merchandising. Courses are given both in French and English.

Niagara College of Applied Arts and Technology. Woodland Rd., Box 248, Welland, Ont.

Tel: (416) 967–1212. Founded: 1967. Dean of Applied Arts: John Giancarlo.

Niagara College has been offering a two-year fashion course since 1971, leading to a diploma.

Ryerson Polytechnical Institute. 50 Gould St., Toronto, Ont. M5B 1E8

Tel: (416) 595–5073. Founded: 1940. Reorganized: 1948. Dean, Fine Arts: D. Sauro.

Established in 1940, coeducational Ryerson is Canada's leading technical institute for a fashion career, although creative design is not taught here. It offers three-year courses in fashion design, styling, fine arts, fashion arts, patternmaking, merchandising, marketing, and retailing.

Seneca College of Applied Arts and Technology. 1750 Finch Ave. W., Willowdale, Ont. M2N 5T7

Tel: (416) 491-5050. Founded: 1967. Pres: W.T. Newnham.

This community college offers three-year fashion design courses, with well-known designers as critics and advisors, leading to a college diploma. Textile design courses are optional.

Sheridan College of Applied Arts and Technology. 1435 Trafalgar Rd., Oakville, Ont. L6H 2L1

Tel: (416) 845-9430. Founded: 1967. Dean: W.E. Firth.

This college offers two-year fashion design courses, leading to a college diploma.

St. Laurence College of Applied Arts and Technology. Portsmouth Ave., Kingston, Ont. K71 5A6
Tel: (613) 544-5400. Founded: 1967. Chmn, Fine Arts: Howard Gilchrist.
St. Laurence has three-year programs in fashion design and also in fashion merchandising, leading to a college diploma.

Costume and Fashion Archives

National Museum of Man. Metcalfe and McLeod Sts., Ottawa, Ont. K1A 0M8
Tel: (613) 992-3497. Founded: 1842. Opened: 1843. Dir: Dr. W.E. Taylor, Jr.
This is Canada's key museum of the country's heritage. It has a large collection of Eskimo and Indian garments and collections of old photographs of Indians and Eskimos in their settings.

Royal Ontario Museum. University of Toronto, 100 Queen's Park, Toronto 5, Ont.
Tel: (416) 928-3692. Founded: 1912. Dir: Dr. Walter Tovell
The museum has a large collection of European, pre-Columbian, American Indian, and Oriental costumes, plus an outstanding collection of antique silks, cottons, and embroideries.

Fashion Publications

Canadian Bride & Fashion. Canadian Bridge Publishing Co., Ltd., 86 Avenue Rd., Toronto 2, Ont.
Founded: 1946. Ed: Judith Campbell. 4 issues/yr.

The Canadian Magazine. The Simpson Tower, 401 Bay St., Toronto, Ont. M5W 2V8
Fashion Ed: Sybil Young.

Chatelaine. Maclean-Hunter Publishing Co. 481 University Ave., Toronto, Ont. M5W 1A7
Founded 1928. Ed-in-chief: Doris Anderson. Fashion Ed: Eveleen Dollery. 12 issues/yr. $4/yr ($6/yr in US). Circ: 1,280,000.

Ego. Ego Publishing Inc., 1396 St. Catherine St. W., Montreal, P.Q. H3G 1P9
Ed-in-chief: Ray Lancashire. Fashion Ed: Virginia Leeming. 4 issues/yr. $6/yr. Text in French and English.

Elan de la Mode; Image of Fashion. Intercol Publishing Co., Ltd., 23 McMider St., Montreal, P.Q. H2V 3X4
Founded: 1967. Ed: Eileen Cooyer. 4 issues/yr. $6/yr. Text in French and English.

Miss Chatelaine. Maclean-Hunter Publishing Co., 481 University Ave., Toronto, Ont. M5W 1A7
Founded: 1964. Ed-in-chief: Mildred Istona. Fashion Ed: Eveleen Dollery. 6 issues/yr. $2/yr ($3/yr in US). Circ: 200,000.

Mode Aujourd'hui. 170 Dorchester Blvd. W., Montreal 108, P.Q.
Fashion Ed: Denise Courtois. Newspaper–magazine in French.

Perspectives. Perspectives, Inc., 231 rue Saint-Jacques, Montreal, P.Q. H2Y 1M6
Women's Ed: Isabelle Lefrançois. Text in French.

Style. Mclean-Hunter Publishing Co., 481 University Ave., Toronto, Ont. M5W 1A7
Founded: 1908. Ed-in-chief: Pat Porth. Fashion Ed: Vivian Wilcox. 26 issues/yr. $8/yr. Circ: 10,900.

CENTRAL AMERICA AND THE CANAL ZONE

It is a Latin American syndrome to inspire the arts and supply many materials that clothe the world, while producing little or nothing in terms of finished goods.

Except for Mexico, which is making a determined bid to increase its contribution to world clothing production, the countries that join North and South America are fashionwise more or less dormant. They have no "name" designers and no resources for fashion research or study.

The beautiful, colorful, and sturdy Guatemalan textiles have inspired many designers and commercial fabric ranges, but Guatemala's major market for fashion fabrics is still the local tourist hotel shops.

The city of Momostenango, the ancient Guatemalan wool center, is a fascinating place to visit and see the work of the handweavers. In contrast, the busy city of Quezaltenango has a modern knitting plant, making garments for domestic use.

Curiously enough, the largest percentage of Panama hats exported from Central America today are not made in Panama, but in Guatemala. The craft of plaiting the straw under water is dying out, however. Most of the output of hats now goes to Italy, where they are blocked, finished, and given Italian labels.

Nicaragua, Honduras, and Costa Rica are among the few remaining

Central American countries where the people continue to wear traditional costume, but no local designer seems to have attempted adapting these for international sale, as has been done in Mexico.

Panama produces gold and silver in small quantities from the pre-Columbian mines of the region. Pearls are also fished around the Pearl Islands south of the Canal.

The Canal Zone, a free port, attracts many travelers to buy hand-embroidered linens and crafts from Mainland China, but it is difficult to find any supply of crafts from the area.

Fashion Publications

Vanidades Continental. Editorial America, S.A.

Founded: 1961. Ed-in-chief: Elvira Mendoza. 26 issues/yr. $1/issue. Circ: 30,000. Most widely read women's magazine in Central America.

MEXICO

Mexico's customs regulations prohibiting the import of anything that is or can be produced domestically have greatly hampered the flow of inspirational fashions and materials which could be prototypes for clothing and textile design. On the other hand, the Indian and colonial costumes of Mexico, preserved in the country's extensive ethnic archives, provide a perennial flow of "Mexicana" into the international pool of fashion ideas.

Designer names well known in Mexico rarely penetrate beyond the borders of the country. Exceptions are a few designers in such resorts as Cuernavaca, Puerto Vallarta, and Acapulco, whose clothes have some international distribution.

Mexican textiles, both hand- and machine-made, are often interesting but apt to be uneven in quality. As yet they are little used in the world market.

Mexican-made leather goods are plentiful, but are often not of fine quality and are noncompetitive in price as a fashion export.

Several interesting jewelry designers have made use of Mexico's still ample supply of precious metals and semiprecious stones. Few of these are as yet known by name, but the activities of competent distributors such as jewelers Emi Fors and the international firm of Stern indicate a future in this area of Mexican design.

The Fashion Group of Mexico, a branch of the United States organization, has made efforts to stimulate design and promote quality in Mexican fashion industries. With the aid of government departments, a committee of the Fashion Group headed by Ana Fusoni, fashion director of *Claudia* magazine, has organized a touring presentation of Mexican fashions and inspirational costumes in a number of foreign countries.

The town of Santa Ana is the wool center of Mexico where yarns are spun and dyed and where woolen and polyester fabrics are woven. Mexican designers and elegant private people, both women and men, travel to Santa Ana to buy fabrics and also to have yarns spun for hand-knitted clothes.

Fashion Designers and Firms

Barbara Amrein. Designer of ethnic-inspired clothes, Mexor, S.A., Oaxaca 30, Mexico, D.F.

One of Mexico's most successful ready-to-wear designers, Mrs. Amrein uses native Mexican fabrics and print motifs in her leisure-clothes collections.

Barbara Angeli. Ready-to-wear designer, Genova 2D, Mexico, D.F.

This creative designer, a former model, makes amusing clothes for Mexican fashion individualists. She is an activist in efforts to promote Mexican fashion on an international scale.

Aries. Leather fashion, Avenida las Torres 178, Mexico, D.F.

Guitierrez Domingo Perez Alonso is design director of this firm which creates fine quality leather fashions in the tradition of Hermes, selling throughout Mexico and in other countries.

Brooke Cadwallader. Print and textile designer, Apdo. 170, Cuernavaca

Born and educated in America, Brooke Cadwallader is a fashion designer on a truly international scale. He was one of the most prominent and successful print creators in the world in the 1940s and 1950s. He made prints for many fashion designers, including Elsa Schiaparelli, for whom he created the first "pop art" dress with an enormous lobster on its front. His print in a facsimile of furniture-caning is a contemporary classic.

Returning to America after a long residence in Paris, Cadwallader contracted tuberculosis. He and his wife Mary, also his business associate, closed their successful firm and moved to Mexico. After his health improved, he returned to designing fabrics, and in the early 1960s set up a studio and small factory in Cuernavaca. He now employs several hundred workers, and his fabrics are exported to decorators and designers in many countries.

Piero Demichelis. Ready-to-wear designer, Arbiter, S.A., Mariano Excobedo 543, Mexico, D.F.

Demichelis is a leading source of higher-priced ready-made women's clothing for distribution in the Mexican market.

Disart. Knitwear designer, Paseo de las Palmas 775, Mexico, D.F.

Disart's two designer-partners, Tere Cortina and Rocio Fernandez, have a wide market for their well-made knits which utilize Mayan and Aztec designs and color combinations.

Esteban (Steven Martin Matison). Designer and boutique owner, Costera Aleman, Acapulco, Gro.

Esteban, a young Colombian-born designer of mixed Hindu, Czech, and American ancestry, was educated in New York at the High School of Music and Art and later at Pratt Institute. His mother, Edith Matison, now a well-known Mexican art dealer, took him to Mexico to escape a spate of childhood allergies.

In 1966 Esteban opened a one-room boutique in Acapulco, designing colorful clothes derived from a single sexy body shape. In 1968 he expanded to the spacious boutique from which he now also conducts an international wholesale business. In 1972 he received the Silver Medal in the International Fashion Week sponsored by the Mexican government to spur more fashion consciousness in the Mexican clothing industry.

Fabrica de Artes de Piel Victoria, S.A. Leather goods manufacturers, Dolores 10-401, Mexico, D.F.

Enrique Lorberfeld is the designer for this firm, Mexico's leading producers of classic handbags by mass-production methods.

Francisco Fernandez. Ready-to-wear designer, Modelos Fernandez, S.A., Plaza 20 Novembre, Mexico, D.F.

This designer is one of Mexico's most proficient producers of good quality clothes in classic styles, selling throughout Latin America.

Pedro Loredo. Evening-dress designer, Salamanca 71, Mexico, D.F.

Loredo's clothes, bright colored and embroidered in large sequin motifs with a Mexican flavor, are bizarre by traditional fashion standards but have a strong appeal to tourists and to foreign shops in search of ethnic fashions.

Gene Matouk. High-fashion designer for the young, Hamburgo 42, Mexico, D.F.

One of the few producers of European- and American-type avant-garde clothes in Mexico, Matouk has a young following among the well-to-do of Mexico City.

Manuel Mendez. Couturier, Hamburgo 150A, Mexico, D.F.

This designer of clothes in the European tradition has a large following of Mexican socialites and actresses. Mendez also designs models to be copied by El Palacio de Hierro, the leading Mexican department and specialty store. In 1971 he received that store's Designer of the Year award, chosen by a panel of 26 judges from the press and the arts.

Mr. Mingo. Leather fashion designer, Calzada de Tlalapan 43, Mexico 55C, D.F.

Mingo is considered one of the best of Mexico's far-out fashion designers with a distinctive flair of his own.

Royer (Louis Royer Hastings). Designer, boutique owner (retired), El Patio, Costera Aleman, Acapulco, Gro.

Born Louis Royer Hastings in Hastings, Nebraska, Royer studied interior design at the New York School of Fine and Applied Arts (now the Parsons School of Design) and the Paris branch of that school.

On his return from Europe, he worked in New York department stores until Dorothy Shaver, president of Lord & Taylor, offered him the then-unusual post of store stylist in 1928. He later designed costumes in Hollywood, and in 1939 went to Mexico to costume Mexican films and the Folklorico Ballet of Mexico.

In 1942 Royer set up a couture house in Mexico City while continuing his theatrical work. In 1951 he retired to Acapulco, only to find himself busier than ever as a designer of clothes for the burgeoning tourist trade in that resort. When he finally retired in 1975 he owned three large boutiques for which he designed the collections.

Fashion Influentials

Rosario Creixell. Fashion editor, *El Heraldo*, Carmona y Valle 150, Mexico 7, D.F.

As fashion editor of one of Mexico's largest-circulation newspapers, Rosario Creixell covers fashion at all price levels and has been an effective prodder toward better quality and styling in mass-produced Mexican clothing.

Ana Fusoni. Teran Publicidad, Durango 247, Mexico, D.F.

Mrs. Fusoni, formerly a *Vogue* editor, works effectively on local and international projects to further the cause of Mexican fashions. Her influence on designers is positive and productive, as is her activity as a leader of the Fashion Group of Mexico.

Charles Kovec, Jr. Fashion director, El Palacio de Hierro, S.A., Apdo. 26, Mexico 1, D.F.

Mexico's most dynamic promoter of domestic and international fashion, American-born and New York-trained Charles Kovec has greatly increased style consciousness in Mexico by originating domestic and foreign promotions and fashion shows for his organization.

He interprets world trends from El Palacio de Hierro's customers by selecting original models from European and American designers to be copied in Mexico for the store's collections.

He is the organizer and director of El Palacio de Hierro's annual fashion festivals, which gain international attention.

Maria Eugenia Moreno. Editor-in-chief, Kena Magazine, 5 de Febrero 246, Mexico, D.F.

As editor of the largest circulation women's publication in Mexico, Mrs. Moreno has been a force in the development of feminine taste in her country. She has also been active in encouraging young fashion talents to think of designing in the lower price brackets, and has brought many promising designers into the volume industry.

She was elected the first president of the World Association of Women Journalists and Writers (AMMPE), the prestigious organization of Western Hemisphere writers.

Hilda O'Farrill. Women's interests advisor, Novedades Publications, Balderas y Morelos, Mexico 1, D.F.

One of the most powerful and dynamic feminine personalities in Mexico, Mrs. O'Farrill, a niece of the Mexican President Manuel Avila Camacho, has brought the readership of her husband's publishing empire into touch with fashion and taste in all phases of their lives. She is also a power in cultural, charitable, fashion, education, and other women's interests in Mexico and Central America.

The O'Farrill's daughter, Hilda O'Farrill de Kelly, is also active on newspapers, magazines, and on television, having her own show.

Hilda O'Farrill de Kelly (Mrs. Paul Kelly). Director of women's sections, Novedades Publications, Balderas y Morelos, Mexico 1, D.F.

Hilda O'Farrill, Jr., was born in Pueblo and has been as absorbed as her parents with the family business, Mexico's Novedades Publications. She is director of women's sections of the newspaper and now edits Claudia magazine.

Both pretty and chic, Hilda O'Farrill de Kelly studied anthropology at the Jesuit University of Mexico and art both in Florence, Italy, and at the Sorbonne in Paris. She familiarized herself with every aspect of the newspaper business and journalism on a newspaper in Miami, Florida. She is vice president of Mexico's Women's Association.

Trixie (Beatriz Lopez Ostoloza). Excelsior, Avenida Paseo Reforma 12, Mexico 5, D.F.

The doyenne of Mexican fashion writers, Trixie is a woman of great dedication to fashion and her readers.

Trade Associations and Organizations

Camara Nacional de la Industria del Vestido. Reforma 403, Mexico, D.F.

Pres: Frederico Diego. Dir: Remigio Gomez-Saltres.

This is the Mexican chamber of commerce for the activities of the country's garment industry. Its activities are mostly internal, but they award scholarships nationally and issue bulletins on trends and colors to their members.

Instituto Mexicano de la Moda (IMMAC) (Mexican Institute of Fashion). Reforma 403, Mexico, D.F.

Founded: 1963. Dir: Victor Vizuett. Exec. Off: Gina Morales.

This government-sponsored association is organized to promote greater skills in the design and manufacturing of high-quality clothing among its membership which includes clothing manufacturers at all price levels, textile producers, and retailers.

Mexican Institute for Foreign Trade (IMCE). Insurgentes Sur 1443, Mexico 19, D.F.

Founded: 1971. Dir: Julio Faesler.

This organization is sponsored by the Mexican government to develop new markets for national products including clothing. The program includes foreign showings of Mexican clothing, participation in international trade fairs, and the encouragement and training of young people suitable for design careers. It sponsors annual competitions for excellence in design, including fashion.

Honors and Awards

IMCE Annual Design Competition Medal

This award established by the Institute of Foreign Trade (Insurgentes Sur 1443, Mexico 19, D.F.) in 1962 involves a national competition for excellence in design in all areas including fashion. It is given more or less annually under the sponsorship of the Institute of Foreign Trade and the method of selection varies with the regimes.

Palacio de Hierro Awards

The Palacio de Hierro Awards (begun in 1967) are given annually to Mexican designers during the Fashion Festival held by El Palacio de Hierro, S.A. (Apdo. 26, Mexico 1, D.F.) and supervised by its director of promotion and publicity, Charles Kovec, Jr.

With the aim of broadening domestic and international appreciation of fashion at all price levels, El Palacio de Hierro presents the collection of one well-known foreign designer, together with a number of Mexican designers, at its annual Fashion Festival usually held in November. The Awards are decided by a jury of 25 personalities from fashion and the arts.

Costume and Fashion Archives

Museo Nacional de Antropologia (National Museum of Anthropology). Calzada de la Milla, Mexico 5, D.F.

Tel: 5-53-62-66. Founded: 1865. New building opened: 1964. Dir: Dr. Ignacio Bernal y Garcia Pimentel.

Mexico's greatest museum, and one of the greatest in the world, has in addition to the rooms of artifacts of various Mexican cultures, an extensive collection of Indian regional and colonial costumes, and has published a large book of costume plates of regional costumes.

Museo Regional de Oaxaca (Oaxaca Regional Museum). Ex-Convento de Santo Domingo, Oaxaca

Tel: 6-29-91. Founded: 1933. Curator: Argueloga Wanda Tommasi de Magrelli.

This museum, originally located on the city plaza, is now re-installed in a beautiful old convent. It contains an outstanding collection of artifacts from the ruins of Monte Alban, a treasury of gold objects, and a good collection of Mexican Indian costumes.

Fashion Publications

Claudia. Mex Abril, S.A., Morelos 16, D.F.

Founded: 1965. Ed: Hilda O'Farrill de Kelly, 12 issues/yr. Circ: 120,000.

Femenidades. Prensa Especializada, S.A., Tenayuca 55-5, Mexico 13, D.F.

Founded: 1946. Ed: Arturo Torres Yanez. 12 issues/yr.

Kena. Ferro, S.A., 5 de Febrero 246, Mexico, D.F.

Founded: 1963. Ed-in-chief: Maria Eugenia Moreno. 24 issues/yr. Circ. 300,000.

Nueva Vida. Mex Abril, S.A., Rio Niagara 64, Mexico 5, D.F.

Founded: 1972. Ed: Graziella Uriarte Lamerens. Associated with Abril Brazil.

Ultima Moda. Publicaciones Herrerias, S.A., Morelos 16, Mexico 1, D.F.

Founded: 1966. Ed: Jose Pichel. 24 issues/yr. Circ. 120,000.

Vanidades Continental. Editorial America, S.A., Publicaciones Continentales de Mexico, S.A., Avenida Insurgentes Sur 421, Mexico 11, D.F.

Founded:1961. Ed-in-chief: Elvira Mendoza. Coordinadora Editorial: Esperanza Brito de Marti. 26 issues/yr. P. 12/issue. Circ: 112,000.

UNITED STATES

With the longest history of ready-to-wear clothing production in the world and the greatest number of professional fashion designers, the United States has nevertheless been consistently introverted and non-aggressive in realizing its potentials to contribute to clothing the world.

Americans consume more than $7.5 billion worth of wearing apparel per year, enough to absorb the national output and to claim about 12 percent of the income of the average family. Apparel manufacture is the fifth largest American industry and the largest in the state and city of New York, its main production center.

Not until the 1960s did it begin to dawn on American clothing producers, apparel unions, and the government that its markets were being successfully infiltrated by foreign-manufactured goods. In the 1950s imports of finished clothing represented only 4 percent of the total retail clothing sales. By 1972 this had grown to 25 percent, largely through the expertise which Americans had shared freely with delegations of foreign manufacturers sent to study the technology of American clothing production, plus vigorous trade promotion by nations such as Great Britain, Italy, France, Spain, the Irish Republic, Scandinavia, and India.

Textile production in America has been reduced to a comparative trickle by the competition of other countries. By 1973, creative textile design in America had become practically nonexistent.

On the bright side, American fashion design, originality, variety, and confidence have flourished on a rising scale since 1928 when the fashionable dressmaker Hattie Carnegie ventured to put her name on a dress label. The United States today has more "name" designers than any other country. Fashion coverage, both editorial and advertising, is more concentrated, widespread, and consistent than anywhere else in the world. Opportunities for a career in fashion are great and constantly increasing. Since the end of World War II when American fashion began to have a strong national image, fashion courses in colleges and the growth of fashion schools have mushroomed.

While America lacks the tradition of fashion apprenticeship, which has immeasurably helped the foreign designer to extend his skills while working, it provides unique opportunities for design education, fashion history, techniques of construction, fashion illustration, and retail management and merchandising.

Note: Alaska, Hawaii, and Puerto Rico are individually discussed immediately following the United States Fashion Publications section

Fashion Designers and Firms

Adolfo (Sardina). Custom and ready-to-wear designer, Adolfo, Inc., 538 Madison Ave., New York, N.Y. 10022

Born on February 15, 1933, in Havana, Cuba, Adolfo was expected to join his family's law practice. His wealthy and elegant aunt, however, encouraged his hopes of a fashion career by taking him to Paris and obtaining a job for him on Balenciaga's staff.

In 1949 he came to New York as assistant to Braagard, a New York milliner. In 1951 he joined the staff of the milliner, Emme, where his flair for small simple hats with character and importance brought him attention.

He founded Adolfo, Inc., in 1963 and in 1968 added dresses to his millinery collections. He now does ready-to-wear sold nationally. His patchwork and peasant evening skirts, Chanel-inspired suits, and luxurious knitted costumes now have the same status-symbol rating his hats originally established. He received a Coty Award in 1955 and 1969.

He is a member of the Council of Fashion Designers of America.

Adri (Steckling). Dress designer, 320 E. 54 St., New York, N.Y. 10022

Born in St. Joseph, Missouri, Adri studied at Washington University in St. Louis and the Parsons School of Design in New York.

After designing sportswear for eight years for B.H. Wragge, she joined Anne Fogarty, Inc., in 1971 as designer of its Clothes Circuit division. In 1972 she organized her own firm, designing young, soft, and graceful dresses, usually with a sheer "floaty" quality.

Adri is a member of the Council of Fashion Designers of America.

Adrian. See Hall of Fame

Ray Aghayan/Bob Mackie. 8636 Melrose Ave., Los Angeles, Calif. 90069

This Hollywood team of theatrical and ready-to-wear clothes designers became associated in 1963, when they designed the costumes for a Judy Garland TV spectacular. Today they create costumes for many large television specials and dress many nightclub and theatre stars in addition to producing luxury ready-to-wear.

Ray Aghayan, an Iranian, was born into fashion. His mother was a couturiere in Teheran. He came to America to study architecture, then went to California and played small roles in the movies before turning to costume design.

Bob Mackie, a native Californian, studied at the Chouinard Institute in Los Angeles and Pasadena City College, then worked as an assistant to Jean Louis designing film costumes.

Together Aghayan and Mackie have won three Emmy Awards for television costuming, an Academy Award nomination, and the Costume Designers Guild Award.

In 1969 they organized their own company to produce fashions in the same dramatic mood as their theatrical clothes.

Ronald Amey. Dress designer, 16 W. 57 St., New York, N.Y. 10019

A designer known for his color sense and the fastidious workmanship of his clothes, Ronald Amey was born May 18, 1932, in Globe, Arizona, and went to high school in the nearby mining center of Superior. His first job was assaying metals in a copper mine.

He studied fashion design at the Chouinard Institute in Los Angeles, but enlisted in the U.S. Air Force and became an electronics instructor, eventually serving with the Air Force in Korea.

With a fellow officer, Joseph Burke, Amey "moonlighted" by designing clothes for army wives.

On his discharge he studied fashion design at the Parsons School of Design in New York, where he was advised by the noted designer and critic Norman Norell to start his own business. In 1959, again with Joseph Burke, he established Burke–Amey, which in 1969 became Ronald Amey, Inc.

Amey has served as a part-time teacher at Mount Mary College in Milwaukee, Wisconsin, and at Moore College of Design.

Jay (James Byrd) Anderson. Designer–owner, Posh, Inc., 50 N.W. 10 St., Miami, Fla. 33136

This designer and manufacturer of day and evening dresses and at-home clothes for resort wear, is one of the best-known producers in the Florida fashion market.

Born in Columbia, South Carolina, on November 1, 1919, he graduated from the University of South Carolina, then came to New York to study fashion design at the Traphagen School there. He served in World War II as captain in the Engineers and was decorated with the Bronze Star with Oak Leaf clusters. In 1946 he moved to Miami and until 1955 designed models for New York dress manufacturers.

Posh, Inc., has been a highly popular operation in stores throughout the country.

Maurice Antaya. Separates designer, Maurice Antaya, Inc., 530 Seventh Ave., New York, N.Y. 10018

This designer of discreetly fashionable clothes that the average well-to-do woman can wear with ease was born in Manville, Rhode Island,

and attended the Massachusetts College of Art and the Rhode Island School of Design.

He came to New York to teach at the Parsons School of Design, where he still is a guest critic.

After free-lancing in the design of leather fashions and evening clothes he joined Ginori to make tailored clothes and later headed Company Five, a division of the Puritan Dress Company. Since 1973 he has had his own independent organization, creating high-quality separates.

John Anthony. Designer–partner of John Anthony, Inc., 550 Seventh Ave., New York, N.Y. 10018

John Anthony, known for dramatic, luxurious fashions, was born April 28, 1938, in New York City. At the High School of Industrial Arts there he won three scholarships for European fashion training. He attended the Accademia d'Arte in Rome for a year, then came home and enrolled in the Fashion Institute of Technology.

At 19, Anthony took his first job with Devonbrook, a wholesale coat firm, where he designed for nine years, followed by three years with Adolph Zelinka.

His own firm was organized in January, 1971, with Robert Levine, a young manufacturer, as his partner. His ultrasleek, rather stately day and evening clothes were an overnight success, even in an epoch when the sportswear feeling dominated fashion. He received the Coty Award in 1971, after his second collection.

He is a member of the Council of Fashion Designers of America.

Jackie Ayer. See Thailand: Fashion Designers and Firms—Design Thai

Jim Baldwin. Crystal Plus, Inc., 498 Seventh Ave., New York, N.Y. 10018

This designer of tailored clothes was born in Caldwell, New Jersey, one of twins in a banking family. After serving in the U.S. Navy Air Corps in World War II, he studied at the Parsons School of Design until Pauline Trigere engaged him as a sketcher. Later he designed for several wholesale firms producing tailored clothes, then formed his own company in 1973. This closed in 1974 and he joined David Crystal of New York to design for its division, Crystal Plus.

Travis Banton. See Hall of Fame

Scott Barrie. Dress designer, Scott Barrie and Barrie Sport, Ltd., 530 Seventh Ave., New York, N.Y. 10018

Born January 16, 1945, in Philadelphia, Pennsylvania, Barrie is one of the group of young black designers who have contributed to the farout fashion scene since the mid-1960s.

He studied at the Philadelphia Museum College of Art and Mayer School of Fashion and designed for several New York wholesale firms before starting his own organization in 1971.

Geoffrey Beene. Designer–partner of Geoffrey Beene, Inc., 550 Seventh Ave., New York, N.Y. 10018

Geoffrey Beene, known for his innovative cuts and unusual decorative touches, was born in Haynesville, Louisiana, on August 30, 1928. He studied medicine for four years at Tulane University before turning to fashion. He prefaced his professional career with only one semester at the Traphagen School in New York, followed by two years at l'Ecole de la Chambre Syndicale in Paris.

He has won three Coty Awards (1964, 1966, and 1974) making him a member of the Coty Hall of Fame, and in 1975 received still another Coty Citation. He received the Neiman–Marcus Award, the Traphagen School Award, and two National Cotton Awards; he was a charter member of the Council of Fashion Designers of America.

Mr. Blackwell (Richard Blackwell). Designer and radio commentator, c/o Robert L. Spencer, Inc., 719 S. Los Angeles St., Los Angeles, Calif. 90014

A former child actor who was one of the "Dead End Kids" and also played opposite Mae West, Richard Blackwell now owns his own wholesale dress business specializing in flamboyant evening clothes.

His chief claim to fame, however, lies in his frequent criticism of well-known personalities and their clothes. Each year he issues his own personal list of "worst dressed" women in the world, and had his own radio show centered on his ideas about dress.

Mr. Blackwell was born in the Hell's Kitchen slums of Brooklyn, New York. He ran away from home after finishing the fifth grade in school, changed his name to Dick Ellis, and played bit parts in off-Broadway shows and in the road company of *Dead End*. Arriving in Hollywood, his career was given a brief boost by Howard Hughes. He also sold used cars, designed toilet-seat covers and, during a stint as a talent agent with a singer client, Wanda Curtis, he designed and made her wardrobe. His career in fashion dates from the mid-1960s.

With Robert L. Spencer, now president of Mr. Blackwell, Blackwell built a successful business with distribution through the United States, Canada, Australia, and Germany.

Bill Blass. Designer–owner of Bill Blass, Ltd. and Blassport, 550 Seventh Ave., New York, N.Y. 10018

Bill Blass is a leading figure in American ready-to-wear who helped to lift its image from the "rag trade" to the level of high fashion. His urbane clothes in soft fabrics with luxurious touches have an international following.

He was born June 22, 1922, in Fort Wayne, Indiana, where his family owned a hardware store. He came to New York to study fashion drawing at the Parsons School of Design, then joined the U.S. Army Engineers and served in the European theatre during World War II.

In 1947 he found his first designing job with Anna Miller Inc. When that firm merged with Maurice Rentner (1959), he remained as designer and in 1962 became vice-president.

In 1970 the name of the company was changed to Bill Blass, Ltd. with the designer as chief executive. He is now sole owner of the firm and its less expensive sportswear division Blassport.

Bill Blass was one of the first "name" designers in America to design men's fashions. His collections for PBM menswear began in 1967. He also designs furs for the French firm, Revillon.

Blass has received the Coty American Fashion Critics' Award five times: for women's fashion in 1961, 1963, and 1970 (Hall of Fame), 1971 (citation to the Hall of Fame), and in 1968 he was given the first Coty Menswear Award. Among his other awards are the Chicago Gold Coast Award (1965), Cotton Fashion Award (1966), and the Print Council Award (1972).

In 1973 he was one of the five American designers who shared honors in the Versailles fashion show in Paris. He designs bed linens and other fashions under license.

Bill Blass is a charter member, vice-president, and member of the board of the Council of Fashion Designers of America.

Ole Borden. 4 Park Ave., Apt. 10H, New York, N.Y.

Born in Elsinore, Denmark, on November 4, 1922, Ole Borden studied art in Vienna and at the Copenhagen Royal Academy of Art. Before World War II and during the seven years following the war, he worked as a fashion designer in London, Paris, and Stockholm. He and his wife came to the United States in 1952.

From 1959 to 1964, he worked exclusively for Lord & Taylor in New York, creating their "Young Look" collections, then joined Rembrandt as designer from 1964 to 1974. He was among the first American designers to export his clothes to the European market.

Brigance (Thomas F. Brigance). Sportswear designer, 122 E. 78 St., New York, N.Y. 10021

Born February 4, 1913, in Waco, Texas, Thomas Brigance studied painting at the National Academy of Art and fashion design at the Parsons School of Design in New York. He later went to Paris, where he

211

sold sketches to couturiers and worked on the staff of a French sportswear house, and for Jaeger in London.

In 1941 he enlisted and served three years overseas with the Air Corps Intelligence. Since 1949 he has designed sportswear for his own and other firms.

He received the Coty Award in 1953, the Cotton Award in 1954, and is a member of the Council of Fashion Designers of America.

Britta (Bauer). Cinnamon Wear, 1411 Broadway, New York, N.Y. 10018

Born June 30, 1944, and a well-known fashion model in her native Germany and the United States before she became a designer, Britta Bauer achieved quick attention as a designer of ultrasimple clothes in ecologically "natural" fabrics and colors.

Her first visit to America was under the auspices of the Eileen Ford Model Agency. In 1972 Britta and her friend Barry Liss formed Cinnamon Wear.

In 1975 Britta was nominated for a Coty Award.

Steven Brody. See Cadoro

Donald Brooks. Fashion and costume designer, 158 E. 70 St., New York, N.Y. 10021

Donald Brooks, now a multifaceted free-lance designer, was born in New Haven, Connecticut, on January 10, 1928. He attended the Fine Arts School of Syracuse University and the Parsons School of Design in New York, where he now serves as guest critic.

After designing for Townley and establishing himself as a major young talent in American fashion, he won a Coty Special Award (1958), the Coty "Winnie" (1962), and the Coty Return Award (1967). He received the New York Drama Critics' Award (1963) for his costumes for the Broadway production No Strings. His clothes for Star, a film biography of Gertrude Lawrence, were widely publicized as spurring the influence of 1930s fashion as the chief inspiration of the early 1970s.

From February, 1965, to December, 1973, Brooks was vice-president and designer for Donald Brooks, Inc., in New York. After his partnership with the fashion entrepreneur Ben Shaw was dissolved, the designer established a couture business of his own and now also designs swimwear, lingerie, foundation garments, loungewear, household linens, and accessories as well as costumes for the theatre and films.

He is a vice-president and member of the Board of Directors of the Council of Fashion Designers of America.

Stephen Burrows. Ready-to-wear designer, 550 Seventh Ave., New York, N.Y. 10018

One of America's most creative avant-garde designers, Burrows was born September 15, 1943, in Newark, New Jersey, to a poor but industrious and affectionate black family. His grandmother was the dominant influence of his childhood and encouraged his interest in art.

He attended Newark High School and the Philadelphia Museum College of Art before going to New York's Fashion Institute of Technology. In 1966 he found his first job as designer for Weber Originals, then he was featured designer for the far-out "O" boutique.

In 1970 Geraldine Stutz of Henri Bendel in New York engaged Burrows as its first "house designer." His inventive use of abstract appliques, uneven hemlines, and his nondressmaking innovations such as the application of the industrial marrow machine to overcast the edges of his clothes helped to change concepts of dress production throughout the world. The Burrows "lettuce hem" became a fashion classic.

Burrows received the Coty American Fashion Critics' Award in 1973 and the same year was established in his own firm designing dresses, separates, and eventually loungewear. He was one of the five American designers in the historic Versailles fashion show in Paris the same year.

In 1974 he received a Coty Special Award for lingerie and loungewear.

Cadoro. Costume jewelry, 389 Fifth Ave., New York, N.Y. 10018

The two associates in Cadoro are Dan Stoenescu, son of the well-known French Impressionist painter Eustace Stoenescu and the nephew of the Rumanian Princess Ghika, and Steven Stuart Brody, a native of Philadelphia. Brody studied business administration at the Wharton School at Pennsylvania University, then became an actor. After playing in radio soap operas and in summer stock with Ethel Barrymore and Barbara Bel Geddes, he went to Paris where he and Stoenescu met. Their plan for a business in industrial plastics switched to costume jewelry, and in 1956 they formed Cadoro.

Both partners share equally in the research, design, selling, and business management at Cadoro. Together they received a Coty Award in 1970 and are members of the Council of Fashion Designers of America.

Jeanne Campbell. Sportswear designer, Sportwhirl, Inc., 498 Seventh Ave., New York, N.Y. 10018

Born in Pittsburgh, Pennsylvania, and brought up at Charter Oak Farm, a landmark and showplace of the area, Jeanne Campbell received an art scholarship to the Pittsburgh Art Institute.

She opened a small sportswear shop in Clearwater, Florida, but joined Sportwhirl in 1947. She was among the first to give separates a high-fashion slant. She is a guest critic of Parsons School of Design, New York.

She won a Coty Award in 1955. Other awards include: Mademoiselle Award, 1951; the Sports Illustrated Award, 1956, 1957, and 1958; and Burdine's Sunshine Fashion Award, 1957.

Capezio. 1612 Broadway, New York, N.Y. 10019

This firm, producing day and evening shoes, stemmed from the dance shoe company founded by Salvatore Capezio in 1887 and is still operating in the theatrical field.

The use of classic Capezio ballet slippers in fashion was launched by American designer Claire McCardell and became an important look of the 1940s. Capezio entered the leisure shoe business while continuing to be a chief supplier of professional dance slippers.

Ben Sommers, the member of Capezio management who nurtured Capezio's link with fashion, is well known in both the fashion and dance worlds. He is a member of the Advisory Board of the Fashion Institute of Technology and the founder of Capezio Awards for dancers.

Patti Cappalli (Taylor). c/o Jerry Silverman, Ltd., 530 Seventh Ave., New York, N.Y. 10018

Designer of easy, young clothes, Patti Cappalli was born May 23, 1939, in Providence, Rhode Island. She graduated (1960) from the Rhode Island School of Design.

She designed for several volume dress and sportswear houses in New York before she joined Addenda, a division of Bobbie Brooks, Inc., in 1968. In 1975 she joined the design staff of Jerry Silverman.

She won *Mademoiselle* magazine's Woman of Achievement Award (1968), served on the Board of Directors of the Fashion Group (1972–1974), and is a member of the Council of Fashion Designers of America.

Albert Capraro. Ready-to-wear designer, Jerry Guttenberg, Ltd., 550 Seventh Ave., New York, N.Y. 10018

A young designer of sound experience, Albert Capraro nonetheless became an overnight "name" in 1975 when Mrs. Gerald Ford, wife of the President of the United States, publicly announced that she had chosen her spring wardrobe from his collection of fashionable yet easy-to-wear clothes.

Born May 20, 1943, in New York City and a graduate of Parsons School of Design there, Capraro worked first for milliner Lilly Dache and then for eight years as assistant and later associate designer to Oscar de la Renta.

In 1974 he joined with three American fashion businessmen, Ben

Shaw, Jerry Guttenberg, and Tony Sciano, in the formation of the dress firm, Jerry Guttenberg, Ltd.

Hattie Carnegie. *See* Hall of Fame

Bonnie Cashin. Sportswear, knits, and accessories designer, 870 United Nations Plaza, New York, N.Y. 10017

Bonnie Cashin has been called America's most "organic" designer. She uses only natural materials for her timeless, deep-country clothes.

Miss Cashin was born in California, the daughter of a custom dressmaker and an artist–inventor. She studied painting in New York at the Art Students League, then returned to California in 1944 to design costumes for 60 motion pictures, among them *Anna and the King of Siam* and *Laura*.

In 1949 she came back to New York to design fashions and promptly won the Neiman–Marcus Award and a Coty "Winnie" (1950). In 1953 she opened her own design studio.

She is both a "designer's designer" and a designer that the outdoors-type woman understands. Her blanket ponchos, leatherbound topcoats, and sleek but flexible pants and bonded sweaters are both basic and decorative.

Bonnie Cashin's were the first American fashions to be sold in a leading European shop, Liberty of London.

While maintaining her own studio and designing for various firms, Bonnie Cashin makes her largest collection of tweed and leather costumes for Philip Sills, Inc. of New York, manufacturers of woolen and leather outerwear.

In 1972 she opened her own knitwear firm, The Knittery, to produce and distribute her own knitted fashions.

She has won numerous honors, including the Coty American Fashion Critics' Award four times: in 1950 (Winnie), 1961 (Special Award), 1968 (Return Award), and in 1972 (Hall of Fame). She received the London Sunday Times Fashion Award in 1966.

Oleg Cassini. Ready-to-wear, film costumes, and accessories designer, 445 Park Ave., New York, N.Y. 10022

This designer, best known as the "official" White House dressmaker of the Kennedy years, was born in Paris on April 11, 1913, of Russian and Italian parentage. He studied at the Accademia di Belle Arti e Liceo Artistico, Florence. He came to the United States in 1938, renouncing his Georgian family title of Count for American citizenship.

Cassini designed for Hollywood studios in the 1940s and married the actress Gene Tierney (later divorced). He opened a wholesale dress firm in 1950 and later was announced as the official White House designer for Mrs. John F. Kennedy. In 1963, he closed his business and went to Italy to design men's fashions and fulfill license contracts to design articles other than fashions. In 1974 he returned to America to design active tennis clothes under his label for Munsingwear and swimwear for Waterclothes.

He is a member of the Council of Fashion Designers of America.

Sal Cesarani. Menswear designer, 12 E. 53 St., New York, N.Y. 10022

This menswear classicist was born September 25, 1941, in New York, the son of Italian parents who both worked in the garment industry. He studied at the Needle Trades High School and the Fashion Institute of Technology, graduating from the latter with honors.

He was assistant to Ralph Lauren for two years before Country Britches, a division of Joseph & Feiss Company and a large menswear group, was set up to launch the Sal Cesarani clothes. In 1975 he founded his own menswear company.

In 1974 Cesarani won a Coty Special Award and in 1975 was nominated for the Coty menswear trophy.

Ceil Chapman. Dress designer (retired), 230 E. 73 St., New York, N.Y. 10021

Ceil Chapman, best known in the 1940s and 1950s for her seductive evening clothes, was born in New York on February 19, 1912. She started Ceil Chapman, Inc., in 1940 with her first husband, Samuel Chapman. In 1946, she was cited by the Coty Awards Committee for her talents in creating seductive yet tasteful dresses with intriguing necklines. The firm was disbanded in 1965. Now retired, she lives in New York with her second husband, Thomas G. Rogers.

Aldo Cipullo. Jewelry designer, 100 Central Pk. S., New York, N.Y. 10019

This designer gained public attention as the originator of gold jewelry made in the form of humble articles such as nails, screws, and paper clips.

He was born into a family owning one of the largest costume jewelry manufacturing firms in Italy and came to New York at 23. He studied painting and graphic arts at the School of Visual Arts in New York, then worked as an assistant to the American jewelers David Webb, Tiffany, and Cartier.

At Cartier he designed a gold "love bracelet," accompanied by a miniature screwdriver which was its only way of being removed. This became a status symbol and was worn by many celebrities. Sophia Loren, Elizabeth Taylor, the Duchess of Windsor, Pierre Cardin, Richard Burton, and Bobby Short were among its famous owners.

After opening his own business in 1974, Cipullo received a Coty Special Award for his men's jewelry.

Jo Copeland. Dress designer (retired), 30 E. 62 St., New York, N.Y. 10021

Jo Copeland was born in New York and attended the Art Students League and the Parsons School of Design. She had her first job with Pattullo and except for a brief try on her own during the Depression, she remained with Pattullo from 1938 until her retirement in 1972. She received the Neiman–Marcus Award (1944).

Victor Costa. Dress designer, Victor Costa, Ltd., 208 S. Lamar St., Dallas, Tex. 75222

Born of Italian parentage in Houston, Texas, on December 17, 1935, Victor Costa at eight sang on the "Stars of Tomorrow" radio program. At 14, when his voice changed, he became guest chef on the "TV Kitchen" program at the same station.

He came to New York to study design at the Pratt Institute and later studied at l'Ecole de la Chambre Syndicale in Paris.

His first designing job was with a bridal dress house in New York. In the summer of 1965 there were 35,000 Costa brides in the United States. The same year he joined Suzy Perette, designing highly fashionable dresses at a low price. In 1974 he resigned to form his own firm in Texas.

He is a member of the Council of Fashion Designers of America.

Lilly Dache (Mme Jean Despres). Milliner (retired), 303 E. 57 St., New York, N.Y. 10022

Lilly Dache, one of the first designers to become a household word in America, was born in Beigles, France. She was apprenticed at 12 to her aunt, a milliner in Bordeaux, and later to the famous milliner Caroline Reboux of Paris.

She came to New York in the early 1920s and worked as a salesgirl until she saved enough from her salary to buy out her employer.

The first Dache made-on-the-head hat was created for a Follies beauty about 1926 and by 1949 the name Dache was known in lingerie, jewelry, decorative household articles, and cosmetics as well as being the acknowledged pacesetter in millinery.

In 1929 she married Jean Despres, a cosmetic executive. Both retired in 1969. The name Lilly Dache is still licensed in cosmetics and accessory fields.

Among her fashion honors were a Coty Award (1943), and the Neiman–Marcus Award (1940). She is the author of two books, *Talking through My Hats* (1946) and *Lilly Dache's Glamour Book* (1957).

James Daugherty. Ready-to-wear designer, James Daugherty, Ltd., 550 Seventh Ave., New York, N.Y. 10018

James Daugherty is an experienced designer with a comparatively new personal reputation. He was first assistant to leading name designers for Hollywood films and also in the New York wholesale fashion industry before New York fashion impresario Ben Shaw formed a successful company around his talents in 1974.

Born in Los Angeles, Daugherty studied fashion design at the Chouinard School there and got his early professional training in the film studios, assisting Edith Head, Walter Plunket, Tony Duquette, and Vincente Minnelli. He came to New York to work with Bill Blass at Maurice Rentner and then designed with Pat Sandler and Shannon Rodgers of Jerry Silverman, remaining at Silverman for seven years.

Daugherty is the only black American designer who does not approach his work from the "far-out" direction. In fact he calls himself "far in," and designs clothes which are quiet and moderate in price.

David Crystal, Inc. Sportswear producers, 498 Seventh Ave., New York, N.Y. 10018

One of the largest American fashion organizations specializing in sportswear, the firm's labels include several divisions of David Crystal, comprising children's wear, Izod, Haymaker Sports, and professional sports clothes signed by tennis star Billie Jean King.

Vincent de Paul Draddy, chairman of the board and powerful figure in American industry, began as a salesman for David Crystal on his graduation from Manhattan College in 1930. His skill and understanding of mass-produced casual clothing rapidly made David Crystal an American fashion giant.

Vincent Draddy received a Doctor of Laws degree from Manhattan College in 1961. A well-known sports fan and high-ranking golfer, he is chairman of the National Football Foundation and Hall of Fame.

Maxime de la Falaise (McKendry). Separates and sportswear designer, Blousecraft Company, Inc., 525 Seventh Ave., New York, N.Y. 10018

This well-known member of the international social and artistic worlds designs chic yet inexpensive casual clothes, including clothes expressly designed for the cook–hostess. She is also a well-known writer on food.

Daughter of the celebrated British portrait painter Sir Oswald Birley, Maxime Birley was brought up in London and the family's country house in Sussex. She also spent much of her youth in Ireland.

She first married the French Comte de la Falaise. Their daughter,

Comtesse Lulu de la Falaise, is a colorful personality of present-day Paris and is associated with Yves Saint Laurent.

She was later married to the late John McKendry, Curator of Prints at the Metropolitan Museum of Art in New York. Her designs for Blousecraft, Inc., carry the Maxime de la Falaise label, the name she signs to her articles and books on cooking and entertaining.

Oscar de la Renta. Oscar de la Renta, Ltd., 550 Seventh Ave., New York, N.Y. 10018

Designer of opulent clothes and accessories for women and men, Oscar de la Renta was one of the first fashion designers in America to have a publicly owned corporation formed around his talents.

Before he was 40, he was made chief executive of four divisions of the Richton International Corporation: Oscar de la Renta Couture, Oscar de la Renta II, Oscar de la Renta Furs, and Oscar de la Renta Jewelry. He was also made a member of Richton's Board of Directors. In 1973 he bought back full control of his organization and compressed its operations into one comprehensive company.

Born in Santo Domingo, Dominican Republic, on July 22, 1932, of Spanish parentage, Oscar de la Renta received his general and university education in Santo Domingo and in Madrid, where he also studied art at the Academia de San Fernando.

After attracting attention in Madrid society for his flair in designing dresses for his young women friends, he joined the design staff of Balenciaga's couture house in Madrid, known as AISA.

In 1960 he was engaged by Spanish-born Antonio Castillo to assist him at Lanvin–Castillo in Paris and in 1963 he followed Castillo as custom designer at Elizabeth Arden in New York.

In 1965, Oscar de la Renta and the American designer Jane Derby formed an alliance which, after Mrs. Derby's death, evolved into the present de la Renta organization.

In 1967, de la Renta married the former Françoise de Langlade, editor-in-chief of French Vogue.

In 1967 he received the Coty Award for his trend-setting Russian and gypsy fashion themes. The following year he received the Coty Return Award and in 1973 the Coty Hall of Fame.

From 1968 to 1973 he designed menswear for After Six and his name has been licenced in other areas of fashion and home furnishings.

In 1972 the President of the Dominican Republic gave him the Order of Juan Pablo Duarte (Grado Caballero) and the Order of Cristobal Colon (Grado de Gran Commandante), as a distinguished citizen.

He is president of the Council of Fashion Designers of America, and was one of the five American designers who participated in the history-making Versailles fashion show in Paris in 1973.

Dimitri (Piero). Menswear designer, 42 E. 57 St., New York, N.Y. 10022

Dimitri, a leading figure in American men's fashion, was born in Palermo, Sicily, on July 1, 1933 and apprenticed to a local tailor at 12. At 20 he entered the Sartotechnica Moda Maschile in Palermo and remained for two years, then started his own business. He became known throughout Italy and was made an honorary member of the Centro Studi Sartoriale.

In 1964 Dimitri came to America with his wife and four children, and in 1969 he became an American citizen. His custom-tailoring business has recently been expanded to include a ready-to-wear division.

In 1975 he was made a member of the Coty Menswear Fashion Hall of Fame, having received the Coty Menswear Award in 1973 and 1974. He is a member of the Council of Fashion Designers of America.

Esther Dorothy. Fur designer, Reiss & Fabrizio, 6 W. 57 St., New York, N.Y. 10019

One of the few women designers in the fur industry and well-known for having launched furs dyed in bright colors, Esther Dorothy was born in Russia and was brought as a child to Boston, Massachusetts. Before she was 20 she had her own custom fur business in Boston and later expanded her salons to other cities.

Her career began in 1940, and she received a Coty Special Award in 1948.

Vincent de Paul Draddy. See David Crystal, Inc.

Florence Eiseman. Children's fashion designer, Florence Eiseman, Inc., 301 N. Water St., Milwaukee, Wis. 53202

One of the few Middle Western designers of international note, Mrs. Eiseman was born September 27, 1899 in Minneapolis, Minnesota. She and her late husband, Lawrence H. Eiseman, founded their children's dress business in Milwaukee in 1945 and rapidly rose to leadership in that branch of the fashion industry.

Mrs. Eiseman won the Neiman–Marcus Award (1955) and the Swiss Fabrics Award (1956).

She is a member of the Council of Fashion Designers of America.

Luis Estevez (de Galvez). Dress and sportswear designer, 122 E. Seventh St., Los Angeles, Calif. 90014

One of the newsmaking American designers located in California, Luis Estevez was born in Havana, Cuba, on December 5, 1930, a descendant of the Spanish de Galvez family. Galveston, Texas was named for his ancestor Count Bernardo de Galvez.

Estevez was educated in Cuba and England and at the School of Architecture at the University of Havana. A summer job in the display department of a New York department store drew him toward fashion.

He went to Paris and apprenticed with Jean Patou, then set up his own ready-to-wear business in New York in 1955. His fashionable but seductive clothes, always with unusual necklines, brought him a Coty Award (1956) and the Sunshine Award of Florida the same year. He received the Chicago Gold Coast Award three times.

Since 1966 Estevez has lived and worked in California. In 1971 he designed a collection of fashions for the actress Eva Gabor, sold under her name. The project was later expanded with a separate division for Luis Estevez's own label.

David Evins. Shoe designer, 9 W. 57 St., New York, N.Y. 10019

David Evins, leader of shoe design in America, was born in London to a family of "highly unsuccessful artists." He was schooled abroad, then studied art at the Chicago University School of Design, and at Pratt Institute and the Art Students League of New York. While doing fashion illustration for Vogue, Harper's Bazaar, and other magazines, an assignment to sketch for a shoe trade publication focussed his interest on footwear.

He served with the U.S. Signal Corps through World War II and on his release worked as "ghost designer" for I. Miller until he founded his own company. He now designs shoes bearing the David Evins and other labels, including Hermes of Paris and Delman.

David Evins received a Coty Special Award in 1949 and the Neiman–Marcus Award in 1953.

He was one of the founders of the Council of Fashion Designers of America and is its treasurer and a member of the Board of Directors.

Anne Fogarty. Women's fashions designer, 45 E. 68 St., New York, N.Y. 10021

Born in Pittsburgh on February 2, 1926, Anne Fogarty studied acting, became a mannequin for couturiere Hattie Carnegie, and later a member of the Carnegie design staff.

She established her own firm in partnership with Leonard Sunshine and soon became known for her young, romantic approach to fashion. She helped launch the petticoat craze of the early 1950s, for which she received a Coty Award in 1951. The partnership was dissolved, and she now designs on a free-lance basis.

She is a member of the Board of Directors of the Council of Fashion Designers of America.

Lisa Fonssagrives (Mrs. Irving Penn). 201 E. 62 St., New York, N.Y. 10021

This designer of lingerie and sports clothes was born May 17, 1911, in Stockholm, Sweden. After studying in Stockholm, Berlin, and Paris, she came to New York as a fashion mannequin and was soon the best known and most imitated in America. She married *Vogue* fashion photographer Irving Penn and now designs special clothes for American specialty shops. The Penns' daughter, Mia Fonssagrives, was a well-known young designer of ready-to-wear in Paris and is now a sculptor in Los Angeles.

Elsie Frankfurt (Pollock). Maternity designer, Page Boy Maternity Co., 2033 Cedar Springs, Dallas, Tex. 75201

Elsie Frankfurt is president and designer of Page Boy maternity fashions. She owns the firm with her two sisters Edna Frankfurt Ravkind and Louise Frankfurt Gartner.

Elsie Frankfurt studied fashion design at Southern Methodist University and later took a degree in business administration.

The now-patented "secret" of the Page Boy maternity garment is a cutout over the abdomen with adjustable tapes to keep it in place.

Miss Frankfurt was the first woman to be made a member of the Young Presidents Organization. She won *Mademoiselle* magazine's Achievement Award in Business (1951).

Diane von Furstenberg. Designer–owner of Diane Furstenberg, Inc., 530 Seventh Ave., New York, N.Y. 10018

A successful socialite designer, Princess Diane von Furstenberg was born Diane Helfin on December 31, 1946, in Brussels, Belgium. She was educated in England, Spain, and at the University of Geneva, where she studied economics.

After her marriage in 1968 to Prince Egon von Furstenberg, of the Austrian branch of the noble von Furstenberg family, she started her dress business, manufacturing her designs in Italy.

The Furstenberg "look," a simple shirtdress made in clinging fabric with a provocatively open neckline, captured the mood of the early 1970s, combining chic and sex appeal with simplicity, lightness, and comfort.

In 1974 Diane von Furstenberg added jewelry and cosmetics to her dress business.

James Galanos. Galanos Originals, 2254 S. Sepulveda Dr., Los Angeles, Calif. 90064

Born James Gorgoliatos on September 20, 1929, of Greek parents in Philadelphia, Galanos left the local public school to study fashion design in New York. He sold original sketches to New York manufacturers, then worked on the staff of couturiere Hattie Carnegie.

In 1947 he went to Paris and trained on the staff of Robert Piguet.

In 1953 he returned to America and opened his own business in Los Angeles. His inventive and highly personal concept, not always in line with current trends, is expressed in the most skillful haute-couture craftsmanship, and his use of beading and embroidery is among the richest in modern fashion.

In 1954 Galanos won the Coty "Winnie", the Neiman–Marcus Award, and the Cotton Fashion Award. In 1956 he received the Coty Return Award and in 1958, the Filene Young Designer Award was given to him. In 1959 he won the NBC-TV "Today" Award as well as the Coty Hall of Fame.

He is a charter member of the Council of Fashion Designers of America and served on its Board of Directors.

Rudi Gernreich. Rudi Gernreich, Inc., 8460 Santa Monica Blvd., Los Angeles, Calif. 90069

America's leading avant-garde designer in the early 1960s, Rudi Gernreich was the first to use the principle of dancers' clothing such as leotards and tights in making the free, lithe body the modern fashion image. He introduced stretch knits and discarded linings and underclothing beneath his transparent clothes.

Born in Vienna on August 8, 1922, Gernreich came to the United States in 1938 and was naturalized in 1943 after attending Los Angeles City College and the Los Angeles Art Center School.

He danced with the Hermes Pan troupe in Hollywood films, working as a fabric salesman on the side. The dresses he designed to demonstrate the firm's material brought him to the attention of California manufacturers.

In 1960 he formed his own company and by 1965, via the publicity given his off-beat fashions, particularly the topless bathing suit, he was the best-known American designer in the world. He won the Sports Illustrated Award (1956), three Coty Awards (1963, 1966, and the Hall of Fame 1967), and the London Sunday Times Award (1965).

At present Rudi Gernreich designs furniture and housewares as well as clothes in his own studio.

Goldworm, Inc. New York knitwear manufacturers, 1410 Broadway, New York, N.Y. 10018

Goldworm, Inc., among the best-known American knitwear firms, was founded in 1928 by Gertrude Goldworm, whose son Robert is now its head.

Robert Goldworm studied business management at New York University and served in the U.S. Air Force in World War II.

In 1956 the mother-and-son affiliation brought Goldworm a Coty Award. In 1959 Robert Goldworm received the Italian government's Star of Solidarity and in 1968 the Premio Mercurio d'Orco.

Bill Haire. Henry Friedricks and Co., 205 W. 39 St., New York, N.Y. 10019

Bill Haire, a designer in the American sportswear tradition with an infusion of romantic and ethnic elements, is a native New Yorker whose entire life seems to have been angled toward his aim to design clothes.

He attended the High School of Art and Design and won a scholarship to the Fashion Institute of Technology, graduating in 1955.

In 1956 he married his classmate in both high school and F.I.T., Hazel Keleher, and the two have had parallel careers ever since.

In 1959, after three years in which the Haires toured the world, Bill Haire joined Victoria Royal to design evening dresses. He remained 14 years, leaving in 1973 to codesign for Friedricks with his wife. In 1975, however, she returned to free-lance designing and he continued at Friedricks as its sole designer.

Halston (Roy Halston Frowick). Couturier and ready-to-wear designer, 33 E. 68 St., New York, N.Y. 10021; and 550 Seventh Ave., New York, N.Y. 10018

Halston, famous worldwide for establishing the "rich uniform" of the 1970s, was born April 23, 1932 in Des Moines, Iowa, and spent his early youth in Evansville, Indiana.

He attended Indiana University, then studied art and costume at the Chicago Art Institute. As a student he designed and made hats for the clients of a friend's beauty salon.

Lilly Dache brought Halston to New York in 1958 to design and manage her wholesale hat division. In 1959 he left Dache to become Bergdorf Goodman's first "name" milliner.

In 1962, Halston won a Special Coty Award for his innovations in millinery, including the world-famous "pillbox" worn by Mrs. Jacqueline Kennedy.

In 1966 Bergdorf Goodman set up a special department for Halston's first venture as a designer of clothes. In 1968 Halston opened his own couture house for private clients and soon opened a wholesale division. In 1975 he added menswear and perfume to his design activities.

He won the Coty "Winnie" in 1971 for "bringing to fashion a Method Actor's ability to project himself into the multiroles of the contemporary wealthy woman." The following year he received the Coty Return Award, and in 1974 joined the Coty Hall of Fame.

In 1973 Halston became part of the Norton Simon organization.

Halston was one of the five American designers who participated in the history-making Versailles fashion show in Paris in 1973.

He is a member of the Council of Fashion Designers of America.

Cathy Hardwick (Kashina Shura). Young fashions designer, Cathy Hardwick 'n' Friends, 1411 Broadway, New York, N.Y. 10018

Kashina Shura, professionally known as Cathy Hardwick, was born December 30, 1937, in Seoul, Korea, a direct descendant, on her mother's side, of Queen Min, the last monarch of Korea.

At 21 she came to San Francisco and in 1959 opened a boutique there. Although untrained as a designer, she created all her own stock and had a successful five years.

In 1974 she organized her own firm, Cathy Hardwick 'n' Friends, in New York where her flair for combining Orientalia with modern fashion trends made her a leader of the young individualistic school of American fashions.

In 1975 she was nominated for a Coty Award.

Sharon Harris. Ready-to-wear designer, Robert Walters, Inc., 4118 S. Clinton, Chicago, Ill. 60616

Fashion editor turned designer, Sharon Harris was born October 4, 1935, in Baltimore, Maryland, and brought up in rural West Virginia. She received a Master's Degree in Political Science at West Virginia University and took postgraduate work at the University of Heidelberg, Germany, and the Sorbonne in Paris. She opened her own dress business in 1965 in Chicago and in 1972 joined Robert Walters.

She received the Chicago Gold Coast Award (1970).

Elizabeth Hawes. See Hall of Fame

Stan Herman. Designer in various fashion fields, Stan Herman Studios, 232 Madison Ave., New York, N.Y. 10016

Stan Herman, one of the designers who became known during the Youth Rebellion of the 1960s, was born in New York City on September 17, 1932. He studied applied arts at the University of Cincinnati Design School and was also a successful "stand-up comedian" in nightclubs before he entered the fashion business. After designing dresses and sports clothes for New York manufacturers, he formed his own design organization, licensing his name in several areas of fashion. He now designs dresses and at-home clothes under his own label and makes lingerie and loungewear for Van Raalte.

In 1965 and again in 1969, Stan Herman received the Coty Award for his fashion-conscious young clothes at a moderate price. In 1974 he received a Coty Special Award for lingerie and loungewear design.

He is a member of the Council of Fashion Designers of America and serves as a guest critic at the Parsons School of Design and as a part-time teacher at design schools in Israel.

Carol Horn. Carol Horn's Habitat, 1411 Broadway, New York, N.Y. 10018

After numerous designing assignments, Carol Horn now has her own company.

Born in New York on June 12, 1936, Carol was educated at Boston and Columbia Universities. Her entry into fashion came as a retail stylist, and she found her first designing job with Bryant 9, a junior sportswear firm. In 1966 she joined Benson and Partners and remained there four years. She was then affiliated with Malcolm Starr International and formed her own organization in 1974.

Carol Horn's Habitat is built around the designer's belief in ethnic influences used in modern but individualistic clothes. In 1975 Carol Horn won the national vote among the three nominees for the Coty American Fashion Critics' Award.

Chuck (Charles) Howard. Sportswear, menswear, and accessories designer, Anne Klein Studio, 205 W. 39 St., New York, N.Y. 10018

Chuck Howard heads the staff of the Anne Klein Studio, established by the late designer Anne Klein and her husband M. N. (Chip) Rubinstein in 1968 as a modern American "Bauhaus" operation, designing in numerous areas of fashion and industry.

The activities under the aegis of Howard and his associate designer Peter Wrigley include Penfold women's active sports clothes, Mark of the Lion menswear, and designs for firms producing costume jewelry, leather accessories, shoes, and home furnishings.

Born March 4, 1927, in Cochran, Georgia, Howard was educated in the South. He started as a sketcher at David Crystal, worked with Bill Blass for two years, six years with Anne Klein, and then designed for Townley before rejoining the Anne Klein Studio in 1974.

In 1975 Howard and Wrigley received the Coty Menswear Fashion Award by a national ballot.

Irene (Gibbons) (1907–1962)

One of the leading film designers of the great days of the Hollywood studios, Irene was also a successful designer of ready-to-wear in the 1950s, the heyday of the Irene and the Adrian suits.

Born in Montana and a graduate of the University of California, Irene opened a small dress shop and then designed the custom collections of Bullock's Wilshire. Her personal stamp of drama coupled with cultivated restraint attracted the more elegant of the movie stars, and she was asked to follow Adrian as designer for Metro-Goldwyn-Mayer when Adrian left to form his own wholesale business.

She was married for many years to the distinguished film set designer Cedric Gibbons.

She died in 1962, having established an organization that continued some years afterward on the luster of her name.

Ishio (Kawamura). Ishio Fashions, Inc., 920 N. Michigan Ave., Chicago, Ill. 60611

One of several Japanese designers bent on developing Chicago as a fashion market, Ishio Kawamura was born in Tokyo on November 28, 1943. He attended Kuazawa Fashion School and was employed by a Japanese ready-to-wear manufacturer before coming to Chicago and opening his own firm. He received the Chicago Gold Coast Award in 1971.

Charles James. Dress designer (retired), Chelsea Hotel, 222 W. 23 St., New York, N.Y. 10011

This British–American dress designer worked from 1928 until the early 1960s, but is now inactive.

A designer's designer, generally regarded as one of the most gifted of the 20th century, Charles James' unusual and daring cuts and his interpretation of Edwardian elegance in somewhat more contemporary terms influenced many other designers.

He was born in Cambersley, England, and spent his early childhood in England where his father was an officer at the Royal Military College. The family subsequently moved to Chicago. He began designing hats in Chicago, then opened couture establishments in London, and later Paris. Lack of administrative control brought failure. James also made several unsuccessful attempts to design American ready-to-wear.

One of his private clients, the late Millicent Rogers, bequeathed her large collection of James clothes to the Brooklyn Museum. He is also represented in the costume collections of the Smithsonian Institution, Washington, D.C.; The Victoria and Albert Museum, London; and the Costume Institute of the Metropolitan Museum of Art, New York. In 1950 he received the Coty Award.

Mr. John (John Pico John). Milliner and fashion designer, Mr. John, Inc., 24 W. 57 St., New York, N.Y. 10019

This long-time personality and designer of hats and clothes was born John Pico John on March 14, 1906, in Munich, Germany. His mother was a well-known milliner there.

Mr. John attended the Sorbonne and the Ecole des Beaux Arts in Paris, then in 1926 came to New York as the milliner to the dressmaking house of Madame Laurel. Later he and an associate, Fred Fredericks, formed the millinery firm of John Fredericks. In 1943 he received a Coty Award for his dramatic and luxurious hats.

Betsey Johnson. 253 Church St., New York, N.Y. 10013

One of the young American designers with their roots in the quaint and sweetly sentimental looks of the Western frontier, Betsey Johnson was one of the sensations of the late 1960s with her pictorially decorated knits and quilted cottons.

Born on August 10, 1942, in Wethersfield, Connecticut, Betsey Johnson graduated magna cum laude and Phi Beta Kappa from Syracuse University, where she majored in fine arts. She was invited to New York as guest editor by *Mademoiselle* magazine, and in 1965 she began designing for Paraphernalia, where her fashions attracted such personalities as Julie Christie, Mrs. Jacqueline Kennedy Onassis, Brigitte Bardot, Françoise Hardy, and Twiggy. In 1968 she helped to open the New York boutique Betsey, Bunky and Nini, and two years later linked up with Alley Cat, a volume-priced junior ready-to-wear firm, where her vervy concept brought her a Coty Award (1971).

In 1975 she left Alley Cat to design in several wholesale fields: dresses for Tric-Trac, Ltd., maternity clothes for Jeanette, children's clothes for Betsey Johnson's Kids, and designer patterns for Butterick.

Victor Joris. Design director of Cuddlecoat, Inc., 500 Seventh Ave., New York, N.Y. 10018

Born in Shreveport, Louisiana, on April 25, 1929, Victor Joris was educated there and came to New York to study at the Traphagen School. He won a scholarship to l'Ecole de la Chambre Syndicale in Paris, and later sold fashion sketches to the French haute couture.

His first job on Seventh Avenue was the one he has today, designer for Cuddlecoat. His tailored designs are often lavished with fur.

Victor Joris was among the first to advocate pantsuits (1962) and also the maxi-coat (1965). He received the Coty American Fashion Critics' Award twice, in 1965 and 1969, and is a member of the Council of Fashion Designers of America.

Mabel Julianelli. Shoe designer, c/o Andrew Geller, 1370 Ave. of the Americas, New York, N.Y. 10019

Born in New York on September 7, 1919, Mrs. Julianelli and her late husband Charles founded their business in 1939. Since 1940 she has designed shoe collections with the Julianelli label for various American manufacturers. She and her husband received a Coty Special Award in

1950. She was given a grant by the Rockefeller Foundation to help develop a shoe industry in India.

Bill Kaiserman. Menswear designer, Rafael Fashions, Ltd., 29 W. 56 St., New York, N.Y. 10019

Bill Kaiserman, one of the leaders in the casual menswear field, was born September 8, 1942, in Brooklyn, New York, in a family known for designing fabric and furniture.

He studied acting and had roles in off-Broadway plays, where he realized he enjoyed the clothes as much as the parts he played. After working as a haberdashery salesman he designed men's hats, the success of which led to designing sportswear under the Rafael label.

In 1974 Kaiserman received the Coty Menswear Award and its Return Award in 1975.

Larry Kane. Free-lance menswear designer, 743 Fifth Ave., New York, N.Y. 10022

Larry Kane, credited with transferring the "separates" concept from women's fashion to menswear, was born in New York City on January 24, 1930. He was a child actor, theatrical agent, and associate of producer Paul Gregory in one-man "evenings" built around Charles Boyer, Hume Cronyn, Charles Laughton, Agnes Moorehead, Tyrone Power, and Jessica Tandy.

After serving in the Korean war, Kane became a stylist of menswear fabrics, then designed masculine sportswear for Stanley Blacker before organizing the Raffles Wear firm in June of 1969. In 1974 he opened his own design studio.

In 1971 he received the Coty Menswear Fashion Award. He is a member of the Council of Fashion Designers of America.

Donna Karan (Mrs. Mark Karan). Anne Klein and Company, 205 W. 39 St., New York, N.Y. 10018

This young designer achieved overnight stardom when Anne Klein, the noted sportswear separates designer who had already named her as codesigner, died suddenly.

Donna Karan was 26 at that time. She was born Donna Faske on October 2, 1948, in Forest Hills, New York, the daughter of a fashion model and a New York haberdasher. She studied for two years at the Parsons School of Design in New York City, but after working during the summer on Anne Klein's staff, decided not to continue school. After a brief hiatus designing for another firm, she returned to Anne Klein and Company in 1968. From 1971 until Anne Klein's death in 1974, Donna Karan was her codesigner.

She is married to Mark Karan, a menswear manufacturer, and has a daughter.

Kasper (Herbert Kasper). Dress and sportswear designer, Joan Leslie, Inc., and J.L. Sport Inc., 530 Seventh Ave., New York, N.Y. 10018

Known as a highly versatile designer of fashionable clothes at a moderate price, Herbert Kasper was born in New York City and attended New York University before serving with the Occupation Forces overseas. He designed costumes for Army shows and on his return studied fashion design at the Parsons School of Design and at l'Ecole de la Chambre Syndicale in Paris. While there he worked for Jacques Fath and Marcel Rochas.

After designing for various Seventh Avenue firms, Kasper joined Joan Leslie, a division of Leslie Fay, Inc., in 1953. He now designs for an added division, J.L. Sport.

In 1955 Kasper won the Coty Award and received the Coty Return Award in 1970.

He is a member of the Council of Fashion Designers of America and a guest critic at Parsons School of Design in New York.

Kenneth (Battelle). Hairdresser, 19 E. 54 St., New York, N.Y. 10022

Kenneth, America's first world-renowned hair stylist, was born in Syracuse, New York, and worked locally as a hairdresser until he joined the staff of Lilly Dache when she opened a beauty salon as an adjunct to her New York millinery business.

Kenneth's creation of the full-topped, shoulder-length hairdo for fashionable women including the then First Lady Jacqueline Kennedy established the fashionable coiffure of the 1960s. In 1963 Kenneth opened his own establishment and is now also president of Kenneth Beauty Products, Inc.

In 1961 Kenneth won a Coty Award for making the coiffure a keystone of modern fashion. On several world tours he designed coiffures for the Empress Farah Diba of Iran, Queen Sirikit of Thailand, and other international personalities.

Omar (Alexander) Kiam. *See* Hall of Fame

Barry Kieselstein (Cord). Jewelry designer, 67 Park Ave., New York, N.Y. 10016

One of the young and potent group of American jewelry designers who are also talented sculptors, Barry Kieselstein Cord was born November 6, 1943, in New York. His father was a top-level jewelry designer, having worked for Faberge and later for Tiffany.

He graduated from the Parsons School of Design, then worked as art director for an advertising company. His urge to sculpt, however, led him to design with silver as his medium. He now sells his signed pieces in gold or silver to jewelers across America and to private clients.

His designs are characterized by bold smooth forms with flowing surfaces of great sheen and tactile quality.

Kimberly. Women's knitwear manufacturers, 1410 Broadway, New York, N.Y. 10018

This American knitwear firm, with husband and wife team Jack and Helen Lazar at the head, pioneered in the development of special yarns, full-fashioned shapings, and knits with a soft dressmaker feeling instead of the usual tailored lines.

Jack Lazar, Kimberly's founder, was born in New Jersey, November 18, 1910, of Alsatian ancestry. At 15, he left school to work in a knitting mill.

After serving in the Pacific in World War II, he founded Kimberly in September 1946 and the same year married Helen Bando, the girl he'd left behind.

In 1962 Jack Lazar was named by President Kennedy one of the 100 leaders of American industry. He is on the advisory boards of the Manufacturers Hanover Trust Company, and the American Arbitration Association, a fellow of Brandeis University, and a donor of its International Library for Foreign Students.

In October, 1972, Kimberly became part of General Mills but retained its family management.

Jack and Helen Lazar are members of the Council of Fashion Designers of America.

Alexis Kirk (Vemian). Costume jewelry designer, 393 Fifth Ave., New York, N.Y. 10018

Alexis Kirk, leading American jewelry designer, has a heritage of art that traces back many generations to the Middle East. One of his Armenian ancestors with the family name of Vemian was a jeweler to the Turkish court and some of his pieces are in the Topkapi Museum in Istanbul. His grandfather was one of the chief artists for Lalique Glass in Paris.

Born Alexis Kirk Vemian in Los Angeles, where his father was an artist with Walt Disney, Kirk came East as a child and grew up in Belmont, Massachusetts.

He studied fine arts at Harvard, the Rhode Island School of Design, and the Boston Museum of Fine Arts school. In Newport, Rhode Island, he set up his first business, an art shop called "Derring-Do."

He began designing jewelry in the mid-sixties, when his understanding of Oriental amulets, occult symbols, and bold but intricate primitive metalwork led the ethnic trend. He won two Swarovski awards, given by the Austrian costume jewelry suppliers, in 1969 and 1970 and a Coty Award in 1970.

Anne Klein (1923–1974)

This international fashion trend-setter was the leader in the move to infuse the casual sportswear feeling into fashion for all hours of the day, and the first to stress the modern idea of a wardrobe composed of interchangeable separate units.

Born August 3, 1923, in Brooklyn, New York, she received a high school scholarship to study fashion designing but gave it up to do freelance fashion sketching. From her first job she was an innovator, changing the firm's production from matronly clothes to a new concept of the "young junior" type, which established a new category of sizing in ready-to-wear.

She helped to form another firm, Junior Sophisticates, and again rewrote wholesale standards by shifting the meaning of "junior fashion" from fussy girlishness to a sleek, fresh, long-legged simplicity.

In 1963 she married Matthew Rubinstein and with him and two other partners, Gunther Oppenheim and Sanford Smith, established Anne Klein and Company and the Anne Klein Studio to encourage and launch other fashion talents. In 1973 both organizations became part of the Takihyo Company, Ltd., of Japan, to produce Anne Klein products internationally.

Anne Klein was made a member of the Coty Awards Hall of Fame in 1971, having won twice before, in 1955 and 1969. She was the only designer to have received the Neiman–Marcus Award twice (1959 and 1969), and also received the National Cotton Award (1964) and the Mademoiselle Merit Award (1954).

In 1973 she was one of the five American designers in the historic Versailles fashion show in Paris.

Anne Klein was a charter member of the Council of Fashion Designers of America.

She died March 19, 1974, in New York.

Calvin Klein. Sportswear designer, Calvin Klein, Inc., 205 W. 39 St., New York, N.Y. 10018

Calvin Klein, one of the most sensational successes of American fashion's recent history, was born November 19, 1942, in New York. After graduating from the Fashion Institute of Technology in 1962, he designed for several New York coat and suit houses. Five years later, he and his childhood friend Barry Schwartz teamed up in their own business,

Calvin Klein, Inc., and soon became a leading resource on Seventh Avenue for young and snappishly tailored sport clothes.

Calvin Klein received a Coty Award in 1973 as a "leader of the contemporary American classic fashion spirit," followed in 1974 by the Coty Return Award and in 1975 he was placed in the Coty Awards Hall of Fame.

He is a member of the Council of Fashion Designers of America, and serves as guest critic at the Parsons School of Design.

Don Kline. Millinery designer, 37 W. 39 St., New York, N.Y. 10018

Don Kline, the first American in recent years to dedicate his talents to reviving high fashion hats, was born in Vandergrift, Pennsylvania.

He attended the Fashion Institute of Technology, graduating in 1969. He joined the staff of Emme, the New York milliner, and tried his hand at sportswear before returning to his first love, millinery, with a small collection of hats in the 1920s mood which he sold one by one to stores and loaned to fashion magazines.

Though his business remains select and his hats have a custom-made quality, they are inexpensive and Kline's influence on fashion has been very pronounced.

In 1973 he won a Coty Special award.

John Kloss. Dress, lingerie, and loungewear designer, John Kloss Inc., 550 Seventh Ave., New York, N.Y. 10018

John Kloss, a free-lance designer who also has his own dress business, was born June 13, 1937, in Detroit, Michigan. He studied architecture at Cass Technical School there and fashion design at the Traphagen School in New York. He worked briefly in Paris for the American-born couturier Bob Bugnand. In 1963 he returned to New York and opened a custom dressmaking business there, soon adding a studio where he designed collections for wholesale manufacturers. Bendel's Studio, attached to the New York store Henri Bendel, arranged to manufacture his designs for national distribution and helped to develop a public for his work.

His clothes, formed of abstract shapes of vivid colors, inspired by abstract paintings, were a prompt success, as was his graceful and seductive lingerie, designed for Cira.

In 1971 and again in 1974 the Cira under-fashions brought John Kloss a Coty Special Award. In 1973 he became one of the Kreisler Group of young designers under the management of the young fashion entrepreneur, Stuart Kreisler. His work now includes his own dress collection and designing, under license, foundation garments, lingerie, loungewear, hosiery, tennis clothes, and home-sewing patterns.

Nancy Knox. Men's leather accessories designer, Intercuerros, 488 Madison Ave., New York, N.Y. 10022

Nancy Knox of Intercuerros, designer of men's fashion accessories, was born April 16, 1923, in North Hollywood, California. She began her fashion career as assistant shoe stylist to Geraldine Stutz at I. Miller in New York, and then became designer for an English shoe firm and in 1963 her firm Renegades became a part of the Genesco shoe affiliates. She resigned in 1972 to design both shoes and other leather accessories with Intercuerros.

She won two Coty Special Awards: in 1971 for men's shoes and in 1975 for her leather accessories for men.

Ronald Kolodzie. Dress designer, Concept VII, 530 Seventh Ave., New York, N.Y. 10018

Ronald Kolodzie, designer of flowing, easy clothes with a high level of sophistication at realistic prices, entered the New York wholesale field as a name designer in 1971 but made his first emphatic hit in 1974.

Born on a ranch near San Antonio, Texas, of Polish parentage, he studied at the Parsons School of Design in New York. After working as assistant to furrier Georges Kaplan and later with dress designer Oscar de la Renta, he designed for Genesis, an avant-garde New York boutique.

He joined forces with young manufacturer Bob Miller in 1971 in their own firm Concept VII.

He is a member of the Council of Fashion Designers of America.

Kenneth Jay Lane. Costume jewelry designer, 115 E. 38 St., New York, N.Y. 10016

Born in Detroit, Michigan, on April 22, 1932, Kenneth Lane studied art at the University of Michigan and the Rhode Island School of Design. He came to New York in 1954 to work on the promotion staff of *Vogue*. In that capacity he met French shoe designer Roger Vivier who recommended Lane as his assistant on a designing assignment for Delman Shoes in America. Later he became Vivier's associate in the latter's Christian Dior shoe collections in America.

In 1963, while still designing shoes, he made some experimental high-fashion jewelry in a new medium, plastic studded with sequins. Within a year his part-time venture had become a full-time business.

His "real jewelry in unreal materials" won for Kenneth Lane a Special Coty Award in 1966.

In 1969, Kenneth Jay Lane, Inc., became part of the Kenton Corporation but Lane repurchased the business in 1972. There are Kenneth Lane boutiques in Paris and London.

He is a member of the Council of Fashion Designers of America.

Hubert Latimer. Dress designer, 300 E. 59 St., New York, N.Y. 10022

A young designer who follows the "high tradition" of perfectionism in ready-to-wear, Hubert Latimer was born in Atlanta, Georgia, and brought up in Arizona. He attended the Wolf School of Design in Los Angeles and worked for Charles Cooper and Irene of California. The American ready-to-wear division of Christian Dior brought him to New York to design there for two years.

Latimer joined Mollie Parnis as designer of her couture collections in 1972 and resigned in 1974 to form his own business.

He is a member of the Council of Fashion Designers of America.

Ralph Lauren. 40 W. 55 St., New York, N.Y. 10019

One of the American leaders of ready-to-wear men's clothing, Ralph Lauren was born in New York on October 14, 1939, and educated at New York's City College. He worked as a salesman at Brooks Brothers in New York, and became assistant buyer on the staff of a retail buying office while attending City College at night.

In 1967, Beau Brummell Neckwear established a division called Polo with Lauren as its designer. The name symbolized Lauren's concept of an elegant, understated gentlemanly look mingling tweediness with a bit of American panache. He reintroduced the wide necktie and boldly patterned shirt, and has made consistent reference to the fashions of the Scott Fitzgerald era. In 1974 he achieved world renown as the designer of men's fashions for the film *The Great Gatsby*, from that Fitzgerald novella.

In 1968 he established Polo as a separate company making head-to-toe men's wear, including shoes and luggage. He added women's tailored clothes in 1972, under the Ralph Lauren label as a division of the Kreisler Group of ready-to-wear designers.

Lauren has won two Coty Awards, the Coty Menswear Award in 1970 and again in 1973, and the Coty "Winnie" for his women's fashions in 1974. He received the American Printed Fabrics Award in 1972. He is a member of the Council of Fashion Designers of America.

Helen Lee (Caldwell). Children's clothes designer, Designs by Helen Lee, Inc., 1375 Broadway, New York, N.Y. 10018

Helen Lee is unique in the realm of children's fashions. She designs for both girls and boys, both expensive and mass-produced clothing, and clothes for infants, youngsters, and teenagers. She is responsible for the largest single volume of children's clothing in the world, the "Winnie the Pooh" collections for Sears Roebuck and Company, and is designer and consultant for numerous large manufacturers of children's wear.

Born in Knoxville, Tennessee, she studied at the University of Tennessee, and in New York at the Traphagen School of Art and the Art Students League.

After designing for several children's wear manufacturers and a partnership in Alyssa, children's dress manufacturers, she formed her own company to create prototype collections for manufacturers chosen by Sears.

She won the Coty American Fashion Critics' Award in 1953, the Nieman-Marcus Award (1958) and the Ethel Traphagen Award (1970). She is a charter member of the Council of Fashion Designers of America.

Judith Leiber. Accessory designer, Judith Leiber, Inc., 14 E. 32 St., New York, N.Y. 10016

This leading American designer of fine handbags is one of the few "name" designers remaining in that high luxury field anywhere in the world. Judith Leiber was born in Budapest, Hungary, on January 11, 1921 and trained in the leathercrafts there. She was made a member of the Hungarian Guild of Handbag Producers in 1939. Following marriage to the well-known artist Gerson Leiber, they came to the United States as war refugees. She designed handbags for Nettie Rosenstein (1947–1960) and briefly for Richard Koret before establishing her own business in 1961.

She received a Coty Special Award in 1973 for her contribution to handbag fashion.

Tina Leser. Dress designer, Tina Leser, Inc., 550 Seventh Ave., New York, N.Y. 10018

Born Tina Shillard Smith on December 16, 1911, in Philadelphia, Tina Leser spent her childhood in the tropics with her wealthy parents. She studied art at the Philadelphia Academy of Arts and the Sorbonne in Paris and in 1935 married and went to live in Honolulu, where she opened a dress shop and remained seven years. Her original beachwear based on the Philippine sarong and Hawaiian native costume made a sensation, but her career there ended with Pearl Harbor, and she returned to America to become a wholesale designer for various firms before establishing her own organization in 1969.

Now married to James Howley, her business associate, Tina Leser continues to design in unique Oriental silks, particularly Indian, and is one of the most informed and romantic interpreters of ethnic-inspired fashion.

She won a Coty Award in 1945. She holds a degree of Doctor of Fine Arts from the Moore Institute of Fine Arts.

Levi-Strauss. Producers of Levi's, 98 Battery St., San Francisco, Calif. 94111

In the near century of their existence, Levi's by Levi-Strauss have become both a worldwide uniform and a word in the dictionary. The Levi look, perhaps more than any other fashion, helped to erase class distinction from modern dress.

Mr. Levi Strauss, a fabric salesman, came to San Francisco during the 1850 Gold Rush to sell tents to the prospectors. Finding that there was a greater shortage of clothing than of shelter, he hired a seamstress and turned part of his stock of tent canvas into work pants. Later he met the demand for Levi's with whatever heavy cotton he could find. The famous metal rivets to prevent tears at stress points in work clothes, now a Levi-Strauss patented trademark, were added in 1873.

As an outgrowth of the Youth Revolution of the 1960s, Levi's invaded every social level and every point on the globe. The company now produces Levi's for men, women, and children and employs designers in many countries for fashion variations. In 1971 Levi-Strauss received a Coty Special Award.

The firm remains under the control of the Strauss family through nephews of the founder, who was a bachelor.

Herbert Levine and Beth Levine. Shoe designers, 161 Ave. of the Americas, New York, N.Y. 10013

An influential husband-and-wife designer–producer team from 1949, until their semi-retirement in 1975, the Levines are credited with contributing in a major way to the fashion for boots through their innovations in stretch materials, and in the feeling of light elegance they achieve in that traditionally heavy-duty article. Conversely, they have been responsible for the introduction of some of the thinnest, wispiest of sandal fashions. For both trends they received Coty Awards in 1967 and in 1973. They won the Neiman–Marcus Award in 1953.

Mr. and Mrs. Levine are members of the Council of Fashion Designers of America.

Jean Louis (Berthault). Fashion and film costume designer, Jean Louis, Inc., 2020 Stoner Ave., West Los Angeles, Calif. 90025

Designer of rich and ultrafeminine clothes for film stars, private clients, and his own luxury ready-to-wear business, Jean Louis was born in 1907 in Paris and trained in ateliers of the couturier Drecoll there. He came to America in 1936 to design for Hattie Carnegie. There, with Claire McCardell and Norman Norell, Jean Louis formed a triumvirate of soon-to-be famous designers.

In 1937 Louis made the first design for the "little Carnegie suit," one of the most widespread American fashion successes, worn by smart internationals such as the Duchess of Windsor and Gertrude Lawrence.

When Louis left Hattie Carnegie (1943) to design for Columbia Pictures in Hollywood, Miss Carnegie brought legal action against the studio's chief executive Harry Cohn for "stealing" her designer.

Jean Louis clothes have been worn in films by Julie Andrews, Doris Day, Marlene Dietrich (whose concert clothes he continues to design), Rita Hayworth, Katharine Hepburn, Marilyn Monroe, and Loretta Young.

In 1956 he won the Hollywood Oscar for the costumes for *The Solid Gold Cadillac*. In all, he has had 22 Academy Award nominations.

Luba (Rudenko Marks). Coat and sportswear designer, Luba Designs, Inc., 512 Seventh Ave., New York, N.Y. 10018

Born in Paris of Russian parents, Luba is known in America for young and dramatic tailored clothes at moderate prices.

Her early career was as a dancer. At 12, she was the youngest member of the Ballet Russe de Monte Carlo and the youngest soloist in its history. She later danced in Broadway productions such as *Annie Get Your Gun* while taking art courses at Columbia University and at the Art Students League. In 1959 she founded her own wholesale firm and in 1968 received a Coty Award.

She is a member of the Council of Fashion Designers of America.

Tzaims Luksus. Fabric designer, 18 Wallcomsac Rd., Bennington, Vt. 05201

This influential textile designer of the 1960s was born in Chicago on January 1, 1932. In 1964 Luksus and his wife, Miriam Fredenthal, his former textile design teacher at the Philadelphia Museum College of Art, bought an abandoned weaving and printing mill in Bennington, Vermont, and began producing handwoven wools and printed chiffons of arresting beauty. In 1965 he received both a Coty Award and the Neiman–Marcus Award for his bold contemporary designs that also conveyed great grace and softness.

In 1968 Luksus stated that he was tired of prints ("I am only copying myself") and briefly became a dress designer, backed by Rebekah Harkness, the wealthy art patron. He now lives and designs on special assignment in a studio in Bennington, Vermont.

Claire McCardell. See Hall of Fame

Marie McCarthy. Dress designer, Lew Prince of Aldrich, Inc., 530 Seventh Ave., New York, N.Y. 10018

Born in Boston and convent-educated, Marie McCarthy was a dress buyer in Boston before joining Larry Aldrich, Inc., as designer in 1943. She remained with the firm when Larry Aldrich retired and sold it to his former sales director, Lew Prince.

Miss McCarthy designs in the contemporary fashion spirit, but her clothes are always realistic and becoming to a wide variety of women.

She is a member of the Council of Fashion Designers of America.

Bob Mackie. See Ray Aghayan/Bob Mackie

Mainbocher. See Hall of Fame

Vera (Huppé) Maxwell. Sportswear designer, Vera Maxwell, Inc., 530 Seventh Ave., New York, N.Y. 10018

Born April 22, 1904, in New York of Viennese parentage, Vera Maxwell trained as a dancer and at 16 joined the Metropolitan Opera corps de ballet. She became interested in designing while working as a part-time model. She designed riding habits and ski clothes, then joined Adler and Adler, Inc. to design tailored day clothes. Her first success was a classic riding jacket revamped for street wear and combined with a grey flannel skirt.

She established her own business in 1946 and has since been both designer and chief executive.

Mrs. Maxwell belongs to the international social circle and is the frequent guest of Monaco's Princess Grace and Prince Rainier.

Among her honors are a Coty Special Award (1951), Neiman–Marcus Award (1955), and a one-man show of her fashions at the Smithsonian Institution in Washington, D.C. (1971).

Mr. Pants, Inc. 550 Seventh Ave., New York, N.Y. 10018

This sportswear firm, operated by husband-and-wife team George and Lynn Stuart, specializes in women's pants and tops. Lynn Stuart also designs menswear and furs for other companies.

Mrs. Stuart studied at the Tobe–Coburn School for Fashion Careers and joined Mr. Pants in 1955.

She was the first designer to receive the Mehitabel Award (1971) given by the Tobe–Coburn School and won the McCall's Magazine Sportswear Award the same year.

Monte-Sano and Pruzan. American coat and suit firm (1924–1969)

Formed in 1924 when Vincent Monte-Sano, Sr. and Max Pruzan became partners, Monte-Sano and Pruzan became one of the leaders in American tailored fashion for the following two decades. They received a Coty Award (1946) and the Neiman–Marcus Award (1952).

The firm dissolved in 1969. Vincent Monte-Sano, Jr., son of the family and Monte-Sano and Pruzan's executive in its later years, now designs rainwear and serves as director of the New York Couture Business Council.

John Moore. Fashion designer (retired), Alice, Tex. 78332

Chiefly rememberd as the designer of Mrs. Lyndon B. Johnson's inaugural gown, John Moore was born in Wilson, Oklahoma, but brought up in Texas. He studied at the Parsons School of Design and was sponsored as a creative designer by that school's leading guest critic, Norman Norell. He worked for Talmack, Inc., where he won a Coty Award (1953), then established his own firm in 1963. In 1970 he closed his business and became designer for a moderate-priced Seventh Avenue house, but retired the next year.

Martin Munkacsi. See Hall of Fame

Morton Myles. Dress designer, Billy Marks, Ltd., 1400 Broadway, New York, N.Y. 10018

Born in New York on June 11, 1929, where his family had been accountants for generations, Myles studied at New York University and the Fashion Institute of Technology in New York, graduating with honors in 1950. He attended the Chambre Syndicale school in Paris and apprenticed at Jacques Fath.

Known for chic dresses at a modest price, Myles has worked for various Seventh Avenue firms and now designs under the label Morton Myles for Billy Marks.

Leo Narducci. Dress designer, The Midtown Farmhouse, 530 Seventh Ave., New York, N.Y. 10018

Born in Boston in a family of clothing contractors, Narducci enrolled in business administration at Boston University, but managed to detour into an art course. After graduating from the Rhode Island School of Design he came to New York and became chief designer of Loomtogs, a large sportswear house, within weeks after being engaged as an assistant designer. On the day he joined a new firm, Guy D., he was informed of winning a Coty Award (1965).

In 1971 he established his own house, specializing in soft clothes with casual outlines and elegant materials.

He is a guest critic for Parsons School of Design and a member of the Council of Fashion Designers of America.

Condé Nast. See Hall of Fame

Albert Nipon and Pearl Nipon. Designers–manufacturers, 530 Seventh Ave., New York, N.Y. 10018

This husband-and-wife business, formed in 1972 by a couple who had already built a highly profitable maternity wear company, became one of the major American fashion success stories of the 1970s.

Both born in Philadelphia, still resident there and the owners of factories in that city, Pearl and Al Nipon were married in 1953. Pearl was already the owner of a local shop selling maternity clothes with emphasis on prettiness. The Nipons decided to sell their product nationally, and it found acceptance.

In 1971 they sold the maternity business and Mrs. Nipon planned to retire. On request from a New York store, however, she and her staff of designers made a collection of 10 dresses for a special promotion. The response was so phenomenal that the firm of Albert Nipon was the logical result.

Nipon clothes, characterized by scrupulously high quality fabrics and dainty detailing such as the signature "Nipon tuck" (rows of fine pin tucking) are notably moderate in price.

In 1975 a separate division, Albert Nipon Everywear, was added to produce knitwear and other clothes in Europe.

Norman Norell. See Hall of Fame

Noriko (Nishi). Blair Fashions, 2650 W. Belden Ave., Chicago, Ill. 60647

This young designer of softly classic clothes with her own original touches was born in Kagoshima, Japan, and educated in the traditional Japanese manner. Her arranged marriage to a Japanese-American brought her to Chicago in 1967. When her husband was killed she supported herself designing clothes and joined Blair Fashions, a firm previously concerned only with foundation garments, when she went to them for technical advice. Noriko now controls most of the Blair production, as well as being its designer.

Olga (Erteszek). Designer of intimate apparel, The Olga Company, 7915 Haskell Ave., Van Nuys, Calif. 91406

Born in Krakow, Poland, Olga Bertram learned the basic techniques of corsetry from her mother, a noted European corsetiere. After a dramatic escape from occupied Poland, she and her husband Jan Erteszek reached America. She designed and sewed her first foundation garments as a means of livelihood for the family.

Today the Olga Company employs 1200 people and produces a multimillion dollar volume of bras, girdles, lingerie, sleepwear, and loungewear.

Olga is responsible for many design patents for girdles, control briefs, panti-slips, divided slips, and figure-shaping nightgowns. She has received a total of 18 State of California Gold Awards from 1950–1967.

She is a member of the Council of Fashion Designers of America.

Frank Olive. Ready-to-wear milliner, 32 W. 39 St., New York, N.Y. 10019

A Mid-Westerner who also worked in California before coming to the

New York fashion world, Frank Olive was born January 20, 1929, on a farm near Milwaukee, Wisconsin, and studied design at two Milwaukee schools, the Layton School of Art and the Hade Fashion School.

His first New York assignment was on the staff of a popular milliner, Chanda. In the mid-sixties he opened a far-out boutique in Greenwich Village but soon established a nationally distributed wholesale business. He now sells his hats under his own and two other labels and also designs and manufactures accessories, blouses, bags, and beachwear.

Holly Park. Holly's Harp, 8605 Sunset Blvd., Los Angeles, Calif. 90069

Holly Park, California designer of amusing, body-conscious fashions, runs her own Los Angeles boutique, Holly's Harp, selling to local luminaries, and her ready-to-wear organization.

She and her husband Jim Park started the business in 1968, and since 1970 Holly Park clothes have been sold throughout the country.

Mollie Parnis (Livingston). Designer and chief executive, Parnis–Livingston, Inc., 530 Seventh Ave., New York, N.Y. 10018

One of American fashion's key personalities, Mollie Parnis is a New Yorker by birth and a devotee of her home city. Her pet philanthropy is the "Dress Up Your Neighborhood" project which she originated in 1971 and funds with $50,000 per year in prizes to encourage New Yorkers in poorer neighborhoods to beautify and improve their surroundings. In 1973 she founded a duplicate project in Israel.

Born in Brooklyn, New York, she went to Wadleigh High School and Hunter College in New York City. A summer job with a blouse manufacturing firm on Seventh Avenue intrigued her to the point of abandoning school for a career in design. She became briefly the blouse firm's salesperson, then its designer—the only job she ever held before 1937, when she and her husband, Leon J. Livingston, started their dress firm, Parnis–Livingston.

Widowed in 1962, Mollie Parnis retired for three months, then resumed her business career. She now controls two divisions, Mollie Parnis Couture and Mollie Parnis Boutique.

Mollie Parnis fashions have a following of smart conservative women throughout the world.

She was a founder member and serves on the Board of Directors of the Council of Fashion Designers of America.

Emeric Imre Partos (1905–1975). Fur designer

Known for his daring treatments of luxury furs, such as multicolored fur mosaics, Emeric Partos was born in Budapest, Hungary, on March 18, 1905. He studied art in Budapest and at the Sorbonne in Paris, then trained as a jewelry designer in Switzerland.

Partos served in the French Army and the French Underground during World War II. After the Liberation, he joined the staff of his former Underground commander, couturier Alex Maguy in Paris.

From 1947 to 1950 Partos worked in France with Christian Dior and then came to the United States as consulting designer at Maximilian furs. In 1955 he joined Bergdorf Goodman as its fur designer and remained until his death December 2, 1975.

In 1975 Partos received a Coty Award.

Sylvia Pedlar. See Hall of Fame

Elsa Peretti. Jewelry designer, 1 E. 57 St., New York, N.Y. 10022

Born in Florence, Italy, on May 1, 1940, to a wealthy family, Elsa Peretti was educated in Rome and came to America as a fashion model. She began to design and make silver jewelry to amuse herself on weekends. To supply the unexpected demand for her gold "tear drop" pendant, her miniature flower vase on a chain, and her large silver loop belt buckle, she sought small artisans in Spain and set up a studio in Barcelona. Her highly original and sophisticated jewelry in polished silver, gold, and ivory was launched by the designer Halston with his couture collection in 1970 and immediately became a high-fashion craze.

She received a Coty Special Award in 1971. In 1974 Tiffany & Company became the headquarters for Peretti jewelry collections and made her "diamonds by the yard" chains interspersed with jewels, the fashion accessory of the following several years.

Alan Phillips. McMullen, 550 Seventh Ave., New York, N.Y. 10017

Former member of the Adolph Bohm Ballet turned fashion designer, Alan Phillips is one of the competent yet nonflamboyant professionals responsible for the great bulk of American clothes production.

Born in Spokane, Washington, on October 15, 1922, and brought up in western Canada, he trained as a dancer with Hermes Pan in Hollywood and then with the Bohm Ballet before returning to Hollywood as assistant to Adrian, designing costumes for films.

He came to New York about 1950, and has since designed for Branell, Malcolm Starr, and Jerry Silverman, always expressing current trends in dresses the average woman can wear and afford. He is currently designing for McMullen and McMullen Sportswear.

Anna Maximilian (Apfelbaum) Potok. Fur designer, Maximilian, Inc., 20 W. 57 St., New York, N.Y. 10019

Mrs. Potok was born in Warsaw, Poland, on June 4, 1907, and until World War II worked there with her brother, the celebrated European fur designer, Maximilian (Max Apfelbaum) who started his fur business in 1918.

In 1940, she accompanied her brother to the United States and worked with him until his death in 1961, when she took over the administration of the family business. Maximilian was part of the Richton Corporation group from 1971 to 1974, when Mrs. Potok resumed control.

Maximilian won Coty Special Awards in 1948 and 1964. Mrs. Potok is a member of the Council of Fashion Designers of America.

Clare Potter (Mrs. J. Sanford Potter). Fashion designer (retired), Lake Nebo, Glens Falls, Port Ann, N.Y. 12827.

Born in Jersey City, New Jersey, Clare Potter studied art at the Art Students League in New York and later attended Pratt Institute in Brooklyn.

Mrs. Potter's ambition was to paint but in 1925 she began designing picturesque clothes for Edward L. Mayer, the leading dress manufacturer of that time. She was one of the first designers to sense the lifestyle shift from formal to casual living and to interpret this in easy, unconstructed designs, equally appropriate for sports or town wear. As one of the designers promoted in Lord & Taylor's drive to establish the American Look, Mrs. Potter received the Lord & Taylor Award for distinguished designing in 1937. In 1939 she received the Neiman–Marcus Award and the Coty Award in 1946.

Priscilla of Boston (Priscilla Kidder). 498 Seventh Ave., New York, N.Y. 10018

America's leading designer–manufacturer of fine-quality bridal dresses, Priscilla Kidder is also one of the few designers in the world to specialize in this fashion area.

Born December 14, 1916, in Quincy, Massachusetts, and the oldest of four children of divorced parents whose mother was their sole support, she opened a small yarn and knitting shop as soon as she was out of high school to help the family finances. At 22 she became assistant buyer of bridal clothes in a Boston department store. In 1940 she married James Kidder, a Harvard graduate and well-known athlete, who is now her business associate. In 1945, after her husband's release from the army, they opened a bridal shop in Boston, selling ready-made and custom-designed dresses for prominent Boston brides. In 1950, her talent began to be noticed by other stores. Today Priscilla wedding gowns are worn by many famous brides.

Lilly Pulitzer (Lillian McKim Pulitzer Rousseau). Creator of the "Lilly," 400 Royal Palm Way, Palm Beach, Fla. 33480

This leading Florida designer had no formal training in fashion. She was born in Palm Beach society, the daughter of Robert McKim and the former Mrs. Ogden Phipps. Yet the "Lilly," the little cotton shift in bright polished cotton chintz made by Lilly Pulitzer (then married to a member of the publishing family) had an elegant flair that made it first a "snob" uniform, then a general fashion craze. Like the Marimekkos of Finland, the Lillys have their own character and their own following of all ages.

Mrs. Pulitzer, now Mrs. Enrique Rousseau, has been president of Lilly Pulitzer, Inc., since 1961, and the business has expanded to include the design of household articles.

Mary Ann Restivo. Genre, 530 Seventh Ave., New York, N.Y. 10018

Born in New Jersey, Mrs. Restivo studied retailing in the convent College of St. Elizabeth (N.J.) and fashion design at the Fashion Institute of Technology, New York.

Her talent for creating young and off-beat fashion brought her the Young Designers Award of the Hecht Company (Washington, D.C.) in 1968 and a 1973 Alumnae Award from the Fashion Institute of Technology.

James Reva. Designer and boutique owner, 9612 Brighton Way, Beverly Hills, Calif. 90210

California designer James Reva was born in Detroit, Michigan, on July 15, 1940, and moved to Monrovia, California, when he was five.

He studied merchandising and design at Woodbury College in Los Angeles.

He opened a dress shop in Monrovia selling dresses of his own design and by 1968 had a chain of three shops in the area. The following year he opened his Beverly Hills shop which established his reputation as a fresh and appealing exponent of the California look. Film and television credits plus a clientele of well-known personalities soon brought his clothes into wider distribution.

Will Richardson and Eileen Richardson. Designers of tie-dyed fabrics, 15907 Gold Blvd., Redington Beach, St. Petersburg, Fla. 33708

This husband-and-wife duo were largely responsible for lifting tie-dyed fabrics from the realm of the artsy-craftsy to high fashion.

Both the Richardsons studied art, Will at the University of Michigan and Eileen (Pendergast) at Cooper Union in New York and the Slade School in London. She received a Fulbright Scholarship and a Huntington Hartford Scholarship for studies abroad.

After their marriage, their experiments in giving a modern aspect to the ancient arts of batik and tie-dying brought them a contract to tour under the sponsorship of the Rit Dye Company.

The Richardsons designed special tie-dyed fabrics for William Theiss films, for Lincoln Center theatrical productions, and for the American Ballet Company's "Pagan Spring." They were introduced to fashion by their designs for Halston's collections.

After winning a Coty Special Award in 1970, the couple moved to Florida and returned to painting.

Youssef Rizkallah. Don Friese, Ltd., 550 Seventh Ave., New York, N.Y. 10018

Rizkallah, an Egyptian of Lebanese extraction, was born in Cairo on February 27, 1934, and at 19 went to Paris, where he worked for couturiers Jacques Griffe and Pierre Balmain. He returned to Cairo and established his own couture house there, with the Queen of Jordan among his clients.

In 1963 Rizkallah came to the United States and worked with Jean Louis and Luis Estevez in California. He joined Malcolm Starr, Inc., in 1969 and in 1975 became affiliated with Don Friese in a business using his name.

Don Robbie. Menswear designer, Don Robbie, Inc., 1271 Ave. of the Americas, New York, N.Y. 10019

Don Robbie, designer of menswear whose work for some years was cloaked behind the labels of Pierre Cardin and Yves Saint Laurent, was born in Cavalier, North Dakota, a town of 700. He graduated from the University of North Dakota and seven years later was advertising manager at Marshall Field and Company, Chicago.

In 1966 he became American interpreter of the Pierre Cardin menswear collections and continued that assignment for five years. Later he adapted Yves Saint Laurent men's clothing for the United States.

He presented his first independent collection in July, 1974, and emerged as a creative entity with his audacious colors and unusual choice of clothing materials, including woven straw.

Shannon Rodgers. Dress designer, Jerry Silverman, Inc., 530 Seventh Ave., New York, N.Y. 10018

A designer of highly sophisticated fashions, Shannon Rodgers was born in Newcomerstown, Ohio, on his family's 18th-century farm, "Buckhorn." His great-great-uncle was Jonathan Chapman, known in American folklore as Johnny Appleseed.

He graduated as an architect from Western Reserve University, Cleveland, and his first job was drafting sets for Broadway plays. After helping out on costume designs for a play, he never went back to the T-square. A Hollywood contract with Cecil B. DeMille followed, in the course of which he designed costumes for *The Barretts of Wimpole Street*, *Stella Dallas*, *Marco Polo*, and other films.

After five years in the U.S. Navy during World War II, Rodgers designed for Martini, a successful New York dress firm, where Jerry Silverman was sales manager. In 1959, Silverman and Rodgers opened Jerry Silverman, Inc., and together they have made it one of the most powerful dress businesses in the field. It is now a division of Warnaco, Inc.

In 1974 Rodgers established a museum of regional crafts in Newcomerstown.

Rodgers is a member of the Council of Fashion Designers of America. He is also a guest critic for Parsons School of Design.

Dominic Rompollo. Teal Traina, Inc., 550 Seventh Ave., New York, N.Y. 10018

Born January 24, 1935, in Detroit, Michigan, Rompollo studied at Detroit's Cass-Tech and School of Arts and Crafts, then spent fourteen years as a professional designer before enrolling at Parsons School of Design in New York. Graduating in 1964, he was assistant designer to Geoffrey Beene and later designer for Teal Traina. He opened his own business in 1971, but in 1975 he returned to Teal Traina.

He is a member of the Council of Fashion Designers of America and is a guest critic for Parsons School of Design.

Helen Rose. Film and ready-to-wear designer (retired), 719 S. Los Angeles St., Los Angeles, Calif. 90014

Best known as a costume designer for 20th Century Fox (1939–1942) and MGM (1942–1963), Helen Rose also conducted a successful wholesale dress business specializing in evening clothes. One of her most famous off-screen dresses was the wedding dress she designed for Grace Kelly when the film star became Princess Grace of Monaco.

She was born Helen Bronberg in Chicago and studied at the Chicago Academy of Art. She married Harry Rose in 1929.

She won Oscars for her costumes for *The Bad and the Beautiful* in 1952 and for *I'll Cry Tomorrow* in 1955.

Nettie Rosenstein. Dress designer (retired), 200 E. 57 St., New York, N.Y. 10022

Nettie Rosenstein was best known from the 1930s to the 1950s as a leading designer of the "little black dress." One of her versions of this fashion, plus the inaugural ballgown she designed for Mrs. Dwight D. Eisenhower are in the permanent costume collection of the Smithsonian Institution, Washington, D.C.

Mrs. Rosenstein was born in Austria and came to America as a child. Her father operated a small dry-goods store in New York. In 1921, she opened Nettie Rosenstein, Inc., one of the first high-fashion ready-to-wear dress houses in the United States. It was soon a leader in the American market and remained so until her retirement. Her business associate was Charles Gumprecht, an astute and far-sighted dress manufacturer who pioneered in making ready-made clothing a major American industry.

Nettie Rosenstein received the Lord & Taylor Award in 1937, the Neiman–Marcus Award in 1938, and the Coty Award in 1947.

Matthew N. (Chip) Rubinstein. Manufacturer and industry leader, Anne Klein and Company, Anne Klein Studio, 205 W. 39 St., New York, N.Y. 10018

Chip Rubinstein is founder and chief officer of two major fashion organizations in the American market, Anne Klein and Company and the Anne Klein Studio, with divisions and affiliations in a dozen aspects of fashion and home furnishings.

Born in New York City on March 7, 1921, Rubinstein graduated from Ohio State University and also holds a degree in economics from Columbia University. He served with UNRA in Europe after the war, and on his return had a business making shopping bags.

Soon after his marriage to the late designer Anne Klein in 1966, he and his wife formed Anne Klein and Company on the then-unheard-of premise that the modern woman should not dress by seasonal trends, but maintain an interlocking wardrobe of components to which she adds parts at intervals, changing the forms, weights, feeling, and coloration of her clothes in a personal way.

In 1967 they established the Anne Klein Studio to employ and groom young fashion designers and to channel their work into modern industry on the Bauhaus and Josef Hoffman principle.

By 1975 Anne Klein rooms were established in 150 stores in the United States and Canada, and the Anne Klein Studio produced menswear ("Mark of the Lion"), women's active sports clothes (Anne Klein for Penfold), and design under license handbags, umbrellas, belts, watches, jewelry, loungewear, lingerie, scarves, and wigs. In 1973 Anne Klein and Company formed a partnership for international expansion with one of the mammoth industrial complexes of Japan, the Takihyo Company.

Clovis Ruffin. Women's ready-to-wear designer, Ruffinwear, 550 Seventh Ave., New York, N.Y. 10018

Clovis Ruffin, an "army brat" who grew up to be one of the bright young American fashion creators, was born in Clovis, New Mexico. His mother named him for that town, where the family was stationed while his father was in the Air Force.

In 1960, having lived in many parts of the world for brief spells, he came to New York to George Washington High School and later attended Columbia University and the Sorbonne in Paris. His mind was fixed, however, on fashion designing and he made T-shirt styles for his friends. The fashion press took notice of his talents and in 1972 he organized his own company, now a part of the Kreisler Group in New York.

Gloria Sachs. Ready-to-wear designer, Gloria Sachs Designs, Ltd., 530 Seventh Ave., New York, N.Y. 10018

This designer of knitted and fabricated clothes was born in Scarsdale, New York, and studied the history of painting at Skidmore College, the Cranbrook Academy, and in Florence, Italy. In Europe she doubled as model and student, working with the painter Léger and with Italian architects, and also modelling for Balenciaga and Balmain.

Her first fashion assignment was designing fabrics for Hans Knoll and Herman Miller. Her handwoven fabrics were exhibited at the Museum of Modern Art in New York and the Art Institute in Chicago.

She worked at Bloomingdale's New York in the interior design department and later as fashion coordinator.

In 1965 she decided to design clothing and was promptly engaged by Saks Fifth Avenue to create teenage clothes. In 1970 she set up her own business, designing knitwear and other handmade clothing, with an enclave of women with the skills to produce them.

In 1974 she received the Woolknit Design Award for Creative achievement in the knit field.

Arthur Samuels, Jr. Shoe designer, Golo Footwear Corporation, 350 Fifth Ave., New York, N.Y. 10001

A native New Yorker, born April 24, 1934, and graduate of Hackley School and Babson College, Arthur Samuels, Jr., now heads the family business founded in 1915. During his tenure, he has changed the firm's "image" from stadium boots and teenage shoes to fashionable footwear, including the well-known Golo boots.

He serves on the style committee of both the National Shoe Retailers and the American Footwear Association. He is a member of the Council of Fashion Designers of America.

Fernando Sanchez. Fur and lingerie designer, 16 W. 57 St., New York, N.Y. 10019

Fernando Sanchez was born in Spain, his parentage Spanish and Flemish. He commutes between Paris and New York and says he "hides out" in exotic places like Marrakech, where he owns a house.

After studying at l'Ecole de la Chambre Syndicale in Paris, he joined Christian Dior to design accessories, sweaters, and lingerie for the Dior boutiques in Europe. An assignment to design lingerie for the Warner Company in America brought him to New York but he returned to

France to design furs for Revillon. In 1974, however, he extended his activities by opening his own firm to produce lingerie and loungewear in New York, while continuing to design furs for Revillon in both France and America.

He received a Coty Special Award for lingerie in 1974 and for his creativity in furs in 1975.

Pat Sandler. Dress designer, Pat Sandler, Inc., 498 Seventh Ave., New York, N.Y. 10018

A native New Yorker, born November 2, 1929, Sandler studied art and fashion design at the Fashion Institute of Technology. After freelance work for New York firms, he joined Highlight, Inc. in 1967, the dress firm which eventually changed its name to his.

Pat Sandler's snappy figure-conscious dresses follow up-to-the minute fashion trends at a moderate price.

He is a member of the Council of Fashion Designers of America.

Giorgio di Sant' Angelo. 6 W. 56 St., New York, N.Y. 10019

A designer of women's clothes and accessories that typify the neo-romantic feeling which entered fashion via the ethnic route of the late 1960s, Count Giorgio di Sant'Angelo was born May 5, 1936, and grew up on his family's estates in Argentina and Spain.

While attending the Barcelona School of Architecture, his extracurricular interest in ceramics won him a scholarship to study that craft in France under Pablo Picasso.

His skill as a graphic artist attracted attention, and Walt Disney Studios brought him to America to work as a film animator. He disliked Hollywood and escaped to New York, where he designed fabrics, plastic jewelry, and gloves before starting his own dress business in 1966.

Sant'Angelo's designs inspired by the American Indian and his other highly personalized versions of ethnic costumes brought him a Coty Special Award in 1968 and the Coty "Winnie" in 1970. He is known for theatrical costumes as well as for the ready-to-wear bearing his label.

Belle Saunders (Mrs. Sigmond Kayne). Ready-to-wear designer, Abe Schrader, 530 Seventh Ave., New York, N.Y. 10018

Belle Saunders is one of the classic American wholesale designers of simple, wearable, and fashion-minded clothes for women with a long record of successful collections since she joined Abe Schrader in 1953.

Born July 15, 1910, on a farm near Nanuet, New York, she pursued an early ambition to design by making clothes for people in her neighborhood. After graduating from high school, she came to New York and worked in a bank, going to art school at night.

She made fashion sketches, then became designer for the International Dress Company and later for other dress houses before joining Schrader.

Arnold Scaasi. Custom-order and ready-to-wear designer, 26 E. 56 St., New York, N.Y. 10022

This designer was born Arnold Isaacs in Montreal, Canada, on May 8, 1931, and studied fashion design at the Cotnoir-Capponi School in Montreal and at l'Ecole de la Chambre Syndicale in Paris. He came to New York in 1951, reversed his name to give it a foreign sound, and worked for couturier Charles James and for Seventh Avenue manufacturers. In 1957 he opened his own business.

Scaasi's daring, dramatic clothes, including a forerunner of the miniskirt, attracted immediate attention and in 1958 he won a Coty Award. He designed film costumes for Barbra Streisand in *On a Clear Day*. In 1971 he designed a collection for French ready-to-wear manufacturer Maria Moutet but now produces his clothes solely in America.

He is a member of the Council of Fashion Designers of America.

Jean Schlumberger. *See* France: Fashion Designers and Firms

Ira Seret. *See* Afghanistan

Susan Sheinman (Mrs. David A. Andelman). Owner–designer of Papillon, Inc. (retired).

Susan Sheinman, known as a designer of young-traditional dresses in interesting prints of her own design, is the daughter of the late Nathan Sheinman, owner of McMullen, one of the more colorful figures of the garment industry.

Born March 13, 1944, in New York, she was educated at Briarcliff College and l'Academie Maxim in Paris and worked as a buyer in two New York stores before establishing Papillon, Inc. in 1970. The firm closed in 1976.

Alexander Shields. Menswear designer, 484 Park Ave., New York, N.Y. 10022

Alexander Shields, designer of colorful yet impeccably tasteful clothes for men and credited with launching the easy luxury look in menswear, is one of the few fashion designers listed in America's Social Register. A member of the Sons of the Revolution, he is a seventh generation American; his forefathers fought under George Washington and in the War of 1812. Still another ancestor was a Confederate general and later Pancho Villa's surgeon-general, having founded the American Hospital in Mexico City.

Shields was born and brought up in San Francisco, studied civil engineering at the California Institute of Technology, then attended the School of Foreign Service in Washington, D.C., before serving in World

War II in the Naval Reserve as commander and chief officer of a merchant ship.

He opened his first shop for men in 1947 in New York. There are now 50 Alexander Shields shops across the country.

He received a Coty Special Menswear Award in 1971 and at that time introduced the caftan fashion for male lounging and beachwear.

Kashina Shura. *See* Cathy Hardwick

Elinor Simmons. Designer for Baron Peters, 530 Seventh Ave., New York, N.Y. 10018

Born in New York City, Elinor Simmons studied costume design at the Parsons School of Design and earned pin money by modeling. Her description of a "dream dress" to a Seventh Avenue manufacturer brought her an offer to design. The dress sold by the hundreds.

She designed for the couture house of Milgrim until she joined Malcolm Starr, Inc., where she remained until 1972, and later joined Baron Peters.

Don Simonelli. Dress and tailored-wear designer, Box 316, S. Salem, N.Y. 10590

A designer with a varied career who now free-lances, Don Simonelli was born in Stamford, Connecticut, on April 11, 1938. His interest in a fashion career stemmed from reading advance copies of *Vogue*, which his father, an electrotyper at the Condé Nast presses, brought home.

He attended Parsons School of Design and spent part of his final year in European study. On his return he graduated from Parsons and began his designing career at a St. Louis, Missouri, wholesale junior dress house.

His first assignment in New York was with P.R.L. designing moderate priced coats. Here he won a Coty Award (1965). Later he worked for Anne Klein Studio and for Modelia.

Adele Simpson. Designer-manufacturer, Adele Simpson, Inc., 530 Seventh Ave., New York, N.Y. 10018

Adele Simpson, creator of ready-made clothes for the sophisticated yet conservative American woman, was one of the first wholesale designers to go "on tour" with her collections in order to meet the customers, now a standard fashion procedure which has aided in establishing a rapport between the designers and the consumer.

Born in New York and graduated from Pratt Institute, Mrs. Simpson began her professional career at 18, and at 21 was one of the highest paid designers in the world. In 1945 she bought Mary Lee, Inc., where she had been chief designer, and gave it her own name.

Mrs. Simpson, an effective crusader for the recognition of American fashion, was one of the founders of the Fashion Group and the Council of Fashion Designers of America. She is on the Board of Governors of the Fashion Institute of Technology. She won the Coty Award (1947) and the National Cotton Fashion Award (1953).

She was married to the late Wesley Simpson, a well-known figure in the American textile and factoring business, and their daughter Joan Simpson Raines and son-in-law Richard Raines are Adele Simpson's business associates.

Stella Sloat. Separates designer, Dalton & Company, 1407 Broadway, New York, N.Y. 10018

Born in New York, Stella Sloat joined her father's sportswear firm as soon as she finished high school. She won one of the earliest of the *Sports Illustrated* "Sporting Look" trophies and in 1970 designed the uniform of the Girl Scouts of America.

She is a member of the Council of Fashion Designers of America.

Willi Smith. Willi Smith Designs, Inc., 49 W. 37 St., New York, N.Y. 10018

Willi Smith is one of several talented black designers to be schooled at the Philadelphia Museum College of Art.

Born February 29, 1948, in Philadelphia where his father was a butcher, Willi came to New York in 1965 with two scholarships to the Parsons School of Design, one from the Philadelphia Board of Education and the other from Parsons. Anxious to get started professionally, however, he dropped out of school and free-lanced for two years, then became designer for Glenora. In 1969 Digits was formed and he became its designer. In January 1974 he formed his own firm.

Eva Sonnino. Shoe designer, Bernardo Sandals, Inc., 1040 Woodland Ave., Columbus, Ohio 43219

Born Eva Moll in Milan, Italy, Mrs. Sonnino and her husband Dino took over in 1950 the footwear firm originally founded by Aldo Bruzzichelli and designer Bernard Rudofsky, noted architect, writer, and early advocate of freedom in wearing apparel. The open, flat Bernardo sandal, based on the classic Greek style, was a major factor in launching the casual shoe shape for all times of day.

Mrs. Sonnino has retained the Bernardo philosophy, while infusing other fashion elements into her designs.

She received the American Shoe Designer Award of the Leather Industries of America in 1963 and is a member of the Council of Fashion Designers of America.

In 1969, Bernardo Sandals became part of the complex of footwear companies of R.G. Barry Corporation of Columbus, Ohio. Mrs. Sonnino and her husband now live most of the year in their country house near Rome and commute between their factories in Italy and in Ohio.

Sophie (Gimbel). Custom designer (retired), 166 E. 64 St., New York, N.Y. 10021

Born Sophie Hass in Houston, Texas, she married the late Adam L. Gimbel in 1931. Her custom salon at Saks Fifth Avenue attracted many wealthy and elegant clients from all parts of the world.

Mrs. Gimbel was instrumental in establishing the Adam L. Gimbel library of fashion and costume archives at the Parsons School of Design in New York.

Stavropoulos (George Peter Stavropoulos). Ready-to-wear designer, Stavropoulos Corporation, 16 W. 57 St., New York, N.Y. 10019

This designer, noted for his classically inspired chiffon evening dresses, was born in Tripolis, Greece. He was a well-known and successful couturier in Athens until his marriage to a homesick member of the American Embassy staff made him close his business and brave the American wholesale industry in 1962.

He is a member of the Council of Fashion Designers of America.

Stella (Hanania). Custom-order designer, I. Magnin and Company, 3240 Wilshire Blvd., Los Angeles, Calif. 90005

One of the few remaining custom designers in America, Miss Stella is a favorite dressmaker of many social and theatrical personalities on the West Coast.

Born in Beirut, Lebanon, she came to America to find a job in fashion. She worked as assistant to Bernard Newman, Bergdorf-Goodman's custom designer, and in 1943 accompanied him to California on a designing assignment. When he returned, Stella remained and became designer for the custom department at I. Magnin and Company, a post she has developed into a powerful element in American fashion.

Marguerite Stix (Mrs. Hugh Stix) (1907–1975). Jewelry designer

Originator of the fashion for real jewelry combining natural shells with gold and precious stones, Marguerite Stix, with her husband Hugh, coauthored The Shell, Five Hundred Million Years of Inspired Design (Harry N. Abrams), the definitive book on seashells.

Born in Vienna in 1907, Mrs. Stix attended European art schools and studied with "Art Deco" artist Joseph Hoffman and at the Academie de la Grande Chaumiere in Paris. She came to the United States in 1941 and made a success as a sculptor. She is represented in the National Collection of Art in Washington, the Hartford, Connecticut, Atheneum, and the Contemporary Arts Museum in Houston, Texas.

Fascinated with the beauty and infinite variety of shells she found on holiday in the Virgin Islands, Mrs. Stix used them as subjects of her drawings and sculpture and eventually in jewelry. Her creations are now sold at Cartier's and other leading American stores.

Mrs. Stix died in New York on January 10, 1975.

Daniel Stoenescu. *See* Cadoro

George Stuart and Lynn Stuart. *See* Mr. Pants, Inc.

Suga (Yusuke). Hairdresser, 132 E. 70 St., New York, N.Y. 10021

Born in China on February 18, 1942, Suga was brought up in Japan and studied traditional Japanese hair arrangement there. He was brought to the United States by Kenneth, the well-known American hairdresser, and now conducts his own business, specializing in original coiffures for fashion magazines and a private clientele.

Morton Sussman. Ready-to-wear designer, Mollie Parnis, Inc., 530 Seventh Ave., New York, N.Y. 10018

A designer well known for making festive clothes that look far more expensive than they are, Morty Sussman was born in New York on April 19, 1931, and trained at the Fashion Institute of Technology there. He designed for Matty Talmack and for Ceil Chapman before joining the newly formed Mollie Parnis Boutique division in 1971.

He is a member of the Council of Fashion Designers of America.

Viola Sylbert. Free-lance fashion designer, 130 E. 63 St., New York, N.Y. 10021

One of America's busiest free-lance designers, Viola Sylbert was born in New York and majored in fine arts at Cornell University before getting her master's degree in retailing from New York University.

Her first job was fashion coordinator with a New York store. She now designs furs for Henri Bendel, dresses for Ciao, furs for Alixandre, and sweaters and related sportswear for Hadley.

She is a member of the Council of Fashion Designers of America. In 1975 she received a Coty Award for her creativity in fur design.

Gustave Tassell. Ready-to-wear designer, Norman Norell, Inc., 550 Seventh Ave., New York, N.Y. 10018

When Gus Tassell was persuaded by the executors of the late Norman Norell to carry on that designer's tradition of luxurious classic fashion, he closed his own dress business in California and came to New York.

Tassell was born February 4, 1926, in Philadelphia and studied painting at the Philadelphia Academy of Fine Arts. Like Norell, Tassell got his early training at Hattie Carnegie in New York, then worked as a free-lance designer in Paris. On his return two years later, he went directly to California and established a successful business there, creating clothes in the haute-couture tradition of perfectionist elegance. He transferred to Norell in 1972.

He won a Coty Award in 1961 and the Cotton Council's Fashion Award (1963).

Bill Tice. Free-lance designer, 750 Park Ave., New York, N.Y. 10021

The son of a hardware merchant in Indianapolis, Indiana, Bill Tice studied fashion design at the University of Cincinnati, where he entered a retail work/study program in which he did everything from selling fishing tackle to designing window displays. He pursued the latter career in Indianapolis stores until coming to New York in the mid-sixties.

He was asked to design clothes for Mam'selle and later worked at Guy D, Teal Traina, and Bobbie Brooks before deciding to go into other fields of fashion.

His sleepwear and leisure clothes, suggesting Watteau and Fragonard with their gentle washes of color and gossamer textures, multilayered, soon brought him his own division, Bill Tice ESP of the Sayour Company, in 1973. It closed in 1975, but he continues to design for lingerie firms, and also creates at-home shoes for Golo.

In 1974 Tice received a Coty Special Award.

Jacques Tiffeau. Ready-to-wear designer, Originala, 512 Seventh Avenue, New York, N.Y. 10018. See France: Fashion Designers and Firms

Leslie Tillett and **Doris Tillett.** Textile experts, 170 E. 80 St., New York, N.Y. 10021

These designers of fabrics are now best known for roaming the world lending their expertise to the establishment of "cottage" industries in underdeveloped areas of the world.

Tilletts training programs inspire and teach native craftsmen to preserve their ethnic skills of weaving and printing fabrics while making them more desirable and practical for commercial sale. Under the sponsorship of governments and charitable foundations, they have worked in Mexico, India, and South America. Their most recent headline-making projects were the Design Works in the Bedford–Stuyvesant area of New York City, and a training program in South Korea which produced $50 million worth of highly salable printed silks.

Monika Tilley. Sportswear and children's clothes designer, Monika Tilley, Ltd., 1407 Broadway, New York, N.Y. 10018

Born in Vienna, Austria, the daughter of a diplomat, Monika Tilley studied at the Academy of Arts in Vienna and had art courses in Paris and Stockholm.

She came to America as a fashion illustrator, became assistant to John Weitz, the sportswear designer, then designed for White Stag, Cole of California, and Mallory before setting up her own design studio. She now creates beachwear, ski clothes, sportswear, at-home clothes, and children's clothes.

She is a member of the Council of Fashion Designers of America. In 1975 she received a Coty Special Award for her swimwear collection designed for Elon.

Teddy Tinling. See England: Fashion Designers and Firms

Julian Tomchin. Textile designer, 400 E. 59 St., New York, N.Y. 10022

One of the leading American fabric designers, Tomchin was born in Brooklyn on April 28, 1932. He was somewhat of a child prodigy, being admitted to the art classes of the Museum of Modern Art at the age of eight. He graduated in fine arts from Syracuse University in 1953 and began designing textiles, working for Vera, Hope Skillman, and Stephanie Cartwright before becoming chief designer for Maxwell Fabrics in 1959. He won the Vogue Fabrics Award (1967) and a Coty Special Award (1969).

Since 1972 he has been an independent textile designer and teaches at Parsons School of Design in New York. In 1976 he was appointed design director of Wamsutta Mills.

Tomchin is a member of the Board of Directors of the Council of Fashion Designers of America.

Pauline Trigere. Designer–manufacturer, 550 Seventh Ave., New York, N.Y. 10018

Highly creative designer of couture-quality ready-to-wear fashions, one of the important names in contemporary American fashion, and a prominent New York personality, Pauline Trigere was born on the Place Pigalle, November 4, 1912, and brought up in Paris. She came to America as a refugee from the threat of Nazi persecution. Her father, a tailor, had taught her the rudiments of his craft, and she had been apprenticed to the couture house of Martial et Armand.

Soon after the family came to America (1937), her marriage broke up and she was left with two infant sons. She found a job on the design staff of Hattie Carnegie, but Pearl Harbor soon closed the Carnegie workrooms. Pauline sold her jewelry, rented one of the abandoned Carnegie workrooms and produced a "collection" of eight dresses. Within a year she was a success in the wholesale business.

Today the Pauline Trigere label also appears on furs, costume jewelry, and simulated diamonds.

She is active in many causes and a leading spokesman on American high fashion.

She is a three-time Coty Award winner (1949, 1951, and Hall of Fame 1959). She is a member of the Council of Fashion Designers of America.

Kay E. Unger. Sportswear designer, St. Gillian Sportswear, Ltd., 498 Seventh Ave., New York, N.Y. 10018

This designer is known for what she terms "soft sportswear." She was born in Chicago on May 22, 1945, and studied at Washington University in Missouri, and at Parsons School of Design in New York, where she won the J. C. Penney and Irish Linen Association scholarships.

After graduating she worked for Pattullo-Jo Copeland, Gayle Kirkpatrick, and Geoffrey Beene. In 1971 she was made designer of the Traina Boutique and Traina Sport collections and did a collection under her own label in Liberty of London fabrics. She was made a partner at St. Gillian in 1972, with manufacturers Howard Bloom and Jon Levy.

Valentina (Nicholaevna Sanina Schlee). 450 E. 52 St., New York, N.Y. 10022

In the 1930s and 1940s the name Valentina stood for soft, flowing, bias-cut clothes in a period otherwise dominated by chunky shoulder padding and waist cinchers.

Born May 1, 1904, in Kiev, Russia, Valentina and her well-to-do family fled the revolution through Turkey, Greece, and the south of France. Valentina married another refugee, George Matthis Schlee, a former Russian army officer working as a theatrical manager. In 1923 the couple came to America with the Russian Chauve Souris Theater, Valentina in the ballet corps and Schlee in the management. They stayed in New York where Valentina's antifashionable clothes inspired by Russian peasant costume and made for herself, attracted attention. Friends backed her in a small dressmaking establishment in 1928, and until her retirement in the mid-sixties Valentina was a dominant voice in American fashion. Her stage costumes for Lynn Fontanne, Judith Anderson, Katherine Cornell, and Katharine Hepburn prompted the *New York Times* critic to write: "Valentina designs clothes that act before a word is spoken." The apron dress, the hooded cape, the snood, the headscarf, and the elegant wraparound silhouette were among her trend-setting innovations.

Valentina's heavy Russian accent and air of melodrama were imitated by the actress Lynn Fontanne in the play *Idiot's Delight*. Her comment "Mink is for football" became a fashion classic.

Vera (Neumann). Textile and home-furnishings designer, Vera Industries, Inc., 1411 Broadway, New York, N.Y. 10018

Born in Stamford, Connecticut, on July 24, 1910, Vera Neumann trained at Cooper Union and the Traphagen School and was a professional painter until 1945 when she and her late husband Serge Neumann, an art director, joined F. Werner Hamm, a textile expert, in founding the Vera Companies for silk-screened prints.

Vera now designs and produces sheets and towels, blankets, bedspreads, draperies, table and kitchen linens, plastics, and needlepoint designs. The Vera Companies, of which she was made president, are a subsidiary of Manhattan Industries, the large textile conglomerate.

Vera is a member of the Board of Directors of the American Crafts Council. The National Home Interiors League and National Society of Interior Designers have given her awards, and the Smithsonian Institution in Washington held an exhibit of her designs in 1972.

Sally Victor (Mrs. Sergiu Victor). Milliner (retired)

Sally Victor, the New York milliner whose name was synonymous with smart hats in the mid-20th century, was born in Scranton, Pennsylvania, and studied painting in Paris. On her return she obtained a job as saleslady in Macy's hat department and was eventually made buyer for the department. In 1934 she started her own hat shop and quickly became a national success. Her styles were often inspired by antique portraits, fashion periods, and themes of current films, books, or news headlines.

She received many awards, including the Coty Award in 1956.

She closed her business and retired in 1968.

Ilie Wacs. 530 Seventh Ave., New York, N.Y. 10018

This designer of tailored clothes for women was born in Vienna, on December 11, 1927, and brought up in China when his family escaped the Nazi invasion of Austria. He was sent to the Ecole des Beaux Arts in Paris and later studied at the Art Students League, New York, where he won the students' prize.

After working for couturier Alex Maguy in Paris, he was brought to New York by Philip Mangone, well-known tailor of the 1950s. He later designed tailored clothes for Originala for five years. In 1972 he became head of his own firm under the aegis of Athlone Industries and later assumed full control.

Dorothy Weatherford. Patchwork fashions designer, Mountain Artisans, 147 Summers St., Charleston, W. Va. 25301

A former artist and teacher, Ms. Weatherford revived the early American crafts of quilting and patchwork as a medium for her own fabric pictures.

She helped to inspire the world revival of patchwork and quilting in fashion and home furnishings through her work with the nonprofit organization, Mountain Artisans.

Born in Knoxville, Tennessee, Ms. Weatherford studied art at Carnegie–Mellon University and later taught art there and at the Art Institute in Chicago. In 1968 she joined Mountain Artisans, the cooperative formed by Jay and Sharon Rockefeller to utilize the local handicrafts of the badly depressed Appalachia area of West Virginia.

Her infusion of fashion elements and modern patterns and colors into the traditional techniques of this American folk art created a new public. By 1973, Mountain Artisans employed several hundred cottage handworkers and maintains a business counted in millions.

Mountain Artisans and Dorothy Weatherford received a Coty Special Award in 1972.

David Webb (1925–1975). Jewelry designer

Born in Asheville, North Carolina, David Webb worked during school vacations for an uncle in the jewelry business who taught him gold work and stone-setting. His grandfather, a well-known metal engraver, taught him the craft that was to bring him fame as a creative and innovative jeweler. He was influential in launching modern jewelry in graceful and precious animal forms. He was a leader in the revival of enamel mixed with colored stones in the Art Deco manner and his long multicolored necklaces were world status symbols.

He came to New York at 17 to work as a jewelry craftsman and at 21 opened his own walk-up shop with three workers.

Today, the house of David Webb occupies an entire building and employs 100 workers at 7 E. 57 St., New York, N.Y. 10022. His fanciful golden animal bibelots, his revival of rock crystal, coral, jade, and enamel in real jewelry brought him a Coty Award in 1964.

He died December 12, 1975.

Chester Weinberg. Chester Weinberg Studio, 419 E. 57 St., New York, N.Y. 10022

Born in New York on September 23, 1930, Chester Weinberg attended New York University and Parsons School of Design.

After an apprenticeship with five different manufacturers on Seventh Avenue, he achieved his great ambition in 1966 when Chester Weinberg, Ltd., was established. In 1974 the name was changed to Chester Weinberg N.O.W. Studio, Ltd.

Weinberg clothes have both impact and gentility. His followers are elegant women who lead active, involved lives.

His awards include the Cotton Fashion Award (1968), the Chicago Gold Coast Fashion Award (1968), and the Coty "Winnie" (1970).

He is a member of the Council of Fashion Designers of America and a guest lecturer and critic at the Parsons School of Design of New York.

John Weitz. Menswear designer, John Weitz Designs, Inc., 40 W. 55 St., New York, N.Y. 10019

Considered the most successful American in international menswear design, John Weitz was born in Berlin, Germany, on May 25, 1923, and educated in England at the Hall School and St. Paul's.

His career as a fashion designer in women's and men's sportswear has been entirely in the United States. He worked for several firms before starting his own business of designing collections for licensees in 1954. Since 1963 he has concentrated on men's clothing in all its aspects. His name and designs are widely promoted in Japan, England, and the United States. He received a Coty Special Menswear Award in 1974.

Weitz is a well-known sailing expert and author of two books, a novel about the fashion business, *The Value of Nothing* (Stein & Day, New York, 1970), and *Man in Charge* (Macmillan, New York, 1974), a dress and manners guide for the modern executive.

He is married to the former actress Susan Kohner, and they have two sons.

Harriet Winter (Mrs. Lewis Winter). Mrs. H. Winter for Yesterday's News Inc., 155 W. 23 St., New York, N.Y. 10011

Harriet Winter gained prominence as a designer who doesn't believe in hems and who is apt to finish a beautiful wool coat by using pinking sheers all around the edges. With her husband Lewis, Mrs. Winter had a shop selling antiques and antique clothing until her fascination with the clingy, diaphanous clothes of other eras led her to up-date them as ultrasoft, wrappy separates. They established Yesterday's News in 1970 to make ready-to-wear. It is housed far off Seventh Avenue in an old building above a fruit market. Their clothes are nostalgic of the early 1930s, but are made in ultramodern synthetic fabrics.

Willie Woo. Free-lance jewelry designer, 853 Seventh Ave., New York, N.Y. 10019

Born in Hong Kong on September 4, 1950, the son of the former editor of the *China Mail* and *Hong Kong Star* who founded the Hong Kong Trade Development Association, Willie came to New York with his parents in 1964.

He attended Manhattan's Collegiate School where his passion was football. He made the team as waterboy and compensated for his slight stature by making plastic football "charms" which were extremely popular with local girls. His football mania culminated when he served for two seasons as waterboy to the famous quarterback, Joe Namath.

On graduating from school he went into business, making off-beat jewelry from unlikely materials: aluminum, plastic, and even hard candy.

In 1971 in partnership with former *Vogue* editor Kezia Keeble, the first full-scale Willie Woo collection reintroduced rhinestone jewelry in pop-art shapes.

Sidney Wragge. Sportswear designer (retired), 800 Lake Dr., Boca Raton, Fla. 33432

Born March 10, 1908, in New York, Sidney Wragge attended New York University and the New School for Social Research. In 1935 after designing men's sports clothes for McGregor, he founded B. H. Wragge and forged a dominant position in classic, understated sportswear. Wragge clothes were a uniform to the elegant, active woman of the 1940s and 1950s.

In 1957 he received the Coty Award. He was one of the founders of the Council of Fashion Designers of America and its first president. He retired in 1972.

Peter Wrigley. Fashion and accessories designer, Anne Klein Studio, 205 W. 39 St., New York, N.Y. 10018

Peter Wrigley, codesigner with Chuck Howard for the Anne Klein Studio, is another in the prolific American group creating sportive fashions for both sexes, accessories, and home furnishings. Peter Wrigley was born October 17, 1934, in Hamden, Connecticut, and studied at the Rhode Island School of Design. He worked with Oleg Cassini and Anne Fogarty before joining Anne Klein's staff in 1970. In 1974 he shifted to the Anne Klein Studio. With Chuck Howard, he shared the Coty Menswear Fashion Award in 1975 for the Studio's "Mark of the Lion" collection as a result of a national ballot by the fashion press.

Ben Zuckerman. Designer–manufacturer of tailored clothes (retired)

The Zuckerman suit was an outstanding status symbol of the 1950s and 1960s,

Born in Rumania on July 29, 1890, Ben Zuckerman came to the United States with his immigrant parents about 1900, landing at Ellis Island. They settled in New Jersey where he went to public school. At 15 he became errand boy and later tailor in the Hoffman coat and suit factory. He bought half the firm and it became Zuckerman and Kraus. In 1949 Mr. Zuckerman retired for a year, then returned to establish Ben

Zuckerman, Inc. Throughout that firm's existence, his designer was Harry Schacter. Both retired in 1959 and live in Palm Beach, Florida.

Ben Zuckerman received the Neiman–Marcus Award in 1951 and the Coty Award three times (1952, 1958, and the Hall of Fame Award in 1961). He and Harry Schacter were charter members of the Council of Fashion Designers of America.

Fashion Influentials

Richard Avedon. Fashion photographer, 407 E. 75 St., New York, N.Y. 10021

This photographer who most successfully captured the image of the young fashion individualist of the 1960s and 1970s was born in New York on May 15, 1923. At 23, after attending Columbia University, he photographed for *Harper's Bazaar* where his work recorded the spirit, the personalities, and fashions of the post-war epoch. He was visual consultant and some said the inspiration for the film *Funny Face*, in which Fred Astaire played a fashion photographer. A number of innovations in film photography were launched in this film.

Avedon's book, *Observations*, published in 1959 in collaboration with black novelist James Baldwin, was a poignant study of the underprivileged as well as the fashion personalities of the day. The Smithsonian Institution and the Museum of Modern Art own collections of Avedon photographs, and a major exhibition of his work was held in New York in 1975.

Bettina Ballard (1908–1961). Fashion Editor, *Vogue*

A scintillating personality and one of America's most brilliant evaluators of fashion trends, Bettina Ballard was born in California about 1908 and brought up in Mexico. She was sent to Paris at 18 to learn French in an exclusive pension and attended the Sorbonne.

Returning to America on the eve of the Depression, she did free-lance writing for the *New Yorker* and *Vogue*, then joined the *Vogue* fashion staff. In 1935 she became French editor of American *Vogue*.

In 1942 she joined the Red Cross and served overseas for the duration of the war.

She returned to her job in 1945, recording the rebirth of the French couture under the spell of Christian Dior and Cristobal Balenciaga and the rise of Italian and American fashion. In the late fifties she left *Vogue* to act as consultant to stores and to write. Her book of memoirs, *In My Fashion* (see Bibliography), contains vivid descriptions of many key style personalities.

She died August 4, 1961.

Betsy Talbot Blackwell. Editor, *Mademoiselle* (retired), 226 West Lane, Ridgefield, Conn. 06877

One of the first to sense the new fashion force of the youth market, Mrs. Blackwell was born in New York and graduated from the Academy St. Elizabeth in New Jersey in 1923. She worked as a fashion reporter for a retail consulting service, then joined *Charm* magazine as assistant fashion and beauty editor. When *Mademoiselle* magazine was established in 1935 she was its fashion editor, and in 1937 became its editor-in-chief. She retired in 1971.

Russel Carpenter. Fashion director for I. Magnin (retired)

Russel Carpenter is credited with bringing the first elegant and sophisticated ready-to-wear fashion to California.

An effervescent personality with an intuitive eye for talent, he discovered a number of now-prominent designers, including Pertegaz of Spain.

He retired in 1971 and lives in Spain.

Irene Castle. See Hall of Fame

Edna Woolman Chase (1877–1957). Editor and fashion arbiter

Editor of *Vogue* for 60 years, Mrs. Chase was a powerful mover in the understanding and appreciation of fashion in America. She made *Vogue* a household word and her influence reached far beyond the limited circulation of *Vogue*.

Born Edna Alloway Woolman in 1877 in Asbury Park, New Jersey, she was brought up in a Quaker household and retained these standards throughout her life.

Hired as temporary help in the circulation department of *Vogue* in the early 1900s, she became its editor three years later. Her marriage to Francis Dane Chase produced a daughter Ilka Chase, the well-known actress and author. She received the French Legion d'Honneur.

Mrs. Chase died March 29, 1957.

Mildred Custin. Retailer, merchandising consultant, 767 Fifth Ave., New York, N.Y. 10022

A pioneering fashion merchant who gave Bonwit Teller, New York, the news flair and fluidity of a high-fashion magazine, Mildred Custin helped to launch numerous now-famous fashion names, among them Andre Courreges, Emanuel Ungaro, Calvin Klein, and James Galanos.

Born in Manchester, New Hampshire, she graduated from the Girls Latin School and Simmons College, Boston, in 1927. She was giftwares buyer in a Boston shop, then came to Philadelphia as a buyer for Wanamaker. In 1958 she was appointed president of Bonwit Teller in Philadelphia and in 1965 assumed the top executive position at Bonwit Teller in New York and its branch stores in other cities. When she resigned in 1970 she was chairman of the board and chief executive officer of the organization, a division of Genesco.

For her service to world fashion Miss Custin received the Croix de la Chevalier de l'Ordre du Merite of France (1970), the Tobe Award for retailing (1969), the Philadelphia Board of Education's Achievement Award (1963), and Man of the Year Award of the City of Philadelphia (1963).

Jessica Daves (Mrs. Robert Allerton Parker) (1898–1974). Editor, Vogue, and writer

Closely identified with the emergence of American ready-to-wear as a factor in world fashion, Jessica Daves' understanding of the new role of ready-made clothing resulted in the first use of the designer's name in Vogue captions, and her editorial coverage of American wholesale showings spurred designers to do more experimental work.

Her books The World in Vogue (Viking, 1963) and Ready-Made Miracle (G. P. Putnam, 1967) (see Bibliography) are highly competent chronicles of American elegance and fashion progress.

For her sponsorship of French fashion through Vogue, Jessica Daves received the French Legion d'Honneur.

She died September 22, 1974.

Baron Nicolas de Gunzburg. Fashion editor, Vogue (retired)

Baron de Gunzburg, an editor with equal knowledge of women's and men's fashions, was born in Paris of aristocratic and wealthy Russian parentage. He spent his childhood and early youth in the utmost luxury in Paris, was a prominent figure in the Paris prewar social whirl, but grew bored with it and came to America in 1934.

He was on the staff of Harper's Bazaar for six years and for two years editor-in-chief of Town and Country.

He joined Vogue in 1949 and through his observations and advice has been closely involved with the rise of important designers in Italy and Spain as well as America. He retired in 1974 and serves as a consultant to fashion firms in New York.

Baron (Gayne) de Meyer (1868?–1946). Fashion photographer

Baron Gayne de Meyer was born in Paris of French and German parentage. He changed his name from Demeyer-Watson to de Meyer when he began to be known as a photographer just before World War I.

His earliest work was photographic landscape; he was a member of the Stieglitz group and of the Linked Ring group of photographers. His fame, however, rests in his luminously lit portraits and fashion photographs.

He is credited with introducing diffused lighting and "mood" to fashion pictures, replacing the explicit "catalog" pictures of the past. He worked in Paris for *Harper's Bazaar* from 1910 to 1940. He died in Los Angeles, poor and depressed, in 1946.

David Dubinsky. Garment industry labor leader (retired)

David Dubinsky, whose leadership in American garment industry labor relations led to many patterns later followed throughout the world, was born in Lodz, Russian Poland, on February 22, 1892. He was the son of a baker and trained with his father. At 15 he was named a Master Baker, and a few weeks after joining the baker's guild he took part in a strike that affected his father's shop.

He was arrested by the Russian authorities and sent to Siberia. He eventually returned to Poland but soon (1911) set out for the United States.

In New York, Dubinsky learned the cutting of garments and also applied his zeal for the labor union cause. By 1922 he was vice-president of the International Ladies' Garment Workers' Union and continued to serve in high policy-making positions that strongly affected clothing production methods—and eventually fashion itself. Mr. Dubinsky retired in 1966.

In 1975 the David Dubinsky Student Center was established at the Fashion Institute of Technology, New York.

Eric (Carl Erickson) (1891–1958). American fashion artist

Born in Joliet, Illinois, in 1891 of Swedish immigrant parentage, Eric studied art at the Chicago Art Institute and went to Paris to pursue painting. He married a fashion artist on *Vogue's* Paris staff, and his casual fashion sketches soon found their way to the pages of that magazine. In the next two decades he introduced the "you-are-there" illusion to fashion illustration by sketching the latest Paris creations against the background of smart restaurants, elegant resorts, and other gathering places of the rich and famous. His influence on smart life and on all of fashion in the 1930s and 1940s was profound, and reemerged in the 1970s.

Eric was probably the first fashion artist to draw fashions from the back view. His ultrathin lady with a fashionable slouch became the elegant posture of his time.

Bettina Ballard, in her book *In My Fashion* (*see* Bibliography), says of Eric, "His drawings over the years evoked a promise of beauty that photographs could never equal."

He died in 1958, but into the 1970s his watercolor sketches continued to be collectors' items.

John Fairchild. Chairman of the board and publisher, Fairchild Publications, Inc., 7 E. 12 St., New York, N.Y. 10003

The stormy petrel of international fashion from the mid-50s to the present day, John Fairchild has been significantly involved in making fashion and the fashion designer subjects of piquant interest to the average newspaper and magazine reader, radio listener and television viewer.

Although Fairchild Publications are officially for the trade, with comparatively small circulations, John Fairchild's insistence on giving fashion news a gossipy, opinionated flavor has made Fairchild's *Women's Wear Daily, W,* and *Daily News Record* major news sources in the consumer press of the world. Fairchild's candid, on-the-street coverage of fashion has had a profound effect on present day style reportage.

WWD, as Fairchild prefers to call his banner newpaper *Women's Wear Daily,* has walked the tightrope of fashion prediction many times, and fallen flat only once, when it made an all-out campaign for the midi length (1970). Although that trend was a dismal flop at the time, its echoes (the persistent young fashion for the ankle length day dress and the 1973 high-fashion revival of skirts well below the knee) showed that *WWD's* prediction was merely premature.

John Fairchild was born March 6, 1927, in New York. His grandfather founded the Fairchild trade publications empire and his father, Louis Fairchild, was head of the organization until his retirement in 1968. John graduated from Kent School and Princeton. From 1955 to 1960 he worked in the organization's Paris bureau. Recalled to the unfamiliar environs of the American garment industry, he succeeded in changing the public image of the "rag trade" to an American counterpart of the tense, creatively turbulent, and personal atmosphere of the Paris couture. In 1968, after his organization was acquired by Capitol Cities Communications, Inc., Fairchild was made chairman of the board of Fairchild and executive vice-president and a director of Capitol Cities.

He is an honorary member of the Council of Fashion Designers of America.

With his wife and four children, he now lives in Bermuda and Gstaad, Switzerland, as well as New York City.

He has written two books, *The Fashionable Savages* (Doubleday) (*see* Bibliography) and *The Moonflower Couple* (Doubleday), a novel.

Arnold Gingrich. Editor-in-chief, *Esquire,* 488 Madison Ave., New York, N.Y. 10022

As an advertising copywriter and then editor of the trade magazine

Apparel Arts, Arnold Gingrich was one of the first in the publishing field to grasp the modern potential of male fashion news. With publisher David Smart he launched *Esquire* in the 1930s and guided it to its present prescience in the menswear field.

Born in Grand Rapids, Michigan, on December 5, 1903, he graduated from the University of Michigan in 1925. Along with his sponsorship of now-famous writers through the pages of *Esquire*, he also promoted men's fashion effectively through expertly presented fashion pages, seminars, and educative fashion shows aimed at the male customer and buyers.

More than any other leader in the field, Gingrich removed male fashion from the effete, effeminate, or gangster doldrums into which it had fallen between the Depression and the 1950s.

Shirley Goodman (Mrs. Himan Brown). Executive vice-president, Fashion Institute of Technology, 227 W. 27 St., New York, N.Y. 10001.

This leading educator in one of the outstanding American fashion training schools has immense prestige and influence as a catalyst in industry matters and in linking the Fashion Institute with all areas of fashion at the highest level.

Born in Portsmouth, Virginia and educated in North Carolina and Washington, D.C., Miss Goodman joined FIT in 1949 after considerable experience in government circles in Washington and New York City. In 1948 she coordinated the Mayor's Committee for New York's Golden Anniversary and became involved in its largest industry, fashion.

In 1973 and 1974 Miss Goodman served as executive director of New York City: Fashion Capital of the World, Inc. She was a member of the Board of Governors and chairman of the Membership Committee of the Fashion Group. In 1975 she was made a trustee of the Coty Awards, and was saluted as Woman of the Year by the Fifth Avenue Association. She is the first woman appointed to the Board of the Phillips—Van Heusen Corporation.

In recognition of her work, FIT has named one of its new buildings the Shirley Goodman Resource Center.

She is the mother of two sons.

Robert L. Green. Fashion director of *Playboy*, 747 Third Ave., New York, N.Y. 10017

A skilled observer and impresario of men's fashion presentations for *Playboy* magazine, Green is an expert persuader of both fashion designers and the masculine consumer.

The son of a Ziegfeld Follies beauty, Green grew up in the theatrical tradition which he has effectively carried over into his fashion presentations.

He is a frequent and always provocative speaker at fashion seminars and on television programs and is a part-time lecturer–consultant at the Fashion Institute of Technology in New York.

Rebecca Stickney Hamilton. See France: Fashion Influentials

George Hoyningen-Huené (1900–1968). Photographer

Baron Huené, a giant in several phases of the history of photography, was first to inject a sense of movement into fashion photography.

Born in St. Petersburg on September 4, 1900, he grew up in the Imperial Russian court where his father, Baron Barthold von Hoyningen-Huené, was chief equerry to Czar Nicholas II. The family managed to escape to Paris during the revolution. George studied art there and was working as a fashion sketcher for *Vogue* (1925) while Main Bocher (later Mainbocher the couturier) was editor. When a staff photographer failed to appear for a sitting, Hoyningen-Huené was drafted to take over and his career with a camera began.

In 1935 he followed his editor Carmel Snow from *Vogue* to *Harper's Bazaar*, but in 1940 he tired of fashion and did a series of travel books which he described as "visual archeology." In 1946 he joined his friend George Cukor in Hollywood where he worked on films and taught photography until his death in 1968.

Eunice W. Johnson. Editor, *Ebony*, 820 S. Michigan Ave., Chicago, Ill. 60605

The editor who most directly influenced the fashion-minded black consumer in America was born Eunice Walker in Selma, Alabama, where her family was prominent in black education and social welfare. Her father was a physician, her mother a teacher, and her paternal grandfather, Dr. Nathanial Walker, a friend of Booker T. Washington and founder of the first black theological seminary in the South.

She finished high school in Selma and attended Talladega College in Talladega, Alabama. She is now a member of its board of trustees.

She came to Chicago to take her master's degree in social service administration at Loyola University. She married a fellow student, John H. Johnson, and together they founded the *Negro Digest*, aimed at the educated black population. *Ebony* was started in 1945 as the first fashion magazine for the black woman.

In 1956 Mrs. Johnson and *Ebony*'s fashion editor, the late Freda de Knight, conceived the idea of a touring fashion show of the work of the most famous international designers to raise money for Negro charities.

In the succeeding years, the Ebony Fashion Fair has become the leading black social event in America. In 1974 it gave 86 performances in 80 cities, and in toto has raised more than $4.5 million for local and national causes.

Since Mrs. de Knight's death in 1961, Mrs. Johnson has directed the fashion activities of Ebony.

She serves on the Board of Trustees of the Coty American Fashion Critics' Awards.

Ann Keagy (Mrs. J. Rodman). Chairman, Fashion Design Department, Parsons School of Design, 70 Fifth Ave., New York, N.Y. 10011

As the leading activist in the education of future American designers, Ann Keagy is to American fashion students what Janey Ironside was to the budding designers in the Royal College of Art in London. She directs the fashion design and technical courses at the Parsons School of Design and is responsible for the close relationship between leading designers and budding talents through the program of guest lectures and guest critics she conducts.

A working designer before she became an educator, Mrs. Keagy has been with the Parsons School since 1947 and remained when it became affiliated with the New School for Social Research in 1970.

Sally Kirkland (Mrs. Frederick Kirkland). Fashion editor (retired) and consultant, 17 E. 89 St., New York, N.Y. 10028

As fashion editor of Life magazine from 1947 to 1969, during which she reported fashion as news that 27 million readers could understand and follow, Mrs. Kirkland's skill at visualizing and pinpointing new trends and her terse, bright text brought new pace to fashion journalism. For this contribution she was decorated by the Italian government with its Order of Star of Solidarity (1954) and received the Neiman–Marcus Award (1955).

Until Mrs. Kirkland retired in 1969, a Life cover was one of the most sought after accolades in international fashion. Today she acts as consultant to numerous fashion events and is the author of a biography on the American designer Claire McCardell, included in the Fashion Institute of Technology's publication, American Fashion, in cooperation with Quadrangle—The New York Times Book Co.

Eleanor Lambert (Mrs. Seymour Berkson). Fashion publicist and writer, 32 E. 57 St., New York, N.Y. 10022

Identified with the emergence of the American designer as a major creative factor in world fashion, Eleanor Lambert was born in Crawfordsville, Indiana.

She planned to be a sculptor, attending John Herron Art Institute in

Indianapolis, Indiana, and the Chicago Art Institute. In 1928 she came to New York and wrote fashion reports for a retail consultant and designed bookjackets. In 1930 she began to handle public relations for artists, helping to make known such artists as Thomas Benton, John Curry, Walt Kuhn, Isamu Noguchi, Jacob Epstein, and Augustus John. In 1934 she added designers to her clients. She was associated with the launching of the American Look and helped to found the Fashion Group and establish the Costume Institute of the Metropolitan Museum of Art. In 1941 she inaugurated the press program of the New York Dress Institute, the newly organized association between management and labor, and established the National Press Weeks for first-hand coverage of American fashion collections by out-of-town reporters.

She has conducted the International Best Dressed Poll since 1940 and in 1942 conceived and was made coordinator of the annual Coty American Fashion Critics' Awards.

In 1936 she married Seymour Berkson, President of International News Service and publisher of the New York Journal-American. He died in 1959.

She was appointed by the U.S. government to produce American fashion shows twice in Russia, in Australia, and on a tour of European capitals.

When President Johnson established the National Council on the Arts in 1965, Eleanor Lambert was named to the first 26-member body—the first time fashion had been listed among the creative arts anywhere in the world. In 1962 she helped to found the Council of Fashion Designers of America, and was made an honorary charter member. She serves on the Advisory Committee of the Costume Institute of the Metropolitan Museum of Art, the Advisory Board of the Fashion Institute of Technology, and the Board of Directors of the Council of Fashion Designers of America.

In 1960, she received the New York Board of Trade's Gold Medal Award for outstanding contribution to the fashion industry.

Eleanor McMillen (Mrs. Niels Olsen). Executive director, The Fashion Group, Inc., 9 Rockefeller Plaza, New York, N.Y. 10020

The director of the Fashion Group, the world's largest fashion organization coordinating all aspects of women's contribution to international fashion, Mrs. McMillen is influential in fashion activities in 31 areas of the world.

Born in Goddard, Kansas, she graduated from Friends University in Wichita and received a master's degree in psychology from Boston University, taught at Tennessee State College, then attended New York University School of Retailing and received a master's degree in that field.

After working in several phases of fashion production and promotion, she became director of the Fashion Group.

In 1963 she served on the John F. Kennedy Status of American Women Commission. She was a member of the former Governor Rockefeller's Committee for Education and Employment of Women in 1966, and was on Governor Rockefeller's Women's Advisory Council.

Stanley Marcus. Retail merchant, Neiman–Marcus, Main & Ervay Sts., Dallas, Tex. 75201

The son of Herbert and Minnie Marcus who made Nieman–Marcus the shopping mecca for the new wealth of Texas in the early 20th century, Stanley Marcus was born in Dallas on April 20, 1905, and trained to succeed his parents by studying business administration at Harvard. His own natural instinct for the beautiful and original, however, led to his world importance as a fashion entrepreneur. He joined the family firm in 1926, becoming its president in 1950. During those years he linked his organization and its customers to the latest developments in fashion throughout the world through his own and his staff's brilliant and farsighted merchandising and through the Neiman–Marcus Award, given to designers from various countries.

He is an overseer of Harvard University and has served on numerous government committees. He has been decorated by the French, Italian, British, and Belgian governments.

Stanley Marcus' autobiography Minding the Store (see Bibliography) is a leisurely and comprehensive history of his noteworthy fashion influence. He is an honorary member of the Council of Fashion Designers of America.

Robert Riley. Fashion historian, Fashion Institute of Technology, 227 W. 27 St., New York, N.Y. 10001

This former curator of costume at the Brooklyn Museum, New York, and writer of fashion history is now affiliated with the Fashion Institute of Technology and the Costume Society of America.

He is the author of numerous articles on fashion history and personalities and his book The Fashion Makers (Crown Press, 1968) is a vivid record of contemporary fashion creators.

Mr. Riley is an honorary member of the Council of Fashion Designers of America.

Mary Russell. Journalist–photographer, 5 place de Furstenberg, F-75006 Paris, France

This young fashion photographer and interpreter of European fashions for American publications was born in Marblehead, Massachusetts. She attended the Ecole des Arts Decoratifs in Nice, France, where her interest in fashion was aroused. He first job was as model–saleswoman for Elizabeth Arden in Washington, D.C. She worked for *Glamour* magazine, setting up a Paris office for the publication in 1964 at the beginning of the Youth Era in fashion. In 1970 she became European correspondent for *Vogue*, covering the couture and ready-to-wear showings in all the fashion centers and reporting on social and art events. In 1975 she established her own office for special assignments and reporting for women's magazines on an international basis. She now reports for American, Brazilian, French, and Italian publications.

Dorothy Shaver (1897–1959). Retail merchant

This powerful and creative fashion merchant, president of Lord & Taylor and original promoter of the term "American look," was born in Center Point, Arkansas, where her father was a judge.

She came to New York with her sister Elsie when they were both in their early twenties. Being a descendant of the famous Stewart family, owners of New York's great 19th-century fashion emporium, Dorothy Shaver had introductions to leading New York retailers. Her first and only job was at Lord & Taylor. Twenty-one years after she began as assistant in the business office she was named the store's president and held the post until her sudden death in 1959.

Miss Shaver's belief in original and independent American fashion talent, together with her capacity for "stirring fact and fantasy" about merchandise to enhance its mystique to the shopper, made her one of the outstanding retailers of her epoch. She was one of the founders of the Fashion Group and instrumental in the establishment of the Costume Institute of the Metropolitan Museum of Art in New York. Through the Lord & Taylor Awards, she established the idea of a department store award for fashion and creative home furnishings and later for individual achievements which added to the quality of life for all people.

Eugenia Sheppard. Fashion editor and columnist, Field Enterprises and *New York Post*, 30 E. 42 St., New York, N.Y. 10017

An outstanding chronicler of the fashionable world, Eugenia Sheppard is credited with having personalized fashion journalism by replacing its stilted phraseology with amusing home truths that make women readers feel less remote from and more involved with fashion as part of everyday life.

She was born near Columbus, Ohio, and educated at the Columbus School for Girls and' at Bryn Mawr College. She worked briefly on her hometown newspaper, then in 1937 came to New York. She was on the staff of *Women's Wear Daily* for eighteen months, then joined the *New*

York Herald Tribune as assistant fashion editor, becoming fashion editor in 1947. In 1949 she inaugurated the first daily woman's page in America, and in 1956, as fashion grew in interest to the average person, she added her now-famous column "Inside Fashion."

Although she is never downright unkind, she always voices her honest opinion. "I guess I was the first to speak disrespectfully of Paris," she once commented.

She was married for many years to the late Walter Millis, a noted editor, scholar, and writer on world peace.

Although frequently honored, she refers only to the fact that she "won the annual Award of the Newspaper Women's Club five or six times."

Jerry Silverman. Manufacturer and industry leader, 530 Seventh Ave., New York, N.Y. 10018

Although Jerry Silverman is a highly successful dress manufacturer (Jerry Silverman, Ltd.), his unique contribution to American fashion has been his enthusiastic leadership of causes and projects aimed at bettering the image of American fashion. He heads the new union–management–civic government cooperative effort, New York: Fashion Capital, Inc., and is on the administrative board of the Fashion Institute of Technology, the Parsons School of Design and many industry committees.

Born in New York and a Harvard-trained lawyer, Silverman served in the U.S. Army but spent his three years' duty sailing the Atlantic on the Queen Mary, then a transport ship. On his return home, he became sales manager of a wholesale dress firm. He formed Jerry Silverman, Inc., with Shannon Rodgers as designer–partner in 1959. All the Silverman enterprises are now divisions of the Warnaco organization.

Carmel White Snow (Mrs. George Palen Snow) (1887–1961). Fashion editor

This eminent editor and fashion authority was noted for fostering the fame of such creators as Balenciaga and Christian Dior. Carmel White Snow was born August 21, 1887, in a suburb of Dublin, Ireland, where her father, Peter White, was managing director of the Irish Woolen Manufacturing and Export Company. The White family came to Chicago in 1893 where Peter White had organized the Irish Village in the World's Fair of that year.

Her mother remained in Chicago and opened a dress shop, then brought her children to New York where Carmel grew up.

From 1921 to 1932 Carmel White was fashion editor of *Vogue*, during which time (1926) she married George Palen Snow.

In 1932 she became editor of *Harper's Bazaar* and established herself as one of the great analysts and interpreters of the haute couture to the feminine public.

Her interest and furtherance of French fashion prestige brought her the Knight's Cross of the French Legion of Honor in 1949.

In 1956, aged 70, she retired and lived briefly in County Mayo, Ireland, but returned to New York to continue her interest, if not her activity, in fashion.

While preparing her memoirs (*The World of Carmel Snow*, McGraw-Hill, 1962) she died in her sleep May 7, 1961.

Edward Steichen. See Hall of Fame

Geraldine Stutz (Mrs. David Gibbs). Retail fashion merchant, Henri Bendel, 10 W. 57 St., New York, N.Y. 10019

One of the world's youngest presidents of a major fashion enterprise, Geraldine Stutz has also been one of the most influential retailers of the 20th century. After revitalizing the venerable but fading New York specialty shop founded by Henri Bendel in the 1890s, Miss Stutz pioneered in making the high-fashion store attractive to the avant-garde youth of the 1960s.

Bendel's organized the first "vertical setup" in the modern retail field, Bendel's Studio, manufacturing and distributing the work of young designers discovered by Bendel's. These included Stephen Burrows and John Kloss.

Born in Chicago, she studied drama and journalism at Mundelein College, graduating magna cum laude in 1945. She joined the staff of *Glamour* magazine and in 1954 became fashion coordinator for I. Miller shoes. In 1956 Maxey Jarman, then chairman of Genesco, asked Miss Stutz to take over the presidency of its new acquisition, Henri Bendel, a store with an honorable but elderly image. By 1975 Bendel's was the leading purveyor and arbiter of young fashion trends known throughout the world.

In 1965 Geraldine Stutz married the British artist, David Gibbs.

Lazare Teper. Research director, International Ladies Garment Workers Union, 1710 Broadway, New York, N.Y. 10019

Dr. Lazare Teper, a well-known economist, and the leading American expert in the compilation of statistics on the garment industry, is apt to be a year ahead of government agencies in compiling the figures on units of clothing manufactured and sold, imports and exports, prices paid, and comparative statistics on family clothing expenditures. His assessment of the fashion industries indirectly but potently affects many facets, from legislation to labor contracts.

Born in Odessa, Russia, January 16, 1908, he studied at the University of Paris. On coming to America in 1927, he attended Johns Hopkins University (PhD, 1931). He joined the administrative staff of the International Ladies Garment Workers Union in 1934 to head its department of statistics.

Susan Train. *See* France: Fashion Influentials

Diana Vreeland (Mrs. T. Reed Vreeland). Fashion editor and special consultant, Costume Institute, Metropolitan Museum of Art, Fifth Ave. and 82 St., New York, N.Y. 10028

Fashion editor for *Harper's Bazaar* and later *Vogue*, and a leading fashion catalyst from the 1930s until her editorial retirement in 1971, Diana Vreeland coined many fashion catch phrases, and her electric personality has been felt through the entire world of chic.

In the mid-1960s, the bizarre fashion poses of *Vogue's* fashion mannequins, particularly such Vreeland discoveries as Verushka and Penelope Tree, furthered the far-out fashion thinking of the times, as well as bringing widespread protest from the more conservative. Her comments such as: "The bikini is the most important thing since the atom bomb," and "Exaggeration is the only reality," are legend.

After her retirement Mrs. Vreeland was appointed advisor to the Costume Institute of the Metropolitan Museum and put together brilliant exhibitions including the fashions of the late Cristobal Balenciaga, a summary of fashions of the first three decades of the 20th century, and a collection of Hollywood designers' outstanding creations.

The late Bettina Ballard, her colleague as a fashion editor, wrote of Diana Vreeland: "Fashion is something she believes enters into everything in life—the way one walks, talks, lives, breathes, eats and thinks, and certainly the way one loves as well as what one wears." Mrs. Vreeland is an honorary member of the Council of Fashion Designers of America.

June Weir (Mrs. Kirk Baron). Vice-president and fashion editor, *Women's Wear Daily*, 7 E. 12 St., New York, N.Y. 10003

The most perceptive fashion eye and pen to emerge in the 1970s, June Weir follows the policy of *Women's Wear Daily* in saturation-type reporting on trends and designers, and yet she has established her own identity as an influential international fashion personality.

Born in Youngstown, Ohio, of Scottish parents, Ms. Weir attended Ohio Wesleyan University, majoring in sociology and psychology. She received a scholarship to the Tobe–Coburn School for Fashion Careers in New York in 1950 and after a year joined the training squad at R.H. Macy, going on to become assistant buyer of women's fashions. In 1954 she joined *Women's Wear Daily* as a fashion reporter, in 1966 was promoted to fashion editor, and in 1969 named vice-president of the parent company, Fairchild Publications.

She married Kirk Baron, an officer of the American Merchant Marine in 1959; they live in Manhattan.

Ms. Weir serves on many fashion committees and is a well-known lecturer on fashion.

Polaire Weissman. Fashion historian, costume curator (retired), 150 W. 55 St., New York, N.Y. 10019

Born and educated in New York, Miss Weissman became associated in 1939 with the late Irene Lewisohn, prominent collector of antique costumes, and helped to organize Miss Lewisohn's collection into The Museum of Costume Art of New York. When the collection was transferred to the Metropolitan Museum in 1946 to form the nucleus of the present-day Costume Institute, Miss Weissman was appointed director and retained the post until she retired July 1, 1971. She is an honorary member of the Council of Fashion Designers of America.

Nancy White (Mrs. Ralph Delahaye Paine, Jr.). Editor, retailer, consultant, 66 E. 91 St., New York, N.Y. 10028.

The former editor-in-chief of *Harper's Bazaar* and later fashion director of New York's Bergdorf Goodman was born to a fashion and editorial career. Her father, Thomas J. White, was a power in the Hearst publishing empire which includes *Harper's Bazaar*, and her aunt, Carmel White Snow, was the creative and authoritative editor of *Harper's Bazaar* for many years.

She was born in Brooklyn on July 25, 1916, and was educated in private schools in New York. She was fashion editor successively for *Pictorial Review*, *Good Housekeeping*, and *Harper's Bazaar*, becoming *Bazaar's* editor-in-chief in 1958. At *Harper's Bazaar* she edited a book celebrating the magazine's 100th anniversary, *100 Women of Accomplishment* (Hearst Corporation, 1967). She was a member of the National Council on the Arts (1966–1972) and is a member of the Board of Directors of General Mills.

Trade Associations and Organizations

American Designer Showings Press Week. 32 E. 57 St., New York, N.Y. 10022

Tel: (212) 688-2130. Founded: 1943. Chmn: Matthew Rubinstein. Coordinator: Eleanor Lambert.

Not a trade organization but a semiannual collaboration of well-known American fashion designers and high-fashion producers in women's and men's fashion, cosmetics, and accessories to show their season's collections by invitation to the international fashion press. A five-day schedule of showings is presented in a New York hotel, with press rooms and wire, radio, and TV facilities set up for news coverage.

Participation is by acceptance of the other members of the group, in the manner of an informal "club."

American Footwear Industries Association. 1611 N. Kent St., Arlington, Va. 22209

Tel: (703) 522-8070. Founded: 1869, Reorganized: 1972. Pres: Mark E. Richardson. Exec. VP. & Secy: Maxwell Field.

Organized in 1869 and taking its present name from a merger in 1972 of The American Footwear Manufacturers Association and The New England Footwear Association, this group has as its purpose the promotion of the general welfare of American footwear manufacturing and allied industries.

Its membership of almost 500 companies is a "who's who" of footwear manufacturers and their supplier companies in America.

American Printed Fabrics Council, Inc. 1440 Broadway, New York, N.Y. 10018

Tel: (212) 564-8505. Founded: 1966. Exec. Dir: Arlene Friedlander.

The American Printed Fabrics Council was organized in 1966 as a non-profit operation by textile and allied companies interested in broadening consumer interest in printed fabrics in apparel, accessories, and home furnishings. Its membership embraces mills, yarn and fiber suppliers, chemical firms, converters, and screen engravers representing over 80 percent of this country's printing capacity.

The Council has a continuing promotion and public relations program aimed at stimulating creativity and new talents in its field, and, through scholarships, to encourage students in major textile colleges and fashion and design schools.

The Council established the Tommy Award in 1970 to honor fashion designers and manufacturers who used prints creatively and printers and fiber makers for special contributions to the textile industry.

California Accessories Guild. *See* California Fashion Creators.

California Childrenswear Guild. *See* California Fashion Creators.

California Fashion Creators. 110 E. 9 St., Los Angeles, Calif. 90015

Tel: (213) 627-1034. Founded: 1943. Pres: Eric Flagg.

This membership organization includes manufacturers of apparel of all types at every price level.

The group carries out a year-round program of promotion and public relations, and also sponsors semiannual press weeks.

Within the overall organization is a smaller group of higher-priced clothing manufacturers: The Los Angeles Fashion Guild (110 E. 9 St., Los Angeles, Calif. 90015). Affiliate organizations at the same address are the California Accessories Guild and the California Childrenswear Guild.

Members of these groups may participate in the activities of the California Fashion Creators, and it also sets dates for showings of member collections in Los Angeles, Dallas, and New York.

Costume Society of America. c/o Costume Institute, Metropolitan Museum of Art, Fifth Ave. & 82 St., New York, N.Y. 10028

Founded: 1973. Pres: J. Herbert Callister.

The Costume Society of America, the U.S. version of the Costume Society formed by the Victoria and Albert Museum in London, provides a center of study and information for individuals and institutions interested in the history of costume.

Its excellent newsletter, edited by Robert Riley, informs members of current happenings in the entire fashion world.

Membership is open to people interested in fashion in all its phases.

Cotton, Incorporated. 1370 Ave. of the Americas, New York, N.Y. 10019

Tel: (212) 586-1070. Founded: 1970. Pres: J. Dukes Wooters, Jr. Dir., Fashion Marketing: Lillian Rosilli.

Cotton, Incorporated (having separated in 1970 from the now defunct Cotton Producers Institute) is a nonprofit organization supported by 250,000 cotton growers of America to promote and market cotton fibers and textiles. It participates in trade fashion presentations such as those of the Men's Fashion Association and the Dallas Apparel Mart.

The organization maintains a center in Raleigh, North Carolina, for technical research in textiles and agriculture and two small branches in Los Angeles and Dallas, where research libraries are available to members.

Council of Fashion Designers of America. 32 E. 57 St., New York, N.Y. 10022

Tel: (212) MU 8-2130. Founded: 1962. Pres: Oscar de la Renta. Coord. Activities: Eleanor Lambert.

The Council of Fashion Designers of America is an honorary, nonprofit society of creative American designers in all fashion fields. Its purposes are to further fashion design as an element of American art and culture, to establish and maintain a code of ethics and practices in professional, public, and trade relations, and to promote and improve international public understanding and appreciation of the American fashion arts.

C.F.D.A. has about 80 members, representing the leading creators in the apparel, footwear, textile, jewelry, and accessory fields. The board of directors has also proposed and had the membership ratify the extension of honorary membership to outstanding fashion personalities other than designers.

Membership is limited to individuals known for their creative force within a fashion firm. Membership is personal and does not extend to the firm or associates.

Fashion Fairs (Cavin and Tubiana, OHG). Organizers of International Trade Fairs, American office: c/o Emron International, 445 Park Ave., New York, N.Y. 10022; German office: Heyes Strasse 20–22, 4 Düsseldorf 12. Branches in London, England, and Haifa, Israel.

Dirs: Dr. Alfred Cavin and Emile Tubiana.

This firm of an engineer–architect and sales and promotion expert is prominent in planning and administering fashion and textile trade expositions for governments or trade groups throughout the world.

Dr. Alfred Cavin is a Rumanian-born architect–engineer who designed and built trade fair layouts before expanding his activities. Emile Tubiana, a Tunisian, was on the sales and promotion side of various trade shows until their association began. They created "packaged" trade shows and developed the Selfexpo visual merchandising system being used in trade shows in Australia, Canada, England, Iran, Poland, Holland, France, and Israel.

They organized and built the Boutique Show which is part of the prêt-à-porter exposition of the Porte de Versailles in Paris. They are advisors to the Igedo and Mode Woche trade fairs in West Germany.

The Fashion Group, Inc. 9 Rockefeller Plaza, New York, N.Y. 10020

Tel: (212) CI 7-3940. Founded: 1931. Exec. Dir: Eleanor McMillen

This association of women executives in every phase of the fashion industry was incorporated in 1931 at the instigation of prominent women fashion personalities including Dorothy Shaver, president of Lord & Taylor, Claire McCardell, designer, and Tobe, retail consultant. The original purpose was to promote more careers for women in fashion.

Today the Fashion Group is international, with 31 regional groups and chapters in Paris, Tokyo, Canada, Mexico City, and Australia added to the focal center in New York.

The Fashion Group sponsors analytical showings of seasonal fashions, career courses, and other projects relating fashion to the professional and to the consumer. It has presented fashion shows in foreign embassies under the aegis of the U.S. State Department and has sponsored an international exchange program of fashion shows with other countries.

Fur Information and Fashion Council. 101 W. 30 St., New York, N.Y. 10001

Tel: (212) 736-4858. Founded: 1958. Pres: Robert Ginsberg. Admin. Secy: Jess Chernak.

This national trade and promotion association was founded in 1958, representing all segments of the fur industries, including manufacturers, distributors, labor, dealers, and dressers.

The organization's purpose is to further the consumer's interest in all types of fur at every price level and to meet challenges such as consumer education on furs in relation to wildlife conservation. Funds are raised by an annual member contribution of a percentage of sales.

International Ladies Garment Workers Union (ILGWU). 1710 Broadway, New York, N.Y. 10019

Tel: (212) CO 5-7000. Founded: 1900. Pres: Louis Stulberg.

This labor union is unique in the fashion world because of its share in fashion industry programs aimed at informing the public and promoting sales through joint efforts and financing.

ILGWU was founded in 1900 by a group of immigrant workers in the clothing trades. Some of them were itinerant, carrying their sewing machines on their backs, and others had given the term "sweat shop" its meaning. The union first came to widespread public notice when a fire in the Triangle Shirtwaist Company on March 25, 1911, killed 146 women in a crowded loft with too-few fire escapes and bolted doors.

Such leaders as David Dubinsky and Julius Hochman led the union into the first labor–management venture, the New York Dress Institute, established in 1941 to promote public appreciation and purchase of American-made dresses. In 1973 a similar pact was made under the name New York: Fashion Capital of the World.

Since 1959 the ILGWU has conducted its Union Label campaign of advertising, booklets, and publicity to make women conscious of clothes bearing the stamp of having been made by unionized workers.

There are now 455,000 members of the Joint Board of the Dress and Cloakmakers Union, affiliated with the AFL/CIO. The organization maintains an excellent research and statistical department under the direction of Dr. Lazare Teper.

Los Angeles Fashion Guild. *See* California Fashion Creators

Men's Fashion Association of America. 1290 Ave. of the Americas, New York, N.Y. 10019

Tel: (212) LT 1-8210. Founded: 1955. Exec. Dir: Norman Carr. Dir., Fashion: Chip Tolbert.

Created in 1955 as the American Institute of Men's and Boy's Wear, the Men's Fashion Association of America (MFA) is now the leading organization for public relations and consumer education in men's wear, with a membership of America's leading manufacturers, textile mills, yarn and fiber producers, converters, selling agents, suppliers, and allied groups plus the 3300 members of the Menswear Retailers of America.

Masculine fashion news is channelled to the fashion press regularly, and a live presentation is made twice a year during the organization's conventions. Through business firms, MFA supplies booklets and color guides on men's dress, and provides local TV stations with fashion films and color slide reports.

Millinery Institute of America. 10 E. 49 St., New York, N.Y. 10016

Tel: (212) 686-2975. Founded: 1959. Chmn-of-the-Bd: Bernard Grossman. Exec. Dir: Burt Champion.

Its membership consists of 200 manufacturers of hats in all price ranges.

The Institute conducts a national publicity campaign and arranges designer tours for members in stores throughout the country. It participates in the educational program at the Fashion Institute of Technology with lectures and presentations.

For several years the organization bestowed Golden Hat awards to personalities, but abandoned the awards in 1969.

National Cotton Council of America. 1918 N. Parkway, Box 12285, Memphis, Tenn. 38112

Tel: (901) 276-2783. Founded: 1938. Exec. Dir: Albert Russell.

Founded in 1938 to promote and protect American cotton-growers, this organization is composed of growers, ginners, merchants, processors, and cotton textile manufacturers. It has representatives in Washington to spur farm bills and other legislation affecting American cotton.

The Council conducts economic studies, research programs, and supports the activities of other allied organizations such as the Cotton Council International, the Cotton Foundation, the Oscar Johnson Cotton Foundation, the International Institute for Cotton, and the Cotton Producers Institute (now Cotton, Incorporated and a separate organization).

The Council has branches and trade representatives abroad and field representatives throughout the cotton-producing areas of America.

National Shoe Retailers Association. 200 Madison Ave., New York, N.Y. 10016

Founded: 1912. Pres: James P. Orr, II. Exec. VP: William K. McGrath.

The only such organization representing all types of shoe retailing, the National Shoe Retailers Association was organized in 1912 and now has approximately 10,000 retail members in the United States, Europe, and the Far East. It promotes the shoe retail industry in the fields of personnel training (both salesman and managerial), public relations, and other activities. Advance fashion forecasts, newsletters, information services on resources for shoes and handbags are supplied to members. Seminars and workshops are held at regional and national shoe trade shows.

New York Couture Business Council, Inc. 141 W. 41 St., New York, N.Y. 10036

Tel: (212) LA 4-0461. Founded: 1967. Pres: Vincent Monte-Sano.

A nonprofit organization, the New York Couture Business Council, founded in 1967, later absorbed some of the functions of the earlier organization, the Couture Group of the New York Dress Institute, the promotional organization founded by the ILGWU and the New York manufacturers in 1941.

The council, composed of about 30 dress, coat, suit, and sportwear manufacturers, established seasonal market weeks and formerly conducted semiannual press weeks for the national fashion press.

Volume Footwear Retailers of America. 51 E. 42 St., New York, N.Y. 10017

Founded: 1944. Exec. V-P: Edward Atkinson. Exec. Sec: Helen Joseph.

This is a nonprofit membership organization of about 50 shoe retailers which deals with merchandising and trade policies and problems.

The Wool Bureau, Inc. (Division, International Wool Secretariat). 360 Lexington Ave., New York, N.Y. 10017

Tel: (212) 986-6222. Founded: 1949. Pres: Felix J. Colangelo.

This promotion and research organization for the U.S.A. is a division of the International Wool Secretariat (established 1937).

The Wool Bureau has its headquarters in New York City. Its purposes are to promote wool fashions and wool fabric production via technical and fashion information aimed at the industry and the press. The commercial emblem, "Woolmark," in sewn-in labels and garment tags, identifies the use of pure new wool and quality processing.

Honors and Awards

Coty American Fashion Critics Award. For a listing of Coty Award winners for the years 1943–1975, see the appendix

The Coty American Fashion Critics Awards were founded in 1942 by Coty, Inc. when Grover Whalen was chairman of the board of that international perfume and cosmetics company. The purpose of the Awards, as they were conceived by Eleanor Lambert (see United States: Fashion Influentials), was to draw attention to the originality, scope and power of American fashion and bring it to equal prominence with European fashion. In the succeeding years, the Coty Awards have become the best known fashion honor in the world and the pattern for similar honors in other countries.

Two committees representing women's and men's fashion act each year to select the designers who are to receive the Coty Awards in certain categories, or who are nominated for a national ballot in other categories. These committees are composed of fashion editors from magazines, news services, newspapers, and television. Their deliberations end in a secret written ballot. Some of the results are announced the same day, but the final results of the national ballot for the annual trophy known as the "Winnie" (for women's fashion) and the Menswear Award are revealed at the presentation itself when an envelope is opened by the presenter. The annual awards were originally given solely to designers of women's fashion, but in 1968 the Coty Menswear Fashion Award was established as well.

To win a Coty Award, a fashion designer must in the previous year have been an outstanding contributor to contemporary American style, or a new talent whose ideas point the way to significant future change in American dress. Winners receiving Special Awards are generally part of a movement to bring attention to one area of dress, such as lingerie, jewelry, shoes, accessories, or furs. Those nominated on the national ballot are designers of clothing. Designers who have previously won the "Winnie" or the Menswear Award are eligible for further honors: the Return Award for repeated excellence, and after that the Hall of Fame Award to a designer of acknowledged leadership and continuous brilliance. In rare instances the committee may give further accolades to Hall of Fame winners whose work is especially influential by awarding the Hall of Fame Citation.

The "Winnie" is a bronze draped female figure designed by the noted American sculptor, Malvina Hoffman. The Special Award is a bronze plaque with the Hoffman figurine in bas-relief. Recipients of the Return Award and the Hall of Fame Award have silver or gold plates attached to their "Winnies." The Coty Menswear Fashion Award carries a trophy in abstract steel sculpture designed by Forrest Myers. The Special Award for Menswear is an aluminum free-form sculpture.

Gold Coast Award

Chicago's largest annual charity fashion show founded in 1955 for the benefit of the Chicago Maternity Center of Prentice Women's Hospital (720 N. Michigan, Chicago, Ill. 60611) involves the presentation of the Gold Coast Award to a designer represented in the fashion show and chosen by popular vote of the audience. About 12 well-known designers are invited to participate each year, representing a selection made by the committee in collaboration with Chicago stores.

International Best-Dressed Poll

This annual international ballot, followed by an announcement of 12 women and 12 men said to symbolize distinguished current taste in dress "without extravagance or ostentation," is an outgrowth of the annual lists of best dressed women announced by Paris couturiers from about 1920 until 1939. When World War II began in Europe, Eleanor Lambert (32 E. 57 St., New York, N.Y. 10022), fashion publicist, picked up the tradition and has maintained it as a personal effort since 1940.

About 2500 ballots annually are sent to fashion designers, fashion and society editors, columnists, and well-known personalities throughout the world. The returned votes are tallied and formally approved by a committee of 20 editors representing the women's and men's fashion press.

In 1959 the committee instituted the Best-Dressed Hall of Fame to which people of consistent style leadership are elevated to permanent status.

In 1968 the growing importance of masculine fashion prompted the Best-Dressed Committee to add an annual men's list.

Neiman–Marcus Awards

These international awards, sponsored by Neiman–Marcus (Main & Ervay St., Dallas, Tex. 75201) were first made in 1938 to fashion designers and personalities in other fields chosen by a jury of executives headed by Stanley Marcus. The awards were discontinued in 1974. The honor carries with it the tribute of having rendered "distinguished service in the field of fashion."

Tommy Awards

The American Printed Fabrics Council Inc. (1440 Broadway, New York, N.Y. 10018) established the Tommy Awards in 1970 to recognize the creative use of prints by designers and manufacturers, and to honor printers and film makers for outstanding contributions in the textile industry.

Fashion Education

The Academie Moderne. 55 Commonwealth Ave., Boston, Mass. 02116

Organized and directed by fashion journalist and commentator Mildred Albert, this school teaches fashion and fashion merchandising. It is helpful to students with talent in either area, although the school owes its reputation more to the dynamism and talents of Ms. Albert than to its scholastic program. An annual award is given to leading American fashion designers.

Art Institute of Chicago. School of Fashion Design, Michigan Ave. at Adams St., Chicago, Ill. 60603

Founded in 1866 and coeducational, the School of Fashion Design offers its degrees in conjunction with a special liberal arts program at the University of Chicago. The school is directly attached to the Art Institute of Chicago, and confers a BFA degree to majors in fashion design.

Bauder Fashion College. 300 Biscayne Blvd., Miami, Fla. 33131. Branches: The Bauder State House, 641 Howe Ave., Sacramento, Calif. 95825. The Bauder Lee House, 508 S. Central St., Arlington, Tex. 76010. 3355 Lenox Rd. N.E., Atlanta, Ga. 30336.

Bauder was founded in 1962 in Miami. The college offers two-year programs in various fashion fields.

Bennett College. Millbrook, N.Y. 12545

An independent junior college for women founded in 1891, Bennett has a two-year program in fashion design. Dormitories are available.

Drexel University. 32 and Chestnut Sts., Philadelphia, Pa. 19104

All Drexel students are required to take part in Drexel's four-year "coop" plan and work the year after their freshman year at a job that parallels their academic majors. The original Drexel Institute of Arts, Science and Industry, founded in 1891, became Drexel Institute of Technology in 1936 and Drexel University in 1970.

It offers a Bachelor of Science major in fashion design and design and merchandising.

The school is coeducational and has dormitories.

Fashion Institute of Design and Merchandising. 323 W. Eighth St., Los Angeles, Calif. 90014. Branches: 13701 Riverside Dr., Sherman Oaks, Calif. 91403. 790 Market St., San Francisco, Calif. 94102

The above is one of three schools, all with the same name and with the same curriculum, founded in 1969. The majority of their students are high school graduates, but they also admit students with college training or degrees.

They offer a two-year nationally accredited (AICS) AA degree, their majors are fashion design and merchandising design, and their concentration is interior design.

They have a work–study program which includes placement service in part-time jobs. For graduates, there is also a placement service.

The school has direct involvement with industry on the West Coast—manufacturers, retailers, and West Coast fashion organizations.

Fashion Institute of Technology. 227 W. 27 St., New York, N.Y. 10001

Founded in 1944 as a community college and operating since 1951 as part of the State University of New York, F.I.T. trains its students for creative, technical, and executive careers in fashion. It has an enrollment of over 5500.

F.I.T.'s two-year programs for high school graduates include fashion design, fashion display, fashion illustration, fashion photography, fashion buying and merchandising, and other related fields leading to the Associate in Applied Science degree. For college graduates and those who have completed the required liberal arts courses it offers one-year programs leading to the same degree.

F.I.T. has an extensive library and the Edward C. Blum Laboratory collection of period and 20th-century fashions for research use by students and professional designers.

Its Educational Foundation for the Fashion Industry is an advisory body of leading representatives of American industry.

F.I.T. has dormitories and maintains a placement office to help its graduates find their first jobs.

Finch College. 50 E. 78 St., New York, N.Y. 10021

This women's college, founded in 1900, makes New York life and culture an integral part of class activities.

The college confers the degree of BA at the end of the four-year program with a major available in fashion design and merchandising. Dormitories are available.

Garland Junior College. 409 Commonwealth Ave., Boston, Mass. 02215

This junior college for women, founded in 1872, aims to provide graduates with marketable skills in fashion design and merchandising. Dormitories are available.

The Harlem Institute of Fashion. 157 W. 126 St., New York, N.Y. 10027

Established in 1966 by Lois Alexander (Mrs. Julius Lane), an employee of the New York Housing and Urban Development Department as a way of encouraging black residents of Harlem to learn to sew and to find employment in the garment industries, this school has meaning in black advancement. The standing of the school owes more to its leadership than its scholastic programs.

Mrs. Alexander has developed courses in Afro-American history, good grooming, and personality as aids to the institute's students.

Laboratory Institute of Merchandising. 12 E. 53 St., New York, N.Y. 10022

This school (founded in 1939) trains students in retail fashion, buying, merchandise, promotion, and fashion appreciation, but not in creative design.

It offers a one-year work–study program (for students with some college training) and two-year work–study program for high school graduates. Both courses include a general liberal arts program combined with the merchandising subjects. Dormitory facilities at nearby colleges are available to students.

Los Angeles Trade Technical College. 400 W. Washington Blvd., Los Angeles, Calif. 90015

This coeducational junior college, originally founded in 1927 and developed to the present status of Trade Technical College in 1949, offers an AA degree in fashion design and special classes for those not qualified to enter the AA program.

Massachusetts College of Art. Brooklyn and Longwood Aves., Boston, Mass. 02215

Founded in 1875, this coeducational college is a professional institution supported by the Commonwealth of Massachusetts. The college confers a BFA degree at the end of the four-year program with a major in fashion design.

Miami Dade Community College. 11380 N.W. 27 Ave., Miami Beach, Fla. 33167

Miami Dade, founded in 1960 with three campuses in Miami, is the largest junior college network in America. The state-supported coeducational school offers career-oriented terminal training courses in fashion design. Out of state students are accepted.

Minneapolis College of Art and Design. 200 E. 25 St., Minneapolis, Minn. 55404

Founded in 1886, this college is coeducational and governed by the Minneapolis Society of Fine Arts, a nonprofit organization which is the parent body for both the college and the Minneapolis Institute of Art.

The college confers a BFA degree after a four-year program with a major in fashion design. Dormitories are available.

Moore College of Art. 20 and Race Sts., Philadelphia, Pa. 19103

America's oldest art college for women, founded in 1844, now confers its BFA and BS degrees in fashion design. The majority of students are full-time degree candidates but there is also a continuing education program. There are both fine arts majors, including jewelry and metalsmithing, and professional arts majors, including fashion design, textile arts, and fashion illustration.

Mount St. Mary's College. 12001 Chalon Rd., Los Angeles, Calif. 90049

This Catholic school for women, founded in 1925, offers a two-year program in art, also transfer or terminal programs, awarding the AA degree with a major in fashion design. Dormitories are available.

Parsons School of Design. 66 Fifth Ave., New York, N.Y. 10011

Originally founded in 1896 and a leading source of education in the fine and applied arts, Parsons has, since 1970, been a division of the New School for Social Research. David C. Levy is dean. Its Chairman of the Fashion Design Department, Ann Keagy, is well-known as an inspired guide and mentor to aspiring design students.

It offers two programs to high school graduates: a four-year curriculum leading to the BFA degree (or three years and three summers) and a three-year program leading to a professional certificate.

Parsons' programs in fashion design and fashion illustration emphasize the availability of faculty from the New York industry; leading fashion practitioners participate in the college's teaching programs as regular faculty members, guest lecturers, and guest critics of student work.

Dormitories are available on a limited basis with priority given to out-of-town students.

Philadelphia College of Textiles and Science. School House Lane, Germantown, Philadelphia, Pa. 19144

This is America's oldest textile college, founded in 1884. It offers a BS degree in fabric design, textile engineering, and other phases of the textile industry. It is coeducational.

Pratt Institute. 215 Ryerson St., Brooklyn, N.Y. 11205

Pratt, founded in 1887, is one of the major American schools for design. It offers a BFA in fashion design, with a minor in merchandising of fine arts. It is coeducational.

Rhode Island School of Design. Providence, R.I. 02903

This coeducational institution, established in 1877, is one of the most prestigious of its kind in the country. The following degrees are conferred: BFA, MFA, and MAT with a major in apparel design and textile design.

Smithsonian Institution. Curator of Costume Course, 1000 Jefferson Dr. S.W., Washington, D.C. 20560

In 1974 the Smithsonian Division of Costume and Furnishings established work–study programs for fashion students interested in being curators of costume collections. Address inquiries to: Mrs. Claudia Kidwell.

Stephens College. Columbia, Mo. 65201

This important women's college, founded in 1833, offers a BA degree in merchandising and a BFA degree in fashion design.

Many Stephens students have been guest college editors on *Glamour* and *Mademoiselle* magazines and have served on Summer Fashion College Boards for leading retail stores across the country. Stephens also has a biannual European fashion seminar and a summer program with various manufacturers to give their students practical experience. It has 16 residence halls.

Stout State University. Menomonie, Wis. 54751

Stout State is part of the University of Wisconsin system, founded originally in 1893 as a manual training school, and is coeducational.

The fashion courses offered at Stout State are in the School of Home Economics and lead to a BS degree major in clothing, textiles and design or in fashion merchandising. The university also gives credit for work experience. Dormitories are available.

Syracuse University. School of Art, Lower Art Center, 309 University Place, Syracuse, N.Y. 13210

Founded in 1870 and coeducational, Syracuse School of Art offers a BFA in a four-year program in fashion design, fabric design, or fashion illustration. An MFA is available in costume design and fabric design in a two-year program. Dormitories are available.

Tobé–Coburn School for Fashion Careers. 851 Madison Ave., New York, N.Y. 10021

This coeducational school was founded in 1937 by two prominent fashion executives, the retail consultant Tobé Coller Davis and Julia Coburn, a fashion editor. It provides work–study courses in fashion merchandising, retailing, fashion promotion, and advertising. The one-year course is for students with two or more years of college, and the two-year course is for high school graduates.

While Tobé-Coburn does not offer courses in fashion design, it does directly link its students to the activities and interests of the fashion world and some students have later become designers.

Traphagen School of Fashion. 257 Park Ave. S., New York, N.Y. 10010

Established in 1923 by Ethel Traphagen, this was the first American school devoted exclusively to fashion technology. The course in fashion design is given as a two- or three-year certificate course; there is also a one- or two-year certificate course in clothing construction and design in which technical dressmaking skills are stressed.

Degree credits leading to a bachelor's degree in fine arts or education may be arranged through a cooperative plan with the New York Fashion Institute of Technology.

University of Cincinnati. College of Design, Cincinnati, Ohio 45221

This coeducational college founded in 1819 confers BA and BFA degrees in art, including fashion design. Dormitories are available.

University of Washington. Seattle, Wash. 98105

Founded in 1861, the University of Washington now offers BA and BFA degrees in fashion design as part of its regular four-year curriculum.

University of Wisconsin. School of Family Resources and Consumer Science, Madison, Wis. 53706

The School of Family Resources and Consumer Sciences is an integral part of the university, founded in 1849.

The apparel design major is a BA program with the junior year spent at the Fashion Institute of Technology in New York.

Virginia Commonwealth University. School of Arts, 901 W. Franklin, Richmond, Va. 23220

Founded in 1838, Virginia Commonwealth University is a publicly controlled liberal arts college, and also offers professional and technical instruction.

The degrees conferred are the AA and BFA, with major in fashion design. Dormitories are available.

Washington University. School of Fine Arts, St. Louis, Mo. 63130

Established in 1853 and coeducational, this school has a very competitive standard for admission. It offers an undergraduate major in fashion design, leading to a BFA. Dormitories are available.

Woodbury College. 1027 Wilshire Blvd., Los Angeles, Calif. 90017

Founded in 1884, this coeducational school offers a BS degree in a three-year program in fashion design and merchandising.

Costume and Fashion Archives

Art Institute of Chicago. Michigan Ave. at Adams St., Chicago, Ill. 60603

Tel: 443-3695 or 3696. Founded: 1879. Curator, Dept. of Textiles: Christa C. Mayer-Thurman.

This museum has large collections of textiles of the Western Hemisphere and metal crafts, and holds periodic special exhibitions. There is no specific costume collection.

The Brooklyn Museum. 188 Eastern Pkwy., Brooklyn, N.Y. 11328

Tel: (212) 638-5000. Founded: 1893. Dir: Michael Botwinick. Curator, Costumes and Textiles: Elizabeth Ann Coleman.

This excellent museum has a permanent collection of exceptionally fine costumes of the 18th, 19th, and 20th centuries up to the present. The Edward C. Blum Laboratory, with the Brooklyn Museum's secondary collection of costumes more freely available for study by designers in the fashion and textile fields, is now housed at the Fashion Institute of Technology, New York City.

Chaco Canyon National Monument. Star Rte., Bloomfield, N. Mex. 87413

Tel: (505) 786-5384. Founded: 1907. Supt: Richard B. Hardin.

American Indian textiles, costumes, and ornaments are on display.

Chicago Historical Society. North Ave. and Clark St., Chicago, Ill. 60614

Tel: MI 2-4600. Founded: 1856. Costume Curator: Miss Elizabeth Jachimowicz.

This society, originally a library of historical data about the State of Illinois, acquired in 1920 a large Americana collection, much of it assembled by Charles F. Gunther, a candy manufacturer.

The costume division includes a few examples from the 18th and early 19th centuries but is strongest in works of the late 19th and early 20th centuries. Many of the fashions by well-known couturiers were worn locally, and all are shown complete with accessories. A small number of men's and children's fashions is included.

The society has both permanent displays and periodic exhibitions.

Cincinnati Art Museum. Eden Pk., Cincinnati, Ohio 45202

Tel: (513) 721-5204. Founded: 1881. Dir: Philip R. Adams. Curator, Fashion: Mary Light Meyer.

This costume collection includes American and European clothes and accessories from the 19th century to 1930.

Costume Institute. See Metropolitan Museum of Art

The Denver Art Museum. 100 W. 14 Ave., Pkwy., Denver, Colo. 80204
Tel: (303) 297-2346. Founded: 1893. Dir: Otto K. Bach. Curator, Textiles and Costumes: Imelda De Graw.

There are American, English, and French costumes from 1750, samplers, textiles of all nations, as well as occasional exhibitions of costumes with a period or designer theme.

Detroit Historical Museum. 5401 Woodward Ave., Detroit, Mich. 48202
Tel: (313) 321-1701. Founded: 1945. Dir: Solan W. Weeks.

There is an extensive collection of clothing for men, women, and children from 1850 to 1900.

Frontier Times Museum. Two blocks north of Courthouse, Bandera, Tex. 78003
Tel: (512) 796-3864. Founded: 1933. Pres: Sandra Doane Turk. Curator: Ruth J. Batto.

There is a permanent display of Western frontier costumes from the 18th century to recent times.

Greenfield Village and Henry Ford Museum. Oakwood Blvd., Dearborn, Mich. 48121
Tel: (313) 271-1620. Founded: 1929. Pres: Donald A. Shelley.

There are 19th and 20th century American costumes and quilts and printed cotton textiles of the 18th and 19th centuries.

Los Angeles County Museum of Art. 5905 Wilshire Blvd., Los Angeles, Calif. 90036
Tel: (213) 937-4250. Founded: 1910. Dir: Kenneth Donahue. Curator, Costumes and Textiles: Mary Kahlenberg.

There is a large collection of women's costumes from 1730, specializing in Parisian couture fashions, and men's clothes dating from the 15th century.

Maryland Historical Society. 201 W. Monument St., Baltimore, Md. 21201
Tel: (301) 685-3750. Founded: 1844. Dir: P. William Filby. Asst. Curator: Eugenia Calvert Holland.

There are costumes, dolls, and jewels from the 17th to the 20th centuries.

Metropolitan Museum of Art, Costume Institute. 82 St. and Fifth Ave., New York, N.Y. 10028
Tel: (212) 879-5500. Founded: 1937 (as Museum of Costume Art). Absorbed by the Metropolitan Museum: 1946. Dir: Stella Blum.

This branch of the Metropolitan Museum was established with funds raised by the American fashion industries after the Museum of Costume Art, founded by Irene Lewisohn, was transferred to the Metropolitan.

The Costume Institute's nucleus, Miss Lewisohn's extensive collection of antique fashions and authentic regional costumes, has been steadily increased by acquisitions of important period costumes and by gifts of recent fashions belonging to fashionable people.

The Costume Institute now contains 17,000 articles of dress dating from the 16th century. The new Costume Institute wing, opened in 1972, has a model repository for the perfect preservation of fragile costumes, protecting them by an advanced system of air conditioning and humidity control. These archives, arranged by period, are available for study and technical analysis by members of the Costume Institute who are professional designers, in a series of work–study rooms on the premises.

The Costume Institute presents a significant exhibition at least once a year on a particular fashion period, inspirational theme, or summarizing the work of one or more famous designers. These are conceived and assembled by Diana Vreeland. See the Fashion Influentials section.

Museum of Fine Arts. 465 Huntington Ave., Boston, Mass. 02115

Tel: (617) 267-9300. Founded: 1870. Acting Dir. and Curator, Classical Art: Cornelius C. Vermeule. Curator, Textiles: Larry Simon.

There are interesting costume and textile collections—American colonial and 19th century, European of the 18th and 19th centuries, and Far Eastern of the 19th and 20th centuries.

Museum of New Mexico. Box 2087, Santa Fe, N. Mex. 87501

Tel: (505) 827-2834. Founded: 1909. Dir: Carlos Nagel.

The collection is dedicated to American folk art from 1800, with emphasis on Spanish colonial textiles and costumes.

Museum of Northern Arizona. Fort Valley Rd., Box 1389, Flagstaff, Ariz. 86001

Tel: (602) 774-2433. Founded: 1928. Dir: Dr. Edward B. Danson. Curator: Barton A. Wright.

There is a collection of Navajo and Hopi Indian textiles and clothing.

Museum of the American Indian. Heye Foundation, Broadway at 155 St., New York, N.Y. 10032

Tel: (212) 283-2420. Founded: 1916. Dir: Dr. Frederick J. Dockstader. Curator: William F. Stiles.

This is an important and extensive collection of American Indian costumes and ornaments documenting the primitive and more recent Indian civilizations and tribal life of both North and South America.

Museum of the City of New York. Fifth Ave. at 103 St., New York, N.Y. 10029

Tel: (212) 534-1672. Founded: 1923. Dir: Joseph Veach Noble. Curator of Costumes: Elizabeth Jachimowicz.

This is a small but fine collection of historical costumes worn by well-known personalities in New York from the 18th century to the present day.

Museum of the Plains Indian and Crafts Center. Box 400, Browning, Mont. 59417

Tel: (406) 338-2230. Dir: Myles Libhart. Acting Curator: Ramon Gonyea.

There are Indian costumes and ornaments dating from the 19th century to recent times.

Ohio Historical Society. Interstate 71 and 17 Ave., Columbus, Ohio 43211

Tel: (614) 469-4663. Founded: 1885. Dir: Daniel R. Porter. Asst. Dir: Charles C. Pratt.

There is a permanent display of American dresses, quilts, and coverlets of the 19th century from donors in the area.

Philadelphia Museum of Art. 26 St. and Benjamin Franklin Pkwy., Box 7646, Philadelphia, Pa. 19101

Tel: (215) 763-8100. Founded: 1876. Dir: Dr. Evan Hopkins Turner. Curator, Costumes and Textiles: Elsie Siratz McGarvey.

There is an interesting permanent display, in period settings, of costumes from the 18th and 19th centuries, as well as a display of period and Oriental textiles.

Phoenix Art Museum. 1625 N. Central Ave., Phoenix, Ariz. 85004

Tel: (602) 258-6164. Founded: 1925. Dir: Goldwaite H. Dorr, III. Curator, Costumes: Jean Hildreth.

There are displays of 20th-century costumes and jewelry.

Smithsonian Institution. 1000 Jefferson Dr. S.W., Washington, D.C. 20560

Tel: (202) 628-4422. Founded: 1846. Secy: Dr. S. Dillon Ripley.

In the Hall of American Costume there is an excellent and in some ways unique collection of American costumes, "viewed as a cultural artifact." The collection includes over 15,000 articles of clothing and accessories worn by men, women, and children. Highlights are clothing of the Pilgrim and Colonial periods, 19th century and such 20th century milestone fashions as early shirtwaist costumes, a typical Hattie

Carnegie suit, Nettie Rosenstein's "little black dress," and clothes of Norman Norell, Anne Klein, Claire McCardell, etc.

The Smithsonian's First Lady collection is naturally its most renowned, being a permanent display of dresses representing the period of every American president, 15 of which are the actual gowns worn by wives of U.S. presidents at inaugural balls, since that of George Washington in 1789.

In 1974 the Smithsonian's Division of Costumes and Furnishings established work–study programs for fashion students interested in being curators of costume collections (see Fashion Education).

The Textile Museum. 2320 S St. N.W., Washington, D.C. 20008

Tel: (202) 667-0442. Founded: 1925. Exec. Dir: Anthony N. Landreau. Assoc. Curator, Middle Eastern Textiles: Louise W. Mackie. Asst. Curator, Western Hemisphere Textiles: Barbara C. Fertig.

There is an extensive and important collection of textile examples from 200 BC to the present day.

Traphagen School of Fashion Museum Collection. 257 Park Ave. S., New York, N.Y. 10010

Tel: (212) 673-0300. Founded: 1923. Dir: Wanda Wdowka. Curator: Florita Raup.

There is a small group of authentic regional and historic costumes and accessories from various countries for public view and the use of design students.

Valentine Museum. 1015 E. Clay St., Richmond, Va. 23219

Tel: (703) 649-0711. Founded: 1892. Curator of Costumes: Mrs. Luther Coleman Wells.

Affiliated with Virginia Commonwealth University and the Richmond Public School System, this museum is composed of a group of early American houses furnished in the period; there is also a large locally worn costume collection ranging from 1668 to the present day.

The collection is said to be the third largest in America. The museum owns also a large photograph collection of many generations of elegant Virginians.

Wadsworth Atheneum. 600 Main St., Hartford, Conn. 06103

Tel: (203) 278-2670. Founded: 1842. Dir: James Elliott. Curator, Textiles and Costumes: Herbert Callister.

There is a large collection of 19th and 20th century costumes from America and Europe.

Fashion Publications

Bride's Magazine. Condé Nast Publications, Inc., 350 Madison Ave., New York, N.Y. 10017

Founded: 1934. Ed-in-chief: Barbara Tober. 6 issues/yr. $3/yr. Circ: 325,000.

California Apparel News. 1016 S. Broadway Place, Los Angeles, Calif. 90015
Founded: 1946. Pub: Ted Levy. Ed: Ms. Freedman. 52 issues/yr. $12/yr.

California Men's Stylist (formerly *Men's and Women's Stylist*). 8732 Sunset Blvd., Los Angeles, Calif. 90069.
Founded: 1937. Pub: Jay Eisenberg. Ed: Paul Roth. 10 issues/yr. $14/yr.

Clothes Magazine. Prads, Inc., 380 Madison Ave., New York, N.Y. 10017
Founded: 1966. Ed: Carolyn Carpentieri Potter. 6 issues/yr. $20/yr. Circ: 40,000. News magazine of the fashion industry.

Cosmopolitan. Hearst Corporation, 224 W. 57 St., New York, N.Y. 10019
Founded: 1886. Ed: Helen Gurley Brown. 12 issues/yr. $12/yr. Circ: 1,900,000.

Daily News Record. Fairchild Publications, Inc., 7 E. 12 St., New York, N.Y. 10003
Founded: 1892. Ed: Sanford Josephson. 5 issues/wk. $32/yr. Circ: 30,000.

Ebony Magazine. Johnson Publication Company, 820 S. Michigan Ave., Chicago, Ill. 10022
Founded: 1945. Ed-in-chief: John H. Johnson. 12 issues/yr. $12/yr. Circ: 1,320,000.

Esquire Magazine. Esquire, Inc., 488 Madison Ave., New York, N.Y. 10022
Founded: 1933. Ed-in-chief: Arnold Gingrich. 12 issues/yr. $10/yr. $1.50/issue. Circ: 1,250,000.

Essence. Hollingsworth Group, Inc., 300 E. 42 St., New York, N.Y. 10017
Founded: 1970. Ed: Marcia A. Gillespie. 12 issues/yr. $7/yr. Circ: 450,000. Black readership.

Family Circle. New York Times Company Publication, 488 Madison Ave., New York, N.Y. 10022
Founded: 1932. Ed-in-chief: Arthur Hettich. 12 issues/yr. 35¢/issue (outside US 39¢). Circ: 8,350,000.

Femme-Lines. Earl Barron Publications, Inc., 15 E. 40 St., New York, N.Y. 10016

Founded: 1957. Ed: Earl Barron. 6 issues/yr. Circ: 14,400. Trade, technical, and merchandising magazine.

Gentlemen's Quarterly/GQ. Esquire, Inc., 488 Madison Ave., New York, N.Y. 10022

Founded: 1957. Ed-in-chief: Arnold Gingrich. 8 issues/yr. $8/yr. Circ: 200,000.

Glamour. Condé Nast Publications, Inc., 350 Madison Ave., New York, N.Y. 10017

Founded: 1939. Ed-in-chief: Ruth Whitney. 12 issues/yr. $8/yr. Circ: 1,710,000. Modestly priced fashions and beauty.

Good Housekeeping. The Hearst Corporation, 959 Eighth Ave., New York, N.Y. 10019

Founded: 1885. Ed: John Mack Carter. 12 issues/yr. $7/yr. Circ: 5,611,420.

Harper's Bazaar. The Hearst Corporation, 717 Fifth Ave., New York, N.Y. 10022

Founded: 1876. Ed-in-chief: Anthony T. Mazzola. 12 issues/yr. $10/yr. Circ: 504,045. *Bazaar Italia* published in Italian. High fashion.

Ladies' Home Journal. Downe Communications, Inc., 641 Lexington Ave., New York, N.Y. 10022

Founded: 1883. Ed: Lenore Hershey. 12 issues/yr. $5.94/yr. Circ: 6,000,000.

McCall's Magazine. McCall Publishing Co., 230 Park Ave., New York, N.Y. 10017

Founded: 1870. Ed: Bob Stein. 12 issues/yr. $6.95/yr. Circ: 6,800,000. Service magazine with fashion pages.

Mademoiselle. Condé Nast Publications, Inc., 350 Madison Ave., New York, N.Y. 10017

Founded: 1935. Ed-in-chief: Edith Raymond Locke. 12 issues/yr. $7/yr. Circ: 807,352. Young sophisticated fashions.

Masculines. Earl Barron Publications, Inc., 15 E. 40 St., New York, N.Y. 10016

Founded: 1957. Ed: Earl Barron. 6 issues/yr. Circ: 10,400. Trade, technical, and merchandising magazine for menswear manufacturers and executives.

Modern Bride. Ziff-Davis Publishing Company, One Park Ave., New York, N.Y. 10016

Founded: 1949. Ed-in-chief: Robert W. Houseman. 6 issues/yr. $5.98/yr. Circ: 350,000. Complete guide for the bride-to-be.

Playboy Magazine. Playboy Enterprises, Inc., 747 Third Ave., New York, N.Y. 10017

Founded: 1955. Ed-in-chief/Pub: Hugh Hefner. 12 issues/yr. $10/yr. Circ: 5,422,343. Also published in German, French, and Italian.

Town and Country. The Hearst Corporation, 717 Fifth Ave., New York, N.Y. 10022

Founded: 1846. Ed-in-chief: Frank Zachary. 12 issues/yr. $15/yr. Circ: 141,800.

Vanidades Continental. Saral Publications, Inc., 605 Third Ave., New York, N.Y. 10016; and Editorial America, S.A., 6401 N.W. 36 St., Virginia Gardens, Fla. 33166

Founded: 1961. Ed-in-chief: Elvira Mendoza. 26 issues/yr. $1/issue. Circ: 57,000 (US); 35,000 (Puerto Rico). Most widely read women's magazine in the Spanish language.

Vogue. Condé Nast Publications, Inc., 350 Madison Ave., New York, N.Y. 10017

Founded: 1892. Ed-in-chief: Grace Mirabella. 12 issues/yr. $10/yr. Circ: 636,323. British Vogue (16 issues/yr, $21.40/yr). Australian Vogue (10 issues/yr, $9.30/yr). French Vogue (in French, 10 issues/yr, $41.15/yr). Vogue Italia (in Italian, 10 issues/yr, $35.45/yr). High fashion.

W. Fairchild Publications, Inc., 7 E. 12 St., New York, N.Y. 10003

Founded: 1971. Ed-in-chief: Michael Coady. 26 issues/yr. $9.50/yr. Circ: 160,000.

Women's Wear Daily. Fairchild Publications, Inc., 7 E. 12 St., New York, N.Y. 10003

Founded: 1910. Ed-in-chief: Michael Coady. 5 issues/wk. $36/yr. Circ: 78,000.

ALASKA

The livelihood of most Alaskans comes from what are known as extractive industries: fisheries, mining, lumbering, and furs.

The trapping of animals for their pelts was the original mainstay of Alaska's economy. Today it is far less important (only about 5 percent of the total national product), and it is now controlled by the government and conducted under the most humane conditions possible.

The chief fur resource is the Alaska seal, now "ranched" in protected waters around the Pribiloff Islands. Under the wildlife preservation program carried out by the government, the seal population has risen from 200,000 to 1,200,000 since the breeding and harvesting controls were established in 1911.

Leather and bead work made by the Eskimos are supple and often beautiful, but unlike the Eskimo sculpture and wood carving, these crafts have not yet been systematically encouraged nor channelled into the commercial world.

HAWAII

Although a part of the United States, Hawaii remains a separate entity in the realm of clothing and design.

The dress devised by Victorian missionaries to cover the nakedness of Hawaiian and Polynesian natives was mutated by each of the islands and has become a form of folk costume. The Hawaiian muu-muu, with its high yoke and loose, easy fullness, was the only one to develop into a local industry and article of export.

The handsome cottons printed with large flowers, originally made in the continental United States for Pacific island trading, have been adapted and somewhat bastardized by local Hawaiian clothing producers. The flowered Hawaiian sport shirt worn by President Harry S. Truman brought the fashion for wild shirts to American men and is credited by some fashion historians with sparking the "liberation" of male attire in color and informality.

While there are numerous clothes manufacturers in Hawaii, few have gone beyond reproducing the muu-muu and native shirt with mildly personalized variations.

PUERTO RICO

While Puerto Rico has not made a name in fashion creativity, it is a consequential source of labor for American manufacturers of foundation garments, lingerie, sportswear, infants and children's wear, and men's shirts, all of whom maintain factories there. Several dozen local manufacturers of clothing are also seeking to extend their distribution to other countries.

In 1973 Puerto Rico produced and exported $185 million worth of corsets, brassieres, and undergarments to the United States, nearly half the entire American production.

The old city of San Juan has numerous custom dressmakers and boutiques whose designers follow current fashions in other countries. Puerto Rican designs in beachwear and evening clothes have an ethnic flavor, using the ruffles, embroidery, and plantation overtones of traditional Caribbean costumes.

The Economic Development Administration of Puerto Rico and the Marketing Development Department of the Commonwealth of Puerto Rico have occasionally sponsored trade showings of Puerto Rican fashions in the Miami, Florida Merchandise Mart.

Among the 28 manufacturers who recently participated were producers of women's and children's apparel, men's pants, and fashion wigs with names as yet unknown but perhaps with a future: Belleza, Caribbean Leisurewear, Creaciones Maria Isabel, Cari, Coamo, Diana, Guemar, Jim, Life, Manet, Mardi Gras, Inc., Maria Boberet, Modas Norma, Modas Sabrina, Ramelia, Rivera Martis, Simpatico, Suevia, Vanessa, and Yoemari Modas.

SOUTH AMERICA

Since this continent is more like a constellation of individual planets than a unit of contiguous countries, it is impossible to assess South America's fashion contribution under one heading. In some countries, it is impossible to uncover any external fashion activity.

Participation in general fashion change reflects inner stability and outward dynamism. In the case of South America, this is illustrated by the almost total fashion blackout in areas undergoing political struggles.

Brazil and Colombia are in a dynamic period, and both are concerned with exporting their textiles and fashions as well as their minerals and agricultural products. Argentina, Peru, Chile, and the others have certain great but unrealized potentials for clothing exports.

Venezuela's rich oil deposits brought prosperity and progress far beyond that of the average South American country. Venezuela has the highest per capita income in Latin America and the highest standard of living. It follows that Venezuela has a highly developed local fashion identity, but as yet this has not reached far beyond its own boundaries—the smart shopping centers of Caracas. This is probably due to the same fact that has kept North American fashion so localized: wealthy and middle-income markets are large enough to absorb the entire production effort.

Venezuela produces diamonds, gold, pearls, some textiles, and dye-stuffs, particularly cochineal.

The growing belief that South America is the land of the future will have as one of its first noticeable reactions the development of a more powerful place in the fashion world.

ARGENTINA

Fashion Publications

Claudia. Surameris Propaganda, Alem 896, Buenos Aires

Founded: 1957. Ed: Mina Civita. 12 issues/yr. Argentina's leading fashion magazine, a localized edition of *Claudia*, which is simultaneously published in several South American countries.

BOLIVIA

Fashion Designers and Firms

Daisy Urquiola de Wende. Artesanias Titicaca, Ltda., Casilla 2933, La Paz

Well-known for her interpretations of native Bolivian costumes and handicrafts in modern fashion terms, Mrs. de Wende was instrumental in the development of a Bolivian fashion industry through obtaining financial aid to artisans from the Alliance for Progress.

BRAZIL

Fashion Designers and Firms

Zuzu Angel (Jones). Boutique designer, Rua Almeida Pereira Guimares 79A, Leblon, Rio de Janeiro

The vibrant, totally Brazilian spirit of this designer has brought her international attention. Her dresses and beach clothes often derive from Brazilian native costume.

Mrs. Angel was born in Curvelo in the state of Minas Gerais, the source of Brazil's gemstones and metals. A wealthy aunt passed on her Paris dresses to the teen-age Zuzu, who remodelled them for herself.

On her marriage to an American, Zuzu moved to Rio de Janeiro. She began to design beachwear after she divorced and assumed the sole support of her three children. Her son, a young teacher, recently was the mistaken victim of political murder in Brazil. One of her daughters, Hildegarde Angel, is a popular young actress, columnist, and TV commentator in Rio. Zuzu owns one of Rio's smartest boutiques, and is one of Brazil's leading fashion exporters.

Dener (Pamplona de Abreu). Couturier, Rua Rego Freitas 289, Sao Paulo

A leading designer with a large following of wealthy Brazilian ladies and the wives of government officials, Dener is known for his highly dramatic and heavily decorated clothes.

Born August 3, 1936, in Belem, near the equator, he designed for fashion houses in Rio de Janeiro and Sao Paulo before opening his own establishment. He is often chosen to represent Brazil at international fashion and trade fairs and won a national popularity prize for 10 consecutive years.

Clementina Duarte (Mrs. Armando Holanda). Jewelry designer, Rua de Aurora 457, Recife, Pernambuco

A designer who specialized in the study of Medieval art during her years at the Sorbonne in Paris, Clementina Duarte was born in Recife and received a diploma in architecture there.

In Paris she began sculpting in silver, creating abstract forms which could be worn as bracelets or necklaces, following the body contours. She was given a one-man show at the Steph-Simon Gallery in Paris, where designer Pierre Cardin saw her work and introduced it with his next fashion collection.

In 1971 she won an award for her jewelry at the International Biennial of Art in Sao Paulo and in 1972 was invited to exhibit her work as an art collection in Milan, Italy.

Joan Guerreiro. Jewelry designer, Avenida Rua Barbasso, Apt. 1702, 300 Rio de Janeiro

Born in Iowa, U.S.A., Mrs. Guerreiro married a young Brazilian banker and lives in Rio. In 1971 she began making her own versions of native Brazilian amulets and charms in gold and Brazilian semiprecious stones. They are sold in jewelry shops in South America and exported to Europe and the States.

Guillerme Guimaraes. Couturier, Rua Sousa Lima 338, Copacabana, Rio de Janeiro

Known for his exquisitely handworked clothes, particularly his elaborate beaded dresses, Guillerme Guimaraes is a designer in the grand tradition who manages to instill a youthful feeling into this usually rather pompous type of dress.

Guillerme's clientele is strictly among the wealthy upper class, film stars, and actresses. Like other designers in South America, his couture collections are sold on a one-of-a-kind basis, with duplicates of each original model only rarely made.

Fernando José. Couturier, Rua dos Ingleses 182, Sao Paulo

One of the most talented of the high-fashion designers in Brazil, José was born in Portugal on November 13, 1937, where he studied fashion design. He came to Brazil in 1957 and worked for five years as a mass-production designer for a Rio de Janeiro manufacturer.

He won a scholarship to l'Ecole de la Chambre Syndicale in Paris. After working briefly in Paris for Nina Ricci, he returned to Brazil in 1966.

Today he limits his production to one of a kind, creating a full collection, then selling it piece by piece to his private clients in Sao Paulo and Rio. He is, however, an influence on all of Brazilian fashion.

Trade Associations and Organizations

Fenit. Comercio e Empreendimentos, Ltda., Rua Brasilio Machado 60, Sao Paulo

Founded: 1970. Founder/Dir: Caio Machado.

Fenit's semiannual expositions are held in Sao Paulo under the auspices of Brazil's national organization of fiber and textile manufacturers. About 400 firms show at the textile fairs held in Sao Paulo's large Exposition Center built and administered by the firm of Caio Alcantara Machado, one of Brazil's most important business leaders. Through his efforts, in collaboration with the government, foreign buyers have been invited in order to encourage and expand the textile standards of the country.

Fashion Publications

Claudia. Editora Abril, Ltda., Av. Otaviano A. de Lima 800, Sao Paulo

Founded: 1961. Ed: Victor Civita. 12 issues/yr (4 additional issues/yr). Circ: 220,000.

Desfile (formerly: *Joia*). Bloch Editores, S.A., Rua Frei Caneca 511, Rio de Janeiro

Dir: Piedro J. Kapeller. 12 issues/yr.

CHILE

Fashion Publications

Vanidades Continental. Editorial America, S.A., Oficina de Ventas, Providencia 711, Santiago

Founded: 1961. Ed-in-chief: Elvira Mendoza. 6 issues/yr. P.16 (US $1) per issue. Circ: 87,000.

COLOMBIA

Fashion Designers and Firms

Olga Ceballos de Amarel. Textile designer, Carrera 7 No. 74-26, Apartado Aerio 22-812, Bogota

Inspired by pre-Columbian textile fragments, Mrs. de Amarel began designing fabrics in 1953 after studying art in the United States at the Cranbrook Foundation in Michigan.

Her designs are now exported throughout the world and are used by well-known couturiers.

Marlene Hoffman. Textile and fashion designer, Avenida 13 No. 70-14, Bogota

Born in the Colombian port of Barranquilla, Marlene Hoffman was trained in architectural drawing, painting, sculpture, and metal-smithing before she decided to make fabric her creative medium. Her work has been displayed many times in international textile showings in leading museums and has been used by such designers as Givenchy of Paris and Mary Quant of London.

Toby Setton. Designer–manufacturer, Jackson Fashions, Apdo. Aerio 16-17, Calle 75 No. 73-43, Barranquilla

Colombia's only fashion tycoon, Mr. Setton started his business in 1956 after having worked as a couturier. He was inspired to design after seeing an Adrian fashion show in California. His popular-priced young fashions are sold widely in South America and also exported to the United States and other countries.

Trade Associations and Organizations

Fondo de Promocio de Exportaciones (PROFEXPO). Carrera 40, No. 22-C27, Bogota

Founded: 1967. Dir: Arturo Michelsen.

This joint association is sponsored by the Colombian government and the Bank of the Republic to promote the export of clothing and textiles.

Fashion Publications

Vanidades Continental. Editorial America, S.A., Oficina de Ventas, Carrera 21 No. 35-53, Bogota

Founded: 1961. Ed-in-chief: Elvira Mendoza. 6 issues/yr. P.16 (U.S. $1)/issue. Circ: 54,000.

PERU

Costume and Fashion Archives

Museo Nacional de Antropologia y Arqueologia (National Museum of Anthropology and Archeology). Plaza Bolivar, Pueblo Libre, Lima
Tel: 234-333. Founded: 1938. Dir: Dr. Jorge C. Muelle.
There is a large collection of pre-Columbian Peruvian textiles and ornamental work.

Fashion Publications

Vanidades Continental. Editorial America, S.A., Oficina de Ventas, Avenida Arenales 1080, Lima
Founded: 1961. Ed-in-chief: Elvira Mendoza. 6 issues/yr. Soles 30 (US $1)/issue. Circ: 38,000.

VENEZUELA

Fashion Designers and Firms

Beachwear and sportsclothes are usually imported into Venezuela from France and Italy, but the boutiques listed here are among those presenting local talent.

Angelo Modas (far-out fashions). Avenida Lincoln, Sabana Grande, Caracas

Biki Bou (bikinis). Chacaito Shopping Center, Caracas

Calzador Tulio (shoes). Chacaito Shopping Center, Caracas

King's Road Beat Time (chic sportswear). Chacaito Shopping Center, Caracas

Nosotras (evening clothes). Avenida Lincoln, Sabana Grande, Caracas

Rina Roth and Mr. Nick. Fashion and textile designers, Ed. Maury, Segunda Avenida, Los Palos Grandes, Caracas
A husband-and-wife team designing for 20 years, Rina Roth and her husband Nicolas are Yugoslavs who worked in Paris before settling in Venezuela. He designs the fabrics; she creates the clothes. Many of their designs are purchased for mass production in the United States.

Fashion Education

Academia de Alta Costura Malena. Edificio Maria Carla, Apto. 19, Avenida Victoria, Caracas
This fashion school offers courses in design and sewing techniques.

Costume and Fashion Archives

Museo de Arte Colonial de Caracas (Caracas Museum of Colonial Art). Avenida El Panteón y Calle Gamboa, Quinta Anauco, San Bernardino, Caracas 101

Tel: 51-85-17. Founded: 1942. Dir: Dr. Mauro Paez Pumar.

There is an interesting collection of colonial, ceremonial, and regional costumes, rooms, and ornaments.

Fashion Publications

Vanidades Continental. Editorial America, S.A., Gerente Internacional de Ventas: Ferrenquin a la Cruz 178, Caracas 101

Founded: 1961. Ed-in-chief: Elvira Mendoza. 6 issues/yr. 3.75 Bolivares (US $1)/issue. Circ: 72,000.

hall
of fame

hall of fame

The record of designers, artists, and nonroyal arbiters of taste who put an indelible stamp on the fashions of their time coincides historically with the rise of a middle class and a world where the artisan who could master the machine was to have creative recognition.

Before the 18th century, fashion was a reflection of royal whim and the slavish imitation of courtiers. The first show of wealth among commoners was ostentation in dress, and that habit was soon subject to rigid restrictions and penalties by law. Dress and personal self-expression thus became interrelated.

The fashion designer who created for the court or theatre is first found as a vague, shadowy figure in the court of the 17th century. Heavy, jewel-laden court dress was worn year round until the frivolous, feckless Queen Marie Antoinette was persuaded by her favorite dressmaker, Rose Bertin, to wear clothes which reversed history by imitating the common people's everyday wools and cottons. The Queen thus gave popular fashion and the "name" designer to the world. Her world showed its gratitude by demanding her head.

This list includes designers and personalities, now dead or retired, whose influence on dress was not only profound in their epoch, but a milestone in the fashion history of their country. It inevitably contains more information on French, American, and British designers, since those countries led the changes in Western costume and in highlighting the creator behind the change.

There is no doubt that some of the more recent figures will diminish in importance as time passes. This book is however for students and researchers into all of the past. The future will judge which names are to be added, which names are to disappear.

Adrian (Gilbert Adrian Greenburgh) (1903–1959)

As a film designer in Hollywood, Adrian strongly influenced world fashion from 1930 to 1952. For the last decade of his life he produced highly imaginative and high-quality ready-to-wear for American stores.

Born Gilbert Adrian Greenburgh on March 3, 1903, in Naugatauk, Connecticut, he studied art at the Paris branch of the Parsons School of Design. In 1921, at the Paris Beaux Arts art students ball, the American composer Irving Berlin spotted the 18-year-old Adrian's prize costume and commissioned him to design for his forthcoming "Music Box Revue" in New York.

After costuming Broadway shows, Adrian signed (1928) a contract with Metro-Goldwyn-Mayer in Hollywood where he quickly became a star in his field. He created the famous wide-shouldered Adrian suit for Joan Crawford, and also the huge puffed sleeve called the "Letty Lynton" for the star's film *Letty Lynton*. His designs for Greta Garbo in *Queen Christina*, *Camille*, and *Anna Karenina* made fashion waves everywhere. He dressed Jean Harlow, innovating the sensuous body look which was to affect fashion for decades to come. His clothes for Katharine Hepburn and Norma Shearer were noteworthy influences. In toto Adrian contributed in a major way to establishing Hollywood as the glamour capital of the world from the 1930s to the 1950s.

In 1939 he married the film star Janet Gaynor. Their son Robin was born in 1940.

In 1942 Adrian opened his couture and ready-to-wear business in Los Angeles and won the Coty Award (1944) for his important contributions to world fashion.

The wide-shouldered Adrian suit with padded shoulders became a worldwide craze and his shoulder pads extended into all areas of dress. They were known in France as "Americaines," although the fashion was equally credited to the Parisian designer Schiaparelli. Adrian also sparked new attitudes in the use of fabrics, introducing checked gingham for tailored suits and cotton organdy for ball gowns.

After a heart attack in 1952, Adrian closed his business and the Adrians retired to a ranch near Brasilia, in Brazil.

Returning to California in 1958, he designed the costumes for the film musicals *Grand Hotel* and *Camelot*, but before the latter was finished Adrian suffered a second heart attack and died September 14, 1959.

Augustabernard (Augusta Bernard)

Augusta Bernard, who elided her name into one for her label was exceptionally well-known between World War I and World War II, specializing in pleated dresses which were a beautiful background for jewels.

Born in Provence, she opened her house in 1919, at 3 rue St. Honoré, Paris, and remained popular until she retired in 1934.

Cristobal Balenciaga (1895–1972)

The most influential as well as the most reclusive French designer of the post war years, Balenciaga retired in the late 1960s, disillusioned by the waning of elegance.

312

During his 30 years of eminence, he was called the "prophet of the silhouette," and launched such classics as the soft-shouldered suit and the straightline chemise silhouette. The latter was an outgrowth of his despised but prophetic "sack" silhouette of 1953.

Born in Guetaria, Spain, on January 21, 1895, to a poor family of fishermen, Balenciaga as a very young child worked with his mother, a seamstress. When a local lady, Marquesa Casa Torres, overheard him murmur "How elegant!" as she passed, she bought him the fabric to copy her French tailleur, and interested herself in furthering his talents. He was 20 when the Marquesa financed his first tailoring shop in San Sebastian. He was soon able to open his own couture house under the name of Eisa in Madrid and Barcelona and, until the Spanish Civil War caused him to leave Spain in 1937, he had a growing reputation. With backing by Spanish refugee friends, Balenciaga opened in Paris on the avenue George V, soon to become the center of world fashion. His name is still over the door, although he retired in 1968.

Obsessed with his work, Balenciaga lived a monastic life, surrounded by a group of equally single-minded disciples whose independent careers he generously fostered. Hubert de Givenchy was a favorite assistant, and Balenciaga helped him start on his own in 1952. Andre Courreges, Philippe Venet, and Emanuel Ungaro are among today's well-known Parisian designers who trained at Balenciaga.

Ungaro said of Balenciaga, "He created a silence around him, an atmosphere of quality."

Balenciaga returned to Spain in 1968 and took an apartment in Madrid, but spent most of his time in Paris. Two months before his death, he emerged from retirement to design the wedding dress of Carmencita Martinez-Bordiu y Franco, General Franco's granddaughter, now Duchess de Cadiz.

Balenciaga died at the seaside resort of Javea, Spain, on March 23, 1972, and is buried in his native fishing village, Guetaria.

Travis Banton (1874–1958)

One of the lesser-known but still potent disseminators of the Hollywood influence on world fashion during the days of great stars and glamour films, Travis Banton was born in New York and studied at Columbia University, the Art Students' League, and the New York School of Fine and Applied Arts.

His first fashion job was on the staff of the New York couturiere, Mme Frances. Producer Walter Wanger gave him a Hollywood contract at Paramount Studios. He remained as chief designer until 1938, working later for other studios.

His film designs were translated in a few wholesale collections, but he preferred to pilot ideas rather than execute them.

One of his last and most memorable efforts was the wardrobe for Rosalind Russell in *Auntie Mame*.

Beaulard

Beaulard was a late 18th-century court dressmaker who was Rose Bertin's only serious rival for the favors of Marie Antoinette and her court ladies. He is credited with inventing tall bonnets with a hidden spring which allowed them to collapse in a carriage, and with doing some of the most monstrous of the scenic headdresses fashionable in the early years of Marie Antoinette's fashion-mad epoch. His creations were expensive even for the times, averaging $1000 each.

Rose Bertin (Marie-Jeanne Laurent) (1744–1812?)

The ancestress of the French couture, Rose Bertin was the first "name" designer in fashion history to wield equal influence over the Queen, the court, and the middle class.

Termed "Minister of Fashion" in court chronicles and French revolutionary pamphlets, Mlle Bertin spanned the reigns of Louis XV, Louis XVI, the Revolution, and Napoleon's empire. Her artistry, beginning with the extravagant headdresses she made a world fashion, is mentioned in memoirs, plays, and literature of the 18th and early 19th centuries. She was the only person allowed to enter the gates of Versailles as she liked without a pass. Louis XVI—followed by the entire court entourage—once doffed their hats to Mlle Bertin as she stood on a balcony of the palace.

She was born Marie-Jeanne Laurent in Abbeville, Picardy, the daughter of a gendarme and a nurse. She was sent to Paris as an apprentice to the milliner Pagalle and by her pert manner and interesting ideas ingratiated herself with the Princess Conti and the Duchesse de Chartres, both fashion leaders of the court. In 1771 the duchess introduced the little *modiste* to the Dauphine Marie Antoinette, then the attractive but shy and uncertain 16-year-old Austrian newcomer to the luxurious French court, where she was intimidated and overshadowed by more worldly and more beautiful women. Rose Bertin's influence helped dramatically to develop the Queen's grace, sense of chic, and her self-confidence.

In 1773 Rose Bertin opened her own shop, Au Grand Mogul, in the rue St. Honoré in Paris. In 1787 she expanded to more luxurious quarters in the rue de Richelieu. From then until 1792, when she fled the Revolution, first to Germany and then England, she had spent the years and her personal funds to give financial and underground support to

French emigrés all over Europe. She continued to aid her old clients from her earnings as a couturiere in London.

In 1800 she was allowed to return to Paris, still famous and respected, a career woman who had bridged the new caste system.

Having, it is rumored, burnt Marie Antoinette's accounts to protect her against the accusations of wanton extravagance, Mlle Bertin spent many futile years trying to collect from other elusive royal customers in Europe. Until 1812 her old Paris shop continued as a chic fashion boutique, run by her nephew.

She died in obscurity, but not in poverty. Only a short time before her death in 1812 (sometimes given as 1813) was she forced to sell her jewelry to live.

Busvine (Richard Busvine)

London couturier from the 1890s to the mid-1930s, Busvine was best known for tailored suits. He designed for both Queen Alexandra and for Queen Mary almost all her life.

Busvine was first known as a maker of riding habits for Edwardian ladies in the 1880s. The craze for tailleurs which followed Queen Alexandra's preference for the tailored look brought Busvine into the fashion field. The house closed shortly before World War II.

Callot Soeurs (1895–1935)

This French couture house, conducted by three sisters, was noted for elaborately trimmed "confection" dresses of chiffon, lace, and embroidery.

Established by the sisters Callot, only one of whom seems to have been known by name, the firm began as a lace shop in the 1890s. The Callot Soeurs couture house at 9 avenue Matignon became a fashion force dominated by the eldest sister, Mme Marie Gerber, and had its heyday from 1916 for about 10 years. Madeleine Vionnet was an employee of the house at one time. The firm closed in 1935.

Hattie Carnegie (Zanft) (1889–1956)

The couturiere Hattie Carnegie may have been the first native American to establish nationwide fashion fame and the first to "copy herself" in ready-to-wear.

Born Henriette Kannengiser in Vienna, she came to the United States with her parents at about 11 years of age. Trained by her mother to sew, she opened a hat shop in 1909 and introduced a full fashion collection in 1918 having chosen the name Carnegie because it symbolized power and success. About 1928 she established her own line of ready-to-wear made in her own factory and sold throughout the United States.

She married John Zanft who with Miss Carnegie's two brothers (both of whom adopted the Carnegie name) remained associates of the Carnegie enterprises, including perfume and jewelry which continued after the designer's death.

The young, molded "little Carnegie suit" was a status symbol of the 1930s and 1940s, worn by a wide circle of international celebrities and a private clientele who regarded the small but forceful Miss Carnegie as their unquestioned arbiter of taste.

Carnegie clothes followed Paris fashion trends, but the house maintained a staff of designers who injected a recognizable Carnegie spirit into each model. Among Hattie Carnegie's young employees were several who were later to have independent fame, among them Claire McCardell, Jean Louis, Norman Norell, and Gustave Tassell.

Hattie Carnegie received the Coty Award (1948) for "consistent contribution to American elegance."

She died February 22, 1956, in New York.

Irene Castle (1893–1969)

This renowned ballroom dancer of World War I days cut her hair in 1915 and established the 20th-century head. Her above-ankle taffeta dance dresses and even shorter day clothes made her "the most influential fashion figure of the post-World War I era," according to Diana Vreeland.

Gabrielle Chanel (1883–1971)

"Coco" Chanel, as both rebel, dictator, and reactionary, is most identified with the clothes which characterized the "new woman" of the 20th century. Her soft-tailored suits and her dresses reminiscent of school-girl uniforms struck the first blow against the overstuffed Belle Epoque.

"She was herself a Chanel creation," observed Marcel Haedrich, one of Chanel's biographers. Given to making up her own vital statistics with impish inconsistency, Chanel, it is fairly well substantiated, was born August 19, 1883, in Saumur, in the Auvergne district of France. (Chanel later falsified her birth certificate by changing 1883 to 1893 and gave her birthplace officially as "near Marseilles.") The correct date was sleuthed out by Marcel Haedrich in birth records at Saumur.

Gabrielle was the second of five children. Her mother died when she was six. Chanel père, who gave her the nickname Coco, left his two sons in an orphanage and took his daughter to his mother in Vichy, where Gabrielle was brought up and sent to a convent at Moulins. She never saw her father again, although she fantasized several poignant meetings with him.

Through her young Aunt Adrienne in Moulins, a cavalry garrison town, she met a wealthy young officer, Lt. Etienne Balsan, and went with him to Paris. In his country house, Royallieu, near Compiegne, Coco shared her love with his official mistress, a famous cocotte of the day.

In 1909, with the help of Balsan and a new romantic interest, "Boy" Capel, she opened a millinery shop in the avenue Gabriel. Successful almost overnight, she moved to 14 rue Cambon and by 1919 leased 25 rue Cambon and the three adjoining buildings. In 1910 she opened a shop in Deauville where her hats and later her clothes were launched by actress Gabrielle Dorziat and the singer Marthe Davelli.

By the mid-twenties the Chanel look had swept Europe, to remain dominant for two generations and then regain popularity in Chanel's old age.

The Chanel fashion spirit permeated every level, from the working girl to the rich woman who discarded emeralds and diamonds for Chanel costume jewelry to wear with her "poor" look, and the girls of every social level who followed Chanel's craze for suntanning.

Chanel's beige and mirror apartment crammed with a mixture of treasures—Coromandel screens, Egyptian sculpture, fur throws, and super-soft sofas—became the mode of interior decor.

Her appreciation for experimental art and music, her wit and arrogance, and her liaisons with famous men made her a headline personality throughout her life. She was reputedly in love with Grand Duke Dimitri of Russia and the British Duke of Westminster, the richest man of his time. She spent several years in London, and many of her fashions are what Haedrich described as the "feminized English masculine style."

Her friends included Picasso, Diaghilev, Cocteau, and Stravinsky.

In 1924 she was the first dressmaker to create her own perfume, Chanel No. 5 (her lucky number). Shortly afterward she sold the rights to the perfume for what she later contended was too little. The settlement out of court assured Chanel financial security for the rest of her life.

In 1939, her supremacy already undermined by more affected chic sponsored by her chief rival Elsa Schiaparelli, Chanel closed her couture house and joined the trek of the French to Vichy. She shortly returned, however, and lived throughout the war at the Paris Ritz, under the special protection of a German officer. This friendship gained her many enemies, and it appeared that her fashion career was ended.

In 1954, however, at the age of 71, she reopened her couture house. The first collection was a critical failure, but a commercial success. Within months her name and power were supreme again.

In 1957, at 74, she made her first and only trip to America to receive the Neiman–Marcus Award.

In 1969, her fictitious life was turned into the musical comedy *Coco*, written by Alan Lerner, with Katharine Hepburn in the role of Coco. Chanel heard the score and approved the book, but never saw the play.

In later life her garrulousness and egocentricity made her increasingly difficult, and her friendships dwindled. She lived in the impersonal "sleeping" apartment she had occupied for years at the Ritz Hotel and went daily to her sumptuous drawing room and dining room on top of her couture house. She also owned a house in Lausanne, Switzerland, the country which to her had come to mean security. There she chose to be buried.

On January 10, 1971, the woman who epitomized modern dress more profoundly than any other designer, and who was the first to break the French social barrier against "persons in trade," died alone but wealthy at the Ritz Hotel in Paris. "The maid who found her said that her face was bathed in tears," comments Haedrich in his book *Coco Chanel, Her Life, Her Secrets* (Little Brown, 1972).

Cheruit (Madeleine Cheruit)

Madeleine Cheruit, a well-known Paris couturiere in the 1920s, was trained at Raudnitz, a Paris couture house of the 1880s. Her rebellion against the flamboyant fussiness of the Edwardian era coincides with that of Chanel, but Cheruit's taste was for severe and ultra-sophisticated dresses, in contrast to the school-girl trend Chanel had launched. Mme Cheruit established her own house about 1914, retired in 1923, but her house at 21 place Vendome continued until 1935 when the premises were taken over by the designer who represented the opposite of the Cheruit creed of simplicity: Elsa Schiaparelli.

The House of Creed (1710–1966)

This family firm of English-based tailors dates back to 1710. In mid-Victorian times Creed was known as "founder of the era of tailor-mades for women."

Henry Creed and his son Henry, tailors at 33 Conduit Street, London, first attracted the attention of the general public during the English Regency through their most flamboyant client, the dandy Comte d'Orsay. D'Orsay's imitators flocked to Creed, and the tailor then branched out, creating riding clothes for ladies. Queen Victoria and Empress Eugenie both commanded Creed to provide their "amazones," as riding habits were then called. Creed's elegant lines were soon utilized for day costumes in general.

The British and French queens eventually exchanged couturiers; Eugenie invited the Englishman Henry Creed to open a branch in Paris, while Queen Victoria asked the great Paris designer, British-born Charles Frederick Worth, to open a branch in London.

Empress Elizabeth of Austria and Queen Alexandra of England wore Creed suits, establishing the tailleur as the correct feminine daytime uniform. In 1910 Henry Creed, grandson of the founder, created the first high-level unisex sensation by making suits for the Duke and Duchess of Alba. Mata Hari "went to her execution and was shot in a Creed suit," according to the memoirs of Charles Creed, last of the family firm.

Born in Paris in 1909, the last Charles Creed was educated in France, England, and Germany. His father sent him to study tailoring in Vienna and also to America to work at Bergdorf Goodman and a Seventh Avenue firm. World War II interrupted and he served with British Intelligence. Following the war he set up his own couture house in London and helped to found the Incorporated Society of London Fashion Designers.

He died in 1966.

Christian Dior (1905–1957)

The French couturier who dominated postwar fashion and built the first international fashion empire, Christian Dior was born in Granville, Normandy, on January 21, 1905. He came to Paris to study diplomacy, but left school in 1928 to work in a Paris art gallery until his fashion sketches brought him a job with Robert Piguet. Prevented by his frail health from war service, in 1942 he joined Lucien Lelong's design staff.

He was recognized as a first-rate talent by the Parisian art circle, particularly Christian Berard and Jean Cocteau.

With Marcel Boussac, the French cotton textile tycoon, as his daring backer, Christian Dior, then unknown to the fashion world, opened his own house at 30 avenue Montaigne on February 12, 1947. The establishment remains there, expanded into a complex of three adjoining buildings. His first theme, termed the "new look," with tiny waist and full skirt inspired by classic ballet, was an overnight world sensation. Following with his A-line and trapeze silhouettes, Dior became the all-powerful, though still unassuming, arbiter of postwar fashion and remained so for the rest of his life.

Known as "Tian" to his intimates, Dior was generous and helpful to young designers, and his choice of assistants, notably Marc Bohan and Yves Saint-Laurent, testify to his sense of the future.

Dior's showmanship was dramatic. He introduced the tiny, pirouetting pony mannequin in a world accustomed to the tall, stately, deadpan type.

Dior died of a heart attack while taking a cure in Montecatini, Italy, on October 24, 1957.

The Dior organization has continued and grown to worldwide scope under the business administration of Jacques Rouet, formerly of the Boussac organization. A portion of the company was sold in 1973 to Moet and Chandon. Marc Bohan is director of design for the house and all its dress collections. The Dior label also appears on perfume, cosmetics, lingerie, shoes, handbags, jewelry, hosiery, and other accessories, as well as menswear and luggage.

The House of Doeuillet (1900–1930?)

This French couture house, located at 24 place Vendome was founded the year of the Paris Exposition by a designer trained at Callot Soeurs and steeped in the feeling of light sheer pastel fabrics in delicate layers. Doeuillet is said to have been the first to create short cocktail and theatre dresses.

In 1928 Doeuillet merged his firm with the House of Doucet and the label Doeuillet–Doucet continued into the 1930s.

Jacques Doucet (the Younger) (1860?–1932?)

The House of Doucet spanned more than 100 years of European elegance, bringing fame and fortune to the grandson and namesake of the founder.

The first Jacques Doucet was a bonnet maker and lace merchant who began with a street stall in 1815 and within a year opened an establishment selling fine lace in the avenue Beaumarchais.

In 1824 with his clientele firmly established, he moved to the rue de la Paix. There his son Jacques introduced a novelty, a laundry for the fine linen and lace-frilled shirts made by the house for the dandies of the day.

Jacques Doucet III, the third generation of the fashion dynasty, was born during the time of Napoleon III and hoped to be a painter. About 1880, however, he took over the family business, determined as he said to paint with fabric. Soon the acknowledged rival of the "king of fashion," Charles Frederick Worth, his clothes were inspired by the 18th century. He was called the "couturier to the seductive woman" and he loved lace dresses with flounces, panniers, and floods of ribbon à la Watteau and Fragonard.

He was one of the first dressmakers to become a renowned art authority and collector. When he suddenly tired of period art, he sold his collection of 18th-century paintings and bibelots for 20 million gold francs and turned his 18th-century mansion and his collection of art books over as a library for art students. He then began collecting the works of his contemporaries, Manet, Cezanne, Degas, Monet, Bracque, Picasso, and le Douanier Rousseau. It is now dispersed to world famous art museums.

During his heyday as a designer, Doucet's most famous client was the actress Rejane, considered the most elegant woman of her day. He dressed her on and off the stage, setting trends in both instances.

In 1928, an old but still vigorous and rich man, Jacques Doucet merged his house with that of the lesser-known designer Doeuillet and retired.

Drecoll (Baron Christopher Drecoll)

This Belgian-born couturier of the late 19th and early 20th centuries was first known in Vienna, but his business was bought and transferred to Paris by his designer Mme Besancon de Wagner, who carried on the name. Drecoll himself retired in 1925, being best known for dresses dramatically draped in two contrasting colors. Drecoll is also said to have invented the harem skirt.

Mme de Wagner's daughter, Maggy, became a couturiere on her own, starting in 1929.

Erté (Romain de Tirtoff)

The first "far-out" designer and illustrator is still influential enough today to merit a place among the all-time fashion greats.

Erté, who contrived his pseudonym from the phonetic pronunciation of his initials, R and T, was born Romain de Tirtoff in St. Petersburg, Russia, on November 23, 1892. His was a wealthy and powerful Czarist family of Tartar descent. His father was inspector of the St. Petersburg Naval School and his uncle was the city's military governor.

As a child he saw the Paris fashions of Poiret when that designer brought his collection to Russia and thereafter pinned his hopes on a fashion career.

In 1912, at 20, he went to Paris, carrying a portfolio of fashion sketches which he shyly left at Poiret's door. He was promptly summoned back and hired to sketch Poiret clothes for circulation to clients and the press. Soon, however, his original designs were incorporated into the Poiret collections. One of his first direct assignments was to create costumes for the dancer Mata Hari.

When Poiret temporarily closed its doors at the outbreak of war in 1914, Erté returned to fashion drawing. His exquisite line drawings of fantastic women wearing impossibly tapered harem skirts, wired lampshade tunics, and pearl-draped turbans, often being led by Russian wolfhounds, helped to intensify a craze for exotic Oriental clothes inspired by the Ballet Russe costumes of Leon Bakst.

From 1915 to 1936, Erté's drawings and his fashion ideas were published under contract to *Harper's Bazaar*. In spite of his reputation for bizarre fashion fantasies, Erté emerges as a farsighted and soundly inventive designer. His use of industrial hardware on clothes predates by half a century the zipper and the current fad for metal touches. He designed the accordian handbag in 1918 and in 1921 presented the first fashion adaptation of the loose Oriental caftan. The same year his one-shoulder dresses with daring cutouts at the sides caused a sensation and forecast the present-day body cult. One of Erté's fanciful inventions was a forerunner of the blank watch face, with a single jewel moving around on a circular slice of onyx.

He was the first fashion designer to think in terms of the whole environment. He designed printed dress and decorator fabrics, bath towels, table linen, and furniture.

Still vigorous and productive in 1975, Erté lives and works in Paris (21 rue Gutenberg, Boulogne-Sur-Seine). In 1971 he collaborated with Yves Saint-Laurent on costumes and sets for a Roland Petit revue starring Zizi Jeanmaire. He has held one-man exhibitions in Paris, London, and New York, and in 1972 wrote his memoirs, *Erté Fashions by Erté* (*see* Bibliography).

Jacques Fath (1912–1954)

The French couturier Jacques Fath was noted during and after World War II for dramatic, ultrachic and body-conscious clothes which stressed the small waist, a draped hipline and his characteristically piquant back-flaring skirts.

Fath was born September 12, 1912, in Vincennes, France. He worked as a bookkeeper and stockbroker before showing his first collection of 20 costumes in Paris in 1937. He enlisted in the French Army in 1939 and was taken prisoner in 1940, later being declared a Hero of France for bravery. On his release he lived in Paris during the remaining war years.

He and his wife Genevieve, formerly the secretary of Chanel, were leaders of the gay postwar social set of Paris, and he often combined an elaborate ball with the showing of his collection at their chateau near Paris. His couture house on the avenue Pierre Premier de Serbie employed 600 craftswomen.

In 1948 Fath made a tie-up with the New York wholesale house of Joseph Halpert for the production of his ready-to-wear.

Fath died of leukemia at the age of 42 on November 13, 1954. His widow continued the business until 1957, then retired. The perfume business they organized is still operating.

Fortuny (1871–1949).

This Hispano-Venetian painter, architect, inventor, and fashion creator is now remembered chiefly for the "Fortuny dress" of finely pleated sheer silk or stencilled velvet which was the height of fashion from 1907 into the thirties.

Mariano Fortuny y Madrazo was born in Granada, Spain, in 1871, the son of a well-known Spanish painter. He died in Venice in 1949, honored as one of its most distinguished citizens.

Although he was a gifted professional in several fields and invented the "Fortuny dome," a predecessor of the cyclorama in stage design, his most sought-after secret was his method of fine pleating and ombre tinting sheer silk, a technique described by one critic as "like breathing rainbows."

The Greek-style dresses devised by Fortuny and his French wife, Henriette, were introduced in Venice about 1907 and quickly became both sex and status symbols. Proust describes his heroine, the Duchesse de Guermantes, as owning many Fortunys. Eleanora Duse, Sarah Bernhardt, and Lady Diana Duff-Cooper were among those who immortalized the Fortuny style.

The Fortuny shop in the Palazzo Pesaro-Orfei in Venice, where the Fortunys also lived, and the shop in New York managed by Elsie MacNeill (now Countess Gozzi) were centers for the clothes and also for Fortuny decorating fabrics which were highly fashionable in the twenties and thirties.

Countess Gozzi took over management of the Fortuny business and workshops in Venice after the maestro's death and now runs it very successfully, producing decorative fabrics of traditional Fortuny designs as well as her own. Fortuny dresses have become rare collector's items, at prices ranging to thousands of dollars.

Louis Antoine Godey (1804–1878)

The founder of the first, most influential, and one of the most long-lasting women's magazines in the world was born in New York. His parents were refugees from the French revolution.

Self-taught and a studious observer of popular taste, Godey saved money from his newsstand and bookshop to establish his *Lady's Book* in 1930, and employed a woman, Sarah Josepha Hale, as its editor.

Godey's *Lady's Book* was the fashion bible to millions of American women for most of the 19th century.

Nicole Groult (188?–1940?)

Groult was a French couturiere with a fashionable following in the 1920s. Mme Groult was the sister of Paul Poiret, but worked independently of her more famous brother. She opened her establishment in 1920 at 29 rue d'Anjou, and closed it about 1932.

Although her success never approached that of her brother, she was his means of support in his old age.

Elizabeth Hawes (1903–1971)

An iconoclastic American designer who helped launch the American look before renouncing fashion as "spinach," Elizabeth Hawes was born December 16, 1903, in Ridgewood, New Jersey of a "genteel poor" family. She made her own clothes from the age of 10 and at 12 designed children's dresses for a local shop.

She went to Vassar for two years, then studied at the Parsons School of Design in New York. In 1925 she went to Paris and worked for a house that "pirated" fashion sketches, then became stylist at the Paris offices of Macy's and Lord & Taylor's.

After a brief stint designing with Nicole Groult, she returned to New York and in 1928 opened a private dressmaking business in partnership with Rosemary Harden. Their soft, easy, bias-cut clothes with natural shoulders, the antithesis of the sharply constructed wide-shouldered silhouette of the time, attracted a small but consequential clientele, including Mary Lewis of Best and Company and Dorothy Shaver of Lord & Taylor, both believers in American talent, and both eventual promoters of Elizabeth Hawes' career.

In 1932 Elizabeth Hawes attempted an ambitious program of designing for a number of manufacturers in varied fields, but after six years gave up disillusioned with what she considered a low level of taste in America. The same year she wrote her opinionated, breezy autobiography, Fashion Is Spinach (see Bibliography). This, at last, put the Hawes name on a bestseller.

Mme Jenny (Sacerdote)

This French couturiere opened her Paris salon in 1911 after being associated with Paquin. She was particularly known for slim dresses with decorative necklines.

Omar (Alexander) Kiam (1894–1954)

This American designer for films and ready-to-wear was born Alexander Kiam in Monterey, Mexico, in 1894. He attended Riverview Preparatory School in Poughkeepsie, New York, and at 18 left school to work as a stockboy for a Poughkeepsie millinery firm. He was soon the firm's designer.

About 1912 he came to New York where he designed furs and clothes under "Omar" Kiam, the nickname his Poughkeepsie classmates had given him. His dramatic clothes gained attention, and in 1935 he signed a contract with Samuel Goldwyn to design for such stars as Janet Gaynor, Merle Oberon, and Loretta Young.

In 1941 he began designing ready-to-wear for Ben Reig in New York, commuting between the coasts for his collections. In 1946 he won a Coty Award. He died of a heart ailment in New York on March 28, 1954.

Laferriere (1825?– ?)

She was a leading Parisian dressmaker of the late 19th and early 20th centuries. Mme Laferriere's couture house was founded in 1849 and she dressed elegantes like Sarah Bernhardt in the 1880s, but she was still flourishing in 1900 when her clothes were featured in the Paris Exposition.

Jeanne Lanvin (1867–1946)

Mme Lanvin, the Paris couturiere most identified with the long-waisted, full-skirted "robe de style" evening silhouette of the 1920s, but a great force generally in the development of French fashion prestige, was born in Brittany, eldest of a family of 10. Her father was a well-known journalist and friend of Victor Hugo. She began by making hats and children's dresses, changing to adult fashion in 1909.

In the post-World War I years, the Lanvin name signified the height of luxurious, formal fashion. Lanvin perfumes were famous and the family estates near Grasse, France, included flower farms for perfume essences.

On Mme Lanvin's death in 1946, the business passed to her daughter, Countess Marie-Blanche de Polignac, an elegant and capable administrator. She engaged the Spanish-born Antonio Castillo to design the Lanvin collections. He remained associated with Lanvin until he went to America to design for Elizabeth Arden.

In 1963, after Countess de Polignac's death, Mme Lanvin's nephew Bernard took over, and Jules François Crahay became designer of the couture and ready-to-wear. A division of men's clothing and accessories was also added.

Crahay, now director of design at Lanvin, was born in Liege, Belgium in 1917. He trained in Liege in his parents' atelier and in Paris with Germaine de Vilmorin and Nina Ricci.

The House of Lanvin on the Faubourg St. Honoré now houses a large shop for ready-to-wear, but the custom dressmaking department continues. Mme Bernard (Maryll) Lanvin, a noted Paris beauty, shares her husband's activities in the business.

Lucien Lelong (1889–1958)

A Paris couturier with his sights on world prestige for French fashion, Lucien Lelong was born October 11, 1889, in Paris where his parents owned a small dressmaking establishment.

Lelong entered the army early in World War I and was wounded. On being invalided out, he opened a couture house on the place de la Madeleine. By 1928 he had an impressive clientele and moved to 16 avenue Matignon.

Lelong was a genial and elegant man with entree to smart Parisian society. His lavish parties became as famous as the quietly elegant clothes he designed. In 1937 he was made president of the Chambre Syndicale de la Couture, and at the outbreak of World War II he worked tirelessly to save the French couture from being blacked out. In 1940 he arranged for American buyers to come to Paris via Italy, and immediately after the Armistice made a government-sponsored mission to the United States to reopen French fashion trade. Ill health forced his retirement in 1947, and he died May 11, 1958.

Several well-known Paris designers trained on Lelong's staff. One of them, Christian Dior, said: "I learned from him that fabrics have personality, a behavior as varied as that of a temperamental woman."

Leroy (Hippolyte Roy) (1763–1829)

The first Parisian couturier to gain a name after the French Revolution, Leroy dressed the great Directoire beauties, including Therese Tallien and Mme Recamier, and became court dressmaker to Empress Josephine.

Leroy's post-Revolution clothes at first were only slight variations on the prototype "national costume" proclaimed by the Revolutionary Committee and designed by Louis David, the official painter of the regime. David made an adapation of antique Greco-Roman dress which dispensed with undergarments and used light cotton and woolen materials. As time went on, however, Leroy's designs reflected the swing toward luxury. The alluring, rich, sometimes diamond-studded gowns that later made him famous were a far cry from his humble beginnings.

Leroy's father was a stagehand at the Paris Opera, and he was apprenticed at 12 to the theater's hairdresser. A short time later (about 1780) Rose Bertin, Marie Antoinette's dressmaker, hired him to work on the Queen's stupendous headdresses, and he later dressed the Queen's coiffures at Versailles. Being a plebeian by birth, he survived the Reign of Terror and emerged as the fashion authority of the Republique, shaping the Citoyenne look of the 1790s.

An extraordinary artist and shrewd, if unscrupulous, businessman, Leroy attracted the most important women of every period in his long

326

career. He served the court at Versailles, then designed for Empress Josephine and for her successor Empress Marie Louise. He dressed her rival Countess Marie Walewska and the ladies of the court of the restored Bourbons.

"Leroy's bills cause as much strife in marriage as illicit love letters," wrote an observer of the 1820s.

In 1824, the house of Leroy made the robes for the coronation of Charles X, but his genius for sheer, erotic clothes could not shift to the wasp waists and balloon sleeves of the Restoration period.

When Leroy died in 1829, he was forgotten.

Louiseboulanger (Louise Boulanger) (1900– ?)

One of the chic Paris dressmakers from 1922 until 1934, Mme Boulanger, who combined her first and last name in her label, received her training with Cheruit and was particularly well-known for her melodramatic clothes with uneven hemlines and in transparent materials, introduced about 1928. She had her own house for only 12 years (closed 1934).

Lucile (Lady Duff-Gordon) (1864?–1935)

Lucile was probably the first fashion designer with an international business, and the first titled personage to achieve top rank in the field of fashion.

Lucile, whose name is still synonymous with the delectable, lightly decorated chiffons in pale colors worn by Irene Castle, Mary Pickford, and the Ziegfeld Follies beauties on and off the stage, was born Lucy Christina Sutherland in England about 1864. Her well-bred and conservative parents also produced the "scandalous" novelist, Elinor Glyn.

At 17 Lucy married an older man, James Clayton Wallace, and shocked her family and their circle by divorcing him after five years. Outside the pale, having to support herself and her daughter, she began to make clothes in the soft, feminine style she had always made for herself and sold them to friends. She was soon such a success that she opened her own establishment in Hanover Square, under the name Lucile. Here again she gained a reputation for shock by introducing gossamer, lace-trimmed underwear which was often returned by irate husbands.

Lucile introduced to England the first fashion parades using live mannequins, and completed her costumes with accessories designed in the house.

In 1890 she married Sir Cosmo Duff-Gordon and reclaimed her social position. But she kept on working, opening branches in Paris, New

York, and Chicago. She wrote frequent articles for fashion magazines and had a fashion column.

Although she herself was pretty, graceful, and petite, her clothes were usually meant to give a tall, statuesque appearance. Her famous models, Hebe and Dolores, were six feet tall and set the standard of the gorgeous showgirl when they later appeared in the Ziegfeld Follies (dressed by Lucile).

The Duff-Gordons were passengers on the fatal voyage of the Titanic. They were saved, but unproven rumors that their places in a lifeboat were gained through bribery caused their social eclipse and affected Lucile's business. Her reputation dwindled and her death in 1935 was little noticed by the press.

The Victoria and Albert Museum in London owns many examples of Lucile's work.

Claire McCardell (Mrs. Irving D. Harris) (1905–1958)

Designer of soft, unconstructed clothes, often with a quaint early American feeling, but also often totally modern and sculpturesque, Claire McCardell was the American designer most closely identified with the term the "American look."

She was born May 24, 1905, in Frederick, Maryland. Her father, Adrian Leroy McCardell, was a prominent banker and state senator. She was married (1943) to the architect, Irving Drought Harris.

She attended Hood College, Maryland, for two years, then came to New York to the Parsons School of Design. Work as a fashion model led to an opportunity to design knitted fashions, and later she joined Hattie Carnegie's design staff. In 1931 she was engaged as model and assistant designer at Townley, Inc. The head designer's death before a seasonal opening brought her the challenge of completing the collection alone.

In 1938 the McCardell "monastic" dress, loose and bias-cut, with a wide separate belt, became a world fashion. She launched the modernized dirndl, the use of wool tweed for evening clothes, the hooded sweater, and the famous "popover," a wrapover dress with side slits and ties.

Time magazine in 1955 devoted its cover to Miss McCardell, citing her "artist's sense of color and sculptor's feeling for form."

She died March 22, 1958.

Mainbocher (Main Rousseau Bocher) (retired)

This American-born couturier in Paris (1929–1939) and New York (1941–1970) is now retired and living in Europe.

Born October 24, 1890, in Chicago, Main Rousseau Bocher was the first American to succeed as a Paris dressmaker. After a public school education, he served in a U.S. Army hospital unit overseas in World War I and remained to study singing in Munich and Paris. He augmented his income sketching fashions for Vogue and Harper's Bazaar, then edited French Vogue until he opened his couture house about 1929.

The Mainbocher corselet, his beaded and fur-lined evening sweaters, his unusual sleeve and shoulder treatments, and his basic black crepe evening dress with a variety of "glamour" attachments which changed its mood and purpose, brought him world recognition. Mainbocher was chosen by Mrs. Wallis Simpson to make her wedding gown and trousseau for her marriage to Edward VIII, Duke of Windsor. The Duchess' wedding gown is now in the Costume Institute of the Metropolitan Museum, New York, and she donated other Mainbochers to the Victoria and Albert Museum in London.

The 1939 outbreak of war forced Bocher to close and return to America. He opened in New York in 1941. During World War II he designed the uniforms of several of the American women's military services: the Waves, Womens Marine Corps, and the Red Cross. He also designed the Campfire Girls uniforms.

On his retirement in 1970 and the closing of his house in 1971, Mainbocher's archives of sketch books were purchased by the Costume Institute of the Metropolitan Museum, New York.

Molyneux (Capt. Edward Molyneux) (1891–1974)

This Paris and London couturier symbolizes the free fashion spirit of the 1920s and 1930s. His willowy, young, yet alluringly feminine clothes, so perfectly worn by Gertrude Lawrence, Ina Claire, and Adele Astaire, brought a breezy English inflection into French fashion.

Born September 5, 1891, in London, he worked in his teens as a sketcher for Lucile (Lady Duff-Gordon) who sent him to Chicago to look after the branch of her dressmaking business there.

He served in the British Army during the First World War and lost an eye. In 1919 he went to Paris and opened a fashion house at 14 rue Royale. With almost instant success, he enlarged his quarters, moving to 5 rue Royale, an address ever since identified with Molyneux.

A talented painter and brilliant collector of art, he amassed a collection of Impressionist works which he later sold for the then record price of $1 million. He promptly formed another collection by newer artists with equal investment acumen.

In World War II Molyneux returned to London, opened his dress house there, and gave all the profits to national defense. He also maintained a refugee camp at Falaise, France. He reopened his Paris house in 1946 but in 1950, threatened with blindness in his remaining eye, he retired and built houses in Jamaica and in Grasse, in southern France. He was persuaded to go back into business in his old Paris quarters in 1964, but gradually withdrew from active participation, leaving the designing to John Tully, a distant relative whom he trained in the Molyneux tradition.

He retired again to Monte Carlo, where he died March 23, 1974.

William Morris (1834–1896)

This English artist, architect, social reformer, and writer was largely instrumental in revolutionizing Victorian taste and launching Art Nouveau. His theories of the grace and beauty of Gothic and medieval forms and colors brought in a new school of fashion thinking.

With painters Edward Burne-Jones and Dante Gabriel Rossetti, his cofounders of the Pre-Raphaelite art movement, Morris helped to create the gentle yet liberated Pre-Raphaelite woman who outmoded the corseted, gussetted, Edwardian beauty. William Morris, in fabrics painted or printed in intricate but clearly delineated designs, gave this woman her special ambiance. They were first produced in the 1870s, and from 1881 until 1940 he had large workshops at Merton Abbey, England.

Morris was a prolific writer and painter, an early environmentalist and crusader for the protection of historic monuments, but the William Morris print pattern is his passport to immortality.

There is now a William Morris Society (founded 1956) for the preservation of his work and the continuance of his precepts. Its headquarters is in the old William Morris house in Hammersmith, London.

Martin Munkacsi (1895?–1963)

This photographer, known as "the high priest of fashion in motion," pioneered in candid fashion photography. His subtly distorted pictures, elongating a woman's figure, captured her movements and expressed the spirit of youth and action from which postwar fashion stemmed.

Born in Transylvania in a working class family (his father was a housepainter), Munkacsi served in the German Army in World War I where he learned photography. Afterward he worked on magazines and newspapers in Budapest and Germany. In 1933 he showed a portfolio of his pictures to Carmel Snow of *Harper's Bazaar*, and together they applied the idea of candid pictures to fashion. He remained throughout his life the master of this phase of his craft, with many followers but no peers.

Condé Nast (1874–1942)

A world leader in establishing fashion as an art form and one of the most elegant and cultivated figures in New York in the first four dec-

330

ades of the 20th century, Condé Nast could also be said to have established, perhaps unknowingly, the framework for an independent American fashion spirit.

From the time he bought a struggling pattern magazine called *Vogue* in 1909 until his death in 1942, aged 68, he advocated many movements aimed at broadening and improving the American lifestyle. His magazines, *Vogue, Vanity Fair, House and Garden,* and later *Glamour* and *Mademoiselle*, sought to show the best in all the arts, and his own way of life and entertaining enhanced the international image of a rich and lively America. In his later years, he expanded his fashion-oriented empire to France, England, Italy, and Australia.

With Irene Lewisohn, Condé Nast established the fashion collection that later became the Costume Institute of the Metropolitan Museum of Art.

Norman Norell (1900–1972)

Called the "dean of American fashion designers," Norell was among the first to employ couture techniques and provide couture quality in ready-made clothing.

Born Norman Levinson in Noblesville, Indiana, on April 20, 1900, and brought up in Indianapolis where his family owned a men's furnishings store, Norell came to New York at 18, after giving himself a "nom de mode" by blending his first name and the initial of his surname. He studied fashion illustration at the Parsons School of Design. His interest in that school remained throughout his career, and he made Parsons the chief beneficiary of his will after his death.

From 1924 to 1928 Norell worked for Charles Armour, a New York dress manufacturer, and in 1932 joined the staff of Hattie Carnegie, where he adapted French models and designed original clothes for the glamorous clientele which included Gertrude Lawrence, Paulette Goddard, and Ina Claire.

In 1941, with manufacturer Anthony Traina, he formed Traina–Norell, a firm which brought a new dimension of luxurious simplicity to ready-made clothes.

After his first year, Norell received the first Coty American Fashion Critics' Award (1943). He won the Award again in 1951 and was the first to be placed in the Coty Hall of Fame (1956). In 1960 Traina retired, and the firm became Norman Norell, Inc., with the backing of financiers from Detroit and Philadelphia. In 1968 Revlon launched Norell perfume, the first major fragrance success linked to an American fashion designer.

On October 15, 1972, the day before a retrospective fashion showing covering his 50 years as a designer was presented by the Parsons School, Norell suffered a stroke. He died 10 days later.

The Norell business continues at 550 Seventh Avenue, New York, N.Y. 10018, with Gustave Tassell as designer.

Paquin (Mme Joseph Paquin)

One of the most prominent Paris couturieres of the early 20th century and a woman of fashion herself, being married to a prominent French banker, Paquin opened her maison de couture at 3 rue de la Paix in 1891. It moved to 120 Faubourg St. Honoré, where it remained until 1954, although Mme Paquin's personal connection ended in 1920.

It was a large, well-organized house and the first Paris establishment to have a London branch (1912) and branches in Madrid and Buenos Aires.

Mme Paquin was an early leader in efforts to unite the top French dressmakers in worldwide promotions. She was chairman of a notable fashion display in the Paris Exposition of 1900.

In spite of her public activities, none of Mme Paquin's vital statistics are known.

Mme Paulette (Mme Jacques de la Bruyere) (retired)

This Paris milliner gained prominence during the early years of World War II when she created wool jersey turbans of great warmth and tremendous chic. Her hats were often small shapes set on a draped scarf. She was still active in the early 1970s.

Sylvia Pedlar (1901–1972)

America's leading designer of lingerie, under the label Iris, Sylvia Pedlar was one of the few American designers whose work had worldwide influence and recognition.

A native New Yorker, Mrs. Pedlar studied art at Cooper Union and the Art Students' League. From the first she concentrated on designing intimate apparel. Her designs and elegant use of easy-care fabrics made "commercial" lingerie both luscious and contemporary and gradually replaced the old concept of frilly, fragile undergarments. Her sleep "toga," her square-necked empire gown, and the short "baby-doll" gown she launched in the 1950s remain worldwide classics.

She won a Coty Award in 1951. After retiring early in 1970, she died February 26, 1972.

She was a charter member of and member of the board of directors of the Council of Fashion Designers of America.

André Perugia (retired)

The leading French shoemaker of the first half of the 20th century and the one responsible for the most delicate and extravagant footwear of his time, Perugia was born in Nice and went to work in his father's shoe shop there at the age of 11. Five years later he opened his own business in Paris, determined to establish shoemaking at an art level. His individually created shoes, with delicate, pointed outlines and intricate, luxurious embroidery in silk and jewels, brought the then unheard-of price of 8000 francs (about $125).

Through a famous Paris demi-mondaine with a passion for shoes, Perugia came to the attention of her couturier, Paul Poiret. Perugia shoes were shown with Poiret collections from 1920 onward and later were designed for Jacques Fath and Givenchy. Until the advent of the low-heeled casual shoe in about 1960, a Perugia shoe was a symbol of elegance.

By World War II Perugia was so famous that the story was told that when his staff was wildly trying to locate German General Rommel to inform him of the Allied landing in Normandy, he was at Perugia ordering shoes for a lady friend.

Perugia retired in 1970 and lives in Cannes.

Robert Piguet (1901–1953)

This French dressmaker of the 1930s was known for his "thin" suits and tasteful day dresses.

Piguet was born in 1901 in Yverdon, Switzerland, and was trained as a banker. He worked from 1918 for Redfern and Paul Poiret before opening his couture house on the Rond Point des Champs Elysées in 1933. In 1951 he became ill and closed his house. He died in 1953.

Piguet was interested in young talent and gave a number of future Paris "greats" their first chance, among them Christian Dior and Hubert de Givenchy.

Paul Poiret (1880–1944)

The French couturier who epitomized the lavish chic of pre-World War I Paris and who "proclaimed the fall of the corset and the advent of the brassiere," was also one of his epoch's most colorful and avant-garde personalities.

The period 1903–1914 was Poiret's heyday. "Artistic" and "exotic" were the two most-used adjectives for his clothes. He adored Persian coloring, seductive Oriental shapes and motifs, and his famous "minaret" tunic harem skirt and exotic embroideries stemmed from Persian miniatures.

Sergei Diaghilev and Leon Bakst were his close friends, and their ballets inspired many of his collections.

In 1911 he established the Martine School of Decorative Arts in Paris (named for his daughter) which fostered much of the art known as Art Deco. He was a patron and sponsor of the painter Raoul Dufy.

Poiret was born in a prosperous bourgeois family of wool merchants in Paris in 1880. He peddled his fashion sketches to Paris couturiers and in 1896 was engaged by the dressmaker Jacques Doucet. Here he designed costumes for the stage, including those of Rejane in *Zaza* and Sarah Bernhardt's for *L'Aiglon*.

Poiret worked at the House of Worth from 1900 to 1904, then opened his own small establishment at 5 rue Auber.

In 1908 Poiret was the first fashion designer to open in the smart Champs Elysées section of Paris. For the next 15 years he was to earn his title "king of fashion," giving the most extravagant fetes and living on a highly lavish scale in his estate Bretard, originally Louis XV's hunting lodge.

His influence waned as the simple fashions of Chanel and others of similar leaning increased. He died poor and virtually forgotten in 1944.

Poiret's work was notably recorded in an exhibition "The Heroic Years 1908–1914," presented by the Houston (Texas) Museum, arranged by James Johnson Sweeney in 1956. Another Poiret show is scheduled for May 1976 at the Fashion Institute of Technology in New York.

Caroline Reboux (1837?–1927)

This Paris milliner of enduring fame from about 1865 to 1927 was nearly 90 when she died. Her designs paralleled fashion trends from Worth to Schiaparelli, and her hats were always slightly outrageous and à la mode.

The daughter of a Parisian journalist, Reboux made hats in an attic from about 1865 and sold them to other Paris modistes for three francs until she was discovered by the elegant Princess Metternich, who also is said to have discovered Worth.

In 1870 Reboux opened a smart establishment at 23 rue de la Paix and became one of the outstanding name designers until her death in 1927. Her latter-day hats for Elsa Schiaparelli and other designers were mere impudent twists of bright satin and felt worn sharply tilted sidewise.

Although Mme Reboux sold to every elegant aristocrat in Paris, her morals were so strict that she barred the famous cocottes of the day from her door.

House of Redfern (1842–1930?)

This couture house, founded in 1842 in London by John Redfern, a court dressmaker to Queen Victoria, was eventually responsible for the tailored look all Europe grew to know as "à l'Anglaise."

In 1881 John Redfern sent his assistant Charles Poynter to Paris to open a branch of Redfern. Poynter became so successful that he added Redfern to his own name. By 1890 the house of Redfern in the rue de Rivoli had 500 employees. It specialized in tailormades of navy blue wool.

Charles Poynter Redfern's period stage costumes were famous and diametrically opposed to his designing for contemporary women. He created the sensationally revealing costumes for Mary Garden in "Aphrodite."

Redfern also designed in 1916 the first women's uniform for the International Red Cross.

House of Reville (1906–1916)

Terry Reville, the London dressmaker particularly known for his elaborate and expensive evening creations, made Queen Mary's court gowns.

The highly temperamental and eccentric Reville got his start designing mourning wardrobes at Jay's in Oxford Circus, but his baroque instincts were asserted to the full in his own ateliers in Hanover Square, where models wandered through the grey Louis XV salons with tall Regency walking sticks.

No two Reville gowns were ever exactly alike.

After being ruined by World War I and his own excesses, Reville died destitute.

Nina Ricci (Marie Nielli Ricci) (1883–1970)

The designer, who founded the still-flourishing house which bears her name, was born Marie Nielli in Turin, Italy, in 1883 and was sent to Paris to work as a seamstress at age 13.

By 1905 she had her own model house and after her marriage to a jeweler, Louis Ricci, she opened Nina Ricci in 1932. This became the center for traditional clothes diametrically opposed to the ease and freedom of the designs of Gabrielle Chanel.

Mme Ricci, a stately and handsome woman who retained her interest in Ricci activities after she turned administration over to her son Robert, was one of the first Paris couturieres to perceive the future of ready-to-wear; she was also the creator of one of this century's most popular perfumes, "Joy."

Maggy Rouff (1897–1971)

This French couturiere, popular in the 1920s, was born Maggy Besancon de Wagner about 1897 in Paris. Her parents administered the House of Drecoll there. Her draped and pouffed clothes were worn by women who clung to elaborate fashion in the face of the new wave of simplicity represented by Chanel.

Maggy Rouff was first established at 136 avenue des Champs Elysées, then after World War II, at 35 avenue Matignon. Mme Rouff retired in 1948 and died August 7, 1971.

Elsa Schiaparelli (1890–1973)

In the frenetic period between the Depression and World War II, this Italian-born Paris couturiere brought appropriate new elements of wit and shock value to world fashion, challenging the entrenched quiet elegance of Chanel, Molyneux, and Mainbocher. Her brand of arrogance was later known as "hard chic."

Elsa Schiaparelli was born in Rome on September 10, 1890, of a well-known intellectual family. Her father, a mathematician and professor of Oriental languages, was dean of the faculty of the University of Rome and her uncle, Giovanni Schiaparelli, was the astronomer who discovered the canals on Mars.

While in her teens Elsa married a Polish ne'er-do-well and went with him to America.

Her marriage broke up in New York, and she was left with a child to support. Her daughter, Gogo Berenson (now the Marchesa dei Cacciapia), produced Schiaparelli's now-famous granddaughters, Marisa Berenson, the model and actress, and Berry Berenson, fashion photographer and wife of actor Tony Perkins.

To eke out a living, "Schiap" began to knit sweaters in New York, then went to Paris, where she made a sensation with the first dressy pullover in history, black silk with a white bowknot knitted into the front. She set up an attic workshop on the rue de la Paix with a few Armenian handworkers. She soon added a few dress models and within months her slim jacket suits and dresses with exaggerated shoulders and nipped waistline, worn with bizarre hats, were the rage of Paris. She made a hat out of an upturned shoe and employed Salvador Dali to design her gigantic surreal prints. She was the first of the ultraexpensive dressmakers to experiment with man-made fibers. Her "glass dress" was in crepe mixing silk and fiberglass.

In 1935 Schiaparelli bought the impressive establishment of Mme Cheruit at 21 place Vendome and became part of the inner circle of Paris social and artistic life.

Among her assistants were the American print designer Brooke Cadwallader (now making fabrics in Mexico), the future fashion great Hubert de Givenchy, and the jeweler Jean Schlumberger, who created buttons and later her amusing and highly successful jewelry, including her blackamoor brooches.

336

"To be shocking was the snobbism of the moment," wrote Bettina Ballard. "Shocking pink was an invention of Schiaparelli and a symbol of her thinking."

When the war came, Schiaparelli closed her house and went to America. She returned to Paris in 1954 to live, but not to work. Her autobiography *Shocking Life* (E.P. Dutton) was published the same year. The proceeds from her perfumes having made her independent, she left postwar fashion to others.

Mme Schiaparelli lived for many years in a handsome 18th-century house on the rue de Berri but sold it and moved to an apartment shortly before her death on November 14, 1973.

Mme Handley Seymour

This ultraexclusive London dressmaker before World War II designed many of Queen Mary's statuesque afternoon costumes.

Edward Steichen (1879–1973)

Steichen is the fashion photographer credited with being the first to use natural light and informal poses for indoor photographs.

Born in Luxembourg but brought up in Milwaukee, Wisconsin, Steichen did aerial photography during World War I and won the Legion of Honor. His photos in *Vogue* from 1923 to 1938 did much to establish "glamorous realism" in fashion coverage.

In his later years Steichen became a portrait and documentary camera artist. His sister was married to the poet Carl Sandburg.

Rose Valois (Mme Fernand Clouet) (retired)

This French milliner flourished in the 1920s and 1930s when she was noted for her side-tilted berets and elaborate evening hats.

Victorine

This French dressmaker was most admired in the 1830s for her "ravishing" dresses inspired by goddesses and romantic heroines of the past. She epitomized in fashion what was happening in all the arts—literature, architecture, and so on in post-Napoleonic Europe—an escape from unrest and readjustment into the more poetic past.

Little is known of her life, and her fame rests chiefly on the references to her clothes made in the romantic French novels of her day.

Madeleine Vionnet (1877?–1975)

This French couturiere, celebrated as the "genius of the soft cut," is also credited with making bias-cut clothes a classic dressmaking technique. Her fluid bias clothes epitomized the willowy elegance of the 1930s.

Born in Aubervilliers, France, about 1877, the daughter of the tax collector of that peasant village, she went to Paris at 12 where she worked as a midinette and later for a dressmaker, Vincent, on the rue de la Paix. At 20 she moved to London, lodging with the family of a doctor who also housed several insane patients. She stuck it out for five years, however, working for the couture house of Kate Reilly.

Returning to Paris, she worked for the then-flourishing house of Callot Soeurs, where she began to discover her own style. In 1907 she joined Doucet as designer, where she introduced her revolutionary one-layer dresses without inner construction. They were shown on barefoot, uncorseted mannequins.

In 1912 she opened her own house, first on the rue de Rivoli and in 1922 at 50 avenue Montaigne. Here she invented the intricate bias-cut styles which swept world fashion.

Mme Vionnet retired in 1939, but kept her apartment above her former fashion ateliers, and continued to follow fashion news and to grant occasional interviews almost until her death on March 2, 1975.

Many of Mme Vionnet's costumes and her design archives are now in the Centre de Documentation du Costume in Paris.

Charles Frederick Worth (1825–1895)

The Paris House of Worth, founded by a Britisher, Charles Frederick Worth, was the leading fashion establishment in Europe for more than 40 years. Charles Frederick Worth was the first "fashion dictator," with a world influence never before felt and rarely equalled since.

Charles Frederick Worth was born in Bourne, Lincolnshire, on October 13, 1825, and at 12 was a salesboy in the London firm of Swan and Edgar, drapers. He taught himself dress design by studying the portraits in the National Gallery and other London museums. At 20, his rich relations provided his fare to Paris where he was hired as salesman at Gaelin and Opigez, fashionable Paris drapers. There he met and married (June 21, 1851) a member of the staff, Marie Vernet. He persuaded the firm to let him dress his wife in his original designs to display new materials, thus launching the idea of live fashion mannequins. The "fashion doll" had been the standard way of selling fashions for centuries.

When Napoleon III and Empress Eugenie restored a glittering court in France, Worth was already well established in his own ateliers on the rue de la Paix—the beginning of that thoroughfare as a legendary fashion center. In 1855 when Empress Eugenie and her ladies-in-waiting sat for the famous Winterhalter group portrait, they wore typical Worth dresses of flower-garlanded tulle.

A critic later wrote of Empress Eugenie, "Her greatest achievement was her collaboration with her couturier."

Worth introduced the hoopskirt and later the crinoline, both of which affected every aspect of Victorian life, from architecture (doors had to be widened) to posture (it was impossible, without creating a scandal, to sit down carelessly in a hoopskirt).

By 1860 Worth was the best-known fashion designer in the world and the founder of the French dressmaking industry's future reputation for style authority. When Queen Victoria paid a state visit to Paris, she invited Worth to open a branch in London, where it existed until the early 1970s (under different management).

During the German siege of Paris in 1871, Worth's luxurious, perfumed salons were turned into hospital wards, but he resumed after the war, launching the bustle and the elaborate ruffled and draped taffeta gowns that now symbolize fashion of the 1870s and 1880s.

Charles Worth continued to design until his death in 1895, on March 10, the date for which he had always had an inexplicable dread. The business passed to his sons Jean and Gaston, who continued it successfully into the 1930s, during which they started Paul Poiret on his career as a fashion designer. Jean Worth was a favorite designer of French actresses, among them Sarah Bernhardt.

appendix:
coty award
winners 1943-1975

1943 Winnie: Norman Norell
Special Awards for millinery: Lilly Dache; John Frederics

1944 Winnie: Claire McCardell
Special Awards: Sally Victor (millinery); Phelps Associates (leather accessories)

1945 Three Winnies: Gilbert Adrian and Tina Leser (at-home clothes); Emily Wilkens (teen-age clothes)

1946 Three Winnies: Clare Potter; Omar Kiam; Vincent Monte-Sano

1947 Four Winnies: Nettie Rosenstein; Mark Mooring; Jack Horwitz; Adele Simpson

1948 Winnie: Hattie Carnegie
Special Awards for furs: Esther Dorothy; Joseph De Leo; Maximilian

1949 Winnie: Pauline Trigere
Special Awards: Toni Owen (sportswear); David Evins (shoes)

1950 Two Winnies: Bonnie Cashin; Charles James
Special Awards: Mabel and Charles Julianelli (shoes); Nancy Melcher (lingerie)

1951 Winnie: Jane Derby
Two Return Awards: Norman Norell; Pauline Trigere
Special Awards: Vera Maxwell (sportswear); Anne Fogarty (prettiest dresses); Sylvia Pedlar (lingerie)

1952 Two Winnies: Ben Zuckerman; Ben Sommers of Capezio
Two Special Awards for their concept of dressing: Karen Stark of Harvey Berin; Sydney Wragge of B.H. Wragge

1953 Winnie: Thomas F. Brigance
Two Special Awards: John Moore of Mattie Talmack (evening wear); Helen Lee (children's designer)

341

1954   Winnie: James Galanos
Special Award: Charles James (innovative cut)

1955   Three Winnies: Jeanne Campbell; Anne Klein; Herbert Kasper
Special Award: Adolfo (millinery)

1956   Hall of Fame Award: Norman Norell
Two Winnies: Luis Estevez; Sally Victor
Return Award: James Galanos
Special Award: Gertrude and Robert Goldworm (knitwear)

1957   Two Winnies: Leslie Morris: Sydney Wragge
Special Award: Emeric Partos (furs)

1958   Hall of Fame Award (posthumous): Claire McCardell
Winnie: Arnold Scaasi
Return Award: Ben Zuckerman
Two Special Awards: Donald Brooks (influence on evening
clothes); Jean Schlumberger (jewelry)

1959   Two Hall of Fame Awards: Pauline Trigere; James Galanos

1960   Two Winnies: Ferdinando Sarmi; Jacques Tiffeau
Three Special Awards: Rudi Gernreich (innovative body
clothes); Sol Klein of Nettie Rosenstein (costume jewelry);
Roxane of Samuel Winston (beaded evening clothes)

1961   Hall of Fame Award: Ben Zuckerman
Two Winnies: Bill Blass and Gustave Tassell
Two Special Awards: Bonnie Cashin (deep-country clothes);
Kenneth (leadership in hair styling)

1962   Winnie: Donald Brooks
Special Award: Halston (millinery)

1963   Winnie: Rudi Gernreich
Return Award: Bill Blass
Two Special Awards: Arthur & Theodora Edelman (leather de-
sign); Betty Yokova of A. Neustadter (furs)

1964   Winnie: Geoffrey Beene
Return Award: Jacques Tiffeau
Special Award: David Webb (jewelry design)
Return Special Award: Sylvia Pedlar (lingerie)

1965   Four Special Awards: Anna Potok of Maximilian (furs); Tzaims
Luksus (fabric design); Gertrude Seperack (foundation garments); Pablo of Elizabeth Arden (leadership in makeup)
Joint Special Award to nine designers of young fashions: Sylvia
de Gay; Bill Smith; Victor Joris; Leo Narducci; Don Simonelli;

Gayle Kirkpatrick; Stan Herman; Edie Gladstone; Deanna Littell

1966 Winnie: Dominic
Two Return Awards: Rudi Gernreich; Geoffrey Beene
Special Award: Kenneth Jay Lane (costume jewelry)

1967 Hall of Fame Award: Rudi Gernreich
Winnie: Oscar de la Renta
Return Award: Donald Brooks
Special Award: Beth & Herbert Levine (shoes)

1968 Two Winnies: George Halley; Luba (Marks)
Two Return Awards: Bonnie Cashin; Oscar de la Renta
Special Award: Count Giorgio di Sant'Angelo (fantasy accessories and ethnic fashions)
1st Coty Award for Men's Fashion Design: Bill Blass

1969 Two Winnies: Stan Herman; Victor Joris
Return Award: Anne Klein
Three Special Awards: Adolfo and Halston (millinery design); Julian Tomchin (fabric design)

1970 Hall of Fame Award: Bill Blass
Two Winnies: Giorgio di Sant'Angelo; Chester Weinberg
Return Award: Herbert Kasper
Menswear Award: Ralph Lauren
Joint Special Awards for costume jewelry design: Alexis Kirk; Cliff Nicholson; Marty Ruza; Bill Smith; Daniel Stoenescu; Steven Brody of Cadoro
Special Award: Will and Eileen Richardson (tie-dyed fabrics)

1971 Hall of Fame Citation: Bill Blass
Hall of Fame Award: Anne Klein
Two Winnies: Halston; Betsey Johnson of Alley Cat
Menswear Award: Larry Kane of Raffles Wear
Four Special Awards: John Kloss of Cira (lingerie); Nancy Knox (men's shoes); Elsa Peretti (jewelry); Levi Strauss (world fashion influence)

1972 Hall of Fame Award: Bonnie Cashin
Winnie: John Anthony
Return Award: Halston
Special Award: Dorothy Weatherford for Mountain Artisans (patchwork and quality)
Four Special Menswear Awards for excitement in menswear: Alexander Shields; Pinky Wolman and Dianne Beaudry of Flo

343

Toronto; Alan Rosanes of Gordonn Gregory, Ltd.; Robert Margolis of A. Smile, Inc.

1973 Hall of Fame Award: Oscar de la Renta
Two Winnies: Stephen Burrows; Calvin Klein
Menswear Award: Piero Dimitri
Menswear Return Award: Ralph Lauren
Special Award: Clovis Ruffin (original young fashion)
Joint Special Awards for accessory design: Michael Moraux of Dubaux (jewelry); Joe Famolare (shoes); Don Kline (hats); Herbert and Beth Levine (shoes); Judith Leiber (handbags); Celia Sebiri (jewelry)

1974 Two Hall of Fame Awards: Geoffrey Beene; Halston
Winnie: Ralph Lauren
Menswear Award: Bill Kaiserman of Rafael
Return Award: Calvin Klein
Menswear Return Award: Piero Dimitri
Special Menswear Award for jewelry: Aldo Cipullo
Two Special Menswear Awards: Sal Cesarani; John Weitz
Joint Special Awards for lingerie design: Fernando Sanchez; Stan Herman; John Kloss; Bill Tice; Stephen Burrows

1975 Hall of Fame Citation: Geoffrey Beene
Hall of Fame: Calvin Klein
Hall of Fame for Menswear: Piero Dimitri
Winnie: Carol Horn
Menswear Award: Chuck Howard and Peter Wrigley of "Mark of the Lion" (Anne Klein Studio)
Menswear Return Award: Bill Kaiserman for Rafael
Special Award for swimsuits: Monika Tilley for Elon
Special Menswear Award for leather design: Nancy Knox
Four Special Awards for fur design: Bill Blass for Revillon America; Fernando Sanchez for Revillon America; Calvin Klein for Alixandre; Viola Sylbert for Alixandre

bibliography

Ackerman, Susa. *Couture in Deutschland*. Munich: Perlenverlag, 1961.

Adburgham, Alison. *A View of Fashion*. London: Allen & Unwin, 1964.

———. *Shops and Shopping, 1800–1914*. London: Allen & Unwin, 1964.

Allen, Agnes. *The Story of Clothes*. New York: Roy, 1958.

American Fabrics Magazine, Editors. *Encyclopedia of Textiles*, 2nd ed. New York: Doric Publishing, 1973

Amies, Hardy. *Just So Far*. New York: Collins, 1954.

Arnold, Janet. *Handbook of Costume*. Springfield, Mass.: Phillips, forthcoming.

Ballard, Bettina. *In My Fashion*. New York: David McKay, 1960.

Balmain, Pierre. *My Years and Seasons*. Translated by E. Lanchbery and G. Young. London: Cassell, 1964. New York: Doubleday, 1965.

Beaton, Cecil. *The Glass of Fashion*. New York: Doubleday, 1954.

———. *Fair Lady*. New York: Holt, Rinehart & Winston, 1964.

Bell, Quentin. *On Human Finery*. Toronto: Hogarth, 1947. Philadelphia: R. West, 1973.

Bergler, Edmund. *Fashion and the Unconscious*. New York: Robert Brunner, 1953.

Bertin, Celia. *Paris a la Mode—A Voyage of Discovery*. Translated by M. Deans. New York: Harper, 1957.

Binder, Pearl. *Muffs and Morals*. New York: William Morrow, 1955.

Brooklyn Museum. *The House of Worth*. Brooklyn, N.Y.: Brooklyn Museum, 1962.

Bruhn, W., and M. Tilke. *A Pictorial History of Costume*. New York: Frederick A. Praeger, 1956. Tuebingen, Germany: Verlag Ernst Wasmuth, 1955.

Burris–Meyer, Elizabeth. *This Is Fashion*. New York: Harper & Bros., 1943.

Byers, Margaretta. *Designing Women*. New York: Simon & Schuster, 1938.

Carter, Ernestine. *With Tongue in Chic*. London: Michael Joseph, 1974.

Centro Internazionale Delli Arti e Del Costume. *International Guide to Museums and Public Collections of Costumes and Textiles*. Venice: Centro Internazionale Delli Arti e Del Costume, 1970.

Charles-Roux, Edmonde. *Chanel: Her Life, Her World—and the Woman behind the Legend She Herself Created*. New York: A. Knopf, 1975.

Chase, Edna Woolman, and Ilka Chase. *Always in Vogue*. New York: Doubleday, 1954.

Chillingworth, J., and H. Busby. *Fashion*. London: Lutterworth Press, 1961.

Collins, Harry. *The ABC of Dress*. New York: Baker & Taylor, 1923.

Crawford, Morris De Camp. *The Ways of Fashion*. New York: Fairchild, 1948.

———. *One World of Fashion*, 3rd ed. New York: Fairchild, 1967.

Creed, Charles. *Maid to Measure*. London: Jarrolds Pub., 1961.

Cunnington, C. Willet, P.E.W. Cunnington, Phyllis Beard, and Charles Beard. *A Directory of English Costume, 900–1900*. London: Adam and Charles Black, 1960.

Daché, Lilly. *Talking through My Hats*. Edited by Dorothy Roe Lewis. New York: Coward–McCann, 1946.

Dariaux, Geneviève A. *Elegance: Etiquette at Home and Abroad*. Translated by M. Stoneridge. New York: Doubleday, 1964.

Davenport, Millia. *The Book of Costume*. New York: Crown, 1948.

Daves, Jessica. *Ready-Made Miracle*. New York: G.P. Putnam's, 1967.

Daves, Jessica, and Alexander Liberman. *The World in Vogue*. New York: Viking Press, 1963.

Dior, Christian. *Talking about Fashion*. Translated by Eugenia Sheppard. New York: G.P. Putnam's, 1954.

———. *Christian Dior and I*. Translated by Antonia Fraser. New York: Dutton & Co., 1957.

———. *Dior by Dior*. Translated by Antonia Fraser. London: Weidenfeld & Nicolson, 1957. Harmondsworth, England: Penguin Books, 1968.

Erté. *Erté Fashions*. New York: St. Martin's Press, 1972.

———. *Erté—Things I Remember*. New York: Quadrangle, 1975.

Evans, Mary. *Fundamentals of Clothing and Textiles*. New York: Prentice-Hall 1949.

Fairchild, John. *The Fashionable Savages*. New York: Doubleday & Co., 1965.

Fairchild Publications, Women's Wear Daily Editorial Staff. *Fifty Years of Fashion: Documented Sketches and Text*. New York: Fairchild Publications, Book Division, 1950.

Garland, Madge. *Fashion*. London: Penguin, 1962.

———. *The Changing Form of Fashion*. London: J.M. Dent & Sons, 1970.

Gorsline, Douglas Warner. *What People Wore: A Visual History of Dress from Ancient Times to 20th Century America*. New York: Viking, 1952.

Haedrich, Marcel. *Coco Chanel—Her Life, Her Secrets*. Translated by Charles Lam Markmann. Boston: Little Brown, 1972.

Hansen, Henry Harold. *Costumes and Styles*. New York: E. P. Dutton, 1956.

Hartnell, Norman. *Silver and Gold*. London: Evans Bros. 1955.

――――. *Royal Courts of Fashion*. London: Cassell, 1971.

Hawes, Elizabeth. *Fashion Is Spinach*. New York: Random House, 1938.

Ironside, Janey. *Janey*. London: Michael Joseph, 1973.

Kybalová, Ludmila, Olga Herbenová, and Milena Lamarová. *The Pictorial Encyclopedia of Fashion*, 2nd ed. Translated by Claudia Rosoux. Feldham, England: Hamlyn Pub., 1968. New York: Crown, 1970.

Langley-Moore, Doris. *The Woman in Fashion*. London: Batsford, 1949.

――――. *The Child in Fashion*. London: Batsford, 1953.

――――. *Fashion through Fashion Plates—1771–1970*. London: Ward Lock, 1971.

Langner, Lawrence. *The Importance of Wearing Clothes*. New York: Hastings House, 1959.

Latour, Anny. *Kings of Fashion*. Translated by Mervyn Saville. London: Weidenfeld & Nicolson, 1958.

Laver, James. *Taste and Fashion*. London: Harrap, 1937.

――――. *Fashion and Fashion Plates*. London: Penguin, 1943.

――――. *Letter to a Girl on the Future of Clothes*. London: Home & Van Thal, 1946.

――――. *Style in Costume*. London: Oxford University Press, 1949.

――――. *Children's Fashions in the 19th Century*. London: Batsford, 1951.

――――. *Clothes*. London: Burke, 1952.

――――. *The Pleasures of Life: Clothes, Fashion and Class Distinction*. London: Burke, 1953.

――――. *The Changing Shape of Things: Dress*. Reprint. London: Murray, 1957.

――――. *Costume through the Ages*. Farnborough, England: Thames & Hudson, 1963. New York: Simon & Schuster, 1964.

――――. *Costume*. London: Cassell, 1963.

――――. *Victoriana*. New York: Hawthorn Books, 1967.

――――. *Fashions from Ancient Egypt to the Present Day*. London: Hamlyn Gray, 1968.

――――. *A Concise History of Costume*. Farnborough, England: Thames & Hudson, 1969.

――――. *Modesty of Dress: An Inquiry into the Fundamentals of Fashion*. London: Heinemann, 1969.

Laver, James, ed. "Early Tudor 1485–1558." *Fashions of the Renaissance in England, France, Spain and Holland*. Costume of the Western World, vol. 3. New York: Harper & Brothers, 1951.

Leggett, William F. *The Story of Silk*. New York: Lifetime Editions, 1949.

Levin, Phyllis Lee. *The Wheels of Fashion*. New York: Doubleday, 1965.

Lieber, Leslie, and Toni Miller. *Fashion's Folly*. New York: Vanguard Press, 1954.

McCardell, Claire. *What Shall I Wear?*. New York: Simon & Schuster, 1956.

McClellan, Elisabeth. *History of American Costume, 1607–1870*, 2nd ed. New York: Tudor Publishing Co., 1942.

Marcus, Stanley. *Minding the Store*. Boston: Little Brown, 1974.

Metropolitan Museum of Art. *The Art of Fashion*. New York: Metropolitan Museum of Art, 1968. (Exhibition Catalogue.)

————. *Fashion, Art & Beauty*. New York: Metropolitan Museum of Art, 1968.

Milinaire, Caterine, and Carol Troy. *Cheap Chic*. New York: Harmony Books, 1975.

Payne, Blanche. *History of Costume: From the Ancient Egyptians to the Twentieth Century*. New York: Harper & Row, 1965.

Pegaret, Anthony, and Janet Arnod. *Costume: A General Bibliography*. London: Costume Society & Victoria and Albert Museum, Publications Department, 1966.

Perkins, Alice K. *Paris Couturiers and Milliners*. New York: Fairchild, 1949.

Picken, Mary Brooks. *The Fashion Dictionary*. New York: Funk & Wagnalls, 1957.

Picken, Mary Brooks, and D. L. Muller. *Dressmakers of France: The Who, How and Why of French Couture*. New York: Harper & Bros., 1956.

Poiret, Paul. *King of Fashion: The Autobiography of Paul Poiret*. Translated by S. H. Guest. Philadelphia: Lippincott, 1931.

Quant, Mary. *Quant by Quant*. London: Putnam, 1965.

Riley, Robert. *The Fashion Makers*. New York: Crown, 1968.

Riley, Robert, Dale McConathy, Sally Kirkland, Bernadine Morris, and Eleni Sakes Epstein. *American Fashion: The Life and Lines of Adrian, Mainbocher, McCardell, Norell & Trigere*. Edited by Sarah Tomerlin Lee. New York: Quadrangle, 1975.

Rochas, Marcel. *Vingt-Cinque, Ans d'Elegance à Paris*. Paris: Pierre 'Tisné, 1951.

Samet, Arthur. *Oddly Enough: From Animal Land to Furtown*. New York. Arthur Samet, 1938.

————. *Pictorial Encyclopedia of Furs. From Animal Land to Furtown*. Rev. ed. of *Oddly Enough: From Animal Land to Furtown*. New York: Arthur Samet, Book Division, 1950.

Saunders, Edith. *The Age of Worth: Couturier to the Empress Eugénie*. Bloomington, Ind.: Indiana University Press, 1955.

Schiaparelli, Elsa. *Shocking Life*. New York: Dutton, 1954.

Settle, Alison. *English Fashion*. New York: Collins, 1948.

Snow, Carmel. *The World of Carmel Snow*. New York: McGraw–Hill, 1962.

Spanier, Ginette. *It Isn't All Mink*. New York: Random House, 1960.

Spencer, Charles. *Erté*. London: Studio Vista, 1970.

Thornton, Peter. *Baroque and Rococo Silks*. New York: Taplinger, 1965.

Tolstoy, Mary Koutouzov. *Charlemagne to Dior: The Story of French Fashion.* New York: Michael Slains, 1967.

Vertés, Marcel. *Art and Fashion.* Translated by George Davis. London: Studio Publications, 1944.

Wilcox, Ruth Turner. *The Mode in Costume.* New York: Scribner's, 1942.

———. *The Mode in Footwear.* New York: Scribner's, 1948.

———. *The Directory of Costume.* New York: Scribner's, 1969.

Williams, Beryl Epstein. *Young Faces in Fashion.* Philadelphia: Lippincott, 1957.

Worth, Jean Philippe. *A Century of Fashion.* Translated by Ruth Scott Miller. Boston: Little Brown, 1928.

name index

354